The Manipulators

By the same author

N.Y.S.E.: A HISTORY OF THE NEW YORK STOCK EXCHANGE, 1935–1975

HERBERT HOOVER AT THE ONSET OF THE GREAT DEPRESSION

THE ENTREPRENEURS

THE MONEY MANIAS

FOR WANT OF A NAIL . . .

THE AGE OF GIANT CORPORATIONS

CONQUEST AND CONSCIENCE: THE 1840'S

MACHINES AND MORALITY: THE 1850'S

AMEX: A HISTORY OF THE AMERICAN STOCK EXCHANGE

THE CURBSTONE BROKERS

PANIC ON WALL STREET

THE GREAT BULL MARKET

THE BIG BOARD

THE ORIGINS OF INTERVENTIONISM

The Manipulators

America in the Media Age

Robert Sobel

ANCHOR PRESS/DOUBLEDAY
GARDEN CITY, NEW YORK
1976

The Anchor Press edition is the first publication of *The Manipulators.*

Library of Congress Cataloging in Publication Data

Sobel, Robert, 1931 (Feb. 19)–
The manipulators.

Bibliography: p. 417
Includes index.
1. Mass media—United States—History. 2. United States—Popular culture. 3. Universities and colleges—United States. I. Title.
P92.U5S62 301.16'1'0973
ISBN: 0-385-08526-5
Library of Congress Catalog Card Number 75–36612

Anchor Press edition: 1976

PRINTED IN THE UNITED STATES OF AMERICA
FIRST EDITION

To

Edward R. Murrow
London, 1940

Contents

Suppose a nation stands apart from the rest of mankind: independently of certain general wants inherent in the human race, it will also have wants and interests peculiar to itself: certain opinions of censure or approbation forthwith arise in the community, which are peculiar to itself, and which are styled honour by the members of that community. Now suppose that in this same nation a caste arises, which, in its turn, stands apart from other classes, and contracts certain peculiar wants, which give rise in their turn to special opinions. The honour of this caste, composed of a medley of the peculiar notions of the nation, and the still more peculiar notions of the caste, will be as remote as it is possible to conceive from the simple and general opinions of men.

Alexis de Tocqueville, *1834*

Summoning artists to participate
In the august occasions of the state
Seems something for us all to celebrate.
This day is for my cause a day of days,
And his be poetry's old-fashioned praise
Who was the first to think of such a thing.
This tribute verse to be his own I bring
Is about the new order of the ages

Robert Frost, *1961*

Introduction

Few civilizations have been scrutinized more carefully than that which was developing in the United States after the Revolution. Americans took delight in dissecting their accomplishments, while scores of foreigners traveled across the Atlantic to do the same. Some concluded that the United States was, in essence, an extrapolation of European society, while others thought the Americans were a truly reborn people; most fell in between the two ideas. Many were shocked by the crudities they found almost everywhere they went, and denied that Americans possessed a true culture as Europeans understood the term. The diversity and formlessness of the new nation amazed them; it appeared the continent was too large to be controlled by a single state and civilization, and that in time several would appear and war with one another. Almost all noted the influence of the land upon the people—a new Garden of Eden was producing an interesting species, so they concluded. In America they saw both an image of their distant past and a preview of what was in store for the rest of the Western world. Some came to spend a season in heaven, and others to witness hell. America seemed to satisfy both.

Perceptive observers were intrigued by the mass nature of the American people. Other countries long had possessed large peasant populations and middle classes of various kinds; in the early nineteenth century there were the beginnings of industrial classes as well. Each had its own values and cultures, methods of satisfying emotions, and forms of work and play. But when those Europeans who had the time and money to travel wrote of cultures and civilizations, more often than not they referred to those produced by and for aristocracies. This was to have been expected, for prior to the Revolution most books were written for that class, and in many cases by its members.

There was no clearly identifiable aristocracy in the United States then, though there were some groups that aspired to such a status. Rather, there were the various mass groups, working and playing in their own ways, and in the process creating their cultures and the vehicles through which they would be expressed. Foreigners came to observe these and the American elites examined them, to find patterns where in most cases none existed as yet.

From the first there were tensions in America—sometimes creative, often destructive—between the masses and the elites. In Europe during and before the eighteenth century the various aristocratic classes had encouraged and made retainers of intellectuals, people who earned their ways through life by developing and using ideas. Lacking such allies and supporters in America, the intellectuals alternated between condemning the masses and attempting to join with them and become their leaders. The former was a sterile pursuit, and the latter proved almost impossible; for while the intellectuals required freedom in order to seek excellence and perfection, the masses demanded equality, not only of opportunity, but also of ideas. The Founding Fathers spoke of liberty and equality, but the conflict between the two ideals antedated the Revolution and provided a leitmotiv thereafter and to this day.

Americans are nothing if not pragmatic. Although the conflict was not resolved in the nineteenth century, the intellectuals and the masses did coexist, each in its own milieu, sometimes coming together in common ventures, but usually remaining apart. This began to change in the twentieth century, and the alteration was due more to developments in the technologies of play and amusement than a conscious effort to alter the civilization. Through new kinds of newspapers and colleges, motion pictures, and most importantly, radio and television, the intellectuals and the masses were able to come together. The original differences did not vanish—the intellectuals continued to have contempt for mass values, while the masses sensed that the intellectuals were somehow aliens in their midst. But they were altered by changing circumstances. In the twentieth century there emerged in America a new culture, based upon play rather than work, organized around consumption instead of production—and concerned more with images than reality. Although a mass culture, it attracted many intellectuals as well. In addition there was a tremendous expansion in the area of higher education, and this contributed to the creation of an enlarged, fairly sophisticated audience for the products of the new society. In any civilization there is a small group that creates ideas, a somewhat larger one that prepares them for dissemination, and a third group that acts as an audience for the "product." It is this last population that has expanded so rapidly during the past three quarters of a century and that has come to dominate the other two and to a large extent force them to its will.

This book is an exploration into how this came about and what it means to the American future.

Alexis de Tocqueville, that perceptive French visitor to America in the 1830s, was one of the first to perceive the existence of cultural divisions here and to explore their implications. "I know of no country in which there is so little true independence of mind and freedom of discussion as in America," he wrote in the classic *Democracy in America*. He offered as a reason for this what later generations would call the tyranny of the majority. "In America, the majority raises very formidable barriers to the liberty of opinion; within these barriers an author may write whatever he pleases, but he will repent it if he ever steps beyond them." To go against the masses would be to invite intellectual obloquy. Thus, said Tocqueville, America could not be expected to produce great writers, or if they did appear, it would reject them. "If great writers have not at present existed in America, the reason is very simply given in these facts; there can be no literary genius without freedom of opinion, and freedom of opinion does not exist in America."

How could it have been otherwise, in a country where so many believed that one man's opinion was as good as another? Americans did not prize excellence; there was no room for an intellectual elite, or for that matter any other special group banded together in a caste that aspired to a major public role. Truth, and taste, would be decided by majority votes. Numbers counted more than absolute truth—indeed, numbers made truths. "If you're so smart, why aren't you rich?" is not only a materialistic question, but one that indicates success is and should be quantifiable. In the realm of ideas, this translated into, "If your concepts, programs, and platforms are so good, why aren't they better known and accepted, and why aren't you in a position of great power?" It was perhaps inevitable that Americans would create best-seller lists in the nineteenth century and pioneer in public-opinion polls in the twentieth. By the middle of this century, such phenomena would become almost as important as political elections.

Tocqueville saw it before anyone else. The Americans were fashioning a mass society, to a large degree undifferentiated, more uniform than those of the Old World, and they were doing so—paradoxically—in the name of liberty and freedom. The rugged individualist who captured the public imagination existed only in fiction; in the "real world" Americans preferred the person who got along by going along. Before Karl Marx, Tocqueville had intimations of the coming of a classless society, not arrived at through warfare and revolution, but through majority pressures for conformity to agreed upon norms. It would not be a society of serfs and rulers; almost all Americans would be propertied. The poor who lacked the will, interests, values, or abilities to make the grade would be despised; those of them who showed the proper spirit would be welcomed, even assisted. As for the very rich, they evoked reactions of dislike and envy so long as they remained aloof from the general population. Should some of them wish to assume a public role, they would have to imitate the middle class and embrace the theology of equality.

This was crucial to an understanding of America, thought Tocqueville. Democratic communities had some taste for freedom, but under special circumstances might relinquish it. "But for equality, their passion is ardent, insatiable, invincible: they call for equality in freedom; and if they cannot obtain that, they still call for equality in slavery. They will endure poverty, servitude, barbarism—but they will not endure aristocracy."

The Founding Fathers, too, had recognized this mass instinct, and as natural aristocrats and intellectuals themselves hoped to preserve their rights and liberties against those of the herd. "It is of great importance in a republic not only to guard the society against the oppression of its rulers, but to guard one part of the society against the injustices of the other part," wrote James

Madison in the *Federalist Papers*. "If a majority be united by a common interest, the rights of the minority will be insecure." The Constitution reflected this view. Madison and his peers believed that the presidency, Senate, and Supreme Court would become the domains of the natural aristocrats, while the masses might obtain control of only the Houses of Representatives. The new government has been viewed by generations of historians as a holding action by the few against the many, and so it was. Of course, the Founding Fathers were mistaken in their belief that this balance could be maintained, for shortly after the Constitution came into being the leveling tendencies were beginning to be felt.

Many American intellectuals of this period professed adherence to the democratic dogmas and swore their affection for the common man. More often than not, however, they were repelled by his actions, especially when the masses obtained power. John Adams, who was well versed in the vocabulary of freedom, shrank from the mob. His son, John Quincy Adams, saw the common man use his freedom to obtain control of the national government, and he viewed the advent of Jacksonian Democracy as the beginning of the end for Western civilization. Even then, in the 1830s, it seemed evident that this common man, and not the elite, would dominate America; numbers would rule, not excellence. There were those who feared this would mean the end for intellectual life in the nation, and some fled to Europe, just as others came to America to enjoy the blessings of the new democracy. But such was not the case. Instead, the intellectuals retreated for a while, emerging upon occasion to lead reform movements. Some served under Presidents elected by the masses, leaders they felt were their intellectual and moral inferiors.

The composition of the masses and the nature of their culture underwent important alterations in the latter half of the nineteenth century and as with all such major transformations, did so for a variety of reasons. Most in one way or another involved the urbanization of America and the powerful thrust of middle-class values into the rapidly growing cities. Dislocations caused by the Civil War exacerbated the situation, accelerating tendencies that already existed. The same was true for immigration, the development of new business forms and industries, and the rapid rise of national power. The urban population doubled in the pre-Civil

War decade, at which time it rose at four times the rate of the rural. One out of every five Americans alive in 1860 lived in cities or large towns; at the turn of the century, two in five were there. Cause and effect intertwined and exchanged roles, but the result was not in doubt: America was evolving into an urbanized, middle-class nation. Increasingly, people were rubbing against one another, and this created friction and change.

Like the people of the older rural America, those of the urban mass society sought norms and exemplars, whether in work or play. Despite the chronic economic dislocations of the postbellum period and the existence of a large underprivileged class that was constantly being replenished from abroad and from the American farms, more people were interested in and capable of paying for play than ever before. Farmers had to adjust their lives to the seasons and weather; urban workers punched time clocks, and after work was done their time was their own. Tourism became an economic and technological possibility for the middle class as well as for the wealthy, and resort hotels and spas catering to such needs made their appearances. Americans went to the country for vacations just as they had left the rural areas to go to the cities for employment. These were vacations in every sense of the word—a time for vacating the year-round routines and seeking different modes of life for a brief period. Resort centers were created in the White Mountains, the Rockies, and the Catskills. Americans went to lake areas as well, while those who could not afford distant travel and lived close by the seaside spent holidays at ocean resorts. The old rich and the new went to Newport for the season in the 1880s; the middle class traveled to Long Branch hotels for a few weeks. President Grant spent his vacations there, in the middle-class atmosphere. An ordinary man in most respects outside of those involved with war, he was considered an inept fool by the elite, especially the intellectuals, while he became an exemplar for the middle-class individuals who saw in him—and in what today we would call his "lifestyle"—a reflection of themselves.

Recreation was developing rapidly, and in the literal sense of the term—re-creation. As early as 1869 there were traveling baseball clubs, which played against home teams that charged admission to the events. The first championship took place in 1871, and baseball was on its way to becoming "the national pastime."

(Again, the word inferred it was a way to "pass time.") Other sports had their vogues; even cricket enjoyed a brief spurt of popularity, though it proved too slow and had too aristocratic an aura for Americans.

Amusement, considered a frivolity by the Puritans, had become a legitimate method by which a person could leave his "real" cares and escape into a make-believe world. P. T. Barnum's traveling circus appeared the same year as the first championship baseball contest, and others followed. No longer were theatrical amusements confined to the major urban centers. Troupes of actors would take to the road, playing in local theaters in small towns, their stock in trade the classics (for edification, but more so as to indicate that civilization had arrived) and melodramas (for entertainment). It was the great age of impresarios who catered to middle-class tastes. Charles Frohman, Abraham Erlanger, David Belasco, and Oscar Hammerstein led the way. Minstrel shows produced by some of them flourished in the 1870s and 1880s and then declined, the impresarios turning to other forms of entertainment. Vaudeville was born, and Benjamin Keith and Edward Albee, leaders in the field, became nationally known.

These were some of the early signs of the development of a modern mass culture. The masses were seeking and finding their voices and means of expression and play—and since they were Americans, they would be organized and structured. Tocqueville had anticipated this, and thought he knew what it would indicate. "But I perceive that the productions of the arts are generally of an inferior quality, very abundant, and very cheap, I am convinced that, among the people where this occurs, privilege is on the decline, and that ranks are beginning to intermingle and will soon be confounded together."

By the late nineteenth century this was taking place in the areas of recreation, entertainment, and amusement. The elites retained their enclaves—the opera, symphony, literary magazines, and the old, established colleges. But everywhere the mass culture was developing its counterparts—vaudeville and the music hall, lurid newspapers, and the newer state universities as well as the public elementary and secondary schools. In time the masses would swamp the elite—numbers would tell—as Tocqueville had predicted would happen. P. T. Barnum understood this. He was reputed to have said, "A sucker is born every minute." On the surface this seems a cynical view of mankind, but it is more, and Barnum knew it—he was hardly a man to insult his customers. Barnum's greatest success and acceptance came from middle-class audiences, individuals whose grandparents and parents hadn't time for such frivolities but who now were in the market for amusement. They liked his extravaganzas, even while the elites scorned them. Barnum outdrew the opera and concerts—there were more of his kind of people than any other—and in time he would attract the elites too, if only as curious onlookers.

The "lower culture" was coming to displace the upper in some cases, while in others it simply absorbed it. That this was occurring was not perceived at the time, however, at least by most observers of the American scene. Henry Adams, the descendant of John and John Quincy, understood well what was taking place, and he feared the implications of this new culture. Would it be controlled by the intellectuals, or would they be swamped by massive mediocrity? Were the Barnums about to inherit the land? He suspected they would, and felt powerless to do anything about it. Out of place in the emerging age of middle-class public values, Adams migrated intellectually, first to the Jeffersonian period, and then farther back, to the Middle Ages.

This middle-class culture, based upon principles of equality and broad enough to embrace the vast majority of Americans, required forms and institutions through which it could be developed and realized. Some already existed, and these would be appropriated and then adapted to meet the needs of the middle class. In addition, several new ones would appear and would be quickly shaped for the use of the mass civilization.

Newspapers and colleges were obvious vehicles for the creation and transmission of culture. In the midnineteenth century, the nation's most important newspapers were under the control of highly individualistic editor-publishers. The printers were considered the most valuable workers at the businesses, while the reporters usually were anonymous and often easily replaced. Some of this changed, however, during the second half of the century, although the alterations were not evident to some of the readers. For one thing, the new editors were concerned with reflecting the interests and desires of their readers, and leading mass crusades.

The printers had been placed in a subordinate position as a result of technological and social change, while the writers—reporters and editors—became increasingly important. They were the forerunners, without fully understanding what was occurring, of the "mass intellectual" of the twentieth century, a hybrid form that has only come into its own in the last generation.

A similar development was taking place in the nation's colleges and universities, where elitist and egalitarian doctrines coexisted, because they were seldom found at the same institutions. The public colleges were usually bourgeois, while the leading private ones held to an elitist position. Yet the drift of higher education was such that while the bourgeois aped the elite's values, the elite bowed to the greater numbers of middle-class students demanding entry into colleges and universities. And there, too, was created the mass intellectual.

Vaudeville remained a stronghold of middle-class entertainment, but the new culture discovered a far more powerful instrument in motion pictures, an evolving technology that still lacked organization, content, and direction. The new class provided all three. Some of the inventors had thought films could be used for education. But the public wanted entertainment, and this was provided, for more people than vaudeville could ever have hoped to reach. As had been the case at the newspapers, the technicians and businessman had most of the power in the early days. Then, just as the newspaper reporter was becoming more prominent in the early twentieth century, so the performing artist came into power after World War II, creations of and exemplars for the mass intellectuals, and members of that class themselves.

Even more pervasive than films was radio, which became a commercial operation in the early 1920s. Some of its pioneers believed radio would remain simply a means of transmitting information; others—like the motion-picture inventors—wanted it to develop into a "university of the air." But the public demanded entertainment, and this was the path taken. Even though radio was far more complex than motion pictures or newspapers, and news and information revived during World War II, the entertainment function was always primary.

Television, which was a confused marriage of radio and motion pictures, at least in the view of the pioneers and early owners of receivers, was the most convoluted of the new institutions, as well as being the prime instrument of mass culture in our time. Here, too, news became subordinate to entertainment, and in television the mass man and the mass intellectual both found problems, confusion, and power.

* * *

Who are these mass intellectuals, this significant subgroup whose coming Tocqueville could not have anticipated, whom Whitman romanticized and did not understand, whom Ortega sensed would inherit leadership in the West but whose influence he could not comprehend, since he knew little of their vehicles for expression? They emerged from the masses, but rejected most of their values. They were products of both the old and new means of communication and entertainment, and their evolution was slow and for a long time went unnoticed. They grew out of different sources, like a plant system whose separate roots merge, intertwine, and then unite at the apex. In order to understand this phenomenon one must start at the roots and then trace their progress, explore their interconnections, and take note of the interaction of form and content that ultimately produced a new kind of perspective, a different culture.

The change took a century to accomplish and followed a pattern of sorts. First came the inventors and innovators, Victorians for the most part, materialists in search of the main chance. Businessmen then took command, organizing their corporations to exploit the innovations, defining and then redefining their industries. They had to hire artists and performers—in the case of higher education, professors who in their own way were performers—who would deal directly with the masses. It was their function to amuse, entertain, and deal in ideas. Then, in each case, the performing artists and professors threw off many of the businessmen's controls. They came to dominate their professions and speak to wider audiences than had been imaginable in the nineteenth century. The implications of this change have not been fully worked out, for the evolution is ongoing. It is, however, the single most important cultural and political force of our times, and pervades all aspects of our lives.

Power—the ability to make people see the world the way you

want them to and then make them act in accordance with your beliefs—is at the crux of the situation. In order to achieve power, retain control, and continue to utilize it, politicians have been obliged to become performers too, to conform with the requirements of these methods of transmitting ideas and entertainment. They, too, have evolved into entertainers, both manipulated by the medium as well as dominating it. This confluence of form and content is hardly new; presidential aspirants had used newspapers since the early national period. But a public raised on motion pictures and television, who have been exposed to ideas at the modern colleges and universities, and faithfully read modern newspapers, is quite different from one informed by local journals and amused by circuses and vaudeville. Part of the difference lies in the fact that in contemporary society, information and entertainment have become one.

The newspaper has been, and is presently, used to transmit fact and opinion. Motion pictures have always been a medium for fiction, while much of radio and television fare is fictional in nature. But the last two were and are used to present facts as well. Here the nature of the media has altered the content, giving news the appearance of circus, resulting in confusion, and also enabling those who understood their techniques to manipulate the public —audience, if you will—far more than any nineteenth-century editor or publisher ever dreamed possible.

In time, those who performed became political forces in their own rights, in effect crossing the line between fiction and nonfiction in their own public lives, and challenged the individuals who had emerged from the older ways of winning support and elections. It could be seen on television and in the movies. The Academy Awards took on a political tone, while national political conventions came to resemble the Awards ceremonies, the nomination (Oscar) going to the best performance. The same people appeared at both, and their roles at each often went unquestioned by people who had not lived through the transformation. Indeed, it was almost expected. Actress Shirley MacLaine, active in both spheres, was asked whether she had abandoned movies for politics. She replied she had never left motion pictures and television. "Well, there was a long period where you were involved in the campaign [of Senator George McGovern for the presidency]." "That's the best show business there is," was MacLaine's response.

Other artists might have answered in the same way, for public life has become a part of show business. Politicians have had to become performers—artists with public-relations men, makeup, and dyed hair. Their campaigns have taken on aspects of a drive to sell a motion picture or a new television show. They are deeply concerned with "image," a term that rapidly became trite, because it was so true and evident. Believability and likability became more important than programs and policies. The new politicians did not have to be told of this—they understood from the start what was required. And the older ones strove to adapt to the new ways.

That this has occurred is fairly obvious, and that it will continue to develop appears reasonably certain. Without an appreciation of the roads taken, however, the future will be more clouded than is necessary. A path through the maze is needed.

And that is the purpose of this book.

GENESIS

1

The Triumph of the Reporter

First came the newspaper. Unlike the book, it was not designed for permanence. It differed from the pamphlet in that it contained a variety of information and ideas, all written for space as well as content. Newspapers bore a resemblance to posters, but they were portable, and could be passed on from hand to hand.

There were no journalists in early colonial America, and so, naturally, no philosophy of journalism or such a profession. Nor were there reporters, editors, critics, reviewers, or any of that group that is so prominent today. Instead there were businessmen, who perceived a demand and acted to fill it. Early on they acted as combination entrepreneur-labor-journalist. Such businessmen organized the company, purchased machinery and set type, and wrote material. No single function was seen as superior to the others; all was of a piece. In time they would draw apart, and each would develop its own interest. But as late as the midnineteenth century no unit of the triad—entrepreneur, laborer, or journalist—appreciated its role; nor could any foresee how the contest among them would emerge, develop, or be resolved over the decades. At that time the publishers still considered themselves newspapermen, in effect employees of the paper they owned, as were the other two groups; they merely performed a different function. Reporters and editors felt a proprietary interest in their journals and, as will be demonstrated, often emerged from the print shop to take places at the front desks. As for the skilled and semiskilled laborers, they had not yet come to terms with their social and economic circumstances, and more often than not felt they had a special kinship with the publisher, one that excluded reporters and those involved with "scribbling."

Yet by the late nineteenth century a separation was taking place, though it would not be fully discernible until much later. There were even alterations in language meant to reflect the coming dispensation. A newsboy, for example, was a laborer, while a newspaperman was a journalist. The latter was not simply an adult version of the former. Yet a half century earlier, the progression from one to the other had been orderly and to have been expected. One joined a newspaper as a newsboy, and then progressed "up the ladder" to emerge a reporter, often combining the two functions throughout. At that time the same person would be known as a publisher, a printer, and a newspaperman, for there were few differences among the functions. Benjamin Franklin had served as all three, as had James Gordon Bennett the elder and Horace Greeley.

Adolph Ochs was one of the breed. He had begun his career as a newspaper boy, then had become a printer's devil, and afterward a reporter. Ochs later purchased an interest in the Chattanooga *Times,* and in 1896, took over the New York *Times.* By then, the divisions among the functions of printer, reporter, and publisher were becoming evident. On the larger papers, reporters knew little of the press rooms and had only marginal contacts with the publishers. Ochs understood this, and made a point of knowing the names of all his reporters at the *Times.* He also went into the composing room to make himself known to the printers. "I'm a printer, as you are," he told them. "I've done my turn at the case with hand-set type. I want to make the *Times* the best example of the printing art in the whole newspaper field, and I know with your help I can do it."[1] Clearly, Ochs spoke their language, but the very fact that he found it necessary to do so indicated the major change that was taking place. The newspapers were the first to feel the full impact of the new dispensation.

Among other things, the newspaper is a product, its shape and contents determined by the same kinds of forces that exist for other products. Paramount among these are technology, the market, the labor force, and the values and desires of management—the last often dictated by the first three. Tradition also played a role, at times as an anchor to the past, on some occasions as a hindrance to desirable change. The interplay of these ingredients provided the backdrop for the colorful publishers, editors, columnists, and reporters, along with the inventors, technicians, and labor unions whose activities and interrelations are discussed and dissected in the many histories of journalism.[2] In all of these the stress is upon the development of the professional staff, editors serving as convenient benchmarks and heroes. The business and labor sides receive consideration in the more encyclopedic works, often as an afterthought, however. Biographies of leading publishers tend to stress their careers as molders of public opinion, not so much as capitalists and entrepreneurs. Reporters emerge as glamorous figures (in varying guises to suit the needs of each period), men and women of action in influential positions—people who possess power, not wealth.

These biographies and histories appeared in an age in which the values of the intellectual sector were coming to dominate the consciousness of all. That such presentations should appear is understandable. But the picture is distorted; for if a newspaper's primary function is to impart news, then there is some question as to whether the nation had many true newspapers prior to the late nineteenth century. The newspapers of the earlier age bore a strong resemblance to those of today. But if the package was similar, the contents and market were strikingly different.

THE ORIGINAL RATIONALE

After several false starts in the late seventeenth century, a handful of men put out successful newspapers. Almost all were printers, the most famous being Benjamin Franklin. They owned print shops, whose primary function was to publish official notices and private advisories of various kinds, as well as playing cards, invitations, and the like. As job printers, their "plant" was idle for much of the week. The publication of a newspaper must have made sense to them, for even if the profits were low, they were better than nothing. Before they could be successful, however, two questions, closely related to one another, had to be answered: What would be in the paper? Who would purchase the sheets?

Some publishers tried to write commentaries upon well-known social and political events, while others attempted short fiction. Neither found a ready market. But America did have a commercial class, especially in the coastal towns, and the printers found that they would subscribe to journals that served their needs. The colonial newspapers would print advertisements paid for by merchants, offering goods and services, in the hope they would be read and acted upon by other merchants. Commercial notices dominated the front pages—the coming and going of ships, the status of cargoes, and foreign news that might affect business. In some there was news of runaway indentured servants and slaves, in others the current prices for selected commodities in nearby towns. The main task of such newspapers was to help the readers conduct their business affairs more intelligently, to gather commercial gossip in one place and so save the readers the trouble of going to the wharves on their own. As far as can be determined, there were no reporters, no staff, no advertising managers. The printer performed all functions, knew all the subscribers and advertisers, and geared his newspaper to suit their needs.

The papers also printed news, but more as filler material than anything else. Usually the printer gathered the material and wrote the stories himself. As political considerations became important late in the century, he wrote editorials as well. But there were no separate news and editorial sections in the early newspapers, and all of this noncommercial material was deemed of secondary importance.

The situation changed somewhat on the eve of the Revolution, when the public was interested in both political news and opinion. The newspapers enabled the printer and others in town to reach a wide audience, larger than any that might be gathered in a meeting hall, and for the first time, the colonial press became more than an adjunct to commerce. During the Revolution itself, printers had to spend more time in gathering and commenting upon the news than they had previously. Still, the printer-publisher remained the key figure, a situation imposed upon him by technology and the market.

Few newspapers had circulations of over a thousand, or subscribers within more than a day's ride of the print shop. Some of the larger ones did attempt to win subscribers in distant places, relying upon the mail to carry the newspapers out of town. But the mail was uncertain and expensive, and even then printers lobbied for better service at lower prices—a reason why Franklin, printer-publisher of the Pennsylvania *Gazette*, sought and obtained the position of deputy postmaster for the colonies in 1753. As for the presses, most were crude affairs, not very different from those developed by Gutenburg three centuries before.

There was a large population of literate Americans in the late eighteenth century, but for most of them, the newspaper was not a handy source of information, but a sizable capital investment—an annual subscription for many papers was in the neighborhood of a dollar a year, and given the different values of money and utilities of that period and our own, the purchase of a newspaper was akin to the purchase of an eight-dollar book today. The newspapers were passed from one reader to another, and retained for months, not hours or even minutes, as would be the practice two centuries later. The news was not only impressed upon the mind, but also could be felt with the hands; it was a product, not a service. This was so even for those subscribers who lived near the print shop and received their newspapers the same day they were printed. They knew another issue would not arrive for at least a week. During the next seven days, then, the newspaper was "current."

The printer-publisher survived the Revolution, but his role changed somewhat in the early national period. With the formation of political parties came a political press, one that existed to serve the interests of the various factions. John Fenno's *The Gazette of the United States*, Philip Freneau's *National Gazette*, Benjamin Franklin Bache's *Aurora*, and other newspapers were allied with political parties and supported by them directly and indirectly. These newspapers carried commercial notices and advertisements, but a large portion of the costs were born by the political notices printed as a matter of course in favored newspapers. As their names indicated, some of the papers were national in scope, even though they were printed at a single location. Improvements in postal deliveries made this possible, while subsidies kept the prices down. Circulations of more than two thousand were obtainable in the early nineteenth century, so that the business of putting out the paper could take up much of the time in a medium-sized shop.

With all of this, the newspapers remained the creations of printers, not newsmen. The printer-publisher might have a government post that required little work and paid a comfortable salary. But he still gathered most of the news himself, wrote it up, and composed the editorials. There was expansion as business picked up, but this took place in the print shop, where additional printers were hired. By the 1820s there were printers' unions and benevolent societies, but none for reporters—the reason being that there were few reporters at work on newspapers, and they were not acknowledged as such at the time.

While newspapers were recognizable businesses in this period by no measure could they be deemed independent, or operating to impart the news. Instead, they served the interests of the commercial readers or political patrons, and could not exist without them. More than half the space in the nonparty press was devoted to advertisements. If politically motivated news and articles can be considered advertisements—as indeed they were—then almost all of the partisan press could be categorized as commercial. Just as infant industries relied upon government for support and existed to serve the agrarian sector of the economy, so the infant press was subsidized by and assisted the political and commercial sectors. In time, of course, the industries evolved, grew, and could thrive without subsidies of various kinds. The same was true for the press. When both did, they took the leap from the agrarian commercial age to the industrial.

"The industrialization of the press" took place during the three decades preceding the Civil War, and as was the case with other aspects of business, involved a different perspective of the national scene as well as an augmented technological base and a changing view of the nature of management.

For one thing, there was a new market for newspapers. Printers who had serviced the commercial interests had sons who had published partisan papers. In turn, their sons came of age at a time when the population was increasing rapidly. There were 12.9 million Americans in 1830, and 31.5 million in 1860. Despite the fact that immigrants accounted for much of the increase, the illiteracy rate fell from 11 per cent to 9 per cent, one of the lowest in the world. Urbanization was increasing. Boston and New Orleans had more than 170,000 inhabitants in 1860, and Philadelphia slightly fewer than 600,000, while New York led the nation, crossing the million mark just before Lincoln's first election.

There had been a financial panic in 1837, followed by a depression. But prosperity returned in the early 1840s; Americans could afford to purchase newspapers, if the price was attractive.

What might they read? The first newspapers existed to provide commercial and political services, but only a small fraction of the general population wanted or needed either. On the other hand, there had always been a market for amusement and entertainment. Furthermore, such developments as the western movement, the Mexican War, immigration, and the great debate over slavery could provide good copy, involving the general population in debates that did not affect them directly. News from distant places might be presented more rapidly too. Not only were transportation and postal services better than before, but also the rates were lowered regularly. The invention of the telegraph in 1832 stirred interest, but it was not until 1844 that the first major linkage—from New York to Philadelphia—was completed. A mass-circulation newspaper, selling for somewhat below the five cents charged by the political press and other papers, seemed possible. And one was founded in 1833.

The New York *Sun*, whose first issue appeared early in the year, was a skimpy four-page daily specializing in human-interest stories, and which sold for a penny. Its founder-publisher-editor-printer-reporter-advertising manager, Benjamin H. Day, had modest hopes for his paper, and so was surprised when circulation reached five thousand within four months and then doubled again in less than a year. The *Sun* could not handle such prosperity and popularity—at least on the technological end of the business. The newspaper utilized a Napier flat press, which turned out a hundred or so impressions an hour. This meant that by the time the last copy of one day's issue was completed, the first of the next had to be placed in the press. Clearly such a situation could not be allowed to continue, and Day was obliged to purchase additional presses and hire a press crew, neither of which he could afford. In 1835 he installed a new Hoe press, which could be pushed to three thousand copies an hour, but which cost over ten thousand dollars. Armed with the new machine, Day was able to expand his operations and attract additional advertisers. Other publishers followed. By the end of the decade the penny press was to be found in every major city in the nation, overshadowing both the commercial and political newspapers in circulation and volume of advertising. What has been called the "Hoe Revolution" was in full swing in the 1840s, as Richard Hoe & Co. was flooded with orders for its machines. By 1847 Richard Hoe was taking orders for a ten-cylinder giant that printed twenty-two thousand pages an hour and sold for twenty-five thousand dollars—more than twenty times the amount of money Day had invested in the *Sun* in 1833.

The enlarged, concentrated population made possible the development of mass journalism, free from commercial and political interests. Without the new technology, however, the penny press could not have been realized.[3]

The new journalism was big business, and although each population center had several newspapers, the industry's focal point was New York, as much due to its population and industry as anything else. No American newspaper of the 1820s had as many as four thousand subscribers, and in 1860, a circulation of five thousand was considered significant. By then the New York *Herald*, with a circulation of seventy-seven thousand, was the world's largest daily. The transformation was sudden; the *Herald* had been founded in 1832 with a capital of five hundred dollars. As late as 1845, it had a staff of thirteen writers of various kinds, but there were thirty-six workers in the press room. The *Herald*'s weekly expense budget was fifteen hundred dollars, while income was slightly more than two thousand dollars on the average.

Horace Greeley founded the New York *Tribune* in 1841, with an investment of one thousand dollars. During the next decade newspapers became big business and required large amounts of capital. In 1850 Henry Raymond organized the New York *Times*, which was capitalized at one hundred thousand dollars, of which sixty thousand dollars was subscribed initially—the same amount as the *Tribune*'s 1849 profits. In its first full year of operations the *Times* spent forty thousand dollars on newsprint alone. As for salaries and wages, the production workers received twenty-five thousand dollars, and the bill for all writers and editors came to thirteen thousand dollars.

The newspapers were also becoming diverse and complex, but relationships within the work force were slower in altering. In the early days, printers also functioned as reporters. Now the full-time reporters appeared, people utilized to collect and write local news at first, and later on, communiqués from Washington and the Mexican War fronts. Most reporters—women as well as men—came from the print shop. It was not unusual for a printer-editor to ask one of his journeymen to investigate a police report, write it up, and then compose the material for the press and finally operate the machine.

The center of the operation, the focus, was the print shop. Most newspapers were located with a mind to transportation and the audience, so that raw materials—paper, ink, machines—could be brought to the shop and the finished product easily distributed. In this respect, the urban newspaper was not much different from the factory. Printing presses and the composing room occupied the ground floor of most newspaper offices, with the editorial staff lodged upstairs, often in an out-of-the-way place. Pressmen and compositors were the aristocrats of the industry, while reporters were considered hangers-on, the most dispensable part of the operation. Indeed, since printers received higher wages than reporters, it was difficult to convince a printer to leave the shop for "upstairs." More often than not, reporters were failed printers.

The key figures in this period were the editors, and they too had printing backgrounds. Horace Greeley had begun as an itinerent printer, advancing to compositor and then to editor. Thurlow Weed, the powerful New York politician and publisher of the Albany *Evening Journal*, had also been a printer. James Gordon Bennett was one of the relatively few who went from reporter to editor-publisher, and for that reason, among others, was considered a maverick and outsider. These men and others throughout the nation—Joseph Buckingham of the Boston *Courier*, William "Parson" Brownlow of the Knoxville (Tennessee) *Whig*, and George Prentice of the Louisville *Journal*, had national power. They dominated their newspapers thoroughly, deciding not only editorial policy (and writing most of the editorials themselves) but also isolating significant events and determining the parameters of debate upon them.

It was a time when the Whig and Democratic parties were in disarray, the former in the process of actual dissolution. Politicians no longer engendered much in the way of trust, while editors did. For a while it appeared that control of a major newspaper, not election to the Senate or a governorship, was to become the path to power and influence in national life. Greeley was courted by Lincoln and later on nominated for the presidency by the Democrats. Bennett's grasp on the mob was stronger than that of any politician in the 1850s—a period when the mob was coming into its own. And there were others, in every city and town and in all sections of the country. As the penny press came to dominate the newspaper scene, and the independent newspapers became near-universal, the editor took his place alongside the clergyman and doctor as a leading citizen and respected figure. After the Civil War, many professional men lost much of their power to a rising business class, but not so the publisher-editor of influential newspapers, who made the adjustment to the new dispensation with a minimum of difficulty.

There were internal changes of major significance as well. Men like Greeley viewed their newspapers as extensions of their personalities, vehicles to be used in sponsoring or opposing causes, crusades, and candidates, and there were many of these to be found in the two decades prior to the Civil War. Editors checked every story that went into print, to make certain they were in line with editorials and not vice versa. "I want to ascertain what reporter of the late Democratic Union Convention talked of that Convention going through the 'farce' of making up a ticket," Greeley wrote in a 1856 communiqué. "Whoever doesn't know what is a reporter's business, and that is not that of editing the paper—ought to find some other place."[4] Should a reporter write several stories that contradicted the editorial policy—no matter how factual or correct they were—he could be fired, and perhaps seek employment on the rival newspaper in town.

And the newspapers of the postwar period were becoming larger, both in size and circulation, and so offered opportunities to young men wanting positions. Most small-town papers had circulations below twenty thousand, but major city newspapers sold over eighty thousand copies of some editions, while issues of one hundred thousand copies, though rare, did exist. The staffs, which grew in size during the war in order to report on military events, remained after Appomattox.

No longer could a major newspaper reflect the views of a single person, simply because no editor or publisher could find the time for the tasks. Greeley's *Tribune*, for example, had a local staff of some thirty reporters in the late 1860s, and was by no means the largest employer of newsmen in the city. Although reporters' salaries remained low, the newspaper's expenditures soared. The *Tribune* raised its price to two cents on the eve of the war and then to four cents shortly before the fighting ended. Still, margins were tight, as the price of newsprint, rent, and all else that went into the business of news rose dramatically. The largest jump in costs came in the area of the news itself, however. In 1863, the *Tribune* spent $49,000 for nonwar editors and reporters and an additional $25,700 for war news. That year, the print shop cost $49,500 in wages. For the first time, the news room and related operations cost the paper more than the print shop.[5] Much of this cost could not be recovered; whenever Greeley raised the price of the *Tribune*, he would expand its number of pages. But the better reporting was reflected in quality, not quantity, and although he understood this, he could not transmit the ideas to his readers, some of whom complained they were being charged the higher price for the same amount of news. Naturally, profit margins declined. On revenues of $736,000 in 1864, the paper reported a profit of less than $12,000.

Public figures as they were, the major publisher-editors spent a good deal of their time in Washington, engaged in politics and war-related activities. While at home, they found that the financial and managerial sides of the business took more time than before, leaving little for actual writing and editing. Some continued their practice of writing for magazines, and a few, Greeley included, went on speaking tours to the back country. And while they did, their journals became larger and more complex, run by the editorial staff, the managing editors in particular. The *Times* and the *Tribune* sent reporters to Europe in 1866 to cover the Austro-Prussian War, and by the end of the decade, these newspapers and others had permanent foreign correspondents, not mere stringers. By then too the larger papers had special writers for fashion news, entertainment, and other amusements the editors thought might draw readers.[6] Some reporters were paid by the word, others by the piece, while a few were out on what amounted to retainers, receiving salaries even though little of what they had written might be printed in any given edition.

The publisher-editors could not be expected to keep track of all this, while still attending to their other interests. So the editorial staffs developed in size as well as power. Where prior to the war the publisher-editor would go over each story, now there were copy editors, trusted men who more often than not came out of the press room instead of the editorial staff. The great publisher-editors had dominated their newspapers; toward the end of their careers, they had institutionalized their positions, many without even realizing what had occurred. By the time Raymond had died in 1869, the *Times* had outgrown him; it had an editorial staff, trained by the publisher, to be sure, but which acted independently of him on a day-to-day basis. The same was true at the *Herald*, where Bennett died in 1872. Toward the end of his life, Greeley was obsessed with politics and allowed the *Tribune* to be run by the staff.

Although newspapers grew, and the large ones prospered in the postbellum period, no new paths of development appeared for two decades. In New York, James Gordon Bennett, Jr., was content to leave the business of news to others. He spent a good deal of his time abroad, and although responsible for some of the *Herald's* more sensational stories of the period—he sponsored reporter Henry Stanley's expedition to find David Livingstone in equatorial Africa—he did little else but draw a large salary and send in ideas from his European residences. There was a brief power struggle at the *Tribune*, after which Whitelaw Reid took charge as editor. Reid was a practical, conservative businessman, who when he needed additional capital obtained it from Jay Gould, the notorious financial buccaneer. But Gould had no discernible influence in the editorial policy, and as far as can be determined, looked upon his investment as just that and little else. Reid understood that the stress in the word "newspaper" had to be on the first syllable. As he put it, "In making a newspaper, the heaviest item of expense used to be the white paper. Now it is the news. By and by, let us hope, it will be the brains." As for the *Times*, control passed to George Jones, one of Raymond's original backers, in 1869. The paper remained independent, somewhat stuffy, and modest in reach and goals.

The younger Bennett had been raised in the atmosphere of the newspaper, but he knew little of the mechanical end of the industry. Reid had been a part owner and editor of Ohio newspapers, a reporter, and had come to the *Tribune* as chief editorial writer in 1868. He was managing editor at the time of Greeley's death and his own promotion. Jones was a businessman who knew Greeley in his youth, had dabbled in newspapers, but always had other interests. Although the newspaper's owner, he did not become its editor. Jones approved several *Times* crusades—one against the Tweed ring in New York in particular—but tended to view the property as a good investment and little else.

The era of publisher-printer-editors was passing, at least in the large cities and at the major American newspapers. The old ways continued in villages and towns, on the weeklies in particular. But as the city continued to emerge as the focal point of American life, its newspapers were viewed as superior to all others. The small-town reader would subscribe to his local gazette, in order to keep informed of gossip and the problems of the town and region. He would also maintain a subscription to a city newspaper, and after he read it he would pass it on to others. The Civil War had broadened the national views; one of its effects was to serve as a combination geography-politics-economics schoolroom for the nation, and the readership habits and desires inculcated in the early 1860s remained after the war. Having found what appeared to be a proper formula for success, the managers of the large newspapers tended to stand pat.

The commercial and political newspapers had been crippled and in the end all but killed by the penny press, itself the product of three significant developments: an enlarged, different kind of readership; a new, improved technology; and the emergence of a unique management and editorial ethic, financed and directed by a handful of extraordinary individuals who understood the situation and were capable of capitalizing upon it. After a season of comparative calm in the 1870s and early 1880s, a similar set of circumstances presented itself, along with opportunities for innovation and power. And as before, they were seized.

The nation's population was changing and growing, in a fashion unexpected at the time of Greeley's death in 1873. There were forty-three million Americans that year; the number doubled by 1905. Although the percentage increase had not been as rapid as that of the 1840s and 1850s, it was most impressive in the aggregate, and more so because so many of the new Americans lived in cities and towns. In 1873, one out of every four Americans lived in an urban area. In 1905, the figure was close to two out of every five.

The cities had changed. By the 1880s the Irish migrants had begun to be absorbed into the national life; the bloody riots were no more, even though major problems persisted. At that time, more than three out of every four Americans had been born in some other country, but the percentage was declining, as it had since the 1860s. By the turn of the century, however, the figure leveled off, and began to rise once more. The 1910 Census indicated that 13.5 million Americans—slightly fewer than one in seven—were foreign-born, and contemporary accounts estimated that a like amount were minor children of immigrant parents. Most of the immigrants lived in cities, which led native-born Americans—some of them, at least—to describe them as more akin to oriental bazaars than centers of American life. Nor were the foreign-born the only strangers in the cities. One in four native-born citizens lived in a state other than that in which he or she had been born, and the majority of the relocations were due to changes from rural to urban settings.

The cities had become the centers of national life. Increasingly, they were the dwelling places and working places of the foreign born. And, of course, they had always been the centers for the nation's largest and most influential newspapers.

Three out of every four immigrants were literate in their native languages, but few understood or could read English. They would learn quickly—citizenship, jobs, and economic well-being depended upon it. In time, almost all would become potential customers for one or several urban English-language newspapers. But the old penny press and its warmed-over successors, geared as they were for native Americans and middle-class in orientation, would not do. A new kind of newspaper was required, one that appealed to the large laboring class that had a substantial immigrant component. The old forms might suffice, but they would require new contents.

JOURNALISM TRANSFORMED

If the requirements of the new market could be ignored for the time being, the technological and economic challenges in the print shop had to be faced. For one thing, Richard Hoe & Co. continued to improve presses and raise prices. An eight-cylinder flatbed press, introduced in 1863, turned out from sixteen thousand to twenty-two thousand copies an hour, each page printed on one side. In 1880, Hoe offered a double-web rotary perfecting press, not only capable of printing thirty thousand pages per hour, but also doing so on both sides, as well as cutting, pasting, and folding. The larger newspapers rushed to order the new machines, for without them they could not keep up with the competition. Increased circulation and advertising more than paid for the installations, and even the enlarged labor bills they brought in their wakes; for the giant Hoes required teams of skilled workers, and with each installation, new workers were hired, often at higher salaries, since greater knowledge was required to run the giants. The colonial print shop, in which the publisher set type and then ran off copies on his flatbed hand press, had been replaced by the print shop of the penny press, in which the functions of typesetter and pressman were separated, with the publisher and editor in different parts of the building. The functions were far more specialized by the late 1880s—the shop had machinists, firemen, paper hustlers, and foremen, as well as compositors and pressmen. The installation of the new machines resulted in quantum jumps in productivity, so that despite the higher costs, profits at the major urban newspapers increased.[7] Additionally, the large-circulation dailies that dominated the scene at the turn of the century would not have been possible without the high-speed press.

Even more important were the changes in the role of the compositor that resulted from the introduction of new machinery and techniques. From the first, the compositor had been considered the aristocrat of the press room. It took brawn to operate the hand presses, and engineering knowledge to master the double webs, but composition required a subtle blend of art and science. With stick in hand the compositor would set type manually, justifying the lines as he went. The fastest could set 1,000 "ems" in an hour—an em being the breadth of the letter *m*—or about 350 words. The press crew would await corrected copy from upstairs, which would then go to the compositor, who would put it into type. The completed material would then be fixed in a stereotype, placed on the press, and the newspaper was "ready to roll." Clearly a skilled compositor was to be prized. In the midnineteenth century, they were wooed from one newspaper to another, in much the same way as popular journalists would in the early twentieth century and television commentators are today. Dozens of inventors attempted to perfect a mechanical composition machine, and when success appeared possible, they would take them to the newspapers and ask for financial backing. Often this was forthcoming, and the large papers lost small fortunes in the failures.

The idea for the successful composition machine originated with James O. Clephane, a Washington court stenographer and promotor, but the machine itself was invented by Ottmar Mergenthaler, a German immigrant. Together they formed the National Typographic Company of West Virginia in 1883, and while Mergenthaler perfected his machine, Clephane sought financial backing.

This was a period of labor unrest at many newspapers. Wages had been cut during the depression that had followed the financial panic of 1873, and although there had been a measure of recovery by 1877, wages had not risen. In addition, the division between the print shop and the editorial offices was growing. Reporters were coming to be recognized as key personnel; they had the visibility and status lacking in the print shop.[8] In order both to restore their wages to their previous level and indicate their power, the typographical union locals called their members out on strike at several large newspapers. The publishers responded by hiring scabs, but the work of the newspapers suffered. Satisfactory scabs could be found for most functions, but not that of composition. Because of this, the work slowed down and the quality deteriorated.

The New York *Tribune* and the Chicago *Daily News* were affected by the strikes. Thus Reid and Melville Stone of the *Daily News* were interested in the Mergenthaler machine. They and others invested in the business, eventually putting some three hundred thousand dollars into it. Encouraged and with sufficient capital, Mergenthaler perfected his "linotype," and the first of them was placed into the *Tribune* press room in 1886. The machine was an instant success. During the next three years, Mergenthaler delivered fifty of them to newspapers, and had a backlog that kept his shop busy and on double shifts. Reid was ecstatic. He would make more money from his investment in the linotype than he would from the *Tribune*; the machines would save his newspaper eighty thousand dollars in labor costs in 1889 alone; and the strikes were broken.

The linotype altered the economics of the print shop and completed the separation of the mechanical from the editorial function. The machines threw hundreds of compositors out of work, so by the end of the century they could not be found on the staffs of "progressive" newspapers in large cities. Linotype operators who could be trained in a matter of weeks took their places. They were considered workers, not artisans, and were so treated by the printers and the publishers. Although other machines were introduced in the next few years, the linotype was the key to the great change to what was called the New Journalism, one hallmark of which was the divorce of those who worked with ideas from the men who worked with their hands.[9]

The print shop workers responded to the change in several ways, the most important of which was the development of new and more efficient unions, which often contested one another for power and members. One of these, the International Printing Pressmen's Union, went from 516 members in 1895 to 17,545 ten years later. It was restricted to skilled workers, unlike some of the others, which accepted the semiskilled as well. "The cost of presses is a serious expense," its leader told a group of publishers, "but if they can be kept fairly employed there need be no loss." He urged the publishers to use men registered with his union. "It is a mistake to allow a machine that costs thousands of dollars to be managed by an incompetent pressman. . . . The superior performance of the qualified workman fairly justifies his higher wages."[10] Workers such as these would seek better conditions in the shop, shorter hours, and higher wages. They would remain workers, and management would be viewed as capitalists, and here too the gulf would grow. In time, some printers would receive higher wages than editors and reporters, but the link between the press room and the editorial office had been broken.

Management, both at the individual newspapers and within the industry, was the final factor in the equation. A new kind of editor and publisher appeared, to capitalize on the enlarged and different kind of market for newspapers as well as the new technology. In fact, there were two forms of leadership, one to reshape the newspapers, the other to help create a businesslike industry. This required different talents, which few men possessed and fewer still were able to develop effectively.

Without a doubt the most influential of the new publisher-editors (as distinct from publisher-businessmen) was Joseph Pulitzer, the son of well-to-do parents, an immigrant who fought on the Union side during the Civil War and who settled in St. Louis after the war. Pulitzer worked on riverboats, performed odd jobs in factories, and tried to find a place in the city's German community. He studied law and was admitted to the bar; for a while he considered a political career. But in 1868, at the age of twenty-one, Pulitzer became a reporter for a German-language newspaper. After an unsuccessful fling at politics and a trip abroad, he returned to St. Louis, where he purchased a failing newspaper and there learned the business side of the industry, while at the same time writing columns for other, larger papers. Pulitzer purchased the St. Louis *Dispatch*, a bankrupt newspaper, in 1878, and shortly thereafter combined it with the St. Louis *Post* to form the St. Louis *Post-Dispatch*. Under his leadership the newspaper initiated crusades against municipal corruption, tax dodging by prominent citizens, and crime. In this, he was little different from the key editors of the prewar period—Greeley, Bennett, and others—except that from the first Pulitzer stressed the news part of the paper, not the editorials. In effect, each news story was a small editorial, or part of the whole. The over-all impression was organic unity, as had been the case with the old New York *Tribune*, but there was a difference. Greeley had insisted that reporters write his kind of news; they were granted little independence, and they understood that the editorial, not the news story, was the central feature of the newspaper.

Pulitzer made certain his reporters believed as he did, were well-trained, incorruptible, and had a respect for truth and a zeal for reform. At a time when the St. Louis press corps had a reputation for shoddy practices and shaky morals, he sought men and women who could be called "professional," and certainly were educated. He chose his people carefully, but then Pulitzer tended to permit them a large measure of autonomy. The result was a newspaper that appeared similar to the penny press, but with a significant difference: The reporter, not the editor, was the central and prominent figure, in fact if not in theory and status. It was a time when many newspapers printed stories without signatures; the *Post-Dispatch*, along with other aggressive journals, utilized by-lines, which gave additional status and prominence to the reporters.

As for the pressmen, they existed to serve the top floor at the *Post-Dispatch*. Pulitzer had never worked in the print shop. To him, the reporter was a person who trafficked with ideas, not a laborer with ink and print once removed.

In 1883 Pulitzer purchased the New York *World*, a failing paper with a circulation of only fifteen thousand, for $346,000. He moved to New York and applied his methods to the paper. Pulitzer fired the hacks that he had inherited, imported several newsmen from the *Post-Dispatch*, raided other newspapers for their better writers, and within a matter of weeks managed to turn the *World* around. This was done not only by producing a better newspaper, but also by catering to the desires of his audience.

The immigrant Pulitzer instinctively appreciated the needs and attitudes of the newcomers to New York, and what he lacked in instinct he made up with intelligence and marketing abilities. In the first issue of the new *World*, Pulitzer wrote, "There is room in this great and growing city for a journal that is not only cheap but bright, not only bright but large, not only large but truly Democratic—dedicated to the cause of the people rather than that of the purse-potentates—devoted more to the news of the New than the Old World—that will expose all fraud and sham, fight all public evils and abuses—that will serve and battle for the people with earnest sincerity."[11] Pulitzer hoped to defend the poor against the wealthy, to support reforms in the political and economic systems, and to present the news fairly and honestly. More important than all of this in terms of the newspaper's orientation, however, he claimed to be the champion of the patriotic immigrant against the nativist, with the *World* functioning as an Americanizing agent. The old *World* was a stodgy newspaper; Pulitzer radically revised the front page, publishing illustrations there and throughout the paper. He featured human-interest stories, specializing in crime and corruption, both of which sold copies. While the city's other major newspapers tended to headline national and even international events, Pulitzer concentrated on the city's problems. The approach worked. Within a year the

World was the city's leading newspaper in terms of advertising and circulation, and was on its way to becoming nationally prominent.

By then, Pulitzer was being compared with the elder Bennett—both men seemed to specialize in sensation, and each set the tone for others in his period. But there were differences, both in editorial content and organization. Bennett was a nativist and a conservative who, among other things, defended slavery, while Pulitzer was identified with almost all the reform movements of his day. Bennett utilized the *Herald* as his own private platform, and considered the paper an extension of his personality. Pulitzer continued the policies initiated at the *Post-Dispatch* at the *World*. His editors were selected with great care, more often than not after a search of rival newspapers for candidates. Other publishers tended to promote senior reporters to editorships, while on the smaller dailies and weeklies, the path from the print shop to the editorial desk still existed. It was different at the *World*. In 1904 Frank Cobb was recommended for the post of editorial writer, and Pulitzer asked, "What has Cobb read in American history, Rhodes, McMaster, Trevelyan, Parkman? What works on the constitution and constitutional law? Has he read Buckle's history of civilization? . . . Search his brain for everything there is in it."[12] Cobb passed muster, accepted the position when it was offered, and in time headed the paper. His initiation was not unusual. Pulitzer rode herd on his reporters, insisting upon accuracy, exciting stories, and efficiency, for which he paid better-than-average salaries. As a result, the *World* became known for its tough approach, while Pulitzer was considered one of the best teachers of journalism in the nation. He regularly encouraged interested and intelligent young people to apply to the *World* for positions. "So far as we know," he editorialized in 1884, "the *World* is the only newspaper in New York that holds out encouragement to developing young men. We are always on the lookout for bright reporters, correspondents, editors, poets, artists &c. We are always willing to give an ambitious young man a trial." So he did, hiring more reporters than he needed, setting them against one another and retaining the winners. Theodore Dreiser, some of whose prose appeared in the *World* in the 1890s, recalled that the reporters there "had a kind of nervous, resentful terror in their eyes as have animals when they are tortured. All were either scribbling busily or hurrying in or out. Every man was for himself. . . . I had never encountered anything like it before."[13] It was tough, but the method worked. By the end of the century the *World* had become a school for the profession; it was not unusual for an ambitious reporter to stay there for a while to learn all he could. Afterward, he would try to find a job on another newspaper, with the *World* experience his best recommendation. Pulitzer often talked of establishing a "school or lyceum for journalists," but never did so in a formal sense. On the other hand, the *World* itself did much to professionalize journalism and oblige other papers to live up to its standards.

Pulitzer was uneasy regarding some aspects of the new journalism he had done so much to create. More than anything else, he feared it prized sensationalism above all. He insisted that the *World* articles had to be important to its readers, significant for the community, help progressive forces, and above all, accurate. Furthermore, his editors and reporters were to present the news and comment upon it; they were not to distort for the sake of faction, or actually make the news. But if the distinction existed, it was a fine one, and the line between the observer and the commentator, and then between the commentator and the propagandist, was a thin one, and often crossed. Pulitzer, who understood the distinctions, was guilty of violations of faith himself. Those who succeeded him, and the many others who imitated the *World*, tended to ignore the line completely.

The most famous of these, of course, was William Randolph Hearst, the flamboyant publisher-editor, certainly the most powerful up to his time. The son of a mining millionaire, Hearst cut his teeth by publishing the San Francisco *Examiner*, which he took over in 1887, when twenty-four years old. Quickly the *Examiner* was transformed into a sensationalist newspaper, one that seemed a West Coast version of the *World*. Seven years later he arrived in New York to take charge of the *Morning Journal* which, ironically, had been founded by Pulitzer's brother, Albert. Spending money lavishly, hiring the best reporters, and revamping the rather staid newspaper—and even changing its name to the New York *Journal*—Hearst created the most talked-about paper in the land.

Where Pulitzer insisted upon facts to substantiate exciting stories, Hearst was willing to twist, ignore, and even create the facts when necessary. His famous telegram to Frederic Remington, who had gone to Cuba in 1897 to investigate the war, found none, and reported the same to Hearst, had been quoted in every history of journalism—"Please remain," said Hearst. "You furnish the pictures and I'll furnish the war."

Whether or not Hearst was responsible for the Spanish-American War, as was once believed, is debatable, but he did father what is known as "yellow journalism." This may be categorized as Pulitzer's sensational approach without undue interest in reform, little in the way of a philosophical base, and an often careless regard for facts and accuracy. Unlike Pulitzer, to whom he was often compared, Hearst did not require his reporters and editors to possess intellectual depth or ideological consistency. All that really mattered was their ability to develop stories faster than the competition and their contribution to circulation. This meant that at times the Hearst reporters were required—or at least encouraged—to make news as well as report it, the most obvious example being the war, when Hearst intruded himself in the area of diplomatic negotiations. Hearst fathered the concept of the reporter as a public figure, and helped set the stage for the muckraking period that followed the Spanish-American War. In time, he became a major public figure, the first publisher since Greeley to entertain serious notions about running for the presidency. But although his work at the *Journal* was important and helped to make him famous, Hearst's influence derived from more than his variations on the themes set forth by Bennett and Pulitzer. It emerged from his abilities to meld the ideas of both with his own, and then combine them with the structure developed by another publisher, Edward Wyllis Scripps.

The Scripps was a newspaper family—three of E.W.'s half brothers and a half sister had entered the newspaper field before him. Brother James founded the Detroit *News*, and all of them worked there for a while in the 1870s. Toward the end of the decade, E.W. decided to strike out on his own. He had little money but great ambition, and a desire to run his own paper. Clearly New York and Chicago were beyond his grasp; he would have to settle for a smaller city. His funds were such that he could not hope to do well in morning newspapers. For the most part, these contained complete news—or at least had aspirations in that direction—and turned out several editions during the morning. The afternoon papers of that time often were thinly disguised rewrites of the morning news plus short items on any stories that might develop during the day and could be featured in headline fashion. Morning newspapers required large staffs of reporters and editors; afternoon papers stressed rewrite editors, men and women who received relatively low salaries and could be hired and fired with ease. Knowing this, Scripps decided to found an afternoon paper, and selected Cleveland as his city.

The Cleveland *Press*, the first issue of which came out in 1878, was a small, unpretentious newspaper. Although it soon led the afternoon field in Cleveland, the competition was minor, and so the honor meant little. But it did show a profit. Scripps, who up to that time had evidenced little interest in journalism as a profession, came to realize that it could be an excellent business. Together with relatives, he purchased the St. Louis *Chronicle*, which performed poorly. He did better in Cincinnati, with the *Post*, and in 1890 he founded the Covington, Kentucky *Post*, another profit-maker. By then, Scripps felt he had come upon the proper formula for success. Like Pulitzer, he would advocate social reforms, but would do so through editorials and columns, which cost less than a staff of reporters. He sought advertisers, but since his costs were so low, he did not have to gear his editorial policies to their dictates. If Scripps had any clear ambitions as a pioneer, it was his dream of a newspaper without advertisements—a dream he never realized.

With the Kentucky *Post* in the black in 1890, Scripps decided to "retire" to a ranch near San Diego and spend the rest of his life on his favorite pursuits—seducing women, drinking whiskey, and playing poker. His business manager, Milton A. McRae, would handle day-to-day operations; Scripps would concern himself only with long-range strategy and any emergencies that might arise.[14] Together with McRae he would select a likely city or town for a newspaper, hire an ambitious young editor to do the work, put him on a strict budget, and offer him a minority interest in the paper if he succeeded. In the period from 1893 to 1926, when Scripps died, the Scripps-McRae chain purchased or founded thirty-five newspapers, of which two were sold off and eight discontinued due to failure. In the process, Scripps amassed a fortune of fifty million dollars.

Frank Munsey, a telegrapher who entered the magazine field, followed Scripps' example, adding to it a few ideas of his own. *Golden Argosy*, which featured Horatio Alger-type success stories, was popular in the early 1880s, and *Munsey's*, a general-interest monthly that became a weekly in 1889, did even better. Munsey found himself with a great deal of money, and he looked for ventures in which to invest. For a while he concentrated on banks and real estate. Then he put a few thousand dollars into a budding grocery chain. Not many of these did well, but the grocery business gave him the idea of creating a newspaper empire. As he later wrote, "Think of the possibilities involved in a chain of five hundred newspapers under a single control! Such a faculty could be so maintained as no college could support; the greatest authors, artists, engineers, essayists, and statesmen could write with authority on every question of importance, each of the five hundred papers getting the benefit of these great minds, while maintaining their individuality on purely local matters." This giant enterprise would bring to a proper height the business of news. "There could be a one-hundred-thousand-dollar or two-hundred-thousand-dollar-a-year man at the head of the editorial force and another God-made genius in charge of the business end," he wrote.[15] And, said Munsey, he would try to bring it about.

Munsey's actions were those of a businessman seeking to maximize profits more than anything else, and he was not very good at it. He began by purchasing the New York *Star* in 1891. Munsey renamed it the *Continent*, tried to win readers by printing sensationalist stories and more pictures than anyone else, but in the end was forced to sell out. During the next thirty-four years he bought and sold many newspapers, usually second-rate operations in major cities, rarely doing well with any of them. Munsey would invest funds, seek qualified editors and reporters, and try to make his mark. If the attempt failed, he would sell the newspaper to the highest bidder, or lacking customers, would simply close it down. Even more than Scripps—who at least tried to develop a common style and approach for his newspapers—Munsey was a businessman, with newspapers his commodities. William Allen White, the editor-publisher of the Emporia *Gazette*, wrote that

Munsey had the talent of a meatpacker, the morals of a money changer, and the manners of an undertaker. "He and his kind have about succeeded in transforming a once-noble profession into an 8 per cent security."

Newspapers had become a business, at least for the publishers, and although Munsey was an extreme case, most publishers were concerned with the dollars-and-cents aspects of the business. Hearst was one of the few publishers able to combine the contents of the revived journalism of the 1890s with the forms of the new big-business structure then developing in the country. He added newspapers to his chain, slowly at first, and then picking up steam on the eve of World War I. He had the money, the ability and the reputation to seek a leading position in the large cities, and he achieved his goal. By 1935, Hearst owned twenty-six daily newspapers in nineteen cities, which accounted for one reader out of every eight in the nation. In addition, he controlled news syndicates, magazines, radio stations, and motion picture firms. What Munsey had dreamed about, Hearst had achieved.

By the early part of the twentieth century, the American newspaper had reached its apogee. There were twenty-two hundred dailies published in 1910; never before or since would there be so many. By then, too, journalism had become professionalized, while the newspaperman was considered a key molder of opinion in his own right, divorced from the publishers in many cases. As for the latter, the age of Pulitzer was not ended, but just as the printer-publisher-editor-reporter had been displaced by the printer-publisher-editor, and he in turn by the publisher-editor, so the businessman-publisher was coming into his own. Hearst was not a prototype for the future, rather a unique individual, a giant who straddled several periods and industries in his long career. The future rested with publishers like Scripps and Munsey. Economic pressures—the high costs of operation, the saturation of markets—dictated consolidation and the formation of chains; publishers had to be at least as concerned with double-entry bookkeeping as with editorials; without a healthy respect for the former, the latter would not appear. The newspaper itself, then, was left to others to run on a day-to-day basis.

THE EMERGING AGE OF THE REPORTER

In the early twentieth century, then, the age of the reporter began. Just as diversity was coming to rule in other branches of American business, so it was happening with newspapers—the first and at the time still the most important means by which Americans received information from outside their own circle. Had the old structure remained—had reporters still emerged from the print shops and retained managerial or even financial responsibilities for their newspapers—their outlooks might have been in harmony with those of laborers or businessmen. Such was not the case, however, even though they tended to sympathize with the former and, for a season at least, castigated the latter. Instead, the journalists as a group tended to form a new entity, one that in time took on some of the trappings of a caste, but that at the turn of the century was just emerging. The journalists were intellectuals, a species that had always existed in America, but in the past had been a rarer, more esoteric breed. They were the forerunners and servitors of the emerging mass intellectuals. Many came from their milieu, and at that time at least appreciated their values and aspirations. As a group they would inherit the mantles of Pulitzer and Hearst; the Scripps and Munseys of their world would have the forms of power alone, not the content.

2

The New Collegians

Joseph Pulitzer was troubled by the low status of reporters and other journalists, as well as the uneven quality of writing and editing found at most newspapers. Although journalism had had a long history in America, the craft still lacked an agreed-upon code of ethics, readily accepted criteria of conduct and performance, and a recognized means of entry into the business and profession. There was no such thing as a philosophy of journalism, although individual publishers and reporters had enunciated their beliefs and in some cases had lived up to them. Reporters still emerged from the print shop at the turn of the century, came from the ranks of failed novelists, or were wastrel sons of wealthy parents, itinerant teachers, or marginal individuals. Some of them did well, and rose to become editors. But who was to judge their qualities, and against what criteria? For the most part, journalism operated by means of the apprentice system, the only certification being performance. It was not an unusual training method; similar ones were traveled by most lawyers, teachers, pharmacists, and doctors in the last part of the nineteenth century. All of this was soon to change. By World War I, individuals in these pursuits would be known as "professionals" and seek the academic credentials that came with the designation.[1]

A man of action who quickly became irritated with delays and could not stand irrationality, Pulitzer was determined to alter the situation in journalism and to professionalize the occupation. He would help create a respectable place where would-be newspapermen could be educated and trained, a center for the profession, where standards could be set that could be spread throughout the land—really a West Point for journalists. Pulitzer thought such a place should be located at Columbia University, a respected but rather impoverished school not too far from the *World's* Manhattan offices. The publisher was not convinced though, that one could obtain an education in such a place. "The best college is the college of the world," he once said, and he preferred the "university of actual experience." From what he had seen of college graduates, Pulitzer was certain the nation's schools were places where idleness and sloth reigned. Yet he wanted his school of journalism. He approached the Columbia trustees in 1892 with his ideas. Not only would he finance the new school, but also it would become a major beneficiary of his estate.

Although the offer was first rejected out of hand, Pulitzer began a twelve-year courtship of Columbia. For once the impatient publisher, who had made and unmade Presidents of the United States, was obliged to be tactful and diplomatic. He told Columbia President Nicholas Murray Butler that he would give the new school two million outright, with more to come later on. He would have no connection with the school, no voice in its direction. However, when Pulitzer tried to establish an advisory board consisting, among others, of the presidents of other universities, Butler became annoyed, and the publisher beat a rapid withdrawal. Finally, in 1903, Columbia accepted the Pulitzer donation.[2] But the "College of Journalism" that Pulitzer so wanted did not open until 1912, shortly after the publisher's death.

By then, journalism was being offered as a subject in more than thirty colleges and universities. Between 1903 and 1912 several state press associations had adopted codes of ethics, and the American Association of Teachers of Journalism had been formed. Sigma Delta Chi, the professional journalistic fraternity, was established in 1909 at DePauw University, and shortly thereafter Theta Sigma Phi, an honorary fraternity for women in journalism, was begun at the University of Washington. In 1912 a National Newspaper Conference, the first of its kind, was held at the University of Wisconsin, and a second one followed two years later at the University of Kansas. A nexus had been formed between the journalists and the universities. Professionalization was on its way.

It was an uneasy alliance, more so on the part of the universities than the newspapers. At the latter the distinct divisions among reporters and editors, the press room, and publishers, were becoming evident. Each group had its functions, problems, and rewards; if the newspaper as product was turned out by the printers, and the newspaper as business was dominated by the publisher as part of a chain of enterprises, the newpaper as information and opinion source was becoming the domain of the editors and reporters.

The situation was far more confused and complex at the colleges and universities, where problems existed that were only then coming to be recognized and that even today have not been fully resolved. Which groups did the colleges and universities exist to serve, and how did they accomplish their goals? Why did each group enter academia? What was the meaning of a "college education"? For that matter, did college necessarily have much to do with education?

Most of these questions seem to be directed at the students for they, after all, were the consumers of whatever it was that colleges produced and offered, the reason for their existence. But is this really the case? And if so, has it always been?

THE ANATOMY OF THE AMERICAN COLLEGE

In the nineteenth century most colleges had five major human components, each of which performed a different task and received its own rewards. The most easily understood were the workers—carpenters, cleaning people, groundskeepers, and the like—who maintained the operation as they might any business. It might be argued that workers at colleges had special affection for the places, and indeed many did; the tale of the gardener who tended the shrubs and retired after a half century was not fiction. In this respect, the college was similar to that other preindustrial organization, the church, in that it retained affections in a semifeudal fashion. Increasingly, however, it was becoming more like the modern corporation, and the newer employees who took the places of the old retainers in the early twentieth century appeared to have accepted that view. There are no data on wages paid each worker category, but given the increases in costs at many colleges in this period, and taking into account charges for other services, it would appear that wages were on the rise—the loss in psychic income being made up by increases in monetary returns, a phenomenon that we have noted appeared in the print shops of major newspapers at the same time.

The second group was comprised of the trustees. In the early and middle years of the nineteenth century most had come from the ministry or had been respected small-town figures. For their efforts they received little but psychic income, in the form of public recognition and inner feelings of satisfaction. In their own small worlds, the power held and exerted by trustees was not to be despised. Nor was the opportunity clergymen had to make certain their ranks were replenished by a steady stream of likely new candidates. After the Civil War, businessmen also appeared on boards of trustees in larger numbers, donating money as well as time.[3] In return for this they achieved a higher status than that to which they had been born, a contact with the arts and sciences that otherwise might have been denied them, and a belief that their lives had been spent in more than "mere money grubbing." Andrew Carnegie thought his fortune worth having only for the good he might do with it, and many of his benevolences were associated with colleges and with education in general. Ezra Cornell, Johns Hopkins, Cornelius Vanderbilt, Leland Stanford, and James Buchanan Duke each gave considerable sums to institutions bearing their names, and directly or indirectly—usually the latter—dominated them, at least in their infancies. The Rockefellers bankrolled the University of Chicago to the tune of thirty million dollars, making it a major institution almost overnight. "I want to save more money than ever for public institutions and purposes," wrote Pulitzer, and other tycoons felt similar impulses. For them, the college was a means of gaining immortality and respectability.

The third component, the faculty, was considered the core of the institution, its source of continuity. Here rewards and tasks became confused, and cannot be isolated or easily identified. In the midnineteenth century the faculties of most colleges were a mixed bag, an assortment of individuals who had been drawn there for one or more of three reasons. There were many who might be termed "vocationalists," for they hoped to inculcate in their students a vision of Christianity that would lead them to the pulpit. To them the college was more a seminary than anything else, a view wholly consistent with the early history of colleges in the colonial and national periods. Vocationalism had two meanings. Not only did they seek students who had vocations for the ministry, but they also considered the college a variety of professional—or trade—school. The students were there not for educations, but to prepare themselves for jobs, the most important of which was that of minister. A second faculty type, divorced from the first, was uninterested in both meanings of the term, at least insofar as the college was concerned. To him, college was a finishing school of sorts, the place where a gentleman-in-embryo might perfect his personality, mingle with others of his social class, and emerge a polite, well-mannered member of his group, prepared for no specific job, but more than able to fill the niche to which he had been born. Finally, there were some faculty who were interested in knowledge, for its own sake if possible, for the students if necessary (as it sometimes was). They were scientists who, in order to survive economically, turned to teaching, but spent a good deal of time furthering their knowledge of their craft, or historians who were interested in exploring the past and perhaps writing about it, but who needed an income at the same time. All three varieties of faculty could be found in the nation's colleges, and although the distinctions among them were not made in the midnineteenth century, they were recognized if not labeled as such by the early twentieth century. In this span of time, the colleges began under the domination of the vocationalists, shifted to the finishing school advocates, and ended with the scholars on the ascendant, but with a new group of vocationalists in the wings.

In many respects, the fourth group, the students, mirrored the faculty, although each would have denied resemblances, and on occasion would have been shocked or insulted by the comparisons. Some students were interested in attending college as a preparation for a clearly defined occupation. The ministry was important in this area, but so were several others. Despite the lack of accrediting facilities, the better secondary schools sought college graduates for their teachers, and this was certainly the case at the well-known preparatory schools, which were conduits to Yale and Harvard. Doctors, lawyers, and others, however, who in the twentieth century would be forced into an educational mold, had a much easier time of it in the nineteenth century. One could enter a medical school or read law without necessarily having attended college; there was a sharp delineation between students who went to college and those who attended professional schools, with the latter clearly a notch behind socially. The majority of students sought a social environment in college, a place where they would be able to live together with their peers for four years, enjoy themselves in a last fling before entering into adulthood. Then there was that small group interested in the college as an educational enterprise, a place where they could explore the wisdom of the past and perhaps make a beginning toward the creation of new knowledge.

Clearly each faculty "type" had his counterpart in the student body and, as might have been anticipated, they tended to find one another. Friendships between faculty who led the glee club and students who spent four years in such organizations lasted beyond the four college years; a minister-president would oversee the career of his neophytes and make certain they found their proper pulpits; the academically inclined student might, if he or she was fortunate, obtain a position at *alma mater* and become a junior colleague of a mentor. Equally obvious, however, was the lack of interest any of the three components had in the other two, and their contacts were rare and at times unpleasant.

The fifth component, the administrative and "professional" staff, was the smallest in the midnineteenth century, but one that would grow rapidly both in numbers and power in the early twentieth century. This branch of the staff was comprised of neither faculty nor trustees, though it emerged from the former and was allied with the latter. Presidents, provosts, deans, principals, and the like also taught classes and attended to other faculty duties. Often the librarian was a senior faculty member, taking on the additional work on a part-time basis. All would be responsible to the trustees for the proper administration of the college, but were not considered administrators—nor did they so consider themselves.

By the end of the nineteenth century, these five general divisions were being altered. There was some awareness of this among the general public, but for the most part, stereotypes were more powerful than actuality. By the late 1890s the "college boy" (or man, or lady, but never girl) had reached the status of a national figure, along with the forceful editor and the daring reporter. At a time of increasing complexity in colleges, as in newspapers, the public sought and found simplified ideals, which would long outlast any reality they once had.

There were more than two hundred colleges in America at the end of the Civil War.[4] Most were in financial difficulties. Rising costs and the absence of students during the war offered some explanation for this condition, but not entirely, for the college population had stagnated and often declined even in the 1840s and 1850s. Foreign observers, including Tocqueville, believed this a result of the leveling aspects of American culture. The educators themselves thought otherwise, with one of them, President F. A. P. Barnard of Columbia, concluding that the colleges were losing ground because they served no discernible need. When and if this changed, enrollments would increase.

It did not appear to be a major national problem. College education had always been for a small portion of the elite, and the situation was no different in 1870. The United States had a population of 40 million, of whom some 3.1 million were between the ages of eighteen and twenty-one. College enrollment that year was 52,000.

These students received a classical education, reciting their lines of Greek and Latin in classes conducted by the college president himself or others of his dwindling staff. The school itself consisted of a few small buildings; some colleges were housed in a single structure. They resembled nothing more than English preparatory schools, both in curriculum and appearance, and no matter what part of the country in which they were located, had a touch of New England about them. This was not surprising; New England was the intellectual center of America, and even then Harvard was the nation's pre-eminent school. Of the 276 college presidents of the pre-Civil War period, 116 were native New Englanders, while another large group came from New York and New Jersey. This area contained the best-endowed schools in the land, and attracted superior faculties and students.[5]

What did this mean? According to college presidents, faculty, and students of that period, the schools were intended to prepare one for a position in the ministry or for the life of a classical scholar. In the emerging industrial age, there was a declining need for the former and an almost total lack of demand for the latter. "For us the college was only a continuation of the school we had just left, with no larger opportunity and with no change in method of instruction," wrote a Columbia student of the 1860s. "We were expected to prepare so many lines of Latin and Greek, or so many problems in mathematics, or so many pages of the textbook in logic or political economy; and in the classroom we were severally called upon to disgorge this undigested information. . . ." The situation was not getting any better, at least among the smaller schools. As late as 1900, a large number of colleges were little more than secondary schools in disguise.

But the situation was changing, and rapidly, in the 1870s and 1880s. In part this was due to the work of a talented group of college presidents—Charles Eliot of Harvard, Noah Porter of Yale, James McCosh of Princeton, Andrew White of Cornell, James Angell of Michigan, John Bascom of Wisconsin, and Barnard of Columbia. Each in a different way was a leader, who if nothing else secularized their schools. Eliot pioneered with the elective system and opened Harvard to nonaristocrats; Porter eased the rigid discipline at Yale; Angell introduced nonclassical subjects into the curriculum in a rapid fashion; Bascom went so far as to say that religion need not be the core of learning; "Religion is not so much the foundation of morals, as morals the foundation of religion."

Intelligent and able as these men were, they could have accomplished little, or perhaps not even have obtained their positions, were it not for a major structural change in the nation's power elites in the post-Civil War period. During the war, but even more so afterward, a new aristocracy of money had emerged to shove aside that of breeding and status. Although they shocked the more genteel by their behavior in the business arena and in society, most of the new entrepreneurs of the industrial dispensation did not emerge from the social depths, but rather from the middle class. Some were college graduates, and those who were not often were self-educated and prided themselves on their learning and private libraries. They had more than a passing knowledge of what college life had been in the prewar period, the subjects required, and the methods of instruction—and what upper-class society deemed a good education.

Almost to a man they disapproved of all four. Such individuals had little use for people whose major talents appeared to be an ability to scan a page of Horace or dispute some fine philosophical point. An education either should equip a person to undertake a task or be a gift offered by parents to their children. The prewar college education was neither. So thought Andrew Carnegie, the leading symbol of the new age and a self-educated man himself. "While the college student has been learning a little about the barbarous and petty squabbles of a far-distant past, or trying to master languages which are dead, such knowledge as seems adapted for life upon another planet than this as far as business affairs are concerned, the future captain of industry is hotly engaged in the school of experience, obtaining the very knowledge required for his future triumphs." As far as the steel tycoon was concerned, "College education as it exists is fatal to success in that domain."

The nation had become great through the efforts of those who worked their ways to the top, lifted themselves by their bootstraps. Colleges seemed a contradiction to the American way as they interpreted it. If classical knowledge could be shown to be an important business asset, and if some secular form of Christianity rather than the uncut version could be offered, their attitudes might change. As it was, however, the businessman saw little worthwhile in colleges.

Despite this, they were willing, and some even eager, to enter into a close relationship with academia, by giving large amounts of money to old colleges and establishing new institutions that would take their names. Why was this so? It could not have been because they hoped the colleges would turn out armies of young men to staff their companies. In a period when industrialists looked for a quick and large return on investments, and these were to be had in a variety of areas, education would have been a foolish place to put surplus cash. Businessmen had criticized the colleges for not offering practical subjects, and yet few of those postwar moguls who did so attempted to establish vocational schools. Had they really desired educational experiences that would serve their narrow interests, they might better have set up such programs within their companies, or even found "captive colleges," with the teachers and staff as employees and the curriculum drawn up by the plant managers.

This was not done, or even attempted. The colleges that received contributions from businessmen in the 1870s and 1880s were not obliged to become vocational schools, or even offer business subjects and engineering. While there was occasional pressure to fire some professors or make changes in the curriculum, these related more to the donors' social and political views than to their business needs.

It was evident that the businessmen did not look upon the colleges as investments. Instead, their participation served a threefold purpose. Involvement with a college enhanced the status of the benefactor, especially if it was a new institution that bore his name. Its work would continue long after he was dead, and so the school had to be "pure" and "elevated" and could not be narrow and corrupt. Too, the college would be the kind of place that turned out what the donor believed to be fine young men and women, not necessarily business machines. It would be a laboratory for his social Darwinist views, the place where the people of the future would be trained and educated, and in some way, his mark would be upon them—at least on their diplomas. Finally, such involvement would enhance the businessman's own reputation. His children and those of his peers would go to college—even if the businessman himself had not—and there mingle with the old aristocrats, on equal terms. To them, college would be a socializing and civilizing experience, with education not necessarily important.

Beset by financial difficulties in the postwar period, the colleges attempted to come to terms with the new power leaders. They wooed them for boards of trustees, gave them honorary degrees, and tried to extract donations. In the process, they discovered the values and desires of the business leaders, and while some academicians agreed with them, others either hoped to convince the businessmen that the old ways were best or sought a middle ground. In 1870, for example, Yale's Porter wrote that the classics increased the student's awareness of life, his powers in "a counting or sales-room," and so permitted him to outperform "in a business capacity" those rivals who had not attended college. Such pleas were not very effective, however. For a while, Yale lost out in the race for funds, and in the process declined as a major institution.[6] President Martin B. Anderson of the University of Rochester was far more in tune with the times when, in 1870, he stated that "Life is for work; youth is for preparation to do work."[7] But this approach was too blunt and outspoken, and in any case, Rochester lacked the status of the older schools, and so did not develop as a major institution until later on.

Charles Eliot of Harvard was most successful in gauging the needs of the business elite and responding to them, while at the same time reforming his institution. His major contribution, the one for which he was most famous, was the elective system, which he set about establishing shortly after arriving in Cambridge in 1869. Eliot scrapped many of the old required courses, most of which were theologically and philosophically oriented, and permitted students a degree of latitude in selecting their own programs. That this was an important educational reform, one that affected the development of higher education, cannot be doubted. But it had implications far beyond education.

In the first place, Eliot signaled the beginning of the attack against the old ways in American colleges. In so doing, he opened the way for new subjects and ideas. The signal for change was given in Eliot's inaugural address. "The endless controversies whether language, philosophy, mathematics, or science supplies the best mental training, whether general education should be chiefly literary or chiefly scientific, have no practical lesson for us today," he said. "This University recognizes no real antagonism between literature and science, and consents to no such narrow alternatives as mathematics *or* classics, science *or* metaphysics. We would have them all, and at their best."[8]

No longer would students march through college in what a future generation of educationalists would call a "lock step." In time the Harvard catalogue would list courses by discipline, not class, with each student relatively free to make his own way through the school. The divisions among classes remained, and in time would become stronger than they had been prior to the Civil War (though for different reasons), but to them were added distinctions among students by interest areas. And this appealed to the social Darwinists, who now saw a competition among subject areas taking shape at Harvard and other colleges that imitated the elective system. Colleges were now free, organically, to develop as the needs of society changed, and in itself this helped revive the institutions, by making them more responsive to social desires than they had been previously.

Beyond that, the elective system was good merchandising. It enabled the customer—the student and his parents—to have a choice, offered them options, and assured them that after a certain number of years the student would receive a degree—the same kind of a degree that had been offered prior to the war. The form was the same, but the content was startlingly different. To the older generation, this appeared a dangerous watering down of education, a lowering of standards; to the "progressives" of 1880, however, the elective system opened a wide area for future development.[9]

Eliot helped alter the course of American higher education, in part through force of personality, intellect, and position, but he could not have accomplished as much as he had were it not for the fact that his ideas were in harmony with those of the people he hoped to influence. Like the businessmen who contributed funds to Harvard and the young men who attended, Eliot was a firm social Darwinist. As far as his patrons and clients were concerned, he combined reform and conservatism in the proper amounts and the correct places. The Harvard president believed in "the system"; he opposed structural political and economic changes and spoke out against socialism and populism. The system needed good men to make it work, he thought, and Harvard would provide them.

This is not to say that Eliot believed that the social order should be frozen. Change was acceptable so long as it was natural, fair, and benefited the whole. So it was that he constantly sought new programs for Harvard and was willing to experiment whenever the demands of society and students called for alterations. "No object of human inquiry can be out of place in the programme of a real university," he wrote. "It is impossible to be too catholic in the matter." He carried this liberality over into the sphere of the student body. "I want to have the College open equally to men with much money, little money, or no money, provided they all have brains," he wrote in 1904. Harvard's students, he implied, should form a natural aristocracy, readily identifiable as such by virtue of their having chosen Harvard and been accepted by the school.

Even those businessmen who opposed Eliot could appreciate that he believed in an aristocracy of performance—and they could assume that this meant they were at the top of the heap. Eliot was no leveler. "Rich people cannot be made to associate comfortably with poor people, or poor with the rich," he said, noting that Harvard had no mandate to change society. "They live, necessarily, in different ways, and each set will be uncomfortable in the habitual presence of the other." This would seem to indicate that Harvard College was a place for the successful of this world, and indeed, Eliot wrote that "The pecuniary capacity of parents is one valuable indication of the probable capacity of their son or daughter." Thus winners begot winners. On the other hand, he admitted "that pecuniary capacity is subject to so many adverse chances which do not really affect the promise of children that I am not disposed to make that indication the most important one."[10]

Eliot's "soft utilitarianism" not only suited the age, but also enabled the liberal arts college to survive, with at least its form intact, and even to thrive. His influence was felt beyond Massachusetts. At the same time, other educational leaders and businessmen came to conclusions similar to Eliot's, and they applied their ideas in much the same fashion as was the case at Harvard.

The curricular revolution in undergraduate liberal arts education was in full swing by the early 1890s, with most presidents and deans of leading institutions taking their stands one way or another on the question of what constituted an acceptable curriculum at their schools. The definition of liberal arts was changing, but it was still considered the major reason for the existence of the colleges. Other kinds of schools were appearing, and colleges were becoming universities, but the debate on the liberal arts attracted the largest share of interest in academic circles.

Throughout the nation educators were saying that the college experience should become more attuned to the world as it existed, and not to the past or to some utopian ideal. The president of Washington State University believed colleges should not produce "a holiness class which is rendered unclean by contact with material concerns," and his Stanford counterpart thought knowledge should be judged by its "ability to harmonize the forces of life." "The college years are no longer conceived of as a period set apart from life," added a New York University professor. "The college has ceased to be a cloister and has become a workshop."

To men such as these, reform meant curriculum changes that would make education less classical and more contemporary. The student would be given his choice of several paths and would be expected to choose "meaningful" programs. But while faculties and administrations discussed educational philosophy, many undergraduates set about creating their own versions of reality on the campuses. More often than not, these had little to do with those matters that concerned the faculties. But like their plans, and all versions of reality set up in a hothouse atmosphere, the students' movements were idealized in both form and content. There was little work and much play in this world; it was a consumption economy, paid for by parents, institutions, and contributors who more often than not shared the undergraduate dream, and in the end accepted a new stereotype. The finished product would not be what in the 1850s would have been called an educated man, but rather a Victorian gentleman. The gist of this was summed up in a popular undergraduate motto of the time, which originated in the Ivy League, and soon spread throughout the country: "Don't let your studies interfere with your education."[11]

Faculty and administrative discipline became slack in the last part of the nineteenth century, to be replaced by a discipline of the students' own making. This could be seen in many changes. At midcentury, for example, the faculty had been responsible for all aspects of student life, including room and board. Faculty members had eaten with their students, and some had roomed in the dormitories. Beginning in the 1880s, however, some colleges permitted students to live in rooming houses near the school. This was not only in keeping with the new liberality, but also permitted the colleges to spend money on classrooms rather than dormitories. As the movement spread, students would band together to purchase rooming houses, with shares being allotted to each, to be sold upon graduation. In a short period of time fraternities and sororities took control of rooming houses, with new ones being formed as the need arose. In the prewar period, the Greek-letter organizations had been social and intellectual groups, not particularly popular except among the more intellectual students. Now they were social clubs that took much of the responsibility for feeding and housing the student bodies. As the intellectual side of college became less important and the social more, the fraternity house replaced the classroom as the symbol of undergraduate education.

The meaning of the term "college spirit" also changed. At one time it had meant that the graduate of a college identified himself as such; it afforded him an intellectual cachet of sorts, set him apart from the rest of the population. According to one story, a pre-Civil War president of Harvard concluded chapel prayers by asking God to "bless Harvard College and all inferior institutions." Whether or not this was so is unimportant, but the spirit was there at the time.

The new collegiate spirit was more along social Darwinist lines; the student was called upon to demonstrate that his school was better than the others. This might be accomplished in several ways, but the most obvious was in sports, especially those requiring bodily contact, which also demonstrated manliness. So it was that football became a national collegiate craze in the 1880s. The sport enabled the "fittest" to compete on the field, while the rest of the school participated in pregame rallies and afterward went to see their teams perform, to cheer them on, to be united with others in a warm glow of fellowship that seemed the essence of college life. Faculties and administrators recognized this. "I want you to develop teams which we can send around the country to knock out all the colleges," said one president to his coach. "We will give them a palace car and a vacation too."[12]

Of course, not all could make the team, but for those who failed, there were athletic managerships, the glee club, campus publications, and the like. After graduation, they would join alumni associations and support the old school. When they returned for reunions, they headed to the stadium and the fraternity house, not the classroom. Those who shirked such responsibilities were pariahs. Dink Stover and Frank Merriwell of Yale—two fictional creations—were the prototype for this generation of collegians. They were clean, honorable, forthright, but decidedly unintellectual. Indeed, excess interest in studies was considered somehow uncollegiate. In one of the Stover books a campus radical, clearly an unpleasant and unsympathetic character, questions the meaning of such an approach. "I came to Yale for an education," he said. "I pay for it—good pay. Work for Yale, go out and slave, give up my leisure and independence to do what for Yale? To keep turning the wheels of some purely inconsequential machine, or strive like a gladiator. Is that doing something for Yale, a seat of learning?"[13] To collegians, of that period and place, no answer was necessary.

Critics claimed that although there was something to be said for college as a socializing center, this was not the reason for their original existences. To them it appeared the colleges were failing in their tasks. But if such matters bothered collegians of the late nineteenth century, they gave little evidence of the fact. The best of them would later agree that they had missed opportunities for learning while at college, but in return they received much more. Henry Seidel Canby, the noted essayist and defender of collegians, as well as a member of Yale, '03, had mixed feelings about the situation, but in the end came down in favor of the college as it was in his day, indicating that the experience was sufficiently broad to serve the interests of many groups, to the benefit of all. At the same time, he believed college life created a new kind of person, who had more in common with his classmates than with those who sent him off to school. "For if he would once place himself in the right college group, his own world would take care of him, provided he did not too egregiously disappoint them in his later career. From henceforth he would not be Jones of Columbus, but Jones of 'Bones' or some other tight-ringed fraternity." Most colleges, said Canby, offered an educational experience, and if the student did not learn much in the classroom, he did come to respect and recognize education when he saw it. This was "very much like the tacit agreement to go to church without being religious which their elders had made with the church. These students were after all to be known as college men, and so they intended to become acquainted, if not familiar, with the best that was being thought and said, able at will to speak of the things of the mind without letting them get in the way of interested action."

Certainly parents seeing their children off to college had some sense of this, perhaps similar to that of their medieval counterparts sending their offspring to monasteries or nunneries. In time they would return, but they would be different. Communication between father and son would be difficult; even those fathers who sent their sons to their *alma maters*, hoping the shared experiences would become a tie, would be disappointed, for there was a major difference between the education of 1860 and that of 1885. As for the collegians, they were certain that their experiences had been worthwhile and made them unique. "We have the pioneer's training in self-dependence, his sense of room at the top, and his certainty that work can get him there," wrote Canby. "The proletariat of the United States has no such experience; the white-collar class of the bourgeoise that did not go to college, have had no such experience." If these people once believed they could achieve success without college, said Canby in the depression year of 1936, "it has already proved an illusion."[14]

Yet the colleges of the late nineteenth century encouraged a different kind of illusion, from the mock Gothic architecture—"instant medieval," in the words of one critic—that was favored by the trustees, to the pep rallies, pranks, and caricatures of the absent-minded professor and the sallow-faced "grind." Novels and rhapsodic tales in popular magazines told freshmen what they could expect and what would be expected of them. The myth became reality for many students, who sought the "gentleman's C," "made contacts," and "did something for the school" in the early twentieth century. Later they would recognize what had actually occurred during their collegiate years. In the 1920s several surveys indicated that most graduates of prestige colleges were doing well, and had no regrets regarding their educations. Then, as the depression struck, their ideas changed. In a 1936 survey of the Harvard class of 1911—which had graduated in an optimistic age—the question was asked, "Did any courses taken in college prove of value afterward?" One third of the respondents replied, "None," and the author of the questionnaire noted, "Whatever it taught these men, four years at Harvard did not teach them to spell."[15]

Had it really been a waste? One study of American businessmen born between 1850 and 1879 indicates that more than half of them had at least some form of higher education, while a 1903 survey showed that 29 per cent were college graduates and another 12 per cent had some college education.[16] Many of these men attended the same schools, often together, while those who went to different ones may have belonged to the same fraternities. Only a small fraction of those in their age group had attended college. Perhaps the experience served them well. It polished their social graces, enabled them to perform as expected in board rooms, gave them a workable set of ethics and friends to go with them, and at the very least exposed them to scholarship, even if the disease was not contagious. On the other hand, it might be argued that most, if not all of this, could have been accomplished at some other place than a school of higher education.

CRACKS IN THE FOUNDATION

Even while this new form of college, this variety of collegian, and this type of education were flourishing and popular, further alterations in the structure were taking place. Historians of higher education usually discuss two significant developments that began in the late nineteenth century and continued on into the twentieth.

The first was the emergence of state and municipal colleges and universities. Given impetus by the Morrill Acts of 1862 and 1890, which provided federal funding for the state schools, these institutions expanded and proliferated. Generally speaking, their standards were lower than those of the established private colleges, as were their tuitions. In 1909, the minimum annual tuition at Yale was $155 and at Harvard, $150, while the University of Illinois charged $24 and the University of Michigan, $30. While most colleges tried to enlarge their student bodies, the leaders of the state schools were impelled to do so, since their very reason for existence was to serve the taxpayers. "My entire political creed, my entire political activity, can be summed up in a single sentence," said Chancellor James H. Canfield of the University of Nebraska. "A thousand students in the state university in 1895; 2,000 in 1900." Ezra Cornell, who founded his school in central New York with state funds, said that it would be "an institution in which any person can find instruction in any study," and from the first, Cornell sought undergraduates with zeal and efficiency.[17] By 1908, Cornell had an enrollment of 3,454 undergraduates, and at that was exceeded by the University of Michigan (4,419 undergraduates), the University of Pennsylvania (3,736) and the University of Minnesota (3,468). In 1900 there were 238,000 college students in America, and ten years later, 355,000. In this period the private college enrollments went from 147,000 to 189,000, while the public institutions of higher education registered 91,000 in 1900 and 167,000 in 1910. By the late 1920s there were more students in public than in private colleges and universities.[18]

The second major development was the emergence of the graduate school, which is usually traced to the establishment of The Johns Hopkins University in 1867, but which really began three years later. The intellectual impetus for such institutions came from Germany. Unlike the colleges, the graduate schools existed to train professionals in their fields, to encourage research from their faculties. In time some established colleges, led by Harvard, Yale, and Columbia, became most involved in graduate and—later on—professional training, and when they did, they changed from colleges to universities. Other schools, among them Clark and the University of Chicago, began as universities, with the stress upon graduate training.

The collegians at the older institutions did not know what to make of these developments, but more to the point, how to consider the students who attended the state and municipal colleges and the others who went on to the graduate and professional schools—often on their own campuses. Each represented a threat, and in a different way, and in some respects the two groups were worrisome.

The undergraduates at the state and municipal colleges were "different" from those at the old private schools. Were it not for low tuition and charges, most students at state and municipal institutions of higher education could not have afforded to enter college, much less remain there for four years. They hoped to achieve status through education, many through entry in one or another of the professions. This meant additional training, after the B.A., in the graduate schools. A 1902 survey at the University of Michigan indicated that the sons of farmers wanted more than anything else to become doctors or lawyers, this at a time when professional schools, not apprenticeship, was becoming required for both occupations. In the same period, students in the old private colleges were turning away from the professions, in part because of the difficulties and hardships of study in such places, but more often because of the lure of a less demanding life in business. As late as 1883, almost 20 per cent of Harvard's alumni were lawyers and another 10 per cent doctors. By 1911, the law alumni had fallen to 13 per cent, and the doctors to 4.3 per cent. In this same period, the percentage in manufacturing rose from 9.6 per cent to 18.5 per cent. No Harvard alumnus was in accounting or advertising in 1883; in 1911, 3.4 per cent were so engaged, more than in the ministry or government service.[19]

A new sense of professionalism was abroad in the graduate schools, along with new faculties and students who were developing codes of ethics. These schools competed with one another for star faculty and bright students. President William Rainey Harper of the University of Chicago raided other schools with abandon—and Rockefeller money—intent on gathering the best and most prestigious minds in the nation for his school. At one point he swooped down on Clark and left with a large fraction of its faculty, operating in much the same fashion as the owner of a football team might toward his counterpart in a rival league.

While it remained true that a college was known for its football team, increasingly the professional and graduate schools at major universities were famous for their faculties. And in many cases, both were side by side on the same campus, the young undergraduates watching the older graduate and professional students, at times seeing them in classrooms, where they served as instructors, quite different from the absent-minded professors of the 1880s. That they were challenges to undergraduate morale could not be doubted. "The central current of American life, as it was then, flowed through the college," wrote Canby, "carrying with it the rich spoils of American prosperity, and also respect and affection for this unique institution." By the turn of the century, however, the university had come to engulf the college, "feeding upon this life stream, eventually [growing] . . . great upon its nourishment." It was "a parasite sucking for it's own excellent purposes the blood of the college, or more accurately, of that college life which engendered the loyalty of gift-giving alumni."

While the liberal arts undergraduates in the prestigious private colleges played football and drank beer, the graduate students were demanding better libraries and laboratories, and getting them. To them the old ways were at best quaint, and worst, archaic, and in any case, were ignored; graduate students would scarcely "do or die for old Ivy." And so, as far as the undergraduates were concerned, they really weren't of their class. "Could an M.A. or a Ph.D. or an LL.B. or an M.D. make a youth into a Yale or a Harvard man?" asked Canby. The answer was obvious. "Never! Only the bachelor's degree with four years of college life behind it gave that almost sacred consecration."[20]

Historians of American education wrote of the difficulties of grafting the German idea of university and professional training upon the English base of the college in America, and certainly this was the case.[21] But the situation was somewhat different from the student's point of view, and certainly from that of society at large. The college-as-entertainment-and-socializer had replaced the college-as-vocational-school after the Civil War. In the 1870s and 1880s the nation's leading schools came under the influence of educators who believed in secularized general education, which students interpreted as meaning an acceptance of the values of Western civilization along with a smattering of actual learning—no more. At the turn of the century the collegians appeared well established, but then this new group of vocationalists appeared—often out of the public schools—to challenge their positions. Suddenly the despised grinds of the 1880s became doctors, lawyers, scientists, and social scientists in training. Others, who hoped to obtain the Ph.D. and then spend their lives as professors, would have far more prestige than the teachers of the 1880s, and would go on to raise a generation like themselves. If the collegians considered the professionals little more than bookworms, the latter had only a slightly masked contempt for the values of the football-oriented sons of the wealthy, even while they aspired to their status.

Being obliged to accept and work with the new professionals was bad enough, but the collegians might have been able to adjust to this in time. After all, the "grinds" had been found in the preparatory schools, and the pale, physically weak scholar was as much a campus caricature in the 1880s as the football hero. But in the early twentieth century a new type appeared that was more threatening, which Canby called the "greasy grind." "The second generation from the East of Europe was beginning to come to college: Polish Jews with anemic faces on which were set dirty spectacles, soft-eyed Italians too alien to mix with an Anglo-Saxon community, seam-faced Armenian boys, and now and then a Chinese." These students were devious, wrote Canby. "Their mein was apologetic; you could see them watching with envious curiosity the courteous indifference of the superior race; they took little part in discussions and asked for no credit. Yet often their more flexible minds could be felt playing round and round the confident Anglo-Saxons, admiring, skeptical, puzzled, and sometimes contemptuous." Canby and others of his group were fearful of the aliens, who were far more serious in their work than the collegians. The greasy grind "had a sneaking cleverness which taught him to snap up the hard questions in easy courses, thus collecting high marks as a protection against a world that, quite properly, wished to keep him down. He would argue with the teacher for ten minutes trying to get a B changed into an A; but he had no intellectual curiosity. Education for him was a coin, useless unless you could buy something with it."[22]

The East European Jews were the main interlopers. By 1913 it was estimated that more than 70 per cent of the students at the City College of New York were Jews, while Columbia University and New York University had Jewish enrollments of around 40 per cent, with Harvard at approximately 15 per cent. By then, their numbers had begun to worry college administrators, especially in the more prestigious schools, which feared a loss of Anglo-Saxon students if they became too alien in tone. In 1901, Harvard's Eliot, who had welcomed Jews, wrote: "It is doubtless true that Jews are better off at Harvard than at any other American college; and they are, therefore, likely to resort to it."[23] Eliot retired eight years later and was replaced by Abbott Lawrence Lowell, who distrusted the elective system and tended to stress graduate work, at the expense of the undergraduate college.

Noting that Harvard had lost students to other schools due to dissatisfaction with Eliot's policies, Lowell sought to change them —and one way to do this would be to shed the reputation it had as a haven for Jews. Along with other schools, Harvard instituted a quota system. It was claimed that this was put forth to guarantee a nationally representative student body, but later on, after much discussion in the press, several college presidents conceded their fears of becoming too Jewish. By 1922 Lowell conceded the point openly. "The anti-Semitic feeling among the students is increasing," he wrote in a letter to the New York *Times*, "and it grows in proportion to the increase in the number of Jews."[24]

What had happened, of course, was the confluence of two streams of historical development. The rapid increase in Jewish immigration at the turn of the century and afterward coincided with the startling expansion of college attendance. Before the doors at leading colleges could be closed, the immigrants had secured their beachheads. And when quotas were instituted, they guaranteed that Jews would be among the brightest students at the prestigious colleges, while the rejects found places without much difficulty in one of the other schools, especially the municipal ones. This too was a blow at the old collegians, an important new ingredient in higher education, and in some respects it backfired. In New York, for example, Columbia University instituted a quota system at its college, and so many immigrants and their children who otherwise might have attended were obliged to go elsewhere. But afterward they would attend the Columbia's graduate and professional schools, which they came to dominate.

Nicholas Murray Butler of Columbia, who instituted the quota system and throughout his professional life feared his school would be engulfed by the newcomers, was in a paradoxical position. His institution's reputation rested with the graduate and professional faculties, and under the new dispensation these people could not be easily controlled; if Butler interfered with a prestigious scholar, he might resign and go to some other school, thus embarrassing Columbia. On the other hand, Butler could and did dominate the undergraduate teachers, as did most other college presidents, and in much the same way as they did in the 1880s and 1890s. The undergraduate school could have quotas; the graduate faculties often were successful in opposing them. Butler accepted the Pulitzer bequest, even though it came from a Jewish publisher, and the aliens would attend in numbers disproportionate to their percentage of the general or even student population. Other donations helped Butler develop graduate education and expand his schools of the law and medicine, but despite quotas, these too served the new professionals, not the old collegians. Not one but several forms and philosophies of education existed at Columbia and other large educational enterprises. In time, said some students of the subject, a rational form would emerge. One never did.

Prior to the Civil War, American higher education had appeared harmonious. Despite student activism for a variety of causes, a small group of scholars with avocations trained those who would, in time, replace them at their posts. Then Eliot and others who shared his beliefs fashioned a new but equally harmonious form of collegiate education, which served the interests and needs of the students, society, and most of the faculty in the last part of the nineteenth century. When attendance increased, the new form was able to accommodate the additional students.

This situation, however, was being altered sharply in the early twentieth century. The numbers of students, faculties, and institutions were growing rapidly, and in diverse fashion. Toward what end? There was no single answer to the question, despite attempts to find one, if only for a single school. The various components of higher education had changed markedly. Only the workers, who kept the places operating and in repair, seemed the same as they had been a generation earlier, and even among them, unionization was growing, and institutional loyalties were weakening somewhat.

As for the trustees, businessmen continued to be prized members of boards, as were eminent professionals. But at public colleges and universities political appointees were the rule, and since the larger portion of their funds came from the legislatures, not donations, their influence would grow.

A professional administrative class had not yet emerged in the early twentieth century, but already there was a gulf between faculty and administration, even though the latter still emerged from the former. Administrators had a variety of tasks, and increasingly those involving fund raising came to dominate their calendars; they were becoming businessmen, even though very little in their training and background equipped most for the tasks of business. They would learn; those who didn't would be replaced.

The changing faculty was an even more important cause for the growing separation between administration and faculty. The "good old prof," somewhat absent-minded, shabby, out of touch with reality, who loved his boys and lived through them—a sort of academic servant—was supposed to have been the hallmark of the old college of the 1880s and 1890s. Like all stereotypes, the picture is exaggerated but also contains elements of truth. Certainly their lives had been more cloistered than most, but they were not that poor and deprived. The average annual salary for a college faculty member in 1893 was $1,470, five times that of elementary and high school teachers and three times that of factory workers.[25] In terms of purchasing power, it was far higher than it had been in the 1850s and about the same as it would be in the 1950s. But there was change in the air, especially for those young people entering the professions at that time. The research-minded universities placed a premium upon originality, research, and publications. They wanted scholars with national—even international—reputations, and would pay dearly for their services. The old prof who spent a lifetime at his school was being shoved aside by the young scholar, who flitted from place to place, obtaining larger salaries and status with each change. This was the case for Edward A. Ross, who noted the change in 1891, when he saw that the American Economic Association meeting of that year was dominated by younger men, many like him under the age of thirty-five. Ross took a job at the University of Indiana, and in less than a year had offers from Cornell and Stanford. Two years after receiving his Ph.D., his annual salary went from $2,500 to $3,500. The money was welcomed, but more desirable was the feeling of being important. "To me the chief thing about a good salary is that it convinced other people about one's success."[26] Able, articulate, and aggressive faculty members were in demand at universities, but also in business and, to an increasing degree, in government. In the early twentieth century, the professor as celebrity was born.

College students, too, were aware of this and related changes, but the new faculty, along with the new university, affected graduate and professional education more than it did the undergraduates. In the early twentieth century it was still possible to be a collegian, to enjoy one's college years, expecting to look back upon them as "the best time of my life." This vision—if it was that—would persist for another half century and never really die. College as entertainment was at its height and did not seem in danger of vanishing.

There was no shortage of students, however, genuinely interested in knowledge for its own sake. Given the veritable explosion in elementary and high school education, an army of teachers would be required. At a time when professional standards were rising and certification of teachers becoming more common, the B.A. was more desirable a possession than ever before.

The most striking change, however, was in the area of professionalization. Colleges and universities had now become places where one went to learn the crafts of medicine, law—and business, journalism, and other professions. The apprentice system had been too casual, the increase in knowledge too great, the requirements for precision too pressing, and the needs of society too complex for the old ways to last. Just as wheat and cotton had certified power in the early nineteenth century and steel and railroads served the purpose later on, so knowledge was coming to signify strength, and the college and university was, after all, a "knowledge factory" and a place where the product was produced, packaged, and dispensed.

As far as the professionals were concerned—faculty as well as students—their freedom knew only the bounds of knowledge, not those of authority. "Academic freedom," an almost meaningless term in the 1880s, was becoming a rallying cry in the early twentieth century. Faculties and administrations battled over the issues, and despite setbacks, the faculties succeeded in establishing their intellectual independence in the better schools—which indeed were considered as such in part because they offered this freedom to scholars. The fight there was not led by the old profs, but rather by the new academics.

The college and university would never achieve a degree of separation between administration and faculty equal to that which existed between the business and editorial functions at many newspapers, but similar forces were at work in both fields. Professionalism was the key, and in each hierarchy the person without financial power or responsibility was starting to earn status and publicity—the editor and reporter at the newspaper, the professor and the grind at the college and university.

There was a nexus here, since the college-educated men and women were at the very least readers of newspapers, and in some cases went on to enter the profession. In every society, a small minority creates knowledge, a somewhat larger group disseminates it, while a third segment of society—often amorphous, rarely cohesive—receives information and knowledge. The colleges and universities, increasingly professionalized, served the newspapers by producing individuals who, in time, would create knowledge and disseminate information. Equally if not more important, institutions of higher learning were helping form a class of mass intellectuals, people who if not capable of creating were able to understand complex issues, especially when formulated by men and women with their own backgrounds. Just as the penny press had spoken to the unwashed masses, and Pulitzer to the outraged, intelligent but relatively uneducated urban middle class, so the descendants of Pulitzer would reach out to the mass intellectuals.

What of the collegian strain in American higher education? Would it be obliterated by the driving force of the new professionalism? In the new kind of society that was developing, the need for colleges as socializing agencies might have been considered less important than was the case in the late nineteenth century. But it was not, and if anything, the collegian atmosphere would increase and became even more desirable in the first half of the new century. In part this was due to the desire on the part of newcomers to ape those who had already "arrived." Thus, the farm boy arriving at an old, established university, would attempt to join the glee club and even try out for the football team, in this way achieving acceptance into this society. The immigrant would introduce fraternities to his city college, attend pep rallies, and become active in his alumni association for the same reason. Although the collegian was more an ornament than a vital unit in the new society, he continued to signify status and power, and so was perpetuated rather than discarded.

And this was an important consideration and development. At the turn of the century, the college graduate had come to be seen as the kind of person who, in time, would dominate business, government, and the professions. This was due at least as much to the kind of people who entered colleges as the products turned out after four years. The sons of the wealthy and powerful were destined at birth to take their fathers' places. Little they learned in college prepared them for the worlds of business, with the exception of the contacts made and social graces acquired, and these might have been obtained at fashionable watering places and a term in a finishing school, rather than Harvard or Yale for four years. People like these might well have viewed college as a luxury—a consumption item, at the very least—and not a prerequisite for success.

The newcomers didn't see things that way. In their view, money and status did not produce the college graduate; rather, the successful completion of a college education would result in financial and social rewards. Because of this, intelligent and ambitious young men and women made great sacrifices in order to obtain their degrees, and with parchments in hand, went into the world seeking their rewards. Often they were disappointed, for although college graduates received higher salaries than did nongraduates, this was not necessarily due to their academic education.[27] The graduates would be frustrated and disappointed. As for the employers, they were able to upgrade standards, realizing as they did that college graduates were applying for trainee positions in management and jobs as elementary and secondary school teachers. The new applicants were not only better qualified than the old, but also had already demonstrated abilities at learning and a certain measure of intelligence, combined with the social graces acquired at college. These people got the better jobs, and with them, additional money and some status.

This situation contained within it the seeds of future troubles. How long would it be until these nonstatus graduates challenged the old collegians for power and money? And what form would the confrontation take? How would society accommodate itself to this increasingly large number of college graduates, certified as having passed a course of study but prepared for no particular position? Would an economy erected on the production of goods be able to absorb thousands of graduates who were not only unable to work in the mills or in the fields, but also unwilling to do so under any but the most pressing of circumstances? On the eve of World War I, there would be some 350,000 students enrolled in the nation's institutions of higher education. The figure would be doubled by 1922, and by the end of the decade there would be more than a million college students—one out of every eight Americans in the eighteen-to-twenty-one-year-old group was in college. What would they do upon graduation, and for the rest of their lives? A developing economy needed education and trained people, but at the same time these kinds of individuals required a special kind of economy and society. In a variety of ways, the new graduates and their instructors would find their places and would remake society during the next half century. Together they would be one of the more creative—and destructive—forces in the nation, as well as its most demanding in terms of recognition and status.

3

Ideas and War: The CPI

In the summer of 1908 Hamilton Holt, managing editor of the *Independent* decided to publish a series of articles on American universities. Given the popularity of collegian novels at the time, the rise of football as a spectator sport, and the growing prominence of college men and women in national life, he was certain such pieces would be well received.

As author of the proposed piece, Holt selected Edwin E. Slosson, a former professor who had recently turned to journalism and letters. The *Independent* would pay Slosson a generous advance, and then he would select the universities, on the basis of interest, importance, and reputation as well as geographic diversity. He would visit the schools during the 1908–9 academic year and write the articles in the autumn and early winter of 1909, after which they would be published in the magazine.

Slosson agreed, and in September 1908 he set out for Harvard. After a week there, he traveled to New Haven for a period at Yale, then on to Princeton and into the Midwest. Slosson was at Stanford in January, after which he started eastward again, winding up in Cornell in May and Columbia in June. He had visited fourteen universities, concentrating on the East and Midwest—the large private schools, the huge public complexes—and ignoring both the Far West, with the exception of Stanford, and the South, traveling only so far as Baltimore to spend two weeks at Johns Hopkins. Still, he could defend his selections. In 1909, American higher education seemed typified by the old and prestigious eastern colleges and universities and the newer, brash state universities of the Midwest. Slosson's articles appeared in 1910 and were gathered into a book late in the year. Both the articles and book were successes; the latter became a minor best seller, and remained the definitive study in its field for years after.

Slosson was most impressed by the state colleges, and especially with the vitality of one. "It is impossible to ascertain the size or location of the University of Wisconsin," he wrote. "The most that one can say is that the headquarters of the institution is at the city of Madison and that the campus has an area of about 56,000 square miles."[1] Like so many others who came to Madison, he was struck by the degree to which the university had infiltrated the daily life of the state, how its influence could be found in all parts of Wisconsin. No one seemed to know how many students were taking courses in various units and subunits of the system, or even how many different locations it controlled. "The laboratories are wherever there is machinery in action, industrial or social, with which the students care to experiment. If we go into a local electric light and power plant in any part of the State, we may happen upon a group of advanced students making an investigation of it," and the same was true of farms and factories.

The main campus was within walking distance of the capital buildings, and Slosson quickly learned that leading professors spent as much time in politics as in academic work. Professor Balthasar H. Meyer, an economist, served as the first chairman of the state Railroad Commission and then left for a post on the Interstate Commerce Commission in Washington. Political Scientist Thomas S. Adams was a member of the Tax Commission, as were William D. Pence, John G. D. Mack, and Halsten J. Thorkelson, all of the University of Wisconsin College of Engineering, and all on the Railroad Commission as well. Geologist William O. Hotchkiss would soon go to the new Highway Commission. Lincoln Steffens, who arrived in Wisconsin weeks after Slosson left, said that forty-one professors were serving in sixty-six state offices and that President Charles R. Van Hise was on five different boards and commissions.[2] The University and the state government appeared to be completely entwined one with the other.

This same kind of situation existed at other state colleges and universities throughout the nation. Under the terms of federal legislation assisting the schools, they were required to become involved in various public services, especially those relating to agriculture. Furthermore, the university could scarcely have expected aid from the state unless it could demonstrate, clearly and directly, that it was serving the interests of its taxpayers and educating its children in worthwhile pursuits. The concept was articulated more clearly and forcefully at Madison than anywhere else, however. Robert LaFollette, who had served as governor from 1901 to 1906, was himself a graduate, and keenly interested in mobilizing the university's resources in the service of the state. He found willing allies in such eminent social scientists as John Commons, Richard Ely, Paul Reinsch, Edward Ross, and others. The politicians required the knowledge of experts, and the latter were eager to put their theories into practice, to have a "social laboratory" at their disposal. It was a fine mating.

While LaFollette spoke of the need for the university to serve all of Wisconsin's citizens, Commons wrote of "utilitarian idealism." "I do not see why there is not as much idealism in breeding a perfect animal or a Wisconsin No. 7 ear of corn, or in devising an absolutely exact instrument for measuring a thousand cubic feet of gas, or for measuring exactly the amount of butter or casein in milk, as there is in chipping out a Venus de Milo or erecting a Parthenon." On accepting the presidency of the school in 1904, Van Hise said: "I am not willing to admit that a state university under a democracy shall be of lower grade than a state university under a monarchy." To become a quality school, Wisconsin would have to select its areas of interest with care, with an eye out to the requirements of the state. Consistently Van Hise spoke of his belief that appropriations for the university were "investments which have been returned manyfold and will continue to be returned in the future in even larger measure," and he promised that the school would be "at the service of the state." To this, LaFollette echoed, "We believe that the purpose of the university is to serve the people and every effort is made . . . to bring every resident of the state under the broadening and inspiring influence of a faculty of trained men."[3]

It seemed so simple and so right. The state would invest funds in its university, and in return see its children educated, its farms and factories benefited by practical knowledge developed at the schools, and its administration assisted by experts on loan from their labors in class and laboratory. The faculty would benefit, both in terms of increased experience and status, and the students would have a better faculty for it. Slosson—the former professor turned journalist—applauded what he saw. "The line that used to be drawn sharply between the scholar and the man of affairs, between those who knew a great deal and could not do anything and those who had to do everything and did not know much about it, is being wiped out in Wisconsin."

But there was a danger, one that Slosson recognized although thought minor. "The offices held by members of the faculty are mostly those classed as non-political positions; that is, they carry with them little money, prestige, or party power."[4] In the narrow, late-nineteenth-century definition of the term, this was doubtless correct, although some might question the prestige aspect. On the other hand, as experts in political life gained power and influence, the academicians would have the best of both worlds—the respect of the academy, the power of the state house. Might not a governor—or a President—call upon the universities to provide him with able, trained experts to help him work his political will? Could not the system as developed in Wisconsin and elsewhere be utilized to impose upon the general population the tyranny of an elitist society? At what point did the expert become a policymaker, thus assuming powers given to elected officials? The academics and reform leaders of the Progressive period did not ask such questions, at least openly. Instead, the difficulties of power without responsibility would be debated by their grandchildren.

POLITICS AND ACADEMIA—THE WILSON YEARS

Slosson admired Wisconsin, which he felt combined the best qualities of liberal arts with professionalism, in such a fashion as to serve the people of the state. But he found Princeton "the most interesting of American universities to study just now," even though it was quite different from Wisconsin. "What I like about Princeton," he wrote, "is that it has an ideal of education and is working it out. It is not exactly my ideal, but that does not matter to anyone but me."

The ideal was Woodrow Wilson's, and at the time of Slosson's visit, Wilson was the university president best known to educated Americans. Through his books, magazine articles, and speeches—and his penchant for publicity—Wilson had become a national figure, who even then was being mentioned as a potential presidential nominee.

Wilson had arrived in academia just in time to benefit from the fresh crosscurrents in the field. He had graduated from Princeton in 1879, when the school had been dominated by the collegians, and although academically inclined, he had belonged to the glee club and took a keen interest in football. Subsequently a graduate of the University of Virginia Law School, he practiced law for a while, but in 1882 entered Johns Hopkins to study political science and history on the graduate level. His first book, *Congressional Government*, was published in 1885, and its success brought job offers from several major institutions. Abandoning law, Wilson went to Bryn Mawr in September of that year, received his Ph.D. in 1886, accepted a chair in history and political science at Wesleyan in 1888, continued to publish widely, and in 1890 took the chair of jurisprudence and political science at Princeton.

Wilson was a popular teacher at Princeton, and also a prolific writer and popular public speaker. In addition, he helped coach the football team—he had served as coach at Wesleyan—and occasionally sang with the glee club. And he spoke of his educational philosophy with members of the faculty. Princeton was a small university in 1890—it had forty-five faculty members and a total student enrollment of 768—and so continuous debate and discussion was possible, and indeed unavoidable.

Under the presidencies of James McCosh and his successor, Francis L. Patton, Princeton had expanded and altered its curriculum. Greater stress was being placed upon the pure sciences, while the administration attempted to raise funds for several graduate and professional schools, which would truly transform Princeton from a small college into a major university, with a national constituency. In 1890, more than three quarters of the undergraduates had come from Pennsylvania, New York, and New Jersey, while the endowment was only $1.5 million. Princeton was a small, local college, with a long but rather undistinguished history. Patton and the trustees thought that a new stress upon graduate and professional education would change this. As for the undergraduates, their education would remain pretty much as it had been before—they would continue to be collegians. Professor of Latin Andrew F. West, who had graduated from Princeton the year before Wilson had entered as a freshman, was committed to Patton's plan. "The college lies very close to the people," West wrote in 1899. "Distinctions of caste may manifest themselves occasionally, and yet the college is stoutly and we believe permanently democratic." In 1900, West was named dean of the proposed graduate college. Two years later, after having turned down the presidencies of several large universities, Wilson was selected to succeed Patton at Princeton.

Wilson's inaugural address, "Princeton for the Nation's Service," was widely reprinted and discussed, for his idea of the meaning of college and university education differed greatly from that of the professionals and the collegians. He strongly favored the liberal arts, not for their utility, but for their own sake. While extracurricular activities were fine, the stress should be on the classroom, not the football stadium. "In planning for Princeton . . . we are planning for the country. The service of institutions of learning is not private, but public. It is plain what the nation needs as its affairs grow more and more complex and its interests begin to touch the ends of the earth. It needs efficient and enlightened men. The universities of the country must take part in supplying them."

This was quite different from the viewpoints of LaFollette, Commons, and Van Hise at Wisconsin, or even West's conception of undergraduate education. "The college is not for the majority who carry forward the common labor of the world, nor even for those who work at . . . skilled handicrafts," said Wilson. "It is for the minority who plan, who conceive, who superintend, who mediate between group and group and must see the wide stage as a whole. Democratic nations must be served in this wise no less than those whose leaders are chosen by birth and privilege."[5]

Wilson believed all should be subordinated to the goal of turning out undergraduates with excellent educations—such that could rival those of graduate students in depth and superior to that which the collegians received in breadth. He strongly supported graduate schools, but wanted them to revolve around the undergraduate college, in hope that the graduate students would form a fellowship with the undergraduates and so help instruct them. Wilson instituted a preceptorial program, bringing in young faculty to meet regularly with students and assist them in their studies. He opposed Princeton's eating clubs, not so much because he thought them undemocratic, but based on his conviction that they distracted students from their main tasks in the classrooms and libraries. "College life in our day, has become so absorbing a thing and so interesting a thing, that college work has fallen into the background," he complained. "The sideshows were swallowing up the circus." Speaking before the University Club in Chicago in 1908, he explained:

> After all, gentlemen, a University has as its only legitimate object intellectual attainment. I do not mean that there should not go along with that a great deal that is delightful in the way of comradeship; but I am sure that men never thoroughly enjoy each other if they merely touch superficially. I do not believe men ever know or enjoy each other until they lay their minds alongside each other and make real test of their quality.[6]

Wilson hoped to apply professional standards to undergraduate liberal arts education, and if some of the trustees were dubious about the necessity of learning for its own sake, they could appreciate the value of professionalism and higher standards. "The fact is, that for some time, a considerable portion of the undergraduate body has looked upon Princeton University as simply an academic and artistic background for the club life that is now such a prominent feature of the place," wrote trustee David B. Jones in 1907. "The clubs will therefore strangle the university unless some radical modification is devised and applied. . . ." And so it was. Wilson strove to eliminate the eating clubs, place the new graduate schools close by the undergraduate institution, and stress basic liberal arts education. He rejected the extremes of Eliot's elective system and the utilitarianism practiced at the University of Wisconsin. Wilson believed America was in a new era, in which expertise would become increasingly important and the nation assume a major world role. He hoped the colleges would educate an elite that was capable of leading the nation, of directing the new experts—a cadre of intelligent, perceptive men who could provide insights for the masses and assume power by virtue of their wisdom and learning. As one whose words and exploits had received wide press coverage, Wilson also respected the powers of publicity. Those who graduated from Princeton in the future would benefit from the insights obtained there, and then bring the message to the world. "Princeton is no longer a thing for Princeton men to please themselves with," he told the University Club. "Princeton is a thing with which Princeton men must satisfy the country."

In the end, Wilson lost many of his battles.[7] But he also managed to create a different kind of school at Princeton. President Lowell of Harvard conceded that Wilson "certainly did raise Princeton very much in grade among the institutions of higher learning in the country. He was also the first, so far as I am aware, who strove to raise the respect for scholarship among the undergraduate body."

Wilson resigned as Princeton's president in 1910, to accept the Democratic nomination for the governorship of New Jersey. But even before then, he had lost several famous battles, and was no longer as effective as he had been at the beginning of his tour there. In 1910, however, Princeton had an endowment of $5.1 million, a student body of 1,444, and a faculty of 174. It had also emerged as the leader of a different kind of college and university from that represented by Wisconsin.

And what of the man? After resigning, Wilson told a friend that his Princeton experience had been a fine preparation for his future career. "I'll confide in you, as I have already confided to others—that, as compared with the college politician, the real article seems like an amateur." By this, he was referring to dealings with the Democratic party's professionals. He felt equipped to lead the masses, but lacked experience and knowledge of the lives and desires of common people. More important, Wilson felt they needed a leader, a person to shape their actions, to help formulate their ideas.

In 1905 Robert LaFollette had asked the Wisconsin state legislature to vote an additional increment to the university's budget. The appropriations was necessary, he said, to provide new buildings for the College of Engineering and the College of Agriculture. Quoting a Board of Regents report, LaFollette explained, "A great institution of learning demands a great and growing income." He recognized the need for economy and prudence, but "the State will not have discharged its duty to the University, nor the University fulfilled its mission to the people, until adequate means have been furnished to every young man and woman in the State to acquire an education at home in every department of learning. . . ."

Wilson had hoped to educate an elite in the liberal arts and have them lead the nation. LaFollette wanted to train and educate the masses in subjects of their own choosing, and in the hope that through additional knowledge they would not only prosper but also become better citizens, more capable of running their own affairs. Both men were leaders, and each considered himself a true democrat, but the difference between them was vast. Wilson was a Princeton graduate, and while the college's leader he often indicated he cared little about expansion. As far as he was concerned, the school could become smaller if that meant its students would be better educated. LaFollette, a Wisconsin graduate, yearned to see his university the largest in the nation. Each man had a philosophy of education that was close to the roots of their beings. In 1912, both offered themselves to the nation as presidential candidates.

Wilson would win.

Although his duties at Princeton had been onerous, they did not interfere with Wilson's speaking tours. These continued, for if anything, the demand for Wilson was growing in 1905–6. In November of 1905 he spoke in Orange, New Jersey, on Princeton's future, and then swept through New York and New England giving talks, sometime at the rate of three a week, on educational, historical, and political topics. On December 16, Wilson was in New York to offer a lecture on politics, in which he said that "governments should supply an equilibrium, not a disturbing force." The remarks were carried in the newspapers and were discussed in columns for several weeks. Then Wilson turned south, speaking in Philadelphia in early January and at Charleston, South Carolina, on January 18. J. C. Hemphill, editor of the *News & Courier*, initiated a correspondence with Wilson soon after. "The whole town is still talking about your lecture as the best delivered in this place for many years." Later that year, Hemphill wrote and published an editorial, "Wanted: a Leader," in which he called Wilson "the most promising of Southern candidates" for the presidency.

In early February, Wilson was in New York again, this time to attend a dinner in his honor at the Lotus Club. George Harvey, the former editor of the New York *World* and a leading Pulitzer protégé, was there to deliver a talk. At the time, Harvey was president of the publishing house of Harper & Brothers and editor of *Harper's Weekly*. He had met Wilson in 1902 and had worked with him on several projects. Harvey quickly became a Wilson enthusiast. In his speech, he all but nominated him for the presidency. Wilson's face was on the cover of the March 12 issue of *Harper's Weekly*, and the full text of the Harvey speech was reprinted inside. With this, a minor Wilson boom was started, led by Harvey, with Hemphill's aid in the South. The Milwaukee *Sentinel* thought the nomination "would be a good thing for the country," and the Trenton *True American* believed Wilson could unite the nation. The influential Henry Watterson of the Louisville *Courier-Journal* thought Wilson would be "ideal," while Adolph Ochs of the New York *Times* read the Harvey speech and thought the Wilson boom a "splendid suggestion." The New York *Sun* noted that a Wilson campaign in 1908 was viewed as "certain" in Washington, while others thought Wilson would be better served to seek the governorship of New Jersey, or a Senate seat from that state, before making a presidential bid in 1912 or 1916. Wilson began receiving letters from all parts of the country urging him to enter politics on the presidential level. Academia and journalism had united to create a national political figure, who had not yet run for public office.[8]

In 1908, Wilson was seriously considered for the vice presidential nomination, but withdrew before any boom could be started. William Jennings Bryan, the Democratic nominee, lost badly to Republican William Howard Taft, who thus succeeded Theodore Roosevelt. The defeat crushed the "radical" wing of the party and opened the way for a moderate candidate in 1912. Even before announcing for the New Jersey gubernatorial race in 1910, Wilson was listed as a Democratic presidential possibility for 1912.

As governor, Wilson received support from Democratic editors and publishers, and his efforts in New Jersey were reported throughout the country. His relations with the Trenton news corps were correct and somewhat stiff, however; some of the older reporters felt he was lecturing them on the arts and science of government on occasion, and they resented it. Generally speaking, the farther reporters were from Wilson—the more they could be influenced by his words rather than his personality—the more impressed they were by the man.

When he won the Democratic presidential nomination in 1912, Wilson received endorsements from the Democratic press as well, including Hearst. The candidate campaigned vigorously, despite his rather fragile health, and delivered some of the most articulate and thoughtful speeches Americans had heard since the Civil War. With the Republican party split between Taft's regulars and Roosevelt's Progressives, there was little doubt from that start that Wilson would win. So he did, with 435 electoral votes, more than any other President had received to that time. But Wilson received only 6,293,019 votes in sweeping the country in 1912, fewer than Bryan had obtained in 1908—6,393,182. Wilson's constituency was mixed—it included regular Democrats, moderate reformers, conservative Republicans hoping to defeat Roosevelt, along with some who admired the coming of the "scholar in politics." How important the last group was cannot be determined; there was no academic voting bloc in 1912, however, and no unity on candidacies or issues on the nation's campuses. The heritage of the Civil War was at least as important as the ties of academia that year. Nevertheless, flawed and uncertain though his mandate was, Wilson became President in 1913.

Wilson had good relations with the press, but such was the norm in this period. William McKinley had been popular with reporters, and his private secretary had been a former editor. Secretary of State John Hay had been a newspaperman, and Postmaster General Charles E. Smith was the former editor of the Philadelphia *Press*. Theodore Roosevelt genuinely liked reporters, had wide experience with editors prior to entering politics, and provided "good copy." He also constructed the first press room in the White House. William Howard Taft had come from a newspaper family; his brother was publisher of the Cincinnati *Times-Star*. He appreciated the power of the press, and inaugurated regular press conferences, which he said were more enjoyable than Cabinet meetings. Wilson inherited this foundation and tradition. He instituted semiweekly press conferences, took reporters into his confidence, and met often with influential editors and publishers.

But there were problems. For one thing, Wilson tended to prepare for his meetings with reporters as he might for a university lecture; he provided information, but answered few questions. Some of the older reporters felt he was preaching to them. When McKinley, Roosevelt, and Taft were misquoted or misrepresented, the result had been anger and irritation. Even when editors took anti-Taft stands, the President remained on good terms with the reporters. All three had what might be called "the common touch." It was otherwise with Wilson, who regarded errors in facts as a sign that the reporter was either professionally incompetent or a dissembler. There was a striking difference between the well-educated President and the self-taught journalists—the last generation of that group of Washington reporters who had come up from the print shop.[9] It was a replay of the Trenton situation; the farther reporters were from Wilson, the more they admired him.

GEORGE CREEL: MASTER MANIPULATOR

In 1896 George Creel, then twenty years old and late of Independence, Missouri, took a position as reporter for the Kansas City *Star*. After serving his apprenticeship there he traveled to New York, where he sought, unsuccessfully, to become a freelance journalist. Then in 1899 he returned to Kansas City to help found the *Independent*, which in time became a leading midwestern newspaper. Creel began writing articles on corruption in Kansas City, which won him a national audience, and in time his pieces began appearing in the muckraking magazines of the day. Along with Ida Tarbell, Lincoln Steffens, and Upton Sinclair, he was considered a major force in the progressive reform movement.

Like Woodrow Wilson, Creel had come to his commitment to reform through a distrust of northern power. As a boy he had sat on the courthouse steps in Independence, listening to tales of the lost cause recited by veterans. Later he looked upon the trusts as an attempt on the part of northern interests to control every aspect of national life. To him, reform was not only humane and progressive, it was also revenge for all the humiliations that had followed Appomattox.

Creel had definite ideas regarding journalism and education, many of which had been inspired by Charles Ferguson, a local pastor. Ferguson was convinced that the nation was on the brink of a major upheaval and that its leaders would come from pure-minded individuals educated at new universities in the Midwest. He wanted to establish one, and as a start, organized the National Fellowship of the University Militant. His new school would be "free from the greeds of private initiative and the raids of the freebooting money-maker." From it would be graduated an elite, which would lead the country into correct thoughts and actions. As for the general public, it would be educated through the newspapers, which Ferguson believed were destined to become the dominant force in national life. He gathered around him a group of young Kansas City leaders, Creel among them, and at one point half convinced the publisher to turn the *Independent* into a new kind of newspaper that would serve the cause.

Creel rejected the idea, but did promise to found "a different kind of journal," to be called *The Newsbook*, which would be "the first link in a projected chain of weekly newspapers localized in the chief cities of the country." It would not be controlled by the "plutocrats," but rather by reporters and editors. *The Newsbook* would be operated as a co-operative venture by the reporters, who would share risks and rewards.

Ferguson contacted his friends in New York, asking them to join in the venture, if only to submit articles. Many indicated an interest. Such leading reform figures as Brand Whitlock, Edwin Markham, Elbert Hubbard, and Ida Tarbell—even Ray Stannard Baker—met in New York with Ferguson and Creel to plan the new journal. According to Ferguson, its aim would be to:

> win and hold the balance of power in American communities, for an institution—the municipal university or university of the people—that shall subordinate all sects, parties, and special interests to the paramount interest of civilization, to wit, the raising of the general standard of living through the practical advancement of science and the humanities. We believe that such an institution is the predestined crown and complement of our national system of free schools.

It was a harebrained scheme, ill-planned and poorly executed. But an issue of *The Newsbook* did appear, on March 7, 1908. It was a monumental flop. Creel and Ferguson had a falling out. Disgusted, Creel gave the *Independent* to two ladies who owned the local job printing shop, and went off to Mexico to recover and forget.[10] He was back in America a few months later, however, and headed to Denver, where he helped lead the reform movement in that city as editor for the Rocky Mountain *News*. Now Creel emerged as one of the nation's most powerful journalists. According to a colleague who met him at this time, Creel was a "humorous, vigorous, laughing human being, pungent, racy, robust, fervidly temperamental in a way that pleased and amused, one of the best story tellers of his day."[11]

Creel had a sketchy education and was not at all certain about the functions of college. He showed contempt for the collegian type, however, and was half convinced they did nothing but sing and play football for four years. On the other hand, he had respect for learning, and stood in awe of professors. "The ideal arrangement, as I have come to see it, is this: after high school a year or so of work so as to give some idea of what is *wanted* out of further schooling. That is what I had in mind for myself, but somehow I could never find either the time or the money."

While in Kansas City, Creel had attended a lecture Wilson gave for a high school audience. The subject was "the meaning of democracy." As was the case with so many who heard Wilson speak, Creel quickly admired the man. "This admiration grew as I read his books and watched him perform as governor of New Jersey." Creel believed then, and later on, that his ideas regarding education were similar to Wilson's. "As Woodrow Wilson complained, most of the colleges and universities fail to relate their courses to life." To be sure, this was an almost total misreading of Wilson's philosophy of education. On the other hand, there was a striking similarity between the ideas of Wilson and those of Charles Ferguson, and as Creel had followed Ferguson in 1907, so he came to admire Wilson.

In 1911, as the governor prepared for the Democratic convention the following year, Creel wrote an editorial in the Rocky Mountain *News* which called for Wilson's nomination. The following year Creel organized a Wilson Club in Denver, and convinced his newspaper's owner, former Senator Thomas M. Patterson, to support Wilson both in print and at the convention. When the candidate arrived in Denver to deliver a campaign speech, Creel was on the committee that greeted him. The two men formed a friendship.

Creel left Denver for New York shortly after the election. While there he wrote free-lance pieces for magazines and was on call as a presidential adviser. The ties between the two men grew, and Creel became one of the army of young reformers who would consider themselves Wilsonians for the rest of their lives.

Creel played a significant role in the 1916 election. He wrote a series of articles outlining the President's stands on major controversies, which were gathered into a small book, *Wilson and the Issues*, and used effectively in the campaign. More important, however, were his organizing activities. In previous presidential elections, journalists, authors, and intellectuals had supported one candidate or another, but unless they joined the official party organization, that was the limit of their efforts. By 1916 Creel knew most of the major journalists in the nation and their politics. With Wilson's blessings, he brought them together in an informal group, and asked them to volunteer to write statements and pamphlets for the cause. Many agreed to do so, and under Creel's direction, such individuals as Tarbell, Steffens, Baker, Irvin Cobb, Samuel Hopkins Adams, Fannie Hurst, Edgar Lee Masters, and Kathleen Norris made significant contributions to the campaign. With the financial backing of several Democratic millionaires, most notably Bernard Baruch and Thomas Chadbourne, Creel was able to run full-page advertisements in major newspapers, attacking Republican candidate Charles Evans Hughes' positions and defending Wilson.

Robert Wooley, who was in charge of publicity for the Democratic National Committee, welcomed this help at first, but then realized that Creel and his group were assuming his role. The two men clashed, with Wilson stepping in as moderator on occasion. Most of the time, however, the President sided with Creel, especially after arguing with Wooley over the use of the slogan "He Kept Us out of War," which Wilson believed deceiving. By the end of the campaign, Wooley was almost powerless, while Creel was invited to come to Washington in an official capacity, but more important, as an unofficial adviser.

Every President has had a kitchen Cabinet of one kind or another. Creel was to become a member of Wilson's in the second Administration; although Creel rejected the offer at first, he changed his mind in 1917, when it appeared that the United States was about to enter the war.

In late March, several newspapers carried stories concerned with the effects of an American declaration of war upon the national life, in which was raised the question of freedom of the press. Most realized that the yellow press had been responsible in part for the Spanish-American War—"Mr. Hearst's War." It had been a short contest, and the matter of censorship had not been seriously considered. But the experience had left a bad taste in government, especially in the War and Navy departments, which felt that full freedom could not be permitted should the United States fight in Europe. The French and Germans had practiced rigid censorship during the Franco-Prussian War, and the British had done the same in the Boer War. All nations involved in World War I were restraining their newspapers. It appeared likely that the United States would follow their leads when and if it became a belligerent.

The Wilson war message was delivered on April 6, and the next day the newspapers indicated that the President favored censorship of one kind or another. Creel learned of this and responded with a brief in which he argued that such a policy would be unwise and counterproductive, as well as of dubious constitutionality. America should not have censorship, he wrote, but rather the press should be asked to accept a series of self-imposed restrictions on the publication of news of troop movements and concentrations in preparations for attacks and withdrawals. The Administration should explain its needs to the nation's publishers and editors, and assuming they were reasonable, all would respond; to do otherwise would be to invite not only the disapproval of their peers but also retaliation from readers who would consider the publication of secret information harmful to the cause.

Creel went on to say that "*expression*, not *suppression*, was the real need." Wilson should organize the nation's opinionmakers and -molders to help in the war effort. It would be "a plain publicity proposal, a vast enterprise in salesmanship, the world's greatest adventure in advertising." Just as the President was mobilizing industry, agriculture, and consumers, as well as the military and naval forces, so should he do the same in the area of propaganda. "What I proposed," wrote Creel thirty years after, "was the creation of an agency that would make the fight for what Wilson himself had called 'the verdict of mankind.'" In the innocent rhetoric of a past age, Creel spoke of the need for a massive propaganda apparatus, which would blanket the nation with official interpretations of events and spread the word to the rest of the globe. Creel wanted a government agency "that would not only reach into every American community, clearing away confusions, but at the same time seek the friendship of neutral nations and break through the barrage of lies that kept the Germans in darkness and delusion."[12]

Wilson was considering just such an organization. Congress had passed the Espionage Act in June, and even before that, several Cabinet members had urged the creation of a propaganda apparatus. Grosvener Clarkson, head of the Council of National Defense, asked leading publishers and editors for suggestions on the censorship issue, and they agreed that such an organization would be in the national good. The only remaining question was that of control. The publishers wanted to make certain that propaganda was in the hands of people like themselves. Frederick Roy Martin, head of the Associated Press, wrote in *Editor and Publisher* that censorship should be administered by "trained newspapermen and not by retired Army and Navy officers, who may suffer from physical or mental gout and antagonize the press at every turn." As he saw it, "Newspapermen cannot command battleships, and military staff officers cannot conduct newspapers."

The Cabinet disagreed. Secretary of State Robert Lansing and Secretary of War Newton D. Baker expected that propaganda and censorship would be in the hands of the military, while all relations with foreign governments—including the release of information—would continue to come under the control of the State Department. Baker was on record as wanting retired officers "to act as censors at the various places where such services may be required," while Lansing had warned Wilson of "grave difficulties" if any outside agency competed with the State Department in releases to foreign governments. For a year the War Department had conducted an "educational service" known as the Bureau of Information, which was in charge of press relations. At its head was an ambitious young officer with a talent for public relations,

Major Douglas MacArthur. Lansing and Baker, together with Secretary of the Navy Josephus Daniels, hoped MacArthur's operation would be expanded, and in time have control over the nation's press and propaganda.

Wilson thought otherwise. After some urging from reformist journalists and intellectuals—among them A. A. Berle, Oswald Garrison Villard, and Norman Thomas (who had also been in Wilson's classes in Princeton)—he offered Creel the position of head of the new Committee on Public Information (CPI), with the other members being Lansing, Baker, and Daniels. As for MacArthur, he would serve as Creel's aide before being transferred to a combat outfit on its way to France.

The battle over leadership of the propaganda apparatus was one of the most crucial that occurred during that first month of American participation in World War I. Given the confusion of the period and the fact that Wilson was calling upon many civilians to take leadership roles in the war effort, the Creel selection appeared part of a general plan, interesting but not worthy of special attention. And yet it was. For the first time in its history, the nation was to have an official propaganda arm. In the past, Greeley, Bennett, Raymond, and other editor-publishers had debated the issues of the Civil War; Lincoln had established no bureau of public information. Hearst and Pulitzer, together with their reporters and editors, had helped lead America into the Spanish-American War, and men like them—not William McKinley—molded public opinion during the conflict. It would be different, however, in World War I. The Wilson administration would not only determine political and military policies, but also possess a stronger instrument of public opinion than that of any publisher or editor.

Creel was in a unique position. The country had had its share of influential editors and publishers, and some had served in Cabinets. One, Horace Greeley, had even been nominated for the presidency. During the muckraking era before the war, journalists like Tarbell, Sinclair, and Steffens had achieved national reputations. Never before, however, had a working newspaperman possessed so much official political power—and with a constituency of one: President Wilson. In an age of information the journalist, not the politician, bureaucrat, or military officer was taking command, and would do so with impressive and effective allies.

Creel had no difficulties in working with Secretary Baker. The two men had met when Baker was mayor of Cleveland, and while Creel admired Baker's progressive programs, the Secretary understood the power of the press and respected it. As for Daniels, he had been publisher of the Rocky Mount *Reporter* and a printer before entering government service. Later on, Daniels had purchased the Raleigh *News and Observer* and had served as a publicity director during the Bryan and Wilson campaigns. He was a shrewd politican who understood men like Creel and had no difficulty in working with them.

Secretary of State Lansing was another matter. A prominent lawyer and unsuccessful politician, Lansing had served in a variety of government posts before assuming his Cabinet position on the resignation of William Jennings Bryan in 1915. An aristocrat by breeding and a conservative by inclination, Lansing had little use for Creel, whom he considered a dangerous radical with "socialist tendencies." Along with other politicians and bureaucrats, Lansing clashed often with Creel, with Wilson usually siding with the former newspaperman. After each confrontation, Creel's power seemed to grow. Lansing believed Creel's views "caused distrust and apprehension among many officials of the Administration." But, Lansing said, Wilson didn't seem to mind; the President "viewed with toleration, if not with a degree of approval, certain socialistic ideas which he termed 'progressive,' although they were utterly hostile to the fundamental principles of his party." In Lansing's view, "Jeffersonian Democracy and Wilsonian Democracy were and will continue to be quite different."[13]

Perhaps it might have been anticipated that Wilson would select a person like Creel to head the CPI. For despite their differences in training, education, and politics, both were individuals who had made their ways through life by developing and expounding ideas.[14] Each man, in his own way, was at home with people who thought, spoke, and wrote for their livings. The CPI that a Creel would establish and manage would be quite different from one headed by a Douglas MacArthur, Robert Lansing, or Newton Baker. Furthermore, its approach, style, and impact were also strikingly different from anything that had gone before or might have developed in the 1917–19 period under a less Jeffersonian variety of President.[15]

The Executive Division of the CPI was headed by Creel and

consisted of him and three associate chairmen. Edgar Sisson, the most important of these, had been city editor of the Chicago *Tribune*, managing editor of *Collier's*, and editor of *Cosmopolitan*. Sisson was sent to Europe after the outbreak of the Russian Revolution, eventually winding up in Moscow, where he was supposed to work against the Soviets. He became director of the CPI's Foreign Section, which distributed domestic releases to European newspapers and governments and created books, pamphlets, and articles for use throughout the world. While Sisson was gone, Harvey J. O'Higgins, an author and playwright, gained power at the committee. O'Higgins was available to assign and write articles that answered specific charges against Wilson and the Administration. Carl Byoir, the third associate chairman, had been circulation manager of *Cosmopolitan* before the war and was considered a brilliant public-relations and advertising man. Among his other tasks, Byoir was charged with maintaining good relations with other agencies of government and the publishers. Next to Creel, he was the most visible member of the Executive Division, and his work there proved a springboard for his postwar activities, which included the establishment of Carl Byoir and Associates, the nation's leading public-relations firm.

Under Creel's direction and with the assistance of Byoir, O'Higgins, and Sisson, the CPI established a division of news, a foreign-language newspaper section, a civic and educational branch, a film division, a bureau of war expositions, a bureau of state fair exhibits, an industrial relations sector, the alliance for labor and democracy, a speaking division, an advertising section, and even a bureau of cartoons.[16] New sections, divisions, branches, and offices appeared daily in 1917, to the point that even Wilson did not understand or comprehend the scope of the organization or its activities. Certainly Creel was afforded a great deal of leeway, with at least as much freedom in organizing propaganda as Bernard Baruch was permitted in mobilizing production. For most of the war Creel functioned on his own, without executive or legislative restraints.

Although most Americans seemed to approve of the declaration of war, there was still a large amount of antiwar sentiment, and even pro-German activity. After all, Wilson himself had campaigned in 1916 on an antiwar platform. LaFollette and others, too, had voted against the declaration. America had large numbers of German and Irish immigrants and children of immigrants, and in 1917, there was some question as to their loyalties. Whether justified or not, Wilson, Creel, and others in government believed a massive propaganda effort in favor of the war was required. To some, it appeared an official version of what Hearst and Pulitzer had done in 1897–98 in respect to the Cuban situation. But it was far more than that. Utilizing his position to the fullest, Creel mobilized a large segment of the nation's intellectuals, writers, artists, and journalists, had them manufacture "products" under his supervision, distributed them and suppressed alternate views. It was the closest America had ever come to control of expression, and given the technology of the period, constituted its greatest effort in that direction. Creel was proud of his accomplishments. In April of 1918, he wrote to the editor of the Birmingham *News* of the scope of his activities:

> Three thousand historians are at our call in the preparation of pamphlet matter; virtually every writer of prominence is giving time to the work of the Committee; the Division of Advertising enlists the energies of every great advertising expert in the United States; there are close to fifty thousand speakers in the Four Minute Men; the war conferences of the states are under our supervision; men and women of all nationalities go from coast to coast at our bidding; the famous artists of the United States are banded together for the production of our posters; the motion-picture industry has been mobilized and is giving us ungrudging support without thought of financial return; and in every capital in the world there are men and women serving with courage and distinction.[17]

Creel was particularly proud of the work done by college professors, a breed he knew little of prior to the war. Given the opportunity to speak before a larger audience than they had ever known, the professoriat responded eagerly. To be sure, academics from some midwestern universities and land-grant institutions in the East had worked with state commissions, but now these academics were listened to as patriotic and influential leaders; for the first time, they tasted the heady wine of power and influence. Hundreds of professors served as Four Minute Men—people prepared to speak for that period of time on topics relating to the war. In the CPI's "Red, White, and Blue Series," Wallace Note-stein and Elmer Stoll of the University of Minnesota wrote *Conquest and Kultur*, an anti-German tract, of which more than 1,200,000 copies were printed and distributed. Professors Dana Munro of Princeton, George Sellery of the University of Wisconsin, and August Krey of the University of Minnesota wrote *German War Practices* (1,500,000 copies); E. E. Sperry of Syracuse University and W. M. West of the University of Minnesota edited *German Plots and Intrigues* (127,000 copies); while the *War Cyclopedia* (200,000 copies) was produced by Frederic L. Paxton of the University of Wisconsin, Edward Corwin of Princeton, and Samuel Harding of Indiana University. In the "War Information Series," William Stearns Davis of the University of Minnesota produced *The War Message and the Facts Behind It* (2,000,000 copies); Professor Charles Hazen of Columbia wrote *The Government of Germany* (1,800,000 copies); Carl Becker of Cornell was the author of *America's War Aims and Peace Terms* (719,000 copies); and Andrew McLaughlin of the University of Chicago wrote *The Great War: From Spectator to Participant* (1,580,000 copies). These scholars, some of them among the leading academic figures in the nation, became, in effect, part-time propagandists for the government. No longer were they the "dear old prof" and "the absent-minded professor." For the duration of the war, at least, they felt themselves to be men of affairs, experts whose knowledge was not as esoteric as previously thought, but instead of great utility—as important to the war effort as guns and ships. For a few years, historians and political scientists were in positions to help sway the entire nation, not merely their college classes and the readers of journals in their fields. They worked under the guidance of a scholar-president; the world was their campus.

It was a heady experience for these men, and some would never recover from it. For the rest of their lives, they would try to function as participants in the nonacademic world. But there would be little call for their talents in the peacetime administrations of Warren Harding, Calvin Coolidge, and Herbert Hoover, or in the business world of the 1920s. In addition, their CPI books and pamphlets, written with such zeal in 1917 and 1918, would seem blatantly propagandistic, hardly respectable history and political science in the cold eye of the postwar period. By the mid-1920s, many professors would come to fear that they had been used, their talents prostituted. Such individuals continued to want a public forum, complete with power, but on their own terms—or as close to them as they could get. In effect, they maintained their loyalties to the Wilsonian dream, but were disillusioned by the practices made necessary in service to the cause. They craved the forms, perquisites, and status that had come with power, but recoiled from the practices necessary to obtain all three. The returning soldiers and sailors of 1910–20 weren't the only ones to have problems of postwar blues during the 1920s. Perhaps instinctively, Creel had discovered that these men had their prices, and he paid them with the coin of status, receiving services and goods in return. Afterward, the professors would wonder whether they had done the right thing.

Creel had a different experience with the newspapermen. Unlike the professors, publishers and editors had known power and at least local influence before the war. They could not be seduced by talk of patriotic duty from a man who, after all, was only one of them, and no plaster saint at that. Hopewell Rogers, head of the American Newspaper Publishers' Association, attacked Creel as "incompetent and disloyal," and other publishers resented Creel's often crude attempts at distorting the news. Creel responded that men like Rogers spoke only for the business end of journalism. "That body of the press which deals with the news itself is without national organization," Creel noted, implying that the reporters would do well to confront their disloyal publishers and their editor lackeys. Reckless journalism, said Creel, "is a positive menace when the nation is at war," adding, "In this day of high emotionalism and mental confusion, the printed word has immeasurable power, and the term traitor is not too harsh in application to the publisher, editor, or writer who wields this power without full and solemn recognition of responsibilities." Later on, Creel claimed he had been talking about information regarding the disposition of troops, convoys, and the like. But at the time he urged those in journalism who had "any doubts" about the propriety of their articles to submit them for approval. Hearst, who was both antiwar and anti-Wilson, was able to withstand Creel's attacks on his patriotism, although on occasion even he bowed to government regulations by killing stories. Lesser editors and reporters simply wrote and published pieces they knew would be in conformity with Creel's desires.[18]

And it was easy to do so. The CPI's News Division, directed by J. W. McConaughy, formerly editorial writer for *Munsey's Magazine* and staffed by experienced editors and writers, was the largest news-gathering and writing press association in the nation, producing some twenty thousand items a week, all of which were available to editors and reporters. It was a simple matter for a reporter to rewrite a CPI release, hand it in, see it published, and then go on to do other things. By the war's end, the "press release," unknown before 1917, had become institutionalized. The practice was continued by government in the 1920s and after, and picked up by businesses, many of which hired public-relations firms—such as Byoir's—to develop and write pieces for release and, hopefully, publication in newspapers and magazines. To be sure, press agentry had its origins before the war, but the CPI experience helped cement the alliances between the new creators in the public-relations rooms of industry and government and the reporters and editors at newspapers throughout the nation. In fact, the two positions often were interchangeable, with talented reporters taking government and business posts, and public-relations men finding employment on newspapers.

During the muckraking period, an independent and powerful press criticized and probed government on all levels. The two came together under Wilson and Creel, and although they separated after the war, the ties were never fully broken. In the years that followed, reformers would criticize the "Lords of the Press," and there would be cries for more independent journalism among other things, for newspapers controlled by reporters and editors and not by publishers. This demand missed the point of the wartime experience. As much as any other group in the nation, reporters had been enlisted into government service, albeit indirectly, by the CPI. For the next generation at least, the nexus would remain intact.

Creel had hoped to mold the American people through propaganda, and certainly his efforts in that direction were impressive. He also worked to sell the Wilsonian dream overseas, and a good deal of the President's popularity can be traced to Creel's vision and prose—spread by the CPI to every corner of the globe. "Creel's enterprise became mainly one of 'building up' Wilson, causing Wilson's ideas to dominate the mind of the world, including Germany, including even the minds of Germany's armies in the field," wrote newspaperman Mark Sullivan. "He, with Wilson; Wilson as forger of verbal thunderbolts, Creel as propagandeer of them; Wilson as Napoleon of ideas; Creel as Marshal Ney of dissemination—the two would conquer the world."[19]

Was this really so? We can trace Creel's efforts through the professors, count the number of pamphlets and articles distributed, note his influence with the press. We can see Creel threatening publishers who printed pro-German books, planting propaganda in textbooks of his own design, helping publish a school newspaper that went to every classroom in the land, and translating Wilson's speeches into all languages. Through Creel's efforts, Wilson did become the best-known, most popular American in history. All of this could rightfully be claimed. The words had been written and distributed. But had they been read? By whom? And what were their effects?

Wilson had been an elitist in education, and Creel a reformer. Yet the congresses of the prewar period had been largely conservative. Americans had elected McKinley with a landslide in 1900; Roosevelt became President after his assassination, and then was elected in his own right only after obtaining the support of a large segment of the business community. Wilson was a minority President. To whom did he speak, and who was listening? In 1918 *Shavings*, a maudlin novel by Joseph C. Lincoln, was a best seller. Gertrude Atherton, Ernest Poole, Irving Bacheller, Mary Johnston—writers of escapist fiction—had fine sales with their novels that year. The first parts of *Ulysses* by James Joyce were banned from the mails in 1918, while *Lightnin'* began a record run on Broadway, and then sent stock companies to the provinces, where *Uncle Tom's Cabin* and minstrel shows were still popular, though not as much as the circus. In all probability more Americans read of Boston Red Sox pitcher Babe Ruth and his World Series exploits than they did the collected—or uncollected—speeches of Woodrow Wilson. What did these Americans think of the propaganda effort, originated and executed by intellectuals and their allies?

The CPI had established a division of labor publications, headed by Robert Maisel, a former labor organizer. It also sponsored the American Alliance for Labor and Democracy, with Samuel Gompers of the American Federation of Labor as its titular chief. Maisel was charged with producing and distributing literature to workers, while the Alliance was supposed to maintain peace and harmony at the unions. In addition, Roger W. Babson, the statistician and economic analyst, headed a division of industrial relations, which provided ideas and assistance for the other two groups. Experts from other sections were brought in to help mobilize the workers. Professor Commons of Wisconsin wrote *Why Workingmen Support the War*, in which he said, "This is an American workingmen's war, conducted for American workingmen, by American workingmen. Never before has democracy for wage earners made so great progress as it has in the six months that we have been at war." Commons predicted that "if this continues" the worker would gain an eight-hour day and higher wages than ever before. "Capitalists are being controlled in their profits and in the wages and hours of laborers by leaders whom the workingmen themselves put on the various war boards."

While the Wilson administration had supported legislation controlling profits, businessmen were, nevertheless, making large profits during the war. In addition, Commons had exaggerated the workers' benefits, both in terms of hours and wages. The CPI urged workers to "enlist in the war effort for the duration." Posters showing workers and soldiers arm in arm were plastered over walls in factories throughout the nation. Firms with high production ratings received awards and publicity. Yet the number of work stoppages increased during the war. There had been 1,593 strikes in 1915, 3,789 in 1916, and 4,450 in 1917. In 1918, with the CPI urging greater productivity, there were 3,353 strikes, and in 1919, 3,630, and the majority were caused by grievances in regard to wages and hours.

What was the reason for this? Some manufacturers blamed "socialistic propaganda" and others spoke darkly of "German plots." "The thing has gone so far that it is going to be a big job to sway the attitude by any educational system," said L. J. Monahan, president of the Universal Motor Company. T. S. Graselli, head of the large Graselli Chemical Company, thought legislation "making it criminal for a man to be idle when any government work has to be done in any community" would be helpful. Economist Chester Wright, who took charge of the division of labor publications in 1918, reported that workers were complaining about excessive overtime and poor wages. "An attempt to proceed with loyalty work without an adjudication of industrial conditions would be pure waste of time," he told Creel. Another commentator wrote that "My two sons in France get $33 apiece per month: Why should Stone, and Armour, and Vanderlip *et al.* be paid more? . . . Unless we conscript wealth to the justifiable limit, all appeals whether by the Four-Minute Men or a letter from the President, to save, to give blood or money, to compose differences, to subscribe for bonds, to stand behind the President—all appeals will fall eventually on deaf ears; and we shall have a sullen, scowling, half-hearted cooperation, instead of a whole-hearted, inspiring to-the-last-ditch united democracy."

Creel was at a loss as how best to proceed. He would not conscript labor, his pleas were unavailing, and no amount of propaganda seemed to do the job. Were the workers simply unpatriotic? After all, a good many of them were foreign-born, and perhaps their sympathies were with the Central Powers, not the Allies. Was the American labor force more radical than had been believed? These were the questions asked, but Creel seemed incapable of coming up with the answers. The attempts to mobilize unskilled and semiskilled labor generally failed; in contrast, Creel's greatest successes had come in his work with intellectuals.

In 1918, H. R. Wade of the Diamond Forging and Manufacturing Company wrote to Creel of labor discontent at his plant. "One of our laborers called my attention to a paragraph in a Polish paper that an individual named Frankfurter, of some college, had been appointed by President Wilson to a position in the Labor Department, and requested enlightenment as to how such a man could use any influence with common labor."[20] In other words, Wilson and Creel might be able to mobilize men like Felix Frankfurter, but they lacked the ability to communicate with manual workers—the nonintellectuals.

We see the war, now, through the eyes of the press, public speakers, officials, and writers—the vision of intellectuals. And it appears a fairly popular crusade, with Wilson capturing the hearts and minds of the nation and then of the world. But was this really so? Given an understanding and appreciation of the Creel effort at the CPI, was this view a truthful one? The histories of the war were written by Wilsonians, often men who worked at the CPI. A generation of American historians were trained in government, and they remained Wilsonians for the rest of their lives.

What did the rest of the country think of the war and of the

Wilsonians? Just how strong was the antiwar movement? There is no way of answering these questions satisfactorily, but there are bits and pieces of information and evidence to consider, such as the number of strikes. Furthermore, antiwar congressmen did not suffer unduly in the 1918 election. Eugene V. Debs and his Socialist party were antiwar. In 1912 Debs received 900,000 votes for the presidency. In 1916, Socialist A. L. Benson ran in Debs' place and obtained 585,000 votes. Four years later, in 1920, Debs was in jail for his opposition to the war and won 919,000 votes. That year Harding—supported by antiwar forces, among others—received 16.1 million votes, while James Cox, with Wilson's blessings, had only 9.1 million.

Then there was Robert LaFollette, who had opposed entry into the war, and spoke for moderation from 1917 to 1919. LaFollette was sharply critical of Creel's propaganda efforts, especially when war resisters were branded as traitors. The CPI issued a series of advertisements urging Americans to "report the man who spreads pessimistic stories. Report him to the Department of Justice." LaFollette branded such activities thought control, and in a Senate speech in late 1917 he urged repeal of the sedition laws. Clearly referring to the CPI, he said, "It appears to be the purpose of those conducting their campaign to throw the country into a state of terror, to coerce public opinion, to stifle criticism, and suppress discussion of the great issues involved in this war." A person of his stature, prominence—and courage as well—could say such things in the superpatriotic atmosphere fostered by the CPI. Other, lesser men remained silent, while a handful in the House and Senate attacked Creel indirectly by attempting to cut appropriations for the CPI. Creel responded by charging them with partisanship, and since most of his opponents were Republicans, there may have been substance to this. Then he would plant stories about the effective work of his committee so as to put pressure on the legislators. When Edgar Sisson returned from Russia with documents purporting to prove that the Germans had encouraged the Soviet Revolution, the news caused a sensation and resulted both in a resurgence of patriotic zeal for the war and new appropriations for the CPI.

By the mid-1920s, the whole nation appeared disillusioned with the war—or at least this seemed the verdict of journalists and other writers. A new generation of them had appeared, one that had not participated in the war effort or had not made moral, professional, and spiritual commitments to the Great Crusade. These men and women criticized those who had involved the nation in the struggle. Their chosen villains were businessmen and foreigners. (Wilson, however, was still praised as a man of vision who even then was taking a place in the pantheon of American saints.) The antiforeign crusade of 1919 that culminated in the Red Raids of 1920 were blamed upon Attorney General A. Mitchell Palmer, not Wilson or Creel. The CPI had done much to create the atmosphere of fear and hate, and even though Creel was repelled by the superpatriots and spoke out against them, he was unwilling or unable to control their work. Later on, in writing his surprisingly candid memoirs, he still failed to discern any significant connection among the anti-German propaganda from 1918–19, the curtailment of civil liberties by superpatriots, and the Red Raids.

Wilson and LaFollette had been leaders of the American reform movement prior to World War I. Despite some surface similarities, they had enunciated differing beliefs and opinions on a variety of issues, from education to the functions of leadership in a democracy. LaFollette trusted the instincts of the common man in most things; he thought Americans could take care of their own interests. Wilson loved humanity in the abstract, but had doubts about the abilities of individuals to select wise and proper courses of action. An elite would be required for this task, a cadre that would create ideas and programs for the rest of the society. These would have to be disseminated among the masses, in a form and a fashion the common people would understand and appreciate. He believed he had found the man for the task in George Creel, the agency in the CPI.

Newspapermen and academics found a perfect conduit into the area of public service in Creel. As chairman, he helped alter the direction of American journalism. Although Creel did not dominate the stage as had Greeley or Pulitzer, he operated on a far wider arena, and for a brief time with greater power than even Hearst. And in the process Creel trained a generation of newspapermen and academics in public service, and fashioned links between journalism and government stronger than any that had existed since the early nineteenth century.

The muckrakers had criticized government from the outside;

Tarbell, Steffens, Sinclair, and others of their group had had no hope of political office; if they had been offered bribes, they were in the form of cash, not power. This changed with the war. From that time on, journalists would attack and defend government with an eye to power—often official power at that. Government and the press would each try to use the other, with often curious results for each.

Most of the professors who worked for and with the CPI and other government agencies returned to the universities and colleges after the war. But the dear old prof, who may have worked for his state or municipal government in one capacity or another prior to 1917, now had had his taste of national, even international status and power. He had mingled with the movers and shakers, and often found the experience heady and to his liking. This would not be forgotten, or the lessons lost on those who took their places in academic affairs and government in the next generation. For example, there was Guy Stanton Ford, professor of European history and dean of the University of Minnesota in 1917, who had become director of the CPI Division of Civic and Educational Co-operation and helped recruit dozens of leading historians and political scientists for Creel, including Andrew C. McLaughlin of the University of Chicago and Carl Becker of Cornell. After the war, Ford returned to Minnesota, soon to become president of the university. Ford, McLaughlin, and Becker all would serve as presidents of the American Historical Association; a majority of those who would hold that position in the 1920s and 1930s had had direct or indirect connection with the Wilson administration.

Men such as these would continue to present the Wilsonian view of the war and defend it. In the past, most historians had liked to think of themselves as impartial observers, standing above the conflict, watching the actors with a cool eye. But the histories of this war would be written by men who had had an emotional, intellectual, moral, and often personal stake in the conflict and its resolution. They may have been better informed than their predecessors for their experiences, but they could now hardly be considered impartial. Wilson may have lost the battle for the League of Nations, but he had long before been victorious in the conflict for the affections of the nation's academic elite.[21]

Some intellectuals spent the 1920s in Europe, where they came to be known as the "Lost Generation." Those who used the term were convinced that America, not the writers and artists in Paris and London, was truly lost, primarily because the nation did not utilize their talents, giving them positions of power and prestige. Those who remained at home railed against those who had succeeded them in government and sneered at the new middle-class culture that emerged after the war. The new people didn't seem to mind, and in fact they appeared somewhat amused by critiques of their ways of enjoying themselves, much to the chagrin and disgust of the attackers. In any case, newspapers and elite colleges were not prime areas of interest for the nation's middle class. Rather, the dominant culture found expression through different instruments, which the intellectuals and reporters initially ignored. The Wilsonians retired to the background—to some newspapers and universities—after the Great War. For a decade it appeared that the age of the mass intellectual had dawned, that if a reform temperament survived it would be that of LaFollette, not Wilson. In 1924 an old, tired, and ill LaFollette ran for the presidency on a third-party ticket, with little publicity or newspaper support. Yet he received 4.8 million votes, an impressive showing under the circumstances. But this was not the age of men like LaFollette or Wilson. Rather, it was best symbolized by the victor in 1924, Calvin Coolidge, and the man he had succeeded, Warren Harding. The differences between them and LaFollette were far greater in most respects than those between the universities at Madison and Princeton.

4

Films from Form to Content

Guy Stanton Ford attended the University of Wisconsin from 1892 to 1896, when the school was becoming deeply involved in the management of the state. He registered for courses with two leaders of the Wisconsin Idea, Paul Reinsch and Richard Ely, but most of his work was with historian Frederick Jackson Turner. After graduation, Ford accepted a teaching position in a local school in order to save money for graduate work, and in 1898 he began to take courses toward a Ph.D. in European history. The following year he went to Berlin to conduct research for his thesis, and in 1901 Ford returned to America, to teach at Yale and complete his doctorate at Columbia. His thesis, finished in 1903, was entitled "Hanover and Prussia, 1795–1803." The work, which dealt with the different traditions within the German Empire, was rather dull and pedantic. As Ford saw it, Prussia was able to dominate the German states because of its abilities at organization, while the other states refused to arm in the face of potential aggression. Ford received his Ph.D. and, after publishing a few articles, was offered a professorship at the University of Illinois, which he accepted. In 1913, he was named dean of the graduate school at Minnesota.

Ford was a solid scholar and an able teacher, but certainly not in the class of a Wilson or a Turner. Rather, he hoped to obtain future administrative appointments and, eventually, the presidency of a major university. While in Minneapolis he worked on several state commissions, helping to bring scholars into government, such as had been done in Wisconsin. If Turner had influenced Ford in his selection of a career, Reinsch and Ely showed him how academia and government could be united.

In 1917, Ford was asked to prepare a list of suggestions as to how Minnesota's schools could assist in the war effort. "I wrote an open letter to school principals about the possibility of using the coming high school commencements for patriotic purposes," he recalled. "I wrote it for the signature of the Commissioner of Education, but he modestly declined to sign it and sent it out, however, over my name." George Creel came upon the letter and was impressed. Within days he had contacted Ford, they met, and the dean was asked to come to Washington to work for the CPI, as head of the Division of Civic and Educational Co-operation. Ford accepted, and during the next two years co-ordinated the largest scholarly effort in the nation's history, mobilizing the academic world in the service of the Wilson administration.[1]

The work was quite different from that of a dean or even of a university president. Although Ford would not have to instruct his corps of professors in the area of content, the teachers and scholars would have to rethink their ideas regarding form. In the past these men had written for their own kind, usually on specialized and often arcane topics, or at best for sophisticated readers of highly literate magazines. Now they would have to aim at a mass audience and write on subjects divorced from their specialties. Finally, the professors would have to learn new techniques, especially those of the films.

Some adapted well. Professor John Tatlock of Stanford wrote commentaries for several successful filmstrips—*Building a Bridge of Ships to Pershing* as well as a fifty-slide set on *The Ruined Churches of France*. Professor George Zook of Pennyslvania State College quickly became the division's star writer, turning out nine series, including *The Call to Arms, The Navy at Work,* and *Airplanes and How They Are Made*. Like many academics who went into government service in this period, Zook liked the work, which was quite exciting after years in the classroom. Later on he became the United States Commissioner of Education, as such drawing additional academics into federal service and perpetuating the work and ideals of the division after the war had ended.

For men like Zook and Tatlock, service with Ford was an education in communications; all the while, the former dean was learning about journalism and public relations from Creel. If the newspaperman appreciated Ford's enthusiasm and erudition, the dean had nothing but praise for his chief's knowledge and abilities. After the war, when he returned to Minneapolis, Ford wrote several books and introductions to many more, and these, unlike his prewar book on Germany, were written in an interesting, journalistic style. By the late 1920s, Ford was turning out articles for popular magazines, as well as editorials for the Minneapolis *Journal.* Creel's influence was evident in these and his other writings, and Ford was always willing to concede his debt, to talk and write of his experiences with the CPI and how much he had learned from them. In particular, he thought Creel had understood, better than anyone else in government, the power of communications and, in particular, the impact of motion pictures. "Here was a man who saw what others had not seen clearly enough in the past, that such a thing has infinite possibilities for good if it is organized in the right way, and that you can teach through the eyes and through these pictures what neither the printed nor spoken word can teach. He caught the idea and he pushed it. . . ."[2]

Among his other prewar accomplishments, Creel himself had been a screenwriter. In 1910, while at the Rocky Mountain *News,* he had met Bronco Billy Anderson, then the nation's leading Western motion-picture actor. Anderson was also a partner in Essanay Film Corporation, and was in Denver to shoot a few stories. "During the summer we make outdoor pictures in and around Chicago," he told Creel, "but when fall comes, I take a photographer, a property man, and two or three principals, and follow the sun. Other people are picked up from local stock companies." This was why Anderson wanted to talk with Creel. He needed stories, and felt the editor could provide them. Would he be interested in writing for Essanay at the rate of twenty-five dollars a story? He would indeed, and for the next few weeks Creel stole time from the newspaper to learn from and write for Anderson. Some of his stories were accepted. These were rather simpleminded, Creel later conceded, but Anderson didn't seem to mind that. "They come to see Bronco Billy," he said. In fact, he thought Creel might have a future in the industry, and he urged the editor to join him and relocate. "Colorado's a great place for scenery and clear light, but some companies are trying to build up a motion-picture center out at a whistle stop in California called Hollywood." Creel rejected the offer, but as was the case with many successful writers, on several occasions he accepted assignments to prepare screenplays.[3] In fact, some of his short fiction was under consideration for film treatment at the time Creel accepted the chairmanship of the CPI.

Shortly after the American declaration of war, the Associated Motion Picture Advertisers, a trade group comprised of leading film manufacturers and theater owners, ran an advertisement in several newspapers that asked, "What Is Your Liberty Worth to You?" America was in danger, it said, and the motion-picture industry "has offered its services to the government to assist in attracting a patriotic activity in behalf of the country in the grave crisis that confronts it, and to stimulate interest in enlistments in the various defensive branches of the government by attractive posters and slides, and by compelling advertising and publicity." Creel met with an industry group shortly thereafter, and he helped form the War Co-operating Committee, which included William Fox, D. W. Griffiith, Thomas Ince, Jesse Lasky, Marcus Loew, Adolph Zukor, and other major industry leaders. Under the committee's direction, the industry would assist in the war effort.

Patriotism had doubtless led to offers of co-operation, but there were other factors as well. The war had all but destroyed the industry's European markets, and several companies were in shaky financial shape. Some hoped for government contracts to tide them over. Although various federal agencies had motion-picture facilities, these would be inadequate for any large-scale propaganda effort Creel might wish to mount, and there was the threat that if the studios did not fill the need, others would. William Randolph Hearst had become interested in motion pictures, and two of his aides, Byoir and Slosson, were close to Creel. In September the CPI established a Division of Films, and on Slosson's recommendation, the chairmanship was given to a Hearst advertising manager, Charles S. Hart. Fearful that Hearst would come to dominate the industry as a result of his contacts, the other producers, managers, and executives rushed to offer their co-operation during the war.

In addition, most of the film industry's leaders had been born in countries with which the United States was at war, and these men spoke with heavy accents. More than a few had been pro-German from 1914 to 1917, and in the summer of 1917 some minor filmmakers and executives had been imprisoned on espionage charges. Felix Malitz, who had specialized in the importation of foreign films, was sentenced to five years in prison for smuggling rubber into Germany, and Frank Godsol, a distributor, was charged with disseminating enemy propaganda. Hollywood buzzed with rumors of other indictments to come. The industry leaders were eager to prove their allegiances.

Already the leaders in film production and distribution were wealthy and successful men. They owned mansions on Long Island, town houses in Manhattan, and California estates, while only a few years before they were petty businessmen who knew little about motion pictures. These individuals were now wooed by Wall Streeters, and their products were known to almost all Americans. They had survived much already, and most would come through the war intact.

By 1921, the estimated gross annual box-office receipts would be approximately $300 million—15 per cent of the money Americans spent for recreation that year. By then, there would be some 14,000 motion-picture theaters, which employed 100,000 men and women to service the 50 million paid admissions per week, or slightly less than half the nation's population. Producers in California and New York, and locations between, would turn out some 700 feature films and many short subjects that year, with the assistance of 15,000 workers of various kinds, artists included. The production payroll would be $25 million; some $15 million would be invested in studios alone. Taken together, the motion-picture complex would be the fastest-growing segment of the economy, increasing at a more rapid rate even than automobiles and electric utilities. A quarter of a century before, there had been no industry.[4]

It had happened so quickly, and in such an unusual fashion, that the outlines of the motion-picture complex could not be drawn, the nature of the business clearly defined, or its impact assessed. The pioneers had been obliged to respond to challenges without completely comprehending their natures, to answer questions before they were fully formulated, and to create large corporations without being certain of the nature of their products. They had relied upon personal friendships to sustain them against outsiders, had drawn upon uncertain precedents from other apparently related industries, and had struggled to understand the relationships among business, education, politics, and art. In the process, they proved to be masters at improvisation, and perhaps without wishing to rise to such positions, had become as important as molders of public opinion as Bennett, Greeley, Pulitzer, and Hearst had been, and more so than any college president or professor.

THE MOVIES COME TO AMERICA

The pioneers were not present at the birth of the industry, in part because no one really knew what it would be until much later. Throughout the nineteenth century inventors and scientists in Europe and America had experimented with devices they hoped would produce "moving pictures." Apparently none had any idea of how the machines would be used once developed; commercial considerations were not involved in the efforts.

Thomas Alva Edison entered the field indirectly and, like the others, did not realize at first the significance of the invention. In 1887 he had patented the phonograph, while one of his assistants, William K. L. Dickson, worked on a companion device. The following year Edison filed a caveat at the Patent Office. "I am experimenting upon an instrument which does for the eye what the phonograph does for the ear, which is the recording and reproduction of things in motion, and in such a form as to be both cheap, practical, and convenient. This apparatus I call a Kinetoscope." Together with Dickson he actually produced a machine, but deemed it little more than a curiosity, with minor practical value. Years later, Edison said, "I figured that after the novelty wore off the camera would either be taken up by the big educators and pushed as a new agency in the schools—or that it would be developed mostly along straight amusement lines for entertainment and commercial purposes." But it wasn't until 1893 that Thomas Lombard, a gramophone dealer, came across the Kinetoscope in Edison's Menlo Park laboratory and, seeing some of its potential, ordered several. These he sold to the Holland Brothers, who ran amusement arcades. In 1894 the Hollands opened a Kinetoscope Parlor on Broadway in New York. Customers would put a coin in a slot, which would activate a fifty-foot spool of film and a light. They then would see a "show," which usually consisted of people waving, a horse running, or almost anything, so long as it was moving. People would stand at the boxes for hours, their eyes glued to the glass viewer, to watch the marvel. The Kinetoscope was a commercial success, and "peep shows" such as the Hollands' opened in cities as far west as Chicago from 1894 to 1895.

Many of the machines were Edison's, but rivals entered the field—American Mutoscope and Biograph (later known as Biograph), Lambda, Kinematograph, Pathé, and others that quickly fell by the wayside. When Edison moved too slowly for his liking, Dickson formed his own company and produced the Mutoscope. By the late 1890s, a trade war among peep-show equipment manufacturers had erupted, to be followed by lengthy patent fights in the courts. The industry had begun.

But what was it? Edison and his rivals produced machines and sold them to amusement park owners and operators. In order to provide product for the machines, they would set up cameras to film natural phenomena and people, often employees. Were the companies engaged in the machinery business? Were the arcade owners involved in the exhibition area—something like sideshows and circuses? Had this been the extent of moving pictures—and the industry stopped at that point—the answers to both questions might have been yes, and that would have been the end of it.

Frank R. Gammon and Norman C. Raff, who worked for Edison, were intrigued with the idea of display. Why have a hundred machines, each with a pair of eyes to the glass, watching the same moving pictures, when a camera might throw the image on a wall, with the same hundred people watching together? In this way, one machine could do the work of a hundred. They urged Edison to work on such a device, but the inventor wasn't interested. Meanwhile, Thomas Armat and C. Francis Jenkins experimented with the idea of projection, and in 1895 produced a combination slide projector-Kinetoscope before deciding to go their separate ways. Gammon and Raff convinced Edison it would be wise to back Armat in his work, for others were developing projectors that might leave the great inventor in the backwash of the new industry. He agreed. Armat was hired, and in 1896 he produced the "Edison Vitascope." The machine was given its first public exhibition at Koster and Bial's Music Hall in April. The audience saw surf breaking on a beach, a burlesque boxing match, a comic allegory based on the Monroe Doctrine, and a woman dancing. It was "all wonderfully real and singularly exhilarating," wrote the New York *Times* in its news story—not review. "For the spectator's [not audience's] imagination filled the atmosphere with electricity, as sparks crackled around the moving lifelike figures." Gammon and Raff were vindicated, and even though the audience applauded Edison, Armat was rewarded. The spectators had come to see an exhibition, a novelty, a curiosity, and they were not disappointed. Other theaters ran Vitascope demonstrations, often in conjunction with vaudeville, which remained the prime draw. Thus an audience would be entertained by live actors and then watch a short film or two, as they might view a display in a museum or a strange animal at the zoo. These were interesting and gave a person something to talk about, but no more.[5]

Charles Frohman, one of the nation's leading theatrical producers, was at the Koster and Bial exhibition. Was it an entertainment? Or even an amusement? By itself, the show was neither. But Frohman did see how films could in time replace other, apparently entrenched entertainments. He saw the moving pictures of nature scenes and, relating them to the stage, said, "That settles scenery. Painted trees that do not move, waves that get up a few feet and stay there, everything in scenery we simulate on our stages will have to go. When art can make us believe that we see actual living nature, the dead things of the stage must go." Frohman thought moving pictures could easily be combined with stage shows. "For instance, Chevalier comes on the screen. The audience would get all the pantomime of his coster songs. The singing, words fitted to gestures and movements, could be done from the wings or behind the curtain. And so we could have on the stage at any time any artist, dead or alive, who ever faced Mr. Edison's invention."[6] Combined with the phonograph, the moving picture could preserve the works of great artists, thought Frohman. As a leading producer of Broadway plays, the idea intrigued him. This, combined with educational considerations, appeared more promising than the entertainment potential of films.

Frohman would not enter the field. Nor would the other major Broadway producers—David Belasco, Sam Harris, the Schubert brothers, and the rest. But if the leaders of the legitimate stage appeared unconcerned with films, might the new medium have appealed to the vaudeville impresarios? Koster & Bial's was a music hall, and films might well supply parts of vaudeville cards, at lower costs and with greater dependability than many acts.

Vaudeville had been the leading American performing art form in the late nineteenth century. Although local and even regional showmen still existed then and held great power, leadership became concentrated in the hands of a few men. An artist could count himself fortunate if he signed with B. F. Keith, E. F. Albee, John Murdock, Percy Williams, or F. F. Proctor. The pay might be low and life on the road difficult, but at least the performer would be certain of a full season of work with more to come.[7] Should a rival impresario make the artist an offer, he or she would try to play one against the other, with the hope of extracting higher salaries and better working conditions. If all went well, the artist would catch the eye of a Broadway producer—a Frohman or a Harris—and become the star of a play that would run a season or two in New York. Afterward, however, it would be back on the road, booked in the better houses, by one of the vaudeville kings.[8]

The impresarios shared certain attributes. They had deep roots in vaudeville, having entered the field early in life. In the late 1890s, most of the major figures were in their late thirties or early forties—middle-aged by the standards of the day—and well established. Almost all were native-born; Albee and Proctor came from the same area of Maine. They knew one another, engaged in friendly competition, and were deeply committed to vaudeville. They would remain in the industry for the rest of their business careers. In varying degrees and in differing fashions, each of the old vaudeville leaders rejected films.

In its infancy, the motion-picture industry might have been controlled or at least dominated by one of four groups already in existence. The inventors of machines, such as Edison, could have assumed power, but they lacked interest, desire, and vision. The powerful show-business tycoons could have entered the scene; Charles Frohman might have become the leader of a major producing firm, for he certainly had similar experience on Broadway. The artists themselves might have become involved in moving pictures, organizing production units around themselves and hiring distributors and perhaps even purchasing theaters with profits. Or the business community could have taken a hand. But the impresarios and artists were wedded to the old ways, while the financiers and tycoons were involved in the creation of major trusts in already existing industries.

The path was clear, then, for others to take leadership, entering the industry at a time when it was still in an embryonic stage, giving it a direction and flavor—and even a content—of their own devising. This was what happened. In its early days, moving pictures, soon to become a major molder of the national character, were controlled by a group of individuals who had no direct roots in the nation, show business, or invention.

The newcomers were immigrants, or men whose parents arrived in America shortly before they were born. Almost all were East European Jews; as was the case with the vaudeville impresarios, they shared similar values, worked with one another while at the same time engaging in competition, and on occasion saw their children marry childhood playmates—the sons and daughters of fellow leaders in the industry. Were it not for the development of motion pictures or their almost accidental entry into the new industry, they might have remained furriers and marginal clothing manufacturers, for their religion and ways of life barred them from entry into established industries and enterprises, while their lack of education prevented them from aspiring to careers in the professions.

Carl Laemmle, the oldest of the group, was born in Germany in 1867, arrived in America at the age of seventeen, and soon after opened a clothing store in Wisconsin. Adolph Zukor, born in Hungary in 1873, emigrated in 1889 and became a furrier's apprentice, and later on owned his own small business. Marcus Loew, born of immigrant parents on Manhattan's Lower East Side, left school at the age of six to take a variety of jobs. He wound up as a fur salesman, and while in Chicago he met Zukor. The two men became friends—Loew helped Zukor move to New York—and later on Loew's son married Zukor's daughter. Jesse Lasky had a different background. The son of Jewish immigrants, he was born in San Francisco in 1880 and tried to make a go of it in vaudeville, but met with repeated failures. His brother-in-law, Samuel Goldfish (later to change his name to Goldwyn) was born in Warsaw in 1882, immigrated to England at the age of eleven, and then came to America in 1897. Goldfish apprenticed himself to a glove manufacturer and then opened his own shop. William Fox, born in Hungary, arrived in America in 1880 when only a few months old and became a cloth sponger on the Lower East Side. Others of the group had similar backgrounds.[9] In one way or another, in different parts of the country, most were raised in the ghetto, and all were highly ambitious and aggressive. Anxious to become Americanized, strongly patriotic, and aware of the opportunities offered them in the New World, they sought vehicles for their ventures into middle-class respectability. The Kinetoscope and its imitators provided them with one such opportunity.

At the turn of the century the motion-picture business offered three possible areas of investment and managerial opportunity. Even then it appeared certain that one would dominate the others, although no individual thought it possible to control all three. The first and oldest might be designated as production—the fabrication of machines and finished films. At the time the two areas were the same, with the machine manufacturers producing motion pictures in order to have a product to offer potential customers. The films were as undifferentiated as the machines, which is to say that clients purchased both on the basis of price, ease of handling, and accessibility. In time the artistic aspects of film would become more important, and some machine companies would concentrate on films instead, but such was not the case in the beginning.

Distribution was separate from production. Patrons soon tired of seeing the same show repeatedly, and demanded variety. Ambitious marginal businessmen realized this, and began purchasing films from one arcade to sell to others. Then they would buy films from the manufacturers and rent them to owners of theaters or arcades. Finally, some distributors set up production units of their own, turning out copies from a single master, in contravention of agreements with the producers. The development of distribution came quickly; a young man who entered the field with only a few dollars and little knowledge in January might have a fairly large-scale operation, complete with a staff to purchase, sell, rent, and copy, by April.

The third area was exhibition, the renting or ownership of an arcade or theater where the films were displayed. Like distribution, exhibition required only a small capital investment, and if all went well, an individual might have a group of theaters in a short period. Then he might rent a film and show it at several locations, in effect bypassing the distributor. The distributors, on their part, would be tempted to open their own arcades and theaters, and so make profits from both sides of the business.

Lack of funds and experience, combined with a knowledge of the opportunities in the business, attracted the immigrants to exhibition and distribution. Chicago, with a large Jewish population, was one center of activity.[10] In 1903, furriers Adolph Zukor and Morris Kohn loaned three thousand dollars to Max Goldstein, an associate, who wanted to open a peep show. The enterprise showed immediate profits, and Zukor opened arcades of his own. When these did well he left the fur business and relocated in New York, where he continued to develop peep shows, while at the same time renting store fronts and turning them into theaters —nickelodeons—to display films on screens. Carl Laemmle also opened peep shows and nickelodeons, and then organized the Laemmle Film Service, a distribution organization. W. N. Rubel, like the others a Jewish immigrant, began the Chicago Film Exchange, which soon became the largest in the Midwest, and later on he opened a chain of theaters. The story was the same elsewhere in the Midwest. In 1904 the Warner brothers pooled their resources and purchased a projector, giving traveling shows throughout Illinois, Indiana, and Ohio. Then they opened a nickelodeon, and with the profits developed others, finally organizing a film exchange. In Haverhill, Massachusetts, junk dealer Louis B. Mayer purchased a nickelodeon in 1907, and soon had a string of them along the eastern seaboard, as well as a distribution service. Marcus Loew opened his first peep show in New York in 1904, after investing in a Zukor operation the previous year and seeing it succeed. Others followed, so that by 1908 Loew was able to open the Royal Theater, one of the finest in the city, which cost four hundred thousand dollars to construct.

Producers of machines and films were aware of the large profits being made in distribution and exhibition. They also realized that most distributors printed copies from masters in violation of agreements—in 1905 a company was actually formed and sold stock on the basis of a plan to make illegal "dupes." Furthermore, distributors and exhibitors showed little regard for contracts, and were proving adept at playing one producer off against the other. They were doing well at it, while the producers were showing losses, and their bankers concern about their futures.

This situation and condition triggered several responses. Many producers changed the specifications of their machines, so that they could run only films produced by the company, in this way hoping to destroy rivals. Others, but only a few, came to realize that once the novelty wore off films would have to become differentiated, that they had to be sold on quality instead of quantity, and they turned to the artistic side of the business. Attempts were made to use strong-arm methods against those distributors suspected of duping operations, and some exhibitors charged that producers had paid arsonists to burn down nickelodeons. Cut-throat competition erupted among the producers, followed by lawsuits and charges of fraud and deceit.[11] None of this worked. The production side of the business was in chaos—a prime area for organization. And the Empire Trust Company, which had loaned two hundred thousand dollars to Biograph and feared for its repayment, joined with the other prime lenders to bring the producers together. In December 1908 they formed the Motion Picture Patents Company, which was to be led by Jeremiah J. Kennedy.

Kennedy had begun his career as a railroad worker, who later on taught himself engineering. Then he went into management, and helped reorganize the Gould railroads. He knew nothing about films, but in 1908 was recognized as an intelligent manipulator, the kind of person bankers used to organize trusts. Empire Trust had hired him to straighten out the situation at Biograph, and he wound up as head of an incipient motion-picture trust. Under his leadership, ten major producers united to pool patents and other resources, and each received a license to manufacture equipment and films. Eastman Kodak, the only large supplier of raw stock, agreed to deal only with the trust. In early 1909, Kennedy issued distribution licenses to 116 independent exchanges, and the producers declared their intention to boycott noncompliers.

Within a year the trust dominated distribution. Then, in 1910, Kennedy organized the General Film Company, capitalized at $2 million, to complete the job and move in on the theater owners. Unless these men accepted trust leadership and schedules, they would be denied both films and equipment. Most fell into line; by October, more than 5,000 of the nation's 9,500 motion-picture theaters were being served by General Film, while all but one of the principal exchanges had bowed to the trust.[12]

By 1911 it had become apparent that motion pictures were not oddities, or even amusements, but a rapidly developing art form. George Melies, perhaps the most original producer-director of his day, and a charter member of the trust, was turning from equipment to art. Edwin S. Porter, a technician at the Edison studios, developed and produced feature-length films, and at the age of forty-one was the "grand old man" of the production end of the industry. D. W. Griffith started as an actor at Edison, sold a few scenarios to Biograph, and in 1908 directed his first films at that company, which like Melies was becoming increasingly interested in production. Thomas H. Ince, a stage actor, arrived at Biograph at the same time, and within two years was known as the best Western director in the business. The inventor-businessman gave such artists great freedom of action, in part because they understood little of the craft themselves, but also because they knew even less about audience desires, and hoped the directors did.

The exhibitors may have known little about film production, but they did study audiences with great care. After all, their futures depended upon their success in divining the tastes of the common man. As Zukor put it, "I would go to a theater, take the first row or sit in a box and then study the audience and see what effect the picture had on them. So I was pretty certain in my mind after the experience I had had in watching audiences that I could use a subject and not go far wrong." Zukor's sometimes partner, Marcus Loew, preferred block booking of pictures, and scoffed at the idea of considering films on their artistic merits. "Such a practice would be analogous to . . . a plum salesman . . . selling one plum at a time."[13] Zukor watched audiences, not pictures, while Loew saw little difference in "product." Later on, when such men did enter production, they would invest large sums of money on instincts, hunches, and "itches in the seats of their pants." And it would be *their* pants, not those of the artists, that would decide the issue.

Would films be dominated by native-born Americans who had artistic tendencies, men who through the trust came to control much of the industry's distribution and exhibition? Or would films be led by the immigrant businessman obliged to enter production in order to have products for display, and who in the process had to educate themselves in the arts? To be sure, investment bankers would have a major voice in the industry whichever way it went, since large amounts of money were needed to open theaters, distribute products, and especially to produce films, and this would be the case no matter which side won. But would the bankers work through artists like Griffith, Ince, Anderson, and Porter, or with businessmen such as Zukor, Loew, Laemmle, and Fox? This was the crux of the struggle between the Patents Company and the independents in the years prior to World War I.

Each distributor and exhibitor reacted differently to the trust and General Film. Some of the smaller operations welcomed structure and security in an industry noted for cut-throat tactics, but the large and growing concerns sought methods of avoiding Kennedy's dictates. Several turned increasingly to vaudeville, which was relatively unorganized. Loew, who combined live and film presentations at his theaters, consolidated with Sullivan and Considine, a large booking agency, and by 1912 Loew's Theatrical Enterprises was the largest force in the backwoods and second-line business. Some experimented with equipment made by new firms, unaffiliated with the trust; a few openly declared their independence and showed films produced by small, nontrust studios. Zukor worked with the trust, but at the same time helped organize the Engadine Corporation, which—with Kennedy's approval—purchased American rights to *Queen Elizabeth*, a film starring Sarah Bernhardt. Out of this came Famous Players Film Company, which Zukor hoped would produce "famous plays with famous players."[14] Kennedy allowed Zukor to produce films in America, so long as they did not compete directly with those turned out by the trust. Famous Players, in time, was transformed into Paramount Pictures. Carl Laemmle, another businessman, had a different experience. He tried at first to work with the trust, but soon after clashed with Kennedy. Laemmle opened the Independent Motion Picture Company (IMP) to produce films, and with others organized the Motion Picture Distributing Sales Company, which went into competition with General Films. The Sales Company failed, but from IMP was formed Universal Pictures Corporation, which soon became a significant force in production. Other independents took a different tack. The Warner brothers farmed out production to small firms. One of these, Bison Live Motion Pictures, which specialized in Westerns, was created by disgruntled employees of trust companies. Other businessmen approached foreign filmmakers, urging them to expand production and importing their products into the United States. Jesse Lasky, Cecil B. DeMille, and Arthur Friend organized Jesse Lasky Feature Plays, one of the first production units to move to Hollywood, and which shortly thereafter merged with Famous Players. William Fox formed the company which, in time, became Twentieth Century-Fox.

The independents had been forced by circumstances to expand and innovate, and they did so in three ways. In the first place, they constructed larger and more ornate theaters, in the hope of drawing customers from those affiliated with the trust. Then they accepted, grudgingly, the idea that films could indeed be sold as art and entertainment. A newcomer, Triangle Films, had shown that the public would pay higher prices to see longer, more ornate films. Zukor's success with *Queen Elizabeth* encouraged him to produce other "classics" for his audiences, and he noted approvingly that the average man was beginning to differentiate among products. When George Kleine, a member of the trust, had a huge financial success with *Quo Vadis?* in 1913, Zukor and others were encouraged to continue along that line, and they proved more innovative and flexible than Kennedy.

Finally, they capitalized upon Kennedy's unwillingness to deal with his artists in a fashion they thought decent. The trust would give them freedom of expression, but would not pay high salaries or offer them billing on programs. The independents reversed this order. Although they insisted upon final approval for their products, they would woo artists from the trust with money and publicity. In this way, Laemmle won Mary Pickford from Biograph, and others followed, while at the same time the independent producers began developing "stars" of their own. John Bunny, Mabel Normand, James Kirkwood, Theda Bara, the Gish sisters, and others of their generation either were introduced by the independents or soon joined them. Florence Lawrence, known only as the Biograph Girl to a public that came to recognize her films, was lured to Universal when Laemmle more than doubled her salary and featured her name on advertisements. Zukor employed stage stars like James O'Neill, James Hackett, and Lily Langtry at Famous Players, and found that their names on advertisements attracted audiences and so justified their high salaries. Charlie Chaplin went from independent to independent, playing one off against the others, and all the while increasing his popularity and price. William S. Hart, Tom Mix, and Douglas Fairbanks rose from relative obscurity to the status of millionaires in a few years. In time, Kennedy and his associates imitated these methods, and the trust too attempted to develop stars. But it was too late.

William Fox used another weapon in the fight. His was the only major film exchange not controlled by the trust. Aided by Rubel and other distributors, he charged the trust with violations of the Sherman Act. At first, Kennedy tried to destroy Fox, and when this failed, he offered to buy him out. In 1914, Fox settled for an out-of-court payment of $350,000, but by then the government had initiated a suit of its own. Discouraged, embittered, and clearly losing business, the trust members ejected Kennedy, and each tried to succeed on its own. But the decline of the individual companies continued, and by 1918, both the trust and General Film were out of business. The independents had won. But the meaning of the victory, its price, and the shape of the industry were not clear.

In order to fight the trust, the small exhibitors and distributors had been obliged to imitate some of its forms. In effect, they became integrated companies—or at least the larger ones did—by moving into all aspects of the industry. Fox went from distribution to exhibition and production. Zukor was in all branches of the industry, and it appeared that he might succeed where Kennedy had failed, by destroying rivals and then taking them over, while Laemmle and some others were not far behind.

The "product" of 1918 was different from that of 1909, the result of changes the independents had been forced to accept. The undifferentiated films with anonymous actors were still being produced, but increasingly the motion-picture industry's leaders were obliged to seek stories from the classics, popular novels, and epic dramas. Theda Bara appeared in *Carmen*, Mary Pickford in *Madame Butterfly*, and Griffith directed *The Birth of a Nation*. Films that cost well over one hundred thousand dollars to produce were no longer unusual, and they came out of studios in California as well as older ones in the East and Midwest. Major productions were shown in ornate theaters, often on a reserved-seat basis—at two dollars each. This was a far cry from the store-front nickelodeons of 1909 and the makeshift facilities of that time. In less than a generation, motion pictures had moved from oddity to lower-class amusement to middle-class entertainment. Needless to say, this transformation cost a great deal of money, which the pioneers lacked.

The money came from investment bankers and old-line businesses. Prudential Insurance backed Fox Films. Goldwyn Pictures was financed by the DuPonts and Chase National Bank. The Liberty National Bank and William Durant of General Motors handled Loew's, Inc.'s flotations. When Laemmle needed money for Universal, he found it at Shields & Co., which took all of his stock and bond issues. First National Exhibitors Circuit sold its shares through Hayden, Stone & Co., while Goldman, Sachs was behind Warner Brothers. American Tobacco was interested in several companies, and in the end invested heavily in Triangle Films and provided some money for Zukor as well. Famous Artists utilized the services of Kuhn, Loeb.

The domestic part of the industry prospered during World War I, and the stock markets boomed, the proper combination to provide the industry with all the money it needed and make its leaders millionaires; the huge salaries received by the stars came from the flotation of securities on Wall Street. After the depression of 1920–21, the flotations would recommence. Tens of millions of dollars would be raised for industry leaders who, before World War I, considered a one-thousand-dollar investment in a nickelodeon worthy of a family conference.

The surviving companies had opportunities, ambitions, and—with the help of the bankers—money. They were in a rapidly expanding industry, and each attempted to become its master. In 1919 Famous Players-Lasky owned more than 200 theaters, had its own booking agencies for vaudeville acts, and produced 139 features. Pathé which merged with DeMille Studios and acquired the businesses of Producers Distributing and the Cinema Corporation of America, released 58 features that year. Loew's, Inc. was one of the largest theater operators in America, as well as a major booker of vaudeville acts; its Metro Studios released 83 features in 1919. Laemmle's Universal accounted for 64 and Fox Films for 70. Together these five large firms released over 82 per cent of the nation's motion pictures for 1919. All were well financed and eager for additional business.

But their leaders could not manage every aspect of their companies. These were men who had emerged from the distribution and exhibition ends of the industry, who a decade earlier were not certain they wanted to be in the field, whose lives were centered around their families in New York and Chicago. As the bankers obtained more control over operations, they had to spend much of their time on Wall Street. Production, on the other hand, was becoming concentrated in Hollywood, a week away by train—and few moguls liked making the trip, or if they did, knew quite what to do once they arrived. So they sought out men like themselves, placed them in charge of studio operations, and hoped for the best. Jesse Lasky, the head of Famous Players-Lasky in Hollywood, had Zukor's confidence, at least at first. Loew had difficulties finding the proper executive, and for a while had to pass on scripts himself. Not until 1924, when he merged with Goldwyn and asked Louis B. Mayer to take command of production—at Metro-Goldwyn-Mayer—was he able to remain in New York, where he wanted to be in any case. After several failures, Laemmle went to Hollywood, and assigned his other interests to assistants. Each leader arrived at his own solution, and each tried to divine the public taste and produce films that would satisfy it.

AN INDUSTRY IN FORMATION

In 1910 the immigrant exhibitors and distributors had faced extinction at the hands of the trust. Ten years later they had to contend with the more perplexing problems that came with success. By uniting with investment bankers and industrialists they had lost a good deal of their freedom of action. These men and their representatives now sat on the boards of directors of major motion-picture companies, and if they did not dictate policy, they at least had an important say in financial matters. This was a price that had to be paid for bigness, and the immigrant tycoons understood the situation and accepted this exchange of power for prosperity. But other problems were not so easily handled.

The first of these concerned the struggle for domination of all aspects of the industry. This was noted by the Federal Trade Commission which, in 1921, brought an action against Famous Players-Lasky, charging the use of unfair methods of competition. Prosecutions of other large firms either were initiated or threatened, and so Washington produced a challenge to the industry's leaders at least as serious as that of the trust before the war. The giant companies had to tread lightly, and some began concentrating on production or exhibition in the hope of avoiding charges of monopoly or excesses of power. Of course, the government could not be challenged as easily as the trust. Industry leaders realized the need for political influence.

In their contest with the trust, the exhibitors had entered the production field, dealing on a regular basis with writers, directors, actors, and other artists. They were uncertain in this area, and uneasy among the people who increasingly were located in Hollywood. It had been so much simpler before the war, when Zukor, Loew, Laemmle, and others of their group had concentrated on theaters and provided "product" for relatively unsophisticated audiences. By 1920 the films, not the theaters, were the main attractions that drew audiences and made for profits, and the middle-class individuals who paid over a dollar to see a feature were quite different from the people who had frequented the nickelodeons. Furthermore, the war seemed to have unleashed new forces and dynamisms within the nation, wild excesses somehow related with Prohibition that the middle-aged and middle-class immigrant showmen neither approved of nor fully understood. Yet the artists did, and their films continued to make money, so the motion-picture industry leaders remained silent though disturbed. A new civilization appeared to be developing in California, and their prosperity depended upon it. Did production control exhibition? Or was the reverse still the case? And what might happen if the older America revolted against the "excesses" of Hollywood? There was the threat of censorship, which might not only result in large-scale losses on particular films, but also the destruction of major studios—and motion-picture companies.

The third problem was one the nation as a whole was experiencing. The conversion from a wartime to a peace economy caused economic dislocation in 1919 and a depression the following year. There were more than 30,000 bankruptcies from 1919 to 1920, almost 500,000 farm foreclosures, and 5 million unemployed workers. In January 1921, the unemployment rate stood at 20 per cent. The gross national product, which reached a record peak of $88.9 billion in 1920, declined to $74 billion in 1921. Along with most other statistics, those for attendance at motion pictures declined. Laden with debt and having to pay large salaries to stars and service mortgages on ornate new theaters, the large companies were in deep trouble. Kuhn, Loeb insisted that one of its men, H. D. H. Connick, take charge of the finance committee at Famous Players-Lasky, and Zukor meekly agreed. The bankers gained power at Metro Pictures, Loew's, Universal, Goldwyn, and Fox. There were rumors of a struggle between the House of Morgan and the DuPonts for the dying carcasses of the major motion-picture companies, and some believed that by 1923 all the large firms would be controlled by one or another investment bank, while the immigrant pioneers would be forced from their creations. The rumors were exaggerated, but in the depths of the depression in 1921, they seemed at least plausible.

The embattled heads of major motion-picture companies once more had to formulate solutions to a set of problems. Those in power in Washington who were intent upon regulating the industry as they might do for steel, oil, or railroads, had to be stymied, and a degree of co-ordination restored among businessmen who had once co-operated so well with one another. The artists, newly wealthy and feeling their power, would have to be throttled; Hollywood would have to learn that New York was the dominant city for the industry. If all of this could be accomplished, then harmony and prosperity might return, and the bankers' grips loosened.[15]

The impetus for change came from reactions to Hollywood, and these had prewar antecedents. The development of the star system led to "cults of personality" for several leading artists, who became heroes and heroines overnight. Fan magazines and clubs were started, and these spread rapidly. *Photoplay*, which specialized in revealing the "inside lives of the Hollywood greats," was one of the nation's most widely read magazines, and there were many imitators. Would-be actors and actresses traveled to Hollywood, even then called "the glamor capital of America," in the hope of being discovered and starring in films opposite their dream idols.

The city boomed, the studios grew, costs of pictures and stars' services increased rapidly, and money flowed freely. This combination of a boom psychology, newness, excitement, money, power, and eager and attractive young people helped give Hollywood the reputation of "sin city," and the fan magazines helped spread the word. Reports of orgies, wild living, crazy antics—the stuff from which the nation would fashion the myth of flaming youth and the jazz decade—started even before the war had ended. News of divorces, seductions, and the use of drugs appeared in the fan magazines. Unwittingly perhaps, the studios established public-relations departments that fed stories to reporters, who then embellished them to make the stars appear almost other-worldly to a nation that was still, for the most part, firmly established in the Edwardian Age. Then Wallace Reid, a major star, died of a drug overdose. So did Olive Thomas, Mary Pickford's sister-in-law. William Desmond Taylor, a leading director, was murdered, and a subsequent investigation involved actresses Mary Miles Minter and Mabel Normand. Fatty Arbuckle, at the time a top Hollywood comic, was accused of the rape death of Virginia Rappe, a starlet. The fan magazines and gossip columns carried stories of wild orgies attended by studio executives and would-be actresses.

The motion pictures turned out by the studios re-enforced the sentiment that Hollywood was an immoral place; during and after the war, many films were released that today would be classified as soft-core pornography. *A Shocking Night, Their Mutual Child, Wife's Awakening, Her Social Value, The Fourteenth Lover, Foolish Matrons, The Good-bad Wife,* and *The Truant Husband* were some in this mold. Cecil B. DeMille, one of the leaders in this kind of film, produced *For Better, For Worse; Why Change Your Wife?; Don't Change Your Husband; Saturday Night; Forbidden Fruit,* and similar films. In them women were "liberated," divorce condoned, and infidelity went unpunished. *The Sheik,* starring Rudolph Valentino and released in 1921, appeared to accept rape, and was the first of a wave of "romances set in the red-hot sands" that appeared the following year.

Censorship may have been inevitable. As early as 1909, Mayor George McClellan of New York ordered all picture houses closed because of the immorality they encouraged. A National Board of Review, founded that same year, tried ineffectually to place restraints upon production. Several states, most of them in the Midwest, established their own boards of review, and although they lacked enforcement mechanisms, the industry's leaders feared a loss of income should these be provided. Then, in 1915, a congressional committee debated the issue of national censorship. The idea died in 1917, when the industry co-operated with Creel and the CPI. But it emerged once more in 1920, as a delegation of churchmen descended upon the Capitol to complain about immorality in films. That year, Senator Thomas Gore of Oklahoma introduced a measure to prohibit films showing or simulating the acts of convicts, desperados, robbers, and outlaws. In 1921, thirty-six states considered censorship regulations of one kind or another, many of which were derived from the CPI experience. Then came the Arbuckle-Rappe scandal, and a senator spoke of the condition of the movie industry. "At Hollywood is a colony of these people where debauchery, riotous living, drunkenness, ribaldry, dissipation, free love seem to be conspicuous." The actors received large salaries and spent them "in riotous living, dissipation, and high rolling." The effects were dire. "These are some of the characters from whom the young people of today are deriving a large part of their education, views of life, and character-forming habits." The conclusion was unescapable. "It looks as if censorship is needed, does it not?"[16]

Some Wall Streeters felt that censorship would destroy the industry, and the securities of motion-picture firms declined, frightening both the bankers and the presidents of large companies. But although the latter group was disturbed, some of its members saw in the attack an opportunity as well. A similar situation had existed in baseball, where the players had gained a great deal of power over the owners, and bankers were entering the sport. Then, in 1921, came the famous "Black Sox" scandal. The owners had banded together to ask Judge Kenesaw Mountain Landis to become commissioner of baseball, and he had accepted. Already Landis was bringing order out of the chaos of baseball, in the process curbing the power of the players, keeping a watchful eye on the bankers, and preventing cut-throat competition among the teams and leagues. What motion pictures needed, the presidents said, was just such a "czar." The right man would keep the artists in line, make certain the bankers did not dominate the industry, and assure the would-be censors of the essential purity of the industry and its products. The moguls had never felt comfortable with the racy films, but none dared stop the artists from producing them, in fear of losing revenues. Now their man would stop their production, by all studios, and help create a more homogeneous product, the combination of art and business. It seemed a proper synthesis for a rapidly maturing industry.

The industry's leaders had decided, then, to select a czar, and they set about finding the proper man. Several people were mentioned—Secretary of Commerce Herbert Hoover and Senator Hiram Johnson of California were among the leaders. After a few meetings, the consensus was to offer the position to Postmaster General Will Hays.

Hays was forty-one years old in 1921, but already had a national reputation. He had risen through the ranks of Republican politics in Indiana, and had been national chairman during the Harding campaign of 1920. He had little knowledge of films, this derived from newsreels and activities during the Republican convention. As Postmaster General he had helped bring order to a department famous for its poor performance, and was well known as a man of integrity and strict Calvinist instincts. In 1921, it appeared the Republicans would remain in power for a generation, at the very least. Hays knew all the important GOP leaders, and through them had connections with New York investment bankers. He appeared to combine the best qualities of the conservative, middle Americans of his state with the belief in modernity; he was, as Sinclair Lewis would say of his fictional character, Babbitt, a "go-getter." "Mr. Hays . . . believes in the form of Government of the United States, the Presbyterian Church of which he is an elder, as was his father before him, and the Republican Party," wrote a journalist. "He accepts and concedes the advantage of such modern things as stem-winding watches, self-starters, and demountable rims. He is not hidebound. And if I may venture to introduce our native speech into these undefiled precincts, I'll tell the world that he wears snappy clothes."[17]

On December 2, 1921, Hays received a letter from several industry leaders, including Zukor, Fox, Laemmle, Goldwyn, and representatives of Metro, Triangle, and Realart. In it he was asked to become "the active head of a national association of motion-picture producers and distributors." Six days later he met with Lewis Selznick and Saul Rogers to discuss details. As Postmaster General, Hays received a salary of twelve thousand dollars a year; the industry offered him one hundred thousand dollars plus expenses. After additional discussions, Hays accepted; he would become head of the newly formed Motion Picture Producers and Distributors of America. Further details were ironed out at a New York meeting on January 14, when Loew and Joe Schenck joined the others. Two months later the industry chiefs hosted a dinner in Hays' honor, at which the new leader said, "I hope to help develop the highest moral and constructive efficiency in films, but will be neither a censor nor a reformer, as the words are properly understood." He claimed to "have no leaning toward eradicating sex from pictures. It would eradicate interest from pictures." Hays conceded that he knew "nothing about the technical end of pictures, either manufacturing, exhibiting, or distributing." He candidly had accepted the job for three reasons. "First, because it offered a chance to engage in a public service; second, because it offered a chance to retire from politics; third, because I needed the money."[18]

Hays' staff included Charles C. Pettijohn, an old Indiana friend who knew most of the industry's leaders, as well as the former postmaster of New York, Thomas Patten, and the former Maine governor, Carl E. Milliken. The staff indicated that an alliance was taking shape between the immigrant Jewish businessmen of New York and Chicago and old-line native-born Republican politicians. It would be directed against those in Washington who hoped to regulate the industry, the Wall Street bankers who were coming to dominate the board rooms, and the Hollywood nexus—including producers, directors, and actors—who would receive direct supervision from the new czar. For example, Zukor had just been served with papers by FTC lawyers, another step in a series of actions aimed at forcing divestiture either of theaters or studios. He was engaged in a controversy with Jesse Lasky, the studio head, over who controlled the company. Finally, Famous Players-Lasky needed additional financing, and the investment bankers were not certain Zukor should have it, demanding concessions in return for any new flotations. Zukor counted upon Hays to silence the lawyers, assist in the fight against Lasky, convince the bankers to float additional bonds and stock but remain away from the board rooms—and end all talk of national censorship and help freeze the status quo within the industry. If he could do all of this, the one-hundred-thousand-dollar salary would have been well earned. The other tycoons had similar shopping lists, though none as large as Zukor's, and in some respects they ran counter to his. Vitagraph, for example, wanted Hays to insist upon divestiture, in this way enabling that company, which had few theaters, to compete effectively in Zukor and Loew theaters. First National and Katz-Balaban, two major exhibitors, hoped Hays would see the wisdom of divestiture and so enable them to crack the Hollywood-New York nexus.

Hays wasted little time in demonstrating his capacity for gratitude. Although the Federal Trade Commission investigation of Famous Players-Lasky continued, it did so at a slow pace. Then two important commission investigators announced their inability to testify due to health reasons. Zukor's rivals among the exhibitors charged that someone had paid hush money to stop the investigation, and Huston Thompson, the FTC chairman, indicated that pressure had been brought to bear upon him to halt the inquiry. George B. Christian, President Harding's secretary, was considered the man who did the work—and Christian was close to Hays. Zukor and Hays refused comment, but the investigation, which had been scheduled to end in 1922, lasted more than six years, more than sufficient time for Zukor to make changes of his own in the company that in part mitigated the unfavorable verdict eventually handed down. Clearly, Hays stood with Zukor and the large firms. In disgust, several distributors quit the Producers' and Distributors' Association, with Vitagraph leaving in 1925.

Wall Street was in the doldrums in early 1922, with brokers and clients uncertain as to which way prices would go or whether the proclaimed economic recovery had indeed taken place. The prices of motion-picture company stocks were low, but worse still, the firms could not attract additional capital. In late February, Hays was the guest of honor at a dinner given by the New York Federal Reserve Bank. Four months later he addressed the American Bankers Association on the subject of the economic future of America—and the film industry. In between he met regularly with leaders of major investment banks. By midsummer, the combination of economic recovery and Federal Reserve actions had made it possible for funds to flow once more into new offerings. The motion-picture companies shared in the general prosperity; perhaps such would have been the case without Hay's efforts. Still, William Brandt, the former president of the New York Theater Owners Chamber of Commerce, credited Hays with restoring confidence in the industry; this effort alone, he said, was worth three years' salary. Zukor, Loew, Laemmle, and Fox agreed. So did George Eastman, who brought his company into the MPPDA at this time.

Hays spent a good deal of his time speaking out against censorship. Conceding that in the past motion pictures had been somewhat racy and perhaps even immoral, he claimed that the best policy would be to permit the industry to regulate itself. Give self-regulation a chance, he said, and if it fails, there will be time to pass restrictive legislation. Hays lobbied for self-regulation in the states and in Washington. The several referenda on boards of control that were voted upon in 1923 indicated that Hays had been successful; only Louisiana and Connecticut introduced boards of review, and the Connecticut one was ended in a short period. More important, the federal measure introduced by Senator Gore was killed in committee.

Meanwhile, Hays acted to make good on his promise of self-regulation. In 1924 he discussed a formula with the presidents of the large companies under which they would reject stories of an offensive nature. From this emerged the Production Code Administration. In 1924 sixty-seven stories were rejected, and of these, almost half were suggested by the Hollywood faction at Famous Players-Lasky. In effect, Zukor was using Hays to assert his domination over both sides of his company, and he succeeded. In 1925, twenty stories were rejected, as the studios took greater care in screening them. The number dropped to two in 1926. By then, most talk of censorship had ended—and New York dominated Hollywood.

The industry appeared mature and fairly settled by mid-decade. Universal, Famous Players-Lasky, Metro-Goldwyn-Mayer, and Fox Films led in production, while Paramount Publix (a Famous Player subsidiary), Fox Films, Warner Brothers, and Loew's were the leading distributors. Zukor, Loew, Laemmle, and Fox stood astride the industry, for the moment at least.

Motion pictures had begun as a technological marvel, and at first had been controlled by inventors and their staffs. In short order, immigrant businessmen went into exhibition and distribution, and they seemed content to let it go at that. Marcus Loew and even Zukor thought of themselves as real-estate managers and small-time impresarios as late as 1909. Then, with the arrival of the trust, these men and others like them were forced to enter production, to come into contact with investment bankers and artists. At the end of World War I it appeared they would bow before these new forces, but the immigrants fought back, and behind the MPPDA and Will Hays, mounted a successful counterattack against their rivals. After a quarter of a century of struggle, they controlled major firms in a large-scale industry. But the contest was not ended. The investment bankers retained important blocks of stock in the motion-picture firms, while the artists, though under the control of New York, still received large salaries and had become significant culture heroes to that generation of Americans. The immigrant businessmen, who had proven to be superb opportunists, now sought stability, for only with such could they hope to contain the bankers and dominate the artists. But the motion-picture industry was too vital and too young to remain stable for long. The combination of technology, art, and finance had transformed a curiosity into a major entertainment force, which already was replacing vaudeville and challenging the legitimate theater. In the late 1920s, when the motion-picture empires appeared secure for the first time, the same three forces would combine in a different way to transform the face of motion pictures and shatter the status quo. In the end, films would come under the domination of a new and even more powerful industry and set of leaders, and the immigrant pioneers from New York and Chicago would fall by the wayside, with only their money and the symbols of power to sustain them.

5

Radio's Age of Organization

Thomas Alva Edison made one of his several fortunes from the Kinetoscope and Kinetograph. His lawyers litigated with rivals, claiming for their client all they could obtain. The Edison interests were represented in the Motion Picture Patents Company, and the litigations continued even after it fell apart. But Edison did not like movies. He accepted the applause and money that came his way, but that was all. In fact, he rarely went to see films, even those produced by his company, and could never understand why they were so popular.[1]

Most of Edison's inventions fell into one of two categories. The first of these, which might be called "industrial," involved power, and included dynamos, electric lights, batteries, and the like. Then there were his "playthings," which he invented and developed because something about them intrigued him. Partially deaf since childhood, he was interested in all aspects of sound, and in 1877 invented the phonograph, a machine to capture voices and preserve them for future listening. For the rest of his life this would be Edison's favorite machine. The Kinetoscope would remain what Edison called it in his 1888 caveat—"an instrument which does for the eye what the phonograph does for the ear." Individuals who purchased his phonographs might also want a Kinetoscope, so they could see the musicians playing while listening to their sounds, or watch dancers performing to music. Thomas Edison could appreciate sound without the visualization, but he saw little purpose in having motion pictures without sound. Had the great inventor been blind rather than deaf, his attitude toward the silent films might have been different.

In 1876, the year previous to the Edison caveat, Alexander Graham Bell filed for a patent on the telephone. Almost immediately he was involved in a series of lawsuits with rival inventors, who claimed to have worked on models prior to that date. But the Bell patents held up, and he is generally credited with producing the first practical telephone, even though others—Edison included—developed improvements during the next few years.

The interests of the two men were intertwined. Like Edison, Bell was concerned with sound. A teacher of the deaf, he hoped someday to construct a device to enable them to hear. Bell married a deaf student, and his father-in-law helped organize the Bell Telephone Company in 1877. The inventor had little to do with business, however, since commerce did not interest him. Instead, Bell continued working with the deaf, experimenting with hearing aides and related equipment. And he fantasized about the telephone. Bell saw a day when all Americans would be tied to one another by his invention, when they could join in song over the wires, in a gigantic chorus. Such music, he thought, would reach to heaven itself.

The sound would have to be amplified, of course, and toward that end Bell worked on an invention he called the photophone and the radiophone. The first transformed light waves into sound, the second was an attempt to utilize light waves to transmit sound—in effect, a wireless telephone combined with an amplifier.

Bell was also interested in the phonograph. Why did he not think of it first? "It is a most astonishing thing to me that I could possibly have let this invention slip through my fingers when I consider how my thoughts have been directed to this subject for so many years past," he wrote his father-in-law. And yet in spite of this the thought never occurred to me to indent a substance and from the indentations to reproduce the sound."[2]

For a while Bell thought about combining the phonograph with the telephone in such a fashion as to enable subscribers to hear music over their lines. Then he abandoned the idea in order to pursue other interests. There is no indication that Bell considered uniting his telephone with the Kinetoscope. Yet both men had the essential ideas for and inclination necessary for the development of talking movies, and in the case of Bell, for a form of radio as well.

SIGHT AND SOUND

William K. L. Dickson perfected the Kinetoscope in the Edison Laboratories in 1888, and shortly thereafter wedded it to the phonograph. Edison was visiting the Universal Exposition in Paris at the time, and when he returned to Menlo Park in 1889 the excited Dickson ushered him into a darkened room in which a camera had been set up. Then a switch was thrown, and the image of Dickson appeared on the screen. "Good morning Mr. Edison. Glad to see you back. I hope you are satisfied with the kineto-phonograph." In effect, Dickson had invented talking pictures, and in deference to Edison, had called it "moving sound."

Edison was not overly impressed, and he did little to encourage his assistant. Not until 1895 did the company produce a "kinetophone," which enabled the viewer of a peep show to listen to music while at his box. The machine broke down regularly, and in any case was deemed too expensive and so was abandoned. Then, in 1904, distributor Sigmund Lubin offered to rent prints of *The Great Train Robbery* for twenty-two dollars, while for an additional two dollars one could have "two Monarch records, playing the music for the above Cineophone Films." For those who took the films, records and "Lubin's 1905 Exposition Model Cineograph and Stereopticon combined" for ninety-nine dollars, he threw in, free of charge, "a Victor Talking Machine Complete, including horn and sounding box."

Few took Lubin up on the offer, and he soon dropped it. But other distributors probed the commercial possibilities of sound movies. Mark Dintenfass of Philadelphia, a former herring salesman, opened "Fairyland," a theater that featured the "Cameraphone." Later on Dintenfass took control of the equipment company, changed its name to "Actophone," and went into the business of producing features. Edison learned of this and had him served with an injunction, in what was a prelude to the war between the trust and the independents. Dintenfass and Lubin abandoned sound pictures soon after, and for the next two years little was done in the field.[3]

From time to time stories appeared of other attempts to create sound pictures, all incorporating the phonograph to play background music. Such devices not only attracted the curious, but also saved money for the exhibitors, who by then had to hire musicians to play during expensive films shown in high-class theaters. Tracking down patent violations kept the Edison lawyers busy throughout this period, and news of prosecutions discouraged potential pioneers. In any case, there was little interest in such matters until after World War I.

It is important to consider that this was a time when *sound* movies, not "talkies," were being discussed by exhibitors and producers. It might be possible to combine the phonograph playing music with the silent film, for synchronization was not necessary. The few attempts to utilize the phonograph to reproduce speech while the film actors talked failed. But by 1920, some in the industry were coming to realize how significant such a development might be. Critic Brander Matthews, writing in 1917, said, "It is because the moving picture has perforce to do without the potent appeal of the spoken word that it can never be really a rival of the drama." Zukor agreed, and in 1920 introduced *Humanova,* which failed. The following year, D. W. Griffith demonstrated talking scenes in his film, *Dream Street,* but this too had no success. During the next few years, exhibitors and producers tried, sporadically, to unite sound and sight, and always they returned to the silents.

Meanwhile, scientists and technicians in Europe and America attempted to develop new methods of producing sound movies. Instead of recording the music on a cylinder, why not run it on the film itself? Eugene Lauste, one of Dickson's associates, worked on the idea for a while, then dropped it, only to return to his experiments later on. In 1906 he obtained a patent on the process in Britain. Thirteen years later a similar process, called the Tri-Ergon, was registered in Germany, and soon after Theodore Case and Earl Sponable obtained their patent on sound movie system in America. Utilizing a different approach, Charles Hoxie of the General Electric Company demonstrated sound on film in 1920 and 1921. Four years later, inventor Lee DeForest produced some short "talk films," prepared a synchronized "track" for scenes in *The Covered Wagon*, and even made a 1924 election film for Calvin Coolidge, which was not, however, shown in theaters. Other firms, among them Westinghouse and the Western Electric Company (a subsidiary of American Telephone & Telegraph), were at work on sound. Yet the major motion-picture firms showed little interest in the various processes. By the mid-1920s the industry appeared secure and stable for the first time, and the businessmen had no desire to initiate a new period of competition and chaos.

Warner Brothers was a small firm, one that was squeezed by the larger ones and on the verge of bankruptcy. Their theaters were doing well, but they lacked films to show in them, and had to depend upon the big studios—which were owned by rival exhibitors. A proposed merger with Columbia Pictures failed, and in desperation, the brothers went to Wall Street seeking new financing. It was a time when motion-picture stocks—even those of marginal producers and exhibitors—were the darlings of the bull market, and Goldman, Sachs was willing to become Warner Brothers' banker. Armed with some four million dollars in new money, the company built new theaters in Hollywood and New York, and for half the money, purchased the old Vitagraph Company, which was to become the nucleus of a production operation.

Vitagraph needed products, and at the same time Western Electric was attempting to interest the filmmakers in its sound process. In early 1925 the two companies concluded an agreement under which the Warners would produce sound movies with Western Electric apparatus, and in return receive a royalty on every sound instrument sold. In a spirit of co-operation, Western Electric agreed the process would be known as "vitaphone."

The other companies watched Warner Brothers with interest and no little trepidation. The new Warner theaters would be wired for vitaphone, and if the process was a success, the older ones might be closed and the company use its earnings to create a new, modern chain. Every other studio in Hollywood was equipped for silent productions. Erected on the Vitagraph foundation, the new Warner Brothers operation was a sound-oriented operation. In effect, the Warners were creating a new kind of company which, if successful, would oblige the older companies to undertake a massive retooling operation. And while this was being done, Warners would go to the fore. If, on the other hand, the sound system failed, Warner Brothers would go bankrupt.

The vitaphone system was demonstrated in August 1926. An audience at the new Warner Theater in New York saw a film of Will Hays, who congratulated the company. "The timing of Mr. Hays' voice with the movement of his lips and his gestures was so perfected that it was as if he himself were speaking from the stage," noted one newspaper reporter the following day. Then followed a series of musical interludes, films of symphony orchestras playing classical pieces, and Giovanni Martinelli singing "Vesti la Giubba." Finally, there was the film *Don Juan*, starring John Barrymore, Mary Astor, and Estelle Taylor. But none of these actors were heard speaking; the sound track was all musical.

It was an impressive display of technology, but was it commercial? The industry did not appear overly impressed. Shortly after the premiere, Joseph P. Kennedy announced the formation of a new company, the Film Booking Offices of America. He claimed that within a year the FBO would be one of the industry's giants. Kennedy showed no interest in talking pictures; the new studios would not be equipped for sound. Then on August 23, Rudolph Valentino died. His funeral was perhaps the most sensational the nation had ever witnessed, complete with suicides of admirers, and film crews to catch the mobs at the funeral home and cemetery. The leading box-office draw of his time, Valentino had shown that sound was not a requirement, that the public did not necessarily want it. Yet experimentation with sound continued. In early 1927, Movietone announced a new sound-on-film system, and later filmed Charles Lindbergh's takeoff for Paris. The reviews were good, and it appeared "talkies" would concentrate on news stories, leaving drama for the silents—the next Valentino would still be seen and not heard. The stage was the proper medium for the spoken word, so it was claimed, while the film was visual entertainment; each had its own art form and content.

Early in 1927 Warner Brothers attempted to lure George Jessel, star of *The Jazz Singer*, to Hollywood to film the show. Negotiations broke down when Jessel insisted upon being paid one salary as a silent actor, another for his singing. The idea that both functions could be united was still novel. The Warners refused to meet these terms, and hired Al Jolson instead. *The Jazz Singer* opened at the Warner Theater in New York in October 1927, and was a sensation, second only to the Lindbergh flight that year. Much of the film was silent, but there were conversations, and Jolson sang. Warners had invested $800,000 in talking pictures, and the film not only returned that amount, but showed a large profit besides. In addition, the company had established itself as the leader in the new technology. In July 1928, it released *Lights of New York*, an all-talking feature. By then, theaters throughout the country were busy adapting to sound. Silent films then in production in Hollywood were either scrapped or remade into talking pictures. Studio heads hired cadres of technicians and voice coaches to convert their facilities, discover whether silent-film artists "had voices," and train those who lacked them. In July 1928, only 200 theaters were wired for sound; by the end of 1929, the number was over 4,000. Marquees no longer proclaimed the titles of films and the names of artists. Instead, they read, "This Theater Is Wired for Sound."

The industry was shaken, more so than at any time in its history. The introduction of sound meant that the large firms had to raise additional capital for conversion efforts, and so rely even more heavily upon investment bankers. Then came the stock-market crash of 1929 and its dreary aftermath, which caused many firms even greater distress. The industry held up well in 1930, when $732 million was collected in admissions, and the figure dipped less than expected in 1931, when $719 million was spent to see movies. But in 1932, admissions dropped to $527 million, and further to $482 million in 1933. Almost all the major studios went into the red, and the immigrant tycoons were under attack. Lehman Brothers, a major Wall Street investment bank, gained control of Paramount, and Zukor was replaced as operating head of the company. Chase National Bank took command at Fox Films in 1933 and merged it with Twentieth Century Pictures to form Twentieth Century-Fox. Fox was shoved aside, bought out for $18 million. Chase and Dillon, Read & Co. became the dominant forces at Loew's the same year, and by 1936, the Bank of America and Standard Capital Corporation controlled Universal Pictures. Even Warner Brothers bowed to the bankers. By the mid-1930s, Wall Street controlled Hollywood; the immigrant tycoons had all been replaced.

Similarly, the artists of the silent era were shoved aside by the coming of sound.[4] According to one poll, the most popular artists in 1929 were Clara Bow, Lon Chaney, William Haines, Hoot Gibson, Colleen Moore, Buddy Rogers, and Richard Barthelmess. None of these had adequate voices. Two years later, a similar poll named Janet Gaynor, Charles Farrell, Joan Crawford, Norma Shearer, and Marie Dressler. They, apparently, had voices.

For a while it appeared that the era of sound movies would be dominated by the major corporation in the area of voice transmission—AT&T. Through Electrical Research Products, Inc. (ERPI), a subsidiary of Western Electric, AT&T signed up almost all the large studios and most of the big chains of theaters. In order to fortify its position, the company forced Warner Brothers to concentrate upon exhibition rather than production, and so it did. Rival equipment manufacturers were silenced through lucrative crosslicensing arrangements. Cash-rich AT&T had no difficulties in the early depression years, when its grip on the equipment field tightened. But it did face a powerful rival.

Radio Corporation of America decided to enter the equipment field in 1928, even though it was tied to AT&T through several agreements. The company, which was partially owned by General Electric, formed the RCA Photophone Corporation, which was designed to exploit several GE inventions in sound, most of which were inferior to those developed by ERPI. So as to obtain a production unit, RCA acquired the Keith-Albee-Orpheum circuit of some two hundred vaudeville theaters, which were then converted to sound, using photophone equipment. To this was added Pathé and several minor studios, also used as outlets for equipment. The Rockefellers entered the combine by taking stock in exchange for properties in what was to become Rockefeller Center. Joe Kennedy's Film Booking Office, a minor and weak firm, rounded out what was to be known as Radio-Keith-Orpheum. It was a decidedly second-rate and shabby enterprise, giving the impression that RCA was not really serious about its foray into films, but merely wanted to use the firm to challenge ERPI.[5] Still, RKO immediately became a factor of some importance in the industry, and for its first two years reported substantial profits. Then, as the depression's force was felt, it showed losses. The company was reorganized in 1931, and two years later, when most of the motion-picture firms went under, RKO filed for bankruptcy. It was taken over by Lehman Brothers and the Atlas Corporation, and remained in receivership until 1941. By 1934, however, RKO had served RCA's purposes. Through it, the mother firm became well entrenched in the industry.

By then, AT&T had become timid about expansion. RCA had long threatened it with litigations and antitrust complaints unless AT&T limited its activities in films. AT&T bowed in 1936, after which RCA mounted a major expansion program. Though the RKO experience had proved unrewarding, the parent firm became a leading factor in the production and sale of services and equipment. It was also recognized as the most innovative and daring force in American business, the leader in new areas of technology. Even more than Ford and General Motors, RCA symbolized the emergence of a new industrial America in the 1920s, and while other companies were crushed in the depression, it continued to grow in the next decade.

Alexander Graham Bell had been obsessed with sound, with its origins and transmission. His inventions were utilized to create AT&T, which was based upon the development, sale, and distribution of what amounted to sound equipment and services. Because of the great capital investments required in telephones as well as other industry factors, the company took on the appearance of a utility. For a while it expanded aggressively, engulfing smaller and weaker rivals. Then, in 1912, it seemed AT&T would be hit by an antitrust action. In order to block this, President Theodore Vail instructed his lawyers to contact Justice Department officials and come to some kind of understanding. This was done.

Under the terms of the Kingsbury Commitment of 1913, AT&T agreed to divest itself of Western Union and restrict further acquisitions, in return for which the antitrust action was halted. AT&T accepted guidance from regulatory agencies and took care to be circumspect in its nontelephone activities. Such was the situation in the 1920s and 1930s. In order to insure sovereignty over its core business, AT&T rejected opportunities to dominate motion pictures, radio, and ultimately television. The company developed essential patents for talking pictures and entered into licensing arrangements thereafter. But the revamped motion-picture industry did not emerge from telephone technology or organization, and the same was true for commercial radio.

Although some of Edison's ideas found their ways into the basic concepts of talking films, the new technology did not proceed from his beloved phonograph. In large part this was due to Edison's own dislike of the idea of "talkies." Abandoning his stance as a younger man, he rejected all suggestions that he attempt to unite the movies with the phonograph. "Americans don't like talking pictures," Edison said shortly before his death. "They prefer the restful quiet of silent film shows." So the next development in sound, the newest stage in the evolution of the new mass culture, would not proceed from the company founded by Bell or that organized by Edison, due to a political consideration on the part of the former and a loss of vision in the case of the latter.

Instead, talking pictures were developed by companies that emerged from a third technological stream, and just as the first two produced the telephone and phonograph, so the third already had created radio. By the early 1930s this industry and device had replaced Edison's phonograph in the home, was as ubiquitous as Bell's telephone, and perhaps was more influential than even the motion picture. In time, radio would become a greater disseminator of information than newspapers and a more pervasive educational medium than the classroom. In retrospect, radio was as revolutionary a force for this century as the steam engine had been for the previous one.

RADIO'S SEARCH FOR STRUCTURE

The pioneer companies, scientists, and organizers of radio technology were not radicals, but then they had no idea of how their discoveries would be utilized by others who were. Throughout the nineteenth century, scientists in several European countries had experimented with electromagnetic waves, which appeared to travel easily through the air and ether. Michael Faraday, James Clerk Maxwell, Heinrich Hertz, Oliver Lodge, A. S. Popoff, and others set down a foundation of theory, from which more practical individuals might conclude that the transmission of sound through the air was possible.

Guglielmo Marconi, a young Italian scientist, read of this in 1894, and soon after began experimenting with wireless communication. By 1896 he was able to send a Morse code message over a distance of almost two miles.[6] Needing both scientific and financial help, he took his invention to Britain, and there conferred with businessmen and officials at the post office. Several demonstrations followed, and in mid-1897 Marconi received an English patent on his device. Then, with the aid of a group of British investors, he formed the Wireless Telegraph and Signal Company, which was later known as Marconi's Wireless Telegraph Company. The firm was capitalized at one hundred thousand pounds, with Marconi receiving half the stock and fifteen thousand pounds in cash. At the time, he was only twenty-three years old.

Before the year was out, Marconi had selected a site for his first production facility. Wireless communication equipment was ordered by the Royal Navy in 1897, and in 1898, was installed on several ships. The Marconi Wireless Company of America was incorporated the following year, with an authorized capital of ten million dollars. Marconi was by then a world-famous scientist and inventor, who was hailed as the Thomas Edison of the coming century.

Although few American scientists had experimented in any important fashion on electromagnetic phenomena, the country had three of the most advanced electrical equipment companies. General Electric, formed in 1892 through a merger of Edison Electric Illuminating and Thomson-Houston, was the dominant force in lighting, while Westinghouse was a major generating equipment producer. Western Electric, since 1881 an AT&T subsidiary, produced power equipment as well as telephones and related devices. At the turn of the century all three were interested in radio wave technology, but lacked the will and imagination to mount major efforts in the field.

Several independent scientists did conduct experiments, however, and one of these, a Canadian by the name of Reginald Aubrey Fessenden, obtained a position at the U. S. Department of Agriculture on the pledge that he would find some method of transmitting weather information by wireless. Fessenden had worked at the Edison laboratories and had been a professor of electrical engineering at Western University. He knew of Marconi's work and hoped to improve upon it. One method would be to find a way to send the human voice over the air. As it was, a person would require a knowledge of the Morse code to use the wireless; voice transmission would make it available to all. If this could be done, a Fessenden device would be as much an improvement over Marconi's as the telephone had been over the telegraph. And in 1901, Fessenden conducted his first successful experiment in voice transmission. Backed by Pittsburgh financiers, he formed the National Electric Signalling Company, obtained technological assistance from Swedish-born scientist Ernst Alexanderson, who was then employed at General Electric, and in 1906 sent his voice over the air in a Christmas Eve broadcast. A second experiment, conducted on New Year's Eve, was picked up by United Fruit Company ships in the West Indies. By any measure, the Fessenden equipment could be deemed workable.[7]

Lee DeForest, an American who in 1899 wrote a Ph.D. dissertation at Yale on Herzian waves, worked for a while at Western Electric, and experimented on his own with several wireless devices. With the help of some Wall Street friends, he organized the DeForest Wireless Telegraph Company in 1902. The firm, which was to produce voice-transmission wireless sets, was capitalized at three million dollars, and quickly sold out; within a year, it was recapitalized at fifteen million dollars, and DeForest was a wealthy and famous man.

The names of these companies are important. DeForest Wireless Telegraph, National Electric Signalling, Marconi Wireless of America—all were concerned with producing a new kind of telegraph, one that would be operable without wires. Marconi constructed sending stations so as to create a link between America and Europe, Fessenden thought in terms of ship-to-shore communication, while DeForest's first devices were used to report stock market quotations and for military purposes. The voice aspects of the DeForest and Fessenden machines were considered important only because they speeded communications and permitted their use by amateurs. At the very most, they might develop into some kind of wireless telephone, and it was on this basis that Western Electric conducted a new series of experiments shortly after the turn of the century. DeForest had the same idea, and in 1907 he formed the DeForest Radio Telephone Company, which would utilize the audion tube, his invention of the previous year. He hoped to attract the interest of AT&T's rivals, who would be able to establish a telephone network with a small investment, since no wires would be required. In time, each house could have a wireless telephone, which might replace the present wired ones.

DeForest was still thinking of radio as a communications technology, sprung from the telephone and telegraph.

For the moment, however, the invention had to be tested and demonstrated. So he obtained some phonograph records and a player, and sent music over the air, to be picked up by receivers at specified locations. His first radio broadcast—the term meaning that the sound was sent out to whoever would pick it up, and not to a specific receiver—was made by DeForest in 1917. The inventor later conceded that he did not recognize the importance of this accomplishment at the time.[8]

Meanwhile, the large electrical equipment manufacturers attempted to adapt the new technology to their own uses. Western Electric scientists met with DeForest in 1912, and for the next five years worked at perfecting the audion tube, in the end buying out some of DeForest's patents. Alexanderson was placed in charge of radio research at General Electric. He came through with a series of important inventions, including a multiple-tuned antenna and several static eliminators. In other parts of the corporation, Irving Langmuir and his associates developed new vacuum tubes. Westinghouse concentrated on the erection of stations and the production of equipment, much of which was based on patents of other firms.

As for American Marconi, it remained supreme in the field. Acquiring the businesses and patents of several failed corporations, it constructed a circle of invention around the others in the industry; transgressors would be met by suits charging patent infringements. A complete marine network was proposed, undertaken, and completed within less than a decade. It was the only company in the field that showed consistent profits. Finally, the Marconi company was the best known to the public. In 1912 one of its operators, David Sarnoff, reported the news of the *Titanic* sinking, becoming famous overnight and awakening the world to the importance of radio telegraphy.

The wireless proved its worth in World War I, as military and naval leaders conceded that the availability of information helped revolutionize warfare. By that time too, American Marconi was so far ahead of its rivals that they could not hope to catch it. Attempting to obtain politically what they could not technologically, the American companies proposed a takeover of Marconi, on the grounds that a foreign-controlled firm should not have so great a stake in such a significant national enterprise. The British financiers who controlled the company protested, noting that the United States and Great Britain were firm allies and likely to remain so, and that a takeover would be, at best, masked confiscation. But the Americans persisted. Owen D. Young of General Electric became the main organizer for the takeover, and he united the other firms behind him. Seeking allies in government, Young contacted the acting Secretary of the Navy, Franklin D. Roosevelt, who favored the creation of a national monopoly of some kind. Others in government spoke in favor of a federally owned corporation that would dominate radio telegraphy, and they might have won their point were it not for the fact that the struggle over the League of Nations was taking place at this time. As it was, Young parried their thrusts skillfully, and in the end obtained approval for the creation of a unique corporation, one that would be privately owned but federally chartered and with government representation on its board.

Young and his General Electric backers organized the Radio Corporation of America on October 17, 1919. Under the terms of the articles of incorporation, its officers would have to be American citizens. No more than 20 per cent of RCA's stock could be owned by foreigners. Finally, a government representative was to be seated on the board. Then American Marconi was obliged to transfer its assets to RCA, receiving in return shares in the new company. Immediately thereafter, General Electric purchased some 364,000 RCA shares from American Marconi. Young was selected as chairman of the board, with several former American Marconi officials, including David Sarnoff, taking important positions at the firm. Within a year, a crosslicensing agreement with AT&T was concluded, part of which involved the transfer of RCA stock to AT&T. Then, with the firm backing of the two major corporations, RCA began erecting new transmission stations, the goal being a worldwide network.

General Electric and American Telephone viewed RCA as a ve hicle through which they could sell their radio-telegraph equipment. Most of the new company's leaders thought in terms of global marine and commercial communications, considering RCA as a combination Western Union-AT&T. Even Young thought the company's interests would be limited to this field, and there were few to dispute him.[9]

Westinghouse was obliged by circumstances to take a different view of the industry. Left out of the new corporation, it faced the prospect of either scrapping radio research or finding some other method of entering the field. For a while it tried to enter the combine by purchasing key patents and then threatening to withhold them unless given a share of RCA. This failed, and so Westinghouse explored other aspects of radio.

Some Westinghouse officials noted the appearance of small groups of amateur tinkerers, and even a few fan magazines devoted to radio. People would construct their own receiving sets and use them to listen in on commercial messages. Some developed crude sending apparatuses and communicated with their fellow radio enthusiasts. Frank Conrad and David Little of Westinghouse's Pittsburgh offices were interested in this aspect of radio. On their own, they constructed a sending unit, given the call letters 8XK. In late 1919 the two men would send music over the air and then invite other amateurs to send in postcards if they picked up the sounds. Thus was born the "broadcast" as we know it. There is no indication that either man understood the implications of their actions at the time, or thought of where they could lead.

Harry P. Davis, a Westinghouse vice president, knew of the broadcasts. In early 1920 he noted that a local department store advertised sales of radio equipment capable of receiving them. This "caused the thought to come to me that the efforts that were then being made to develop radio telephony as a confidential means of communication were wrong, and that instead its field was really one of wide publicity, in fact, the only means in instantaneous collective communication ever devised."[10] Davis met with Conrad and Little and offered them company support for the construction of a larger station. They accepted, the work was begun, and the new station, called KDKA, was ready for transmission on October 21. After a brief shakedown period, it was able to broadcast the results of the Harding-Cox presidential election. Sales of receiving equipment rose, and encouraged, Westinghouse decided to make its move into this side of the industry. New stations were added—WBY in Springfield, Massachusetts, WJZ in Newark, New Jersey, and KYW in Chicago—and each opening resulted in higher sales of sets in the area. While General Electric concentrated on sending equipment and RCA upon the erection of telephony communication, Westinghouse opened new stations in order to sell receiving sets to the general public.

Westinghouse's success in this area, combined with the company's control of several patents, led to a conference with the RCA leaders. United Fruit, which had developed a new antenna and in addition utilized radio communication among its Caribbean ships, also attended. On June 20, 1921, the parties agreed to a restructuring at RCA. Now GE controlled 30 per cent of the stock and AT&T slightly more than 10 per cent. Westinghouse received 20.6 per cent, and United Fruit 4 per cent, with the other 35 per cent in the hands of the public. What might be called "the radio trust" was completed. Among them, RCA and its parent companies controlled almost all of the major patents in the industry, and although small firms were beginning in manufacturing, and minor stations emerging in broadcasting, none had the assets and power of Big Radio.

Thanks to the Westinghouse contribution, radio was set upon a new path. RCA would continue to dominate marine and wireless, but now the company's attention was drawn to the private market for broadcasting equipment. The huge profit potentials of broadcasting can be seen retrospectively. At the time, most of RCA's attention was focused on the market for home receivers, with broadcasting supported only so the purchasers of radio sets would have something to listen to. Even in its new corporate form, RCA still thought of itself as a manufacturing company, not one in the business of entertainment and information.

In 1920, Sarnoff sent a memorandum to E. W. Rice, Jr., president of General Electric, predicting that great profits would be made from the sale of "radio music boxes." Assuming an average price of seventy-five dollars each, he thought one hundred thousand could be sold the first year, three hundred thousand the second, and six hundred thousand the third, for a total sales of seventy-five million dollars.[11] Sarnoff moved ahead with his plans after Westinghouse was brought into RCA. As general manager he opened new stations, sought interesting events to report upon, and attempted to win publicity in the newspapers, all with the objective of selling receivers. Others entered the field, so that by late 1921, a full-fledged boom had developed, with the airwaves around some major cities clogged with stations.

It was then that the question of control was first raised. As late as 1920 it appeared the government would take no role in the new industry, except through representation on the RCA board. President-elect Harding had no ideas on the subject, and few members of his Administration spoke out on radio and related topics. But Herbert Hoover, the incoming Secretary of Commerce, was becoming involved. One of the very few authentic heroes to emerge from the war, Hoover was looked upon as a potential President, a vigorous individual, and—most importantly—a man not willing to allow his interests to be bound by his department. Within a few months of taking office, Hoover had antagonized most Cabinet members by invading their areas, and in 1921 he assumed powers in the new field of radio. The Commerce Department declared that broadcasting was a separate function from telephony, and would have to be licensed. In the first eleven months of 1921, it issued 5 licenses, all for 360 meters on the radio dial, though in different parts of the country so there would be no overlap. The difficulties began in December, when 23 licenses were given. There were 8 in January 1922, 24 in February, and 77 in March, while for the year as a whole, 430 were given. And all of this to sell radio sets.

As interest in radio grew, Hoover decided to convene a Washington radio conference, which assembled in late February 1922. The conference was confused, aimless, and little more than exchange of opinion among government and industry leaders. For a while there was talk of a "radio czar," on the order of Landis in baseball and Hays in films, but Hoover discounted the idea, preferring instead to attempt co-operation between industry and government. The Secretary did warn that he might change his mind should commercial interests invade radio. Hoover did not elaborate upon this, but he might have been referring to a plan set forth by AT&T about to be placed into operation.

American Telephone was ambivalent regarding radio. The company was not involved in the manufacture of receiving sets; it obtained no benefits from the sales of RCA "radiolas." Nor did it have sending stations, as did RCA and, to a lesser degree, GE and Westinghouse. AT&T had concentrated upon the manufacture of sending apparatuses, and was more interested in radio as a new variety of the telephone than as a vehicle for selling consumer equipment. The company hoped to establish some stations, but with a quite different approach from the other electrical equipment firms. These would be a form of public telephone. "Anyone who had a message for the world or wished to entertain was to come in and pay their money as they would upon coming into a telephone booth," recalled a AT&T executive several years later. He would then "address the world, and go out," to be followed by the next person with a message. President Walter Gifford of American Telephone called the service "radio-telephone broadcasting," and had no intention of producing programs. Music would be played on phonographs between announcements, merely to indicate to listeners that the station was broadcasting. "For my own part," said Gifford in 1944, "I expected that since it was a form of telephony, and since we were in the business of furnishing wires for telephony, we were sure to be involved in broadcasting somehow." Gifford believed that "perhaps people would expect to be able to pick up a telephone and call some radio station, so that they could give radio talks to other people equipped to listen."[12] This even had a name—toll broadcasting. True to the pattern set down in telephones, AT&T planned to have many stations, each linked to the others in a fashion similar to the way local telephone companies were united by long-distance wires.

The plan was made public in February 1922, and work begun on the first station, WBAY in New York, which opened for operation in July. WBAY experienced many operating difficulties, so that a month later American Telephone started another New York outlet, WEAF. This was more successful, but at the same time the company found itself in many difficulties in programming. There were some "advertisers" (as they were called from the start), but the musical interludes failed to hold the attention of audiences. In addition, WEAF had troubles with the American Society of Composers, Authors, and Publishers (ASCAP), which insisted upon payments for the music played, since the station was a commercial venture. The telephone company agreed to pay a small sum for the music, and in addition began scheduling talks on various subjects and even sports events in order to hold audiences for the advertisers. The motion-picture industry had undergone a similar development a few years before, when the public began to tire of merely witnessing the novelty of films and insisted upon content as well. Now it was happening in radio.

The RCA, GE, and Westinghouse stations might judge the success of their broadcasts by the amount of equipment sold;

AT&T was interested in the sale of transmission equipment, but was not involved in the manufacture of radiolas. Drawing upon the telephone pattern, it hoped to obtain revenues from selling a service, not a product. And so it had to convince potential advertisers that people were listening to their messages, and this in turn resulted in a need to develop interesting programs. *Printer's Ink*, the leading advertising journal, took note of this in the early 1920s. "Station WEAF has built up its reputation on the fine quality of its programmes. Radio fans who tune in on this station are accustomed to get high-class entertainment." But what of the advertising? "If they are obliged to listen to some advertiser exploit his wares, they will very properly resent it. . . . An audience that has been wheedled into listening to a selfish message will naturally be offended." As the magazine saw it, "The man who does not want to read a paint ad in the newspaper, can turn the page and read something else. But the man on the end of the radio must listen, or shut off entirely. That is a big distinction that ought not to be overlooked."[13] But for the time being, AT&T did not explore the problem, instead concentrated upon the development of new stations and interconnections among them.

Secretary Hoover felt otherwise. In early 1923 he called a second Washington radio conference and declared that due to overcrowded airwaves and chaos in the industry, some kind of control might be needed. Already there were several bills in various stages of preparation, and all were geared at either nationalization of broadcasting or government control. Unless the industry proved capable of self-regulation, said Hoover, such action might be necessary. The conferees did agree to allocations of airwaves, times of broadcasting, and standardization of certain equipment. But there was no significant decision on commercial broadcasting. The year before, Hoover had warned that it was "inconceivable that we should allow so great a possibility for service to be drowned in advertising chatter." Now he said that airwaves belonged to the nation and not to the commercial broadcasters. Licenses could be taken away as well as granted, he said. Still, AT&T continued to open new stations, all with commercial broadcasting.[14]

By this time AT&T on the one side and RCA, GE, and Westinghouse on the other had found they no longer could co-operate with one another. American Telephone initiated several suits against its rivals, claiming infringements of patents, and at the same time complained that RCA was purchasing most of its equipment from GE and Westinghouse and not enough from Western Electric. On occasion, RCA utilized Western Union and Postal Telegraph lines, when those of AT&T subsidiaries were available. AT&T's stations were competing with RCA's, especially in New York, where their signals overlapped on occasion. As purchases of radio equipment by consumers increased—going from $60 million in 1922 to $136 million in 1923—AT&T considered putting out a set of its own, and indeed actually produced a prototype, which was presented to President Coolidge early in 1924—a year when sales of radio sets reached $358 million. If and when they were marketed, a major struggle between the "radio group" and the "telephone group" might commence, with the result being the entrance of government in one form or the other.

AT&T began selling its RCA stock in 1923, and the following year stepped up its program of connecting stations, thus forming a "network," which could offer advertisers a larger audience and so obtain higher fees. The radio group retaliated by transferring most of its stations to RCA and forming a second network, while converting stations to commercial broadcasting. In 1925 Secretary Hoover intimated that self-regulation had failed and that a federal agency might have to be formed, which would be charged with regulating the industry. Later in the year AT&T charged the radio group with violations of the antitrust acts, and this resulted in a flurry of countercharges. To further complicate the situation dozens of small companies producing receivers had been organized, some using radio group patents illegally, and their securities were being marketed on Wall Street to investors and speculators eager to get in on the radio boom. The industry was in a state of chaos, while growing and evolving at a rapid pace. Clearly some kind of order was called for.

At this point David Sarnoff, who for over a decade had been known as one of the more knowledgeable figures in the industry, became its commanding figure. His background was similar to that of the motion-picture tycoons. Sarnoff had been born in Russia in 1891 and arrived in America at the age of nine. Soon after he obtained a job as a delivery boy, attending school primarily to learn English. After working at a variety of menial tasks, he was hired as an office boy at American Marconi, where he learned telegraphy. In 1908 he went to Nantucket as a marine operator, and two years later was transferred to New York. The *Titanic* telegraphy took place when Sarnoff was only twenty-one and provided his career with an aura of glamor. He moved up in the company's hierarchy and had no difficulty in finding a place at the newly formed RCA. But Sarnoff was always in a subordinate position; unlike Zukor, Loew, and the others in motion pictures, he did not create an empire but rather served one. Even in its early days, huge sums were needed in order to make a mark in radio; a hundred dollars or so sufficed to start a film exchange or a nickelodeon empire.[15] The industry, including RCA, was dominated by native-born Protestants, most of whom had backgrounds in law or engineering. The self-educated, young, immigrant Jew was decidedly an odd man out in the industry—again, a marked difference from the situation in films. Owen Young was the chairman of RCA. Edward J. Nally, an American Marconi engineer-businessman, was its first president, and he was succeeded in 1923 by General James Harbord, a man with excellent Washington connections. These men needed Sarnoff, and they even liked the man and socialized with him. For the time being, however, they would not give him too much power or place him in a position where he would speak for the company. As for Sarnoff, he understood the situation and accepted it. During the rest of the decade he concentrated on making himself indispensable and removing all doubts regarding his fitness for eventual leadership of the corporation.

In 1925 Sarnoff was named head of a committee charged with developing a "peace plan" for the industry. The group met regularly, and toward the end of the year recommended the creation of a broadcasting corporation, wholly owned by RCA, GE, and Westinghouse, to include "all stations of all parties." The new entity would purchase the AT&T stations and in return pledge to utilize telephone wires. Sarnoff moved among the involved firms, attempting to iron out differences. He succeeded. On July 7, 1926, the firms signed twelve agreements and contracts, which created a new entity, National Broadcasting Corporation, which was to dominate the field. Some thought that Sarnoff would be named president of NBC, a move that would remove him from RCA headquarters but at the same time give him a command of his own. Had he pressed for the appointment, it might have been his. But Sarnoff held back. Instead, the presidency went to Merlin H. Aylesworth, managing director of National Electric Light Association, who at the time did not even own a radio. Under his direction, NBC organized two networks. The first of these, known as "red network," was centered around WEAF, while the second—the "blue network"—was erected around WJZ, RCA's New York flagship station.

With the formation of NBC, it appeared that RCA had become the sole significant force in the industry.[16] The company dominated broadcasting, was the prime producer or radios, owned most of the major patents in the field, and employed the most talented and experienced personnel in the industry. For the moment at least, advertisers posed no threat to RCA domination, though they would in the future. Nor was the artist a major force, as he was in films. Radio performers received low salaries—five dollars for the recitation of a poem or the singing of a song was not unusual—and they would never reach the high status of their counterparts in films. It was little wonder, then, that RCA common stock was one of the darlings of the stock market in 1926.

But the company was not without challenges and problems, which at this time came from three sources: rival networks, competitors in set production, and the government itself.

Arthur Judson, a violinist turned agent, visited Sarnoff in 1926, at a time when the creation of a national broadcasting network appeared certain. He hoped to establish a new talent agency, which would work with the network and help end competition. Sarnoff appeared interested, but he did nothing. Angered, Judson and an associate, George A. Coats, decided to start their own network as a vehicle for the talent agency. They organized the United Independent Broadcasters in early 1927, vowing to fight both NBC and ASCAP, both of which Coats charged with being monopolies. United Independent was able to sign up a few stations, but was no more than a marginal operation.

At the same time, small manufacturers of radio sets found themselves stymied in their attempts to compete with the RCA radiolas. The company dominated its field, initiating patent infringement cases against all who threatened it. Some rival firms sought government help against RCA and in 1926 several legislators appeared interested in having the company indicted under the antitrust laws. In response, RCA offered to license its competitors, and soon after entered into such arrangements with Philco,

Atwater Kent, Zenith, and several others. Still, its continued domination appeared assured.

While Judson and Coats organized their network and RCA attempted to come to terms with the independent set manufacturers, Secretary Hoover worried about industry chaos and crowded airwaves. "I can see no alternative to the abandonment of the present system," he told conferees at the fourth Washington radio conference, held in late 1925. Several draft proposals for a radio control act reached the floor of Congress in 1927, and in the following year, a comprehensive Radio Act was finally passed. Under its terms, a five-man Federal Radio Commission was established and given powers over the industry. Among these was the right "to refuse a license to any applicant found guilty by a federal court of unlawfully monopolizing 'or attempting unlawfully to monopolize' radio communications." The Act set forth the principle of public ownership of airwaves; the stations could use them under licensing arrangements and retain licenses during periods of good behavior. Advertising was mentioned as an afterthought; even then the government wasn't convinced commercial radio would be significant. But implicit in the Act was the idea that stations would never be fully independent, and certainly be more regulated than were newspapers. In theory at least, freedom of speech was more limited in radio than in the press, or even in movies under Will Hays.

As this was happening, Judson and Coats sought backing for their network. Both men were interested in providing talent for radio; neither knew much about the medium, and they lacked funds. They met with Atwater Kent, and even Adolph Zukor, both of whom showed some interest but then backed down. For a while Bernarr Macfadden, then a radio personality as well as a publisher, considered entering the United Independent, and there were meetings with Victor Talking Machine Company as well. All ended unsatisfactorily, the Victor deal collapsing when that firm merged with RCA.

The union of these two firms threw Victor's leading competitor, Columbia Phonograph Record Company, into United Independent's arms. Together they formed the Columbia Phonograph Broadcasting System, but even with additional capital, the new network was unable to attract interest. Discouraged, Columbia Phonograph withdrew support, and it appeared the network might have to close down. Then William S. Paley, whose family owned the Congress Cigar Company, which advertized occasionally on radio, became interested in the network. The son of an immigrant Jew who like Sarnoff was deemed an outsider, Paley was believed a dilettante, and at the age of twenty-eight showed little promise. In 1928 he became president of CBS. Paley set the firm's house in order and then lured Zukor into purchasing 49 per cent of its stock. With the additional capital, Paley expanded. Now NBC had a competitor, even though CBS remained weak for a decade.[17]

The small radio set manufacturers were not troublesome in this period, and as for the government, its powers were more potential than real. Rivalry and regulation were not serious matters in the late 1920s. RCA thrived, with Sarnoff given much of the credit. He received his reward in January 1930. Young resigned, Harbord became chairman, and Sarnoff, not yet thirty-nine, was named president of RCA.

RADIO: A MEDIUM IN SEARCH OF A MESSAGE

Sarnoff had spoken out regarding radio's future throughout the 1920s, exploring the medium's potential. He continued to believe that music would dominate programming. When occasion demanded, radio could cover special events. There would be room for drama and cultural programs. But in public at least, Sarnoff denied that radio could ever challenge newspapers. "Insofar as radio may attempt to serve the listening public with a digest of current news it is the herald of the newspaper," he said in 1925. "It announced in 'headlines,' as it were, that which impels millions of listeners to seek in the press the necessary details or the raw material of public opinion." The most powerful man in the industry added that although radio "has a great cultural and educational destiny," it could never replace the newspaper "in giving a historical record of the news of the day." He concluded by saying that "there is no more likelihood that the broadcasting station will displace the newspaper as a chronicler of the news than that the public will ever be willing to abandon written history for the word-of-mouth records of times gone by, or that it will desert the classroom for a radio lecture course or abandon the opera for a general musical program through the air."[18]

What did Sarnoff mean by this? The man who quickly recognized radio's unique possibilities could scarcely have wished to limit its scope and range so early in its development. Perhaps a clue can be had in the fact that Sarnoff spoke of the newspaper as a historical record of the past more than a source for information regarding current developments. Even in 1925, some radio stations carried news programs of two varieties. The first consisted of an announcer reading Associated Press or United Press bulletins—a kind of "talking newspaper." Then there were on-the-spot reports, more often than not of sports events, which would be reported in the newspapers the following morning. Both challenged newspapers, and often effectively. Possibly Sarnoff realized that radio could pose a threat to the printed word, though the time for a confrontation had not yet arrived. But several newspaper publishers understood the shape of the challenge, and it bothered them. If radio attempted to develop its own news programs, the newspapers would retaliate by not printing stories of radio, or logs of shows to be heard. Sarnoff and others in the industry might have felt that the matter would best be pursued at some future date.

In 1925, some 3.5 million American homes had radios; by 1929 the number was 9 million. In this same period expenditures on radio sets and parts rose from $430 million to $843 million. And throughout this period, music, both live and recorded, accounted for well over 65 per cent of all programming. In 1925, radio stations paid $130,000 to ASCAP under the terms of an agreement regarding the use of copywritten music, and the following year, radio royalties accounted for well over a quarter of ASCAP's total take of $2 million. Radio royalties rose to $450,000 in 1927, and in 1929, stood at $667,000.[19] Radio music was causing declines in attendance at musical events, in contradiction of Sarnoff's statements on the subject. Sales of sheet music, instruments, and phonographs were declining, and this too was blamed on radio.

In their perceptive study of the city of Muncie, Indiana, at the end of the decade, sociologists Robert and Helen Lynd recorded statements from residents as to their uses of radio. "The radio is hurting moviegoing, especially Sunday evening," said the owner of a theater. "I don't use my car so much any more. The heavy traffic makes it less fun," said a middle-aged man. "But I spend seven nights a week on my radio. We hear fine music from Boston." When asked, "In what thing that you are doing at home this fall are you most interested?" high school students answered "listening to radio" more than any other occupation.[20] In effect, the radio had become Sarnoff's "household utility," his "radio music box."

This was radio's primary content as late as 1928. Musical programs, interspersed with commercial messages, were standard fare. There were talks by authorities on various subjects as well, and some educators thought radio might in time develop into a "classroom of the air." On occasion a play or a novel would be dramatized, but this was unusual, and more or less limited to larger stations.

There were several reasons for this. The radio pioneers had concentrated upon learning the technology of their business and working out patent and related arrangements among themselves and with the government. Programming was not their primary interest. These men, who emerged from manufacturing for the most part, looked to radio and equipment sales for their profits, and not to broadcasting itself—which as late as 1928 was still viewed by RCA's leaders as a means by which additional radiolas might be sold.

But the situation was changing. The novelty of radio was wearing thin, and even though owners of sets marveled at the idea of hearing events and music that were broadcast from hundreds of miles away in their own homes—and for no charge—they were becoming restless with unimaginative programs. Advertising revenues were growing, and with the coming of networks—making it possible to charge higher rates for larger audiences—the companies were willing to spend more money for artists. When NBC put its first major program on the air on November 15, 1926, it enticed leading artists for the event—the New York Symphony, Metropolitan Opera star Tito Ruffo, the vaudeville team of Weber and Fields, and the Vincent Lopez and Ben Bernie orchestras. Mary Garden sang a song, and Will Rogers imitated President Coolidge. It was a major event, one that cost the network some fifty thousand dollars, according to some newspapers. But President Aylesworth told an announcer that it cost "hardly a cent," since the artists had worked gratis. He knew, however, that this situation would not last for long. "Hereafter advertising will pay for the elaborate broadcasts we plan to present," and Sarnoff agreed. In time, radio would challenge all other mediums of entertainment. "The richest man cannot buy for himself what the poorest man gets free by radio."[21] In 1928, however, few radio actors and actresses received more than token payments for their services, while announcers—considered the top of the profession—often worked for less than a hundred dollars a week.

Aylesworth and Sarnoff were convinced that radio had a sparkling future, although its final dimensions could not be appreciated toward the end of the 1920s. The Lynds wondered about radio's impact upon the population of Muncie; in 1929, it was not "wholly clear." "As it becomes more perfected, cheaper, and a more accepted part of life, it may cease to call forth so much active, constructive ingenuity and become one more form of passive enjoyment." The sociologists had no doubt that radio would play a "mighty role" in widening the outlooks of Muncie's citizens; together with the motion picture and the automobile, it was "reshaping the city." Even then, radio was recognized as a major force in American life. But to what end? The Lynds believed radio would furnish "diversified enjoyment," but at the same time operate, "with national advertising, syndicated newspapers, and other means of large-scale diffusion, as yet another means of standardizing many . . . habits."[22]

This was for the future. Advertising was still undeveloped in the late 1920s, when RCA's Aylesworth believed sponsors should limit their messages to a brief identification at the beginning and end of a program, and most of CBS's programs were unable to attract sponsors. Programming was still the most undeveloped part of the industry in 1928–29, with radio's leading figures uncertain or unwilling to make major steps in the field. Technology and business still predominated. For the time being, art and content would be subordinated to science and form. On the eve of the Great Depression, radio—like motion pictures—was about to be reshaped, and in a fashion as significant to the nation's future as anything that occurred in the field of politics.

DEVELOPMENT

6

Images of an American Depression

On March 4, 1933, Franklin D. Roosevelt took the presidential oath. His Inaugural Address was reprinted in many newspapers the following day, along with analyses of the event. For two or three cents, Americans might have obtained a morning paper and read the speech and commentaries. But this was a depression period, when even such a small expenditure was considered carefully. In 1933, newspaper circulation was 12 per cent below what it had been three years before, and in the same period, advertising income had dropped by 45 per cent. In many parts of the country small newspapers were closing, medium-sized ones merging with others, and the larger newspapers cutting down on size and personnel.

One could have attended the local motion-picture theater on a weekday in early March for the price of a dime, and seen a double feature, coming attractions, a short subject, and, if the night was right, played bingo. In addition, there was the newsreel. A week after the event, Americans saw and heard parts of the Inaugural in the theaters. But like the newspapers, the motion-picture theater suffered in the early years of the Great Depression. In March of 1933, attendance receipts were 40 per cent of what they had been in January 1931, while several companies were in the hands of receivers.

The Inaugural was broadcast on radio as well, and those who had sets could have heard it in its entirety for next to nothing, and at the time of delivery, not a day or a week later. In 1933, 20.4 million American homes had radio sets—there were 22 million in use that year. In 1929, only 9 million households had had receivers, and in that last predepression year, there were 10.5 million in use. In every year of the 1930s, the number of sets and households with radios would increase. In time the newspapers and motion pictures would recover, but this was to be a radio decade.

Roosevelt seemed to understand this, and he appreciated the power of radio and the new opportunities it offered those who would use it intelligently. Unfriendly journalists easily might distort his words or their meanings, and newsreel editors could do the same. Although many in the press had been friendly to him during the campaign, Roosevelt had no idea how things would develop now that he was in the White House. But through the wise utilization of radio, he could speak to the nation over the heads of the journalists, and hopefully do so effectively.

On March 11, Roosevelt issued a statement that he believed he had an obligation "to convey to the people themselves a clear picture of the situation at Washington itself whenever there is danger of any confusion as to what the government is undertaking." In order that there "may be a clear understanding as to just what has taken place during the last two days . . . it is my intention, over the national radio networks, at ten o'clock Sunday evening, to explain clearly and in simple language to all of you just what has been achieved and the sound reasons which underlie this declaration to you."

Sunday was a big night on radio. The NBC Red Network featured "The Eddie Cantor Show" at eight o'clock, followed by a half hour with tenor John McCormack at nine, and a half-hour concert at nine-thirty. The Roosevelt talk would displace an analysis of "current government" by David Lawrence, scheduled for ten o'clock. The Blue Network had "The Gladys Rice Concert" from eight to nine, a half-hour drama, "The Man Who Didn't Get Rich" and then Walter Winchell's commentary at nine-thirty, followed by music with the Pickens sisters at nine forty-five. D. W.

Griffith's "News from Hollywood" would not be heard due to the President's address. The CBS network started with a fifteen-minute sketch by John Henry at eight, a half-hour concert by the Kostelanetz Orchestra, and then another fifteen minutes with John Henry. The Katzman Orchestra came on at nine (with a comedy skit featuring Fred Allen), and at nine-thirty, the Hal Kemp Orchestra played. On CBS, Roosevelt would displace "Ernest Hutchins, Piano."

Why did the President choose this late hour for his talk, when he knew that those workers who had jobs would have to rise early the next morning? Time zone considerations may have had something to do with it, for this was a coast-to-coast broadcast, and ten o'clock Washington time would be seven o'clock in Los Angeles. In addition, he may not have wished to replace one of the more popular shows. In 1933 the networks were not obliged to cancel commercial programs in order to broadcast presidential addresses, and Roosevelt may have wanted to avoid any difficulties in this area. He wasn't concerned with what a later generation would term "instant analysis," for it was not the practice then or later for discussions of content to follow presidential speeches. Nor would the Roosevelt speech be subjected to much in the way of analysis the following day, for in early 1933, the tradition did not exist. There were a few former newspapermen hired by the networks to write what were in effect columns and read them on the air, and although some of these had larger audiences than their counterparts at major newspapers, they were not as yet considered influential. Not until late in the year would the networks give them a title—"commentator"—and only four of them had significant reputations: H. V. Kaltenborn, Lowell Thomas, Boake Carter, and Walter Winchell.

The Roosevelt speech was released to the newspapers prior to the broadcast in order to receive front-page attention the following day, and so it did. Radio news programs, which ranged from five to fifteen minutes, consisted of an announcer reading selections from the Associated Press, the United Press, and the International News Service. In March, when the news services were threatening to discontinue selling their wires to radio stations on the grounds that they competed with newspapers, none of the broadcasters had even the foundation for a separate news operation. It didn't seem necessary or even desirable. The most popular radio programs of 1933 were constructed around recognized vaudeville stars. Eddie Cantor, Ed Wynn, and Ken Murray had their own variety programs, as did Jack Benny, Fred Allen, and the Marx brothers. Rudy Vallee's "Vallee Varieties," one of the most popular nighttime shows, had a "card" quite similar to that at prestige vaudeville houses and might have served as a model for later television programs, including Ed Sullivan's. Entertainment, not news, was still the programming rationale early in 1933.

The Roosevelt talk of March 12 was a special event, then, and was considered as such. But it was not entirely anomalous, even though many Americans stayed up late to hear it and invited friends who did not have sets to listen with them. Politicians on all levels, from candidates for local office to those seeking the presidency, had used radio in their campaigns for almost ten years. In 1924, when he hoped to obtain the Democratic nomination, William Gibbs McAdoo had purchased his own station in California in preparation for the event. Father Coughlin and Huey Long both used radio effectively, understanding how to reach an audience and how to manipulate sentiments. John R. Brinkley, one of the many fake medicine men who utilized radio to sell his products and services—before medical and broadcasting agencies cracked down on the practices—turned to politics in the early 1930s, and with little in the way of a platform but high recognition from his radio audience, announced his candidacy for the governorship of Kansas in 1932. Republican Alfred M. Landon won, with 278,000 votes, beating Democrat Harry Woodring, who received 273,000. But Brinkley, who did little campaigning except by radio, and ran as an independent, captured 245,000 votes. Throughout the nation, in the late 1920s and early 1930s, politicians had been noting the impact of radio and trying to use broadcasting effectively. Few succeeded, however, perhaps because the public did not know how to listen to radio addresses, but more probably because of the inability of politicians to prepare and deliver the right kinds of speeches for the medium.

The American politician of the 1920s had been raised, trained, and probably even first ran for office in preradio days, when the ability to bellow out to a large audience was prized. William Jennings Bryan's famous Cross of Gold speech had electrified the

Democratic convention of 1896, and won him the presidential nomination that year. But the words would not have been heard above the din had Bryan not been able to shout them out—without amplification—so as to reach the rear of the huge hall. Bryan and his generation provided models for the politicians of the 1920s who, upon attempting to speak to a radio audience, tended to shout into the microphone or, if they managed to hold down their voices, still talked as though in a hall.[1] This was certainly the case with Warren Harding, the first President to use radio. Calvin Coolidge was a decided improvement. He had a small voice to begin with, and a precise New England pronunciation, both of which were drawbacks on the stump but advantageous on radio. More natural and at ease than most politicians of his time, "Silent Cal" sounded almost professional on radio, and he knew it. "I am very fortunate that I came in with the radio," he once remarked. "I can't make an engaging, rousing, or oratorical speech . . . but I have a good radio voice, and now I can get my message across to them without acquainting them with my lack of oratorical ability."[2] In a poll rating radio personalities conducted during his Administration, Coolidge came in fourth, behind John McCormack, Walter Damrosch, and Madame Schumann-Heink (all musicians) but ahead of Will Rogers. Yet Coolidge did not utilize radio as much as he might have, perhaps because he did not feel the need to do so during his Administration. "I don't think it is necessary for the President periodically to address the country by radio," he said at a press conference in 1925. Coolidge got along well with newsmen, and felt no need to speak to the country directly. "The newspaper reporters do very well for me in that direction," he conceded.

The situation was different with his successor, Herbert Hoover, who didn't like reporters and made no secret of the fact. He tended to ignore the press corps after his first year in the White House, and when he did hold press conferences, he lectured reporters on their responsibilities. On occasion Hoover played favorites, and he neglected to stay on the good side of prominent journalists. Rarely did he try to win their understanding and respect, not to mention friendship. "A former President once told me that the relationship between the White House and the press could never be solved satisfactorily," Hoover told his secretary. "He said that there never would be a President who would satisfy the press until he had been dead for twenty years."[3] With the exception of Richard Nixon, no American President in this century had worse press relations than Hoover.

Radio might have enabled him to overcome this, but Hoover did not understand the medium. He had a booming voice for speeches before large audiences, and on occasion could be dramatic in front of a crowd, rolling his *r*'s and gesturing like an old-fashioned politician. Hoover was given to delivering long speeches, not too unlike those of pre-Civil War politicians, the kind that were reprinted in the press the following day for all to read. Radio demanded short, intimate speeches, and Hoover either could not or would not prepare such addresses. Instead, he lectured the American people in his radio talks just as he did the reporters. These were long, complicated, and usually boring. To make matters worse, Hoover delivered them in a dull monotone. On one occasion during the 1932 campaign, the President spoke on NBC for more than two hours, when the speech had been advertised as being one hour in length. In the process, he displaced "The Ed Wynn Show" and further angered his audience. Those who were bored or angered by the speech were lost to Hoover, but the many millions of angry Wynn fans were probably more important. The following week, the stations received six thousand letters of protest.[4]

Roosevelt, however, possessed both an understanding of radio and an excellent voice for the medium. His March 12 talk was only fifteen minutes long. It was not billed as an address or even a speech. Instead, the President referred to the talk as a "fireside chat." The idea of warmth was important, as was that of illumination. More significant was the image of the radio as a fireside, around which the family gathered in the evening. Unlike Hoover and most other politicians, Roosevelt spoke to the people informally, as though he were in their living rooms. He began, "I want to talk with the people of the United States about banking—with the comparatively few who understand the mechanics of banking but more particularly with the overwhelming majority who use banks for the making of deposits and the drawing of checks," and then went on to describe what his Administration had done in the field of banking and what it intended to do in the future. "We had a bad banking situation," he said. "Some of our bankers had shown themselves either incompetent or dishonest in their handling of the people's funds." But this was over, and all would soon be better. "It has been wonderful to me to catch the note of confidence from all over the country," he said toward the end of the first fireside chat. "Confidence and courage are the essentials of success in carrying out our plan. You people must have faith; you must not be stampeded by rumors or guesses. Let us unite in banishing fear. We have provided the machinery to restore our financial system; it is up to you to support and make it work." Roosevelt concluded by saying, "It is your problem no less than it is mine. Together we cannot fail."

In fact, the New Dealers lacked the time, experience, and personnel to make certain the banks were in sound shape. The financial crises had been compounded by an emotional one, however, and Roosevelt did help restore a sense of confidence through the fireside chat. In large part this was done by making the radio listeners feel they were being told the entire story by a kind, wise, and powerful friend, who happened to be President, but who took time out from his work to deliver an informal talk. It was, in effect, a throwback to the idea first propounded by Alexander Graham Bell—Roosevelt used the radio as though it were a telephone hooked up to each listener. He did not speak to an audience, but instead to a group of individuals. John Dos Passos, not then or later an admirer of the President, characterized the fireside chat best.

> There is a man leaning against his desk, speaking clearly and cordially to youandme, painstakingly explaining how he's sitting at his desk there in Washington, leaning towards youandme across his desk, speaking clearly and cordially so that youandme shall completely understand that he sits at his desk there in Washington with his fingers on all the switchboards of the federal government, operating the intricate machinery of the departments, drafting codes and regulations and bills for the benefit of youandme, worried about things, sitting close to the radio in small houses on rainy nights, for the benefit of us wage earners, us homeowners, us farmers, us mechanics, us miners, us consumers, retail merchants, bankers, brokers, stockholders, bondholders, creditors, debtors, jobless and jobholders. . . .

And it worked. "When the cordial explaining voice stops, we want to say: Thank you, Frank; we want to ask about the grandchildren and that dog that had to be sent away for biting a foreign diplomat. . . . *You have been listening to the President of the United States in the Blue Room . . .*"[5]

Roosevelt spoke over the radio twenty times during his first ten months in office, but only four of these were fireside chats. Yet a decade after the last of them was delivered, many who heard the talks were convinced the President had spoken to the nation at least once a week, and in prime time, during that crisis period. Roosevelt believed the restoration of national confidence a prerequisite for all else he hoped to accomplish, and he succeeded in his efforts in March 1933.[6] This could not have been done so rapidly, or as well, were it not for the President's mastery of radio. Fortuitously, the man and the medium were united at the proper time. No other political figure, before or after, was as attuned to radio as was Roosevelt, or utilized it more intelligently.

THE ELECTRICAL SOPORIFIC

The Great Depression erupted at a time when the United States was the most powerful nation in the world, after a decade of unusually rapid growth in the industrial and service sectors of the economy and society. Secondary school and college attendance had risen in every year of the 1920s. By 1932, there were over 900,000 public-school teachers and more than 100,000 college and university teachers in America; almost one out of every fifty workers was a teacher. During the decade of the 1920s, the annual production of bachelor's degrees rose from 48,000 to 122,000, while that of master's and doctor's degrees also tripled. Though the number of newspapers declined in this same period, falling from 2,042 dailies in 1929 to 1,944 in 1929, total circulation increased, from 28 million daily copies to 39 million. The silent film displaced vaudeville as the nation's leading middle-class entertainment in the 1920s, and toward the end of the decade, the talkies promised still greater growth and influence. By the time Roosevelt entered the White House, of course, the radio had joined the telephone as a necessary "household utility."

What might be expected from this depression? Although the

farmers had done poorly through most of the 1920s, and the coal miners were not much better off, urban Americans—a majority of the nation as indicated by the 1920 census—had little to guide them. There had been a minor slump in 1926, and a sharp, short, though brutal economic collapse earlier, in the aftermath of World War I. The economy had been in the doldrums prior to the war, and there had been financial panics as recently as 1901 and 1907. But the last prolonged and widespread depression had begun in 1893 and continued into 1896. This period was one of social upheaval and saw the emergence of a powerful native radicalism, led by farmers and self-educated intellectuals. For a while it appeared the country might fall, or at the very least, be the victim of a class war.

The Great Depression of the 1930s was far more severe than that of the 1890s; not since the Civil War had Americans undergone such a traumatic and damaging experience. But despite claims that the New Deal was a disguised form of communism, the movement was more conservative than might have been anticipated. Roosevelt was not as radical as Bryan had been in 1896; the New Dealers were more moderate than Bryan's "Popocrats." More than anything else, Roosevelt strove to preserve the nation's essential economic and social institutions, and capitalism was one of these. He succeeded. Considering the nature and dimensions of the problems of the 1930s, the alterations made in government and society were not very jarring at all.

Much of the credit (or blame, depending upon one's point of view) for this belongs to Roosevelt and the people he attracted to Washington. Bryan had relied upon the "socialism of the heart" for the foundation of his beliefs. Roosevelt's men—who clustered around the "brain trust," itself a significant part of the anatomy to stress—were quite different. A large majority of them had fathers who were businessmen, successful ones at that. They attended leading colleges—the top three in terms of numbers by one count were Harvard, Yale, and Wisconsin—and from there went on to graduate schools (to major in economics or political science) or law school (preferably in the Ivy League). Roosevelt raided the faculties of prestigious colleges, universities, and law schools for talent. When he finished he had assembled a bureaucracy of academics, the first in the nation. What Creel had done for a few sections of the CPI in World War I, Roosevelt accomplished for Cabinet departments in the 1930s.

The President spoke of the "forgotten man," the person who he claimed was ignored by government, passed over by life, and in this he echoed the democratic and leveling sentiments of Robert LaFollette. But in fact he was closer to the tone and content of his mentor, Woodrow Wilson, insofar as his concept of leadership was concerned. The New Deal was manned by the well-born, the well-educated, and the well-connected. Old-line Protestants and the Ivy League-educated children of East European Jews were leaders in the movement; Irish Catholics and blacks were underrepresented, as were the uneducated and uncouth, the kinds of people who had marched with Bryan in 1896. As one team of scholars put it, "The New Deal intellectuals originated as an urban elite in a rural society."[7] *Noblesse oblige*, not rustic radicalism, was the hallmark of the New Deal, in all of its phases. This accounts for its moderation as well as its innovativeness.

There had been no radio in Bryan's glory days, and motion pictures had been little more than a curiosity. Now, individuals who might have marched with Coxey's Army or joined in protest demonstrations learned of what was happening from their radios, or were entertained by movies. One of the reasons the reactions to the two depressions were so different lay in the image of each disaster received and reflected upon by people of the periods.

Rural Americans of the 1890s had learned of urban life through farm newspapers, friends and relatives, their ministers and political leaders, and hearsay. City dwellers might have emerged from the countryside, but many immigrants had never seen farming areas, or for that matter ventured much beyond a few miles of their Atlantic Coast dwellings. Individuals such as these tended to see two civilizations in conflict, and the potential for class warfare was there to be exploited, as did Bryan and many of his followers.

The situation was quite different in the 1930s. Both urban and rural Americans listened to the same network radio shows and saw motion pictures produced for all classes, regardless of geographic area and occupation. In these good was rewarded and evil punished; the endings invariably were happy, and the moral made evident—work hard, accept the system, and all would be well. In the 1890s American farmers stayed at home, where there was little to do after working in the fields but ponder their cruel fates. Or they might attend meetings in which hardships were discussed and actions contemplated. For them, amusements were minor and occasional, and certainly not an everyday part of life.

It was different for their grandchildren. In their homes they could listen to radio, which concentrated upon escapism and music, and when they ventured from their rooms after work, it was to go to the movies, and not political rallies, and there too the messages were subdued and escapism the rule. It was an age of soporifics in radio and motion pictures, and many Americans literally were diverted from their darker thoughts.

Clearly people exposed to this kind of message had a different view of their lots and the future than did their grandparents. It was the first great age of mass amusements via electricity, and the medium of radio and that of motion pictures did as much as Roosevelt to prevent chaos. The pains of the 1930s were as great or greater than those of the 1890s, but the perceptions were different.

The motion-picture industry was in shambles in 1933. The studios continued to release films—*State Fair, Forty-second Street, Little Women, King Kong, The Private Life of Henry VIII*, and *Dinner at Eight* were the major productions that year, and none reflected protest or even the cry for change. But the companies that produced them either were bankrupt or on the verge of declaring insolvency. Wages were slashed down the line. The artists blamed the high costs of admission for their difficulties, while the theater operators responded that Hollywood's films no longer drew patrons. Studio technicians went on strike to protest the cuts, and some executives welcomed the walkouts, since they gave them an excuse to close down unused facilities. The performers formed a union, the Screen Actors Guild, but at first it drew few members, as much for an inability to pay dues as anything else.

Despite this, the industry's essential structure remained intact. The large companies were in the hands of New York investment bankers and businessmen who, while they might have regretted paying high prices for properties, realized that Americans would continue to desire films and that in time the industry would recover. What was required, they thought, was an end to waste and inefficiency, and a rationalization of films far beyond what had existed before. There had been a start in this direction in the late 1920s, when the leading exhibitors acquired studios and distribution facilities, thus becoming integrated firms. Then, with the arrival of the talkies and the investment bankers, followed by the depression, there was disorder and regrouping. From 1933 to 1934, the old order and structure was still intact and in the process of being strengthened. In the end it was transformed into what some called a motion-picture trust, others a community of interests.

Five major firms—Paramount, Loew's, Twentieth Century-Fox, Warner Brothers, and RKO—led the industry. Each had its own studios, complete with rosters of artists and work forces, and each was under the control of New York banking and related business interests. In 1933–34, Hollywood turned out 480 feature films, and of these, the five majors accounted for 248, including all of those with budgets over $500,000. Of the approximately 16,000 motion picture theaters in the nation, the large firms owned or controlled 2,700. The first-run houses in the downtowns of large cities were their flagships and showcases, and they had chain operations in other parts of the cities and in the countryside. The majority of independent, nonaffiliated theaters were small, and few had good locations. There were some local chains, just as there were independent film producers, but these were obliged to work with the big five and accept their dictates. This was true even for such studios as Universal, Columbia, and United Artists, and for such prominent industry figures as Samuel Goldwyn and Walt Disney. The big five would compete for properties and concepts, but they would unite in the face of threats to their hegemony, either from inside the industry or without.

Given the situation at the time and the state of the economy, there was no effective way for independent exhibitors to combat industry leaders. The major means of control were devices known as "block booking" and "blind buying." Under the former the independents purchased the rights to show films in package deals, rather than on an individual basis, while blind buying meant they had no idea of what they were getting; on occasion films were identified only by numbers in catalogues, without even titles or an indication of their stars. The contract might have a clause permitting the exhibitor to reject 5 per cent or so of the features, and refuse another 5 per cent with half payment made. A third 5 per cent need not be shown, but had to be paid for. These "5-5-5" contracts became standard in the early 1930s and were the cause of bitter complaints by independents. The big five firms argued that the device gave the exhibitor a measure of freedom, and that without block booking, the studios could not survive. Feature films cost at least $300,000 to make in this period, and risks would not be taken unless the studios were reasonably certain they would be purchased. Without block booking and blind buying, there could be no motion-picture industry.

In practice, the studios would produce only a handful of major films each year, and advertise each extensively. These would be shown in their own showcase theaters, and all the while demand for them would grow in the neighborhoods. The independent exhibitor knew, from experience, that he would do well with the film once it was available. And in order to make a large profit for that one week, he would accept the risk of low profits, even losses, on some of the studio's lesser films. With block booking and blind buying, the major studios could function like factories, taking orders in advance, turning out products, and distributing them to an assured market. The devices brought a measure of security and stability to a shaky industry, enabled the businessmen and bankers to continue their control, and resulted in large profits during the depression. But at the same time, the artistic side of motion pictures was subordinated to the commercial. Each major studio took pride in its few important productions, and hoped they would go on to win awards and critical acclaim, both of which enhanced the firm's reputation. Some of these films also made a good deal of money, but more profit could be obtained from the many "B" films turned out in a matter of weeks on budgets of below $100,000, and which were block booked into theaters that were obliged by contract to accept them.

The studio system kept the artists in check, and also prevented the smaller industry units from achieving major status, or the independents from becoming too powerful. Before an actor or actress could hope to achieve any importance in Hollywood, he or she would have to sign a long-term contract with a studio, complete with options and clauses designed to protect the studio in any eventuality. All the studios hired talent scouts, maintained dramatic schools, and employed publicity staffs. Once an artist was signed, he or she would be groomed, trained, made the object of a publicity campaign, and then placed either in a supporting role in a major production or given a more prominent place in a B picture. If all went well, the artist might become a star or "a starlet." And if this happened, he or she would receive salary increases but remain under studio control. If the artist refused to accept an assignment, he or she would be suspended without pay, unable to work for another studio in an age when work was hard to come by and in an industry where fame was fleeting and memories short. Should the artist accept work from an independent, the resulting film might not be accepted for showing in theaters controlled by the home studio. Each studio maintained "backups" for major stars. At Warner Brothers, for example, Ida Lupino would replace Bette Davis when that actress rebelled. The star system would remain, for the public wanted it, and stars insured profits. But the artists would be kept under control at all times.

On occasion, the artist might be permitted to buy his or her way out of a contract, but the company could refuse to sell, in which case the artist either would capitulate or leave the industry. Contracts could be sold by one studio to another, but this was rare. And in no case would one major studio challenge another for an established and signed star. The industry was based on business control of all aspects of production and distribution. The front office spoke for Hollywood, deciding which artists would be featured, which stories would be made into films, and where and how they would be displayed.

If the motion-picture company executives had little to fear from artists, industry rivals, or exhibitors, they were concerned with governmental actions that might alter their activities. The government had been litigating against various film companies ever since 1928, concentrating attention on the then leader of the industry, Paramount, charging it with violations of the Sherman Antitrust Act.[8] The case went through many appeals, motions, and countermotions, and by the early 1930s involved all of the majors. By then the Federal Trade Commission was charging these companies with monopoly practices and demanding that they divest themselves of theaters and related enterprises. The cases were still in the courts at the time of the 1932 election, and it appeared then that the motion-picture trust might be destroyed within a matter of a few years.

The antitrust action was suspended in 1933, as the New Deal attempted to stabilize business by halting prosecutions temporarily. Under the terms of the National Industrial Recovery Act, each industry was required to assist in drawing up a code of fair competition, and as far as the New Dealers were concerned, motion pictures constituted an industry, not an art form or information medium. The code was completed in November, and a Code Authority selected to administer it. Selected by the National Recovery Administration, the Authority was dominated by the nominees of the major studios.[9] It named the personnel for local grievance boards, which acted to strengthen the large firms against the independents. The Administration valued recovery more than reform in 1933, and so permitted the Authority to coerce the smaller firms into waiving rights under antitrust laws and dropping old complaints. In this fashion, the large studios were able not only to continue to hold power, but also to solidify and enlarge upon their positions, all in the name of recovery and the preservation of jobs. Block booking arrangements were strengthened, but here a concession was made to the exhibitors: Under the NRA code, they would be permitted to reject 10 per cent of films in packages instead of 5 per cent. The Authority also accepted the NRA's mandate of minimum wages, maximum hours, and collective bargaining, but since the theaters and some aspects of studio activity were not considered to be in interstate commerce, federal laws did not apply. And to make up for any additional payments made to workers, the Authority gave the major firms a measure of control over the admissions charges of independent exhibitors, though only when they were showing studio-produced and -contracted films.

The independent exhibitors retaliated. Professor Thomas Irwin of Columbia drafted a measure designed to end block booking, which was introduced in the Senate by Matthew Neely of West Virginia and in the House by Samuel Pettengill of Indiana. Clarence Darrow, the famous attorney who at this time was charging the NRA with instituting a form of native fascism, was retained to lead the fight for the Neely-Pettengill Bill and organize local support. The independents received additional help when A. Lawrence Lowell, president emeritus of Harvard, refused to serve on the Code Authority Board, citing as his reason opposition to the block booking practices. But the bill died in committee, in large part due to the efforts of Will Hays, who had retained his political connections in Washington long after going to Hollywood. Hugh Johnson, head of the NRA, had selected a New York lawyer, Sol Rosenblatt, to be division administrator of the Code, in part because although he did not know Hays, he accepted the point of view of the big companies. Rosenblatt dismissed Darrow's complaints as "the vicious mouthings and conjecture" of an NRA enemy, and he defended block booking vigorously. Then, in 1935, the U. S. Supreme Court invalidated the NRA, and the Code Authority was closed down. The following year the Justice Department instituted a new suit against Paramount, but throughout the New Deal, the industry remained in the hands of the big five.[10]

There is no indication that the New Dealers intentionally worked to help the major studios; in 1933–34 Roosevelt and his top aides had more on their minds than the structure of the film industry. Still, this structure was approved by the economic and social planners then dominant in the White House.[11] It enabled the large studios to standardize their products as much as possible, and among them, to subordinate the performers and writers to the studios.

After the depression had ended, and several years after the conclusion of World War II, the nation would learn that a fairly substantial number of Hollywood writers and performers had what was then deemed to be "left wing" connections, interests, and proclivities. Some, a small amount, had belonged to the Communist party or one or more of what were then called "front organizations." In the terminology of the early 1950s, Hollywood's creative and artistic element had been laced with "pinkos."

In the 1930s, however, little of this was known or even suspected by the general public. At a time when writers and intellectuals were making their positions known and working for radical solutions to the nation's problems, there was little political content in films. The reason was clear: business and studio domination of the medium and its artists. Actors and actresses were made to understand that outside political activities—for almost any candidate, but certainly for the more radical ones—would lead to losses at the box office and a subsequent lowering of salaries, and perhaps even the cancellation of contracts. If this occurred—if a performer was fired for political reasons—he or she could not hope to obtain employment elsewhere, at least among the major Hollywood studios. The position of the motion-picture star of the 1930s was not unlike that of the football or baseball player of the 1960s—well-paid, adulated, imitated, but under the control of the front office and bound by a contract that forbade the athlete from negotiating with a rival club. The relationship baseball club owners had with their commissioners was similar to that of studio heads with the presidents of the Motion Picture Producers and Distributors of America; the "czars" had been named by business to control the performers. Will Hays performed this function admirably, as did his successors.

The New York investment bankers, operating through their studio heads, had a major voice in determining the content of films in the 1930s. For the most part, these men were anti-New Dealers, though not extremely so; in 1940 they would support Wendell Willkie, and four years later Thomas E. Dewey against Robert Taft. The Hollywood studio heads were, to a man, old-fashioned "dreamers of the American dream," though in different ways. Louis B. Mayer of Metro-Goldwyn-Mayer was a conservative Republican, while Jack Warner of Warner Brothers was an ardent New Dealer. But with the exception of William Randolph Hearst, whose Cosmopolitan Studios released its films through MGM, there were no potential fascists at the heads of studios. Warner Brothers was deemed the radical studio at the time, even though its films were hardly revolutionary.

These men, not the writers and performers, decided which films would be made, who would write them, and how they would be cast. Although some members of a future generation would call this Hollywood's "red decade," this could not have been determined by the films released. The movies of the 1930s did not stir the population to revolution, but rather helped lull Americans into a sense of security, offering what for the most part was a message of hope. With few exceptions, Hollywood's films had happy endings, or at least concluded with justice being done to all concerned. If anything, the films issued a call for community, not an order to the barricades. They provided what the *Daily Worker* frustratingly called "the circuses to go with Roosevelt's bread, which crushed hopes of revolution in the United States."

There had been little political activity in Hollywood in the late 1920s and early 1930s. As Dorothy Parker remarked, the only "ism" the film colony believed in was plagiarism.[12] Conditions changed with the coming of the New Deal, but even then politics occupied a fairly minor part in after-work activities for the vast majority of artists and performers. Considering the times, the wealth of the community's leaders, and their proclivities, motion-picture artists were either nonpolitical or limited their activities to financial contributions. There had been hardly a stir in Hollywood during the 1932 elections. But two years later, when Upton Sinclair won the Democratic nomination for governor of California and ran on a radical platform, the studio heads united to support his Republican rival, Frank E. Merriam, and went so far as to threaten to move the industry to Florida if Sinclair won. They also "suggested" that artists and performers donate a day's pay to the Merriam campaign, and did so themselves. Most went along with the forced contribution, although a few—James Cagney, Jean Harlow, and writer Gene Fowler among them—refused to do so. This, and the organization of a small, largely ineffectual Upton Sinclair Committee, however, was the limit of their opposition. Under the direction of the studio heads, anti-Sinclair newsreels—essentially made up of faked footage—was released in the theaters, showing radicals who supported Sinclair (usually speaking with foreign accents) and average Americans who planned to vote for Merriam. For the first time since the end of World War I, the motion pictures were consciously being used for propaganda purposes, and in favor of conservatism, not radicalism.

In 1936 many artists and performers joined and attended anti-Nazi and anti-Communist organizations, often with the co-operation of such groups as the American Legion. In addition, some appeared at rallies in favor of Loyalist Spain. The temper of the times was such that this was not considered radical, or even very much left of center. A trade paper poll that year showed that the performers were in tune with the executives insofar as the election was concerned. Writers supported Roosevelt over Alfred Landon by a margin of five to one, the same ratio as executives. Directors were eight to one for Roosevelt, and the figures for agents was twenty-four to one, while Hollywood as a whole was six to one in favor of Roosevelt's re-election. Four years later the executives would vote for Wendell Willkie, while if anything, the artists were more strongly for Roosevelt than before. But this was hardly a sign of radicalism that year. Little of this came over in the films of the era. Melvyn Douglas and James Cagney, often outspoken in favor of progressive causes and critical of what they considered repression, made those pictures their studios assigned them. Cagney in particular looked upon filmmaking as simply a job, one that was divorced from reality. For the most part, Douglas appeared in light comedies. His one film that had some political content, *Ninotchka*, poked fun at life in the U.S.S.R., and for this he was attacked by the radical press.

In 1939 and 1940, Congressman Martin Dies of Texas, chairman of the newly formed House Committee on Un-American Activities, charged that Hollywood was filled with Communists and subversives. Buron Fitts, the Los Angeles district attorney, claimed to have evidence of Communist cells at the studios. The Fitts charge was dismissed as campaign rhetoric, but the Dies accusations troubled the heads of the major studios, who feared that should they be proven, their valuable properties would be worthless. Y. Frank Freeman, president of the Association of Motion Picture Producers, demanded that Dies investigate Hollywood, and Freeman offered his full co-operation. The Screen Actors Guild, by this time part of the Hollywood establishment, did the same. Dies accepted the invitation, and upon his arrival indicated he wanted to talk with Cagney, Douglas, Fredric March, Humphrey Bogart, and Franchot Tone, among others. Meetings were arranged, and afterward Dies announced he was satisfied that these men "were not or never have been Communists or Communist sympathizers." In addition, he cleared the major studios of charges that they had engaged in a program of inculcating radicalism in America through the medium of films. Hollywood's first brush with congressional censors ended on this note.

The industry turned out more than three thousand films from the time of Roosevelt's inauguration to the end of the 1930s.[13] Generalizing about so large a number is difficult. As might have been expected, most were transient pictures, which had little impact at the time and were forgotten soon after. According to one study, over half of the films produced in 1939 cost less than $250,000 to produce, while only nineteen that year were million-dollar extravaganzas.[14] During the late 1940s and early 1950s, all of these were combed through by investigators intent on discovering radical messages or themes. Only a handful were discovered to fall into that category; some had been made at the suggestion of

Washington, while others were written by and starred individuals of conservative persuasion. The most popular stars of the decade, according to polls taken of theater audiences, included Marie Dressler, Will Rogers, Janet Gaynor, Clark Gable, Wallace Beery, Fred Astaire, Ginger Rogers, Joan Crawford, Shirley Temple, Sonja Henie, Mickey Rooney, Tyrone Power, none of whom were deemed radical at the time or later, and all of whom appeared in pictures of an essentially escapist variety.

There were several basic categories of films produced and popularized in the depression era.[15] Musicals were very popular. They were not only escapist, but also required little in the way of composition, since many were taken from stage shows or contained flimsy plots, relying instead upon what amounted to feature numbers by the stars. Musicals also provided a link between motion pictures and radio; if a radio personality became very popular, he or she would be asked to come to Hollywood to make motion pictures, and of course the reverse was also the case, with well-known movie stars appearing on radio programs, not only to make more money, but also to publicize their films. The two mediums united in a series of motion pictures, based on the idea of a coast-to-coast radio show—the "Big Broadcast" films, which usually starred minor players to carry the plot, and the highlight of which was the broadcast itself, complete with songs and comedy routines by the radio stars.

More familiar were the Fred Astaire-Ginger Rogers musicals, all with essentially the same plot, highlighting their dancing and Astaire's singing of songs by such composers as George Gershwin, Irving Berlin, Jerome Kern, and Cole Porter. Jeanette MacDonald and Nelson Eddy did the same for Sigmund Romberg and Rudolph Friml operettas. Shirley Temple and Deanna Durbin starred in children-oriented musicals. The Warner musicals, often starring Ruby Keeler, Dick Powell, and Cagney, were considered to have some social content, perhaps because they portrayed struggles to succeed and depicted businessmen in subsidiary roles—*Gold Diggers of 1933* and *Footlight Parade* are two examples. But these, like all other musicals of the period, had happy endings, and taught that success was possible by working through the system. By the late 1930s, when Mickey Rooney and Judy Garland were starred in a series of MGM musicals, the message was even broader: The next generation could have hope, for the depression would be "licked."

Crime films were in vogue early in the decade, with Warner Brothers their most important producer. *Little Caesar*, *The Public Enemy*, and *Scarface*, all produced before Roosevelt's inauguration, were extremely popular, and made stars of Edward G. Robinson, Cagney, and Paul Muni. In all the gangster-heroes were killed, and in a fashion, justice triumphed. Still, the lawbreakers were central figures, and clearly meant to be admired, or at least respected through fear. *I Am a Fugitive from a Chain Gang*, Muni's next film, depicted an honest man, in trouble through no fault of his own, who was continually thwarted by a cruel society. In the end he was forced to remain outside the law. That such a story had social content cannot be denied, although it is questionable whether the audiences in Herbert Hoover's America saw it and similar films as mythic sagas, as they appeared to have been to some of the more esoteric critics of later years.[16] Furthermore, the studios, responding to criticism, made certain that in the later gangster films, the central figure was often balanced by a priest (apparently Warner's and other studios thought most criminals were Irish Catholics), played by Pat O'Brien, William Gargan, or some other minor star, who survived, and is present to intone the final message: Crime does not pay. With the coming of the New Deal, the studios strengthened the message. In *G-Men* and *Bullets or Ballots*, Cagney and Robinson played law-enforcement officers, while the Hays Office pressed for further glorifications of law and order. When the criminal appeared as a sympathetic figure in the mid-1930s, it was usually made clear that he turned to lawlessness because agencies of government had broken down; somewhere along the line, the belief that understanding and sympathetic judges, district attorneys, and lawyers could correct abuses was made evident. The system needed reforms—and Roosevelt was providing them—and not revolution; this was the implicit message.[17]

Toward the end of the decade, when it had become clear that there would be no major social protest movement in America, several highly popular films appeared to celebrate the ideals of community and democracy. *Mr. Deeds Goes to Town*, *Mr. Smith Goes to Washington*, and *Meet John Doe*, all directed by Frank

Capra at Columbia Studios, present the common man as a hero beset by crooked politicians, corrupt newspapermen, and cynical lawyers. These and other films of the genre implied that with love anything was possible. All thought of revolution was gone; the heroes were out to correct specific abuses, to set loose forces they believed were essentially conservative. Gary Cooper, who played Deeds and Doe, and James Stewart, as Smith, were purified, kindly, almost saintly, and in these and similar pictures, asexual figures. Cagney and Robinson were rebels with causes in the gangster films—whichever side of the law they were on—while Stewart and Cooper were the grown-up boys next door, who one suspects would vote for Roosevelt in 1932 and 1936, but before and after were solidly conservative Republican in sympathies and actions.[18]

Some critics of the art believe that films had reached their peak in the 1930s. Whether or not this was so is unimportant here. What is interesting is that the medium that V. I. Lenin considered to have prime propaganda potential was utilized as a diversion in this period. The Westerns, college humor films, and comedies, along with those already discussed, were considered entertainment and little else. Whatever messages existed were not subliminal, but clear for all to see: Love and kindness were important, and forbearance was a virtue. There were no important rebels without causes in 1930 films; their causes included social justice, but these could be accomplished through the system, not by revolution. Laws had to be obeyed, or if they were bad laws, changed. In *Dead End* the life of the slum was criticized, as were the forces that made it, but the gangster who chose to fight the system in his way dies an inglorious death, while the architect who kills him—also a product of the slum—ends by showing the juvenile delinquents the proper path. *I Am a Fugitive from a Chain Gang* is one of the few exceptions, and it was produced before the New Deal. There would be none like it afterward. In the 1930s, the studio system dominated Hollywood, and the businesses were headed by conservative men, with a handful of New Dealers thrown in. The artists and performers contained some individuals who were politically active in what at the time appeared to be radical causes, but for the most part, their energies were satisfied by the New Deal too. If anything, the Roosevelt programs and personality detracted from revolution and provided a focus for most movements desiring reform and substantial change. The motion picture of this decade, for these reasons, was not a call to action, but a means for sublimation of tensions.[19]

THE DEPRESSION AND RADIO

While one may argue that the silent films of the 1920s and the *avant-garde* products of the earlier generation were superior to the studio-made motion pictures of the depression period, there is near-universal agreement that radio reached its programming peak in the 1930s and during World War II. Before then, live and recorded music had been the staple fare for most stations, even the networks; music accounted for more than 67 per cent of NBC's programming in 1933 and 54 per cent at CBS.[20] The medium reverted to recorded popular music in the 1950s, while around-the-clock news programs and telephone talk shows became popular in the next decade.[21] Network radio, high-priced and influential soon after its birth, bowed to network television in the 1950s, and although its form persisted, the content was no longer there.

The depression accentuated but did not account for radio's greatness; all of the prerequisites had been there before the bad times. CBS and the NBC Blue and Red networks were solidly established by 1933, and their successes encouraged local and regional stations to unite to share costs and so increase advertising revenues. In 1934 the Bamberger Broadcasting Service and the Chicago *Tribune*'s station joined to form the Mutual Broadcasting Service, which grew from four stations that year to over one hundred in 1939. The rise of networks—the creation of national and regional mediums for entertainment and news—predated the New Deal, while economic fluctuations did not hinder their growth once the initial impact had passed. A 1933 CBS survey showed that there were over 16 million sets in operation; after a major sales decline in 1931–32, over $300 million worth of receivers were sold in 1933, and $350 million in 1934. Network revenues rose from $27 million in 1932 to $43 million the following year, and in 1935 they were $86 million and rising. Toward the end of the decade, the public was spending upward of $900 million a year on radio and related equipment and service.

Set sales remained steady, even in those parts of the country where the depression struck hardest; there is evidence that Americans did without adequate nourishment and shelter in order to maintain their radios. Writing about Muncie, Indiana, at the bottom of the depression, Robert and Helen Lynd contrasted it with what they had seen in the mid-1920s. "Everywhere the blare of radios was more pervasive than in 1925." Radio, they wrote, "is now almost entirely a passive form of leisure in [Muncie]. . . . It is likely that this inexpensive form of leisure, like the reading of free library books, has involved a relatively larger amount of time per radio during the depression, and it is also possible that it has constituted a mild cohesive element in family life through the greater association of family members in this common activity within the home."[22]

The programming of the late 1930s was quite different from that at the beginning of the decade. There was a decline in the amount of music—especially classical and semiclassical—played on network radio. This was not due to costs, for there were few programs more inexpensive to maintain than recorded music shows. Rather, this was because the stations had come to understand that the enlarged audiences, seeking alternatives to movies (which they could not afford as often as before), sought variety on radio, in particular, drama. This kind of programming accounted for little more than 11 per cent at NBC in 1933; by 1939, it was over 20 per cent. In the same period, drama time at CBS increased from 18 per cent to almost 26 per cent. Variety and quiz shows also became popular in this period, as did the broadcasting of special events.[23] In the mid-1920s, talks on esoteric subjects and concerts by amateurs were used to fill time by most stations; there was none of this on network radio in the 1930s, or at the more important independent stations in large-market areas.

Just as Hollywood's major studios concentrated on "formula films" during the depression, so the networks featured a limited variety of programs, each at a certain time of day. In the morning and early afternoon "soap operas"—so called because of their sponsorship by soap companies—took up much of the time. These fifteen-minute programs, the favorites of housewives, dealt with the problems of people in all walks of life, although the stress was upon white-collar workers and professionals, especially doctors, lawyers, and clergymen. CBS had "Big Sister," "Brighter Day,"

"David Harum," "Guiding Light," "Hilltop House," "Ma Perkins," "Our Gal Sunday," and "The Romance of Helen Trent," among others, while at NBC "Backstage Wife," "Just Plain Bill," "Life Can Be Beautiful," "Lorenzo Jones," "Pepper Young's Family," "Portia Faces Life," "Right to Happiness," "Stella Dallas," and "Young Widder Brown" were favorites. The many characters in each faced difficulties, which were resolved over a period of weeks in daily episodes. These included illnesses, divorce, financial failure, false charges of crime, and similar problems. If they so wished, listeners in depression America could tune in on a dozen or so of these continuing dramas—as many did—and hear the fictional tales of people in worse shape than most of them. More important, the soap opera heroines remained brave, optimistic, and patriotic in the face of their problems. No matter how severe their difficulties, they all appeared confident that things would work out well and for the best. Although quite different from the gangster films of the period, the soaps had the same moral: Justice will triumph in the end.

The soaps were followed in the late afternoon by children's adventure programs, usually featuring a dashing hero or group of them, engaged in exciting pursuits of various kinds. "Jack Armstrong," "Captain Midnight," "Terry and the Pirates," "Superman," "Gang Busters," and "The Lone Ranger" offered to children the same message the programs earlier in the afternoon had for their mothers, that good triumphs and clean living pays. Some of the adventure programs were based upon comic strips—"Dick Tracy" and "Little Orphan Annie," for example—and the children could follow the exploits of their heroes and heroines in two separate stories, one on radio, the other in newspapers—and perhaps a third in comic books.

Drama, variety, music, and quiz programs succeeded children's tales at 8 P.M. on most weekdays. It was here—in "prime time"—that the competition was keenest, with shows and concepts replaced regularly if they did not attract a sufficiently large and broad audience. Those that did were widely imitated, of course. "Major Bowes' Amateur Hour" which featured a telephone poll to determine winners of talent contests, also demonstrated that the show was widely followed, and so it spawned several similar programs—"True or False," "Hobby Lobby," and "Professor

Quiz" among them. The success of the NBC horror program "Lights Out" led to dozens of competing shows. In the late 1930s NBC and CBS competed in the area of Shakespearean drama, as they did in other areas of programming.

Toward the end of the decade the film-radio nexus was strengthened when both NBC and CBS erected palatial studios and broadcasting centers in Hollywood. Film stars and studios, eager to enhance their popularities and exploit pictures and performers, supported the move. "Silver Theater," "Screen Guild Theater," "Hollywood Star Theater," "Hollywood Hotel," and "Lux Radio Theater" presented motion-picture stars to radio audiences, just as movies utilized radio personalities such as Bing Crosby, Burns and Allen, and Edgar Bergen and Charlie McCarthy in films. Hollywood also drew upon radio-trained writers such as Arch Oboler, Irving Reis, and Norman Corwin. Orson Welles, of course, became a major personality in several mediums, and in a variety of functions. By the end of the decade, performers often were introduced as a "star of stage, screen, and radio," though in many cases the designation of two of these was only a courtesy. In this fashion, the new mediums of film and radio came to maturity and, in a fashion, were united in the midst of the depression. The American people suffered economically, but never before had a nation in such misery been diverted by so much in the way of extremely inexpensive entertainment.

Like the motion pictures of the period, radio programs offered escapism, fantasy, hope, amusement, and morality tales. If anything, radio was even less contentious than films, and radio artists more fearful of espousing their political and social beliefs.

There were several reasons for this situation, but three were of overriding importance insofar as the performers were concerned. As the Hollywood-radio nexus grew, artists came to realize that if they insisted upon attracting publicity that the studio—be it radio or movie—thought unfavorable, they would be blacklisted. NBC, CBS, and Mutual were every bit as conservative as Paramount, MGM, and Twentieth Century-Fox, and indeed they often worked together. Paramount, which at one time owned a large interest in CBS, was particularly interested in exploiting radio stars created by that company. To earn disfavor at one would mean rejection at the other. Too, although the major radio stars and personalities could not be readily replaced, the lesser ones might. One could scarcely replace a motion-picture actor in a series with ease—there was the matter of looks to consider. It was easier on radio, however, where voices alone had to be imitated, and often were, both when convenient and necessary due to firings or death.[24] Henry Aldrich, the central character on "The Aldrich Family," was played by Ezra Stone, who was succeeded by Norman Tokar, and in turn by Raymond Ives, Dickie Jones, and Bobby Ellis; the role of Mary Aldrich, his sister, was created by Betty Field, and she was followed by Joan Allison, Mary Mason, Charita Bauer, Mary Shipp, and Mary Rolfe, with Ann Lincoln ending the line. The role of Lamont Cranston on "The Shadow" was played by Robert Hardy Andrews, Orson Welles, Bill Johnstone, and Bret Morrison in succession, and "Cranston's friend and companion, the lovely Margot Lane," first was played by Agnes Moorehead and then Marjorie Anderson, Gertrude Warner, Grace Matthews, and Lesley Woods, while Commissioner Weston was played by Dwight Weist, Arthur Vinton, Kenny Delmar, Santos Ortega, Jimmy LaCurto, and Ted de Corsia.[25] The knowledge that they could easily be replaced must have made artists more tractable. At the same time, the inexacting demands of soaps and even evening drama programs—preparation for a show, in which the artists could read scripts, was usually limited to a single run-through—meant that an actor or actress could appear on several in the same week, often playing continuing roles on both children's programs and soaps. Santos Ortega, Ruth Perrott, George Petrie, Irna Phillips, Frank Readick, Ken Roberts, Pat Ryan, Anne Seymour, and Cliff Soubier would rush from one studio to another, appearing on four or five shows a day on occasion, with few of the listeners aware of them, and not knowing their names. The availability of this kind of work and the great supply of performers eager for the jobs meant that salaries for such people were low on the individual-performance basis. But when contracted for several programs at a time, they could do quite well financially. In the process, however, radio took on the character of an assembly-line operation, and the soaps and children's programs at least suffered from an acute lack of imagination for the most part.[26] From this stable of radio performers came many fine character actors, who had long careers in Hollywood and even the legitimate stage, but few important stars were created from this kind of milieu.

"The radio industry lives in fear of the FCC and in love with the sponsors of its commercial programs," wrote a perceptive newsman of the period. "Whereas a newspaper must please only two groups of people—its readers and its advertisers—a radio station must please four—the listeners, the sponsors, the government, and the National Association of Broadcasters, which is the trade association to which most of the better stations belong."[27] Part of the statement was oversimplified and exaggerated. The National Association of Broadcasters was no more than an industry lobbying association, formed in 1923 to fight ASCAP's demands for higher payments for recorded music played on the air, and which in 1933 represented the radio businessmen in the writing of the NRA radio code. Small stations might have been somewhat concerned about NAB attitudes, but the bigger ones and the networks controlled the Association. As for the Federal Communications Commission, during most of the 1930s its powers were more potential than real. Set up by the Communications Act of 1934 as a replacement for the Federal Radio Commission, the FCC took office in 1934 and immediately was embroiled in charges and countercharges regarding time allocations for commercials and the future of noncommercial radio. At first it appeared that drastic curbs would be placed on the amount and variety of commercials, but the NAB utilized delaying tactics with skill, and little happened in the end. The networks and large stations promised to air more educational and public-service programs and to cut back on advertising, and the FCC accepted this form of self-regulation. Fearful of charges of government thought control and wary of its own power, the Commission refused to censor programs. On the other hand, it would take into account the merits of programming when reviewing applications for renewals of licenses. Failures to renew could be challenged in the courts, but in 1935 and 1936, in almost all such cases the Commission's decisions were upheld. Stations were made to understand that if they behaved responsibly, they would have no difficulties with the FCC. But they were not given clear guidelines as to what constituted good behavior. Should their licenses be canceled, they would have to go out of the business. Faced with this kind of situation, most stations adopted cautious policies, while the networks were in constant communication with the Commission. Thus the FCC acted as a watchdog over the industry, even though the sharpness of its teeth was hardly tested in the 1930s.

As indicated, the sponsors were a major force in radio, and had no real counterpart in films. At first, most interested parties indicated dissatisfaction with commercial broadcasts; Herbert Hoover, Sarnoff, and Aylesworth all came out in favor of public-service radio in the early 1920s. But even then, broadcasters experimented with ads, and the real question was what form they would take, not whether radio would or would not be commercial.

The clearest model was the newspaper. Although advertisers exercised great power in the early days of newspapers, by the 1920s they were more or less content with purchasing space in the more popular journals, realizing that they would have little influence on editorial and news content by so doing. And this was imitated on local radio in the early 1920s. Some stations experimented with the sales of blocks of time to advertisers; on January 1, 1922, WAAT sold an hour to a local company for the purpose of transmitting New Year's greetings. Two years later, station WHB originated "The Invisible Theater" and urged listeners to purchase "tickets" by sending in donations, in this way discovering whether or not listener-sponsored radio was possible; the idea was soon abandoned as unworkable. New York's WEAF, an avowedly commercial venture, hit upon the idea of naming programs and even artists after sponsors. Thus there appeared the Cliquot Club Eskimos, the Gold Dust Twins, the A&P Gypsies, and others. Billy Jones and Ernie Hare became the Happiness Boys for the Happiness Candy Stores, and then the Interwoven Pair for Interwoven Socks, the Best Foods Boys for Best Foods, and the Taystee Loafers for Taystee Bread.[28] In these instances, the advertiser had no control over content. But the station discovered it could sell popular programs and had little luck with the unpopular ones. Thus it was impelled to investigate public tastes, and the first surveys were made in this period.

The advertising firm of N. W. Ayer pioneered in this field. Ayer executives would listen to WEAF and other stations, attempting to find proper vehicles for clients' products. In 1923 the agency packaged several musical and dramatic programs as "The Eveready Hour" for Eveready Batteries, which set the pattern for a while. The agency would locate the proper show by "auditing" station created products. In this fashion, the stations were placed in the business of developing and putting wares on the air, hoping for a taker. The next step in the process came in 1925, when the La France Company agreed to sponsor regularly scheduled half hours of music, complete with commercial messages at the beginning, middle, and end of the program, a format quickly adopted by other advertisers.

By 1938, some advertising agencies had begun putting together their own shows for clients. There were several reasons for this: unsatisfactory programs from the stations, lower costs resulting from dealing directly with artists, the desire to create an even closer bond with clients and to tailor-make shows for their products and tastes, and, of course, the matter of power. The large advertising firms had come to dominate programming by the early 1930s, while the stations, in effect, leased their facilities to them, exercising vetos over some programs—but not many, in fear of angering powerful agencies.

This transition of control from the stations and even networks to the leading advertising agencies, accomplished with little notice and no real debate in New York and Washington, was a key development for radio. In this way, power over content passed from men like Sarnoff and Paley to the leading figures at the advertising agencies, most of which seemed to be concentrated on Madison Avenue in New York, with branches elsewhere, and the leader of which—as far as radio was concerned—was Albert Lasker of Lord & Thomas. Along with most leading advertising executives, Lasker was opposed to the New Deal. Representing as they did important business advertisers, the industry's official position could scarcely have been otherwise. Lord & Thomas, for example, represented American Tobacco, General Electric, Cities Service, Commonwealth Edison—and RCA and RKO—in the early 1930s, as well as many of the leading soap and toothpaste firms. Companies such as this put together shows for their clients; both would make certain the messages of their presentations were conservative—or at least without political content—and that their performers and writers were nonpolitical insofar as their public lives were concerned.

In 1928, some $1.115 billion had been spent on advertising in major media, and of this amount, only $20 million went to radio. Newspapers received the major share of the advertising budget, some $760 million, while magazines were in second place with $215 million, and outdoor billboards had $85 million. Even farm journals, with $35 million in 1928, were deemed more important than radio. The situation changed greatly when the depression began, as all forms of advertising expenditure declined. By 1933, only $665 million went for advertising. In that year, however, radio advertising was $65 million, down from the $80 million of 1932, but still far ahead of the pre-1929 figures. The industry recovered ground in the early New Deal years, so that by 1937, the billion-dollar figure was reached, for the first time since 1930. But the advertising dollar was divided quite differently from what had been the case in 1928. Radio advertising sales were $145 million, the same figure as magazine sales, and the following year radio would pass magazines in this area. Meanwhile, newspaper advertisements slipped badly in almost every depression year, coming in at $600 million in 1937, and $520 million in 1938.[29] Clearly, radio was becoming more appealing to advertisers than any other medium.

The attractiveness of radio as a means of communication in depression America was clear. But what would be communicated, and how? Most publishers and editors of newspapers were opposed to Roosevelt in the 1930s, and their thoughts were reflected on the editorial pages. On the large dailies, and for major columnists, such restrictions, though significant, could be overcome. But advertisers in such journals had little influence over content, and in the case of the larger papers and journals, rarely sought to use it. This was not the condition with radio. Like the motion pictures, it entertained and diverted the American people in a time of great distress, all the while urging them to purchase various goods produced by business firms, in a fashion dictated by the advertising agencies. The two great electronic means of communication performed as stabilizing forces, due in large part to the structures of their respective industries and to their close relations in this period.

The situation was different with newspapers, which offered a far wider spectrum of opinion. Radio easily might have competed much more with the newspapers in the depression era. Sarnoff had spoken of newspapers "printed" by radio impulses on paper inserted in receivers as early as 1922; within less than an hour, he believed, set owners who subscribed to such a service could have an eight-page newspaper, complete with pictures—and advertisements. A more obvious means of competition was the news show, also sponsored, although the matter of control by advertisers was troublesome. Yet for most of the decade, news programs were scanty on radio. In 1933, only 2 per cent of NBC's programming was in the news area, and the figure was less than 5 per cent at CBS. The amount of news coverage expanded slowly through the New Deal period; more time was granted to quiz programs in 1935 than to news on all three networks.

In part this situation was the result of sponsors' unwillingness to accept such shows, which were bound to be more controversial than music or drama. On the other hand, given the anti-New Deal proclivities of Madison Avenue and its clients, sponsorship of conservative commentators and shows might have been an ideal way of getting messages across to the public; if Roosevelt could speak to the American people over the heads of the newspapers, why couldn't they, through selected commentators, do the same? Of course, the FCC would prevent abuses, while the National Association of Broadcasters took strong stands against the presentation of opinion on the air; an NAB Code, promulgated in 1939, stated, "Since the number of broadcasting channels is limited, news broadcasts shall not be editorial." Still, much might have been accomplished by the President's opponents through news shows.

This approach was rejected. The reasons were not prudence, a sense of fair play, or even commercial considerations, though the last was a matter of some concern. The agencies' conviction that news programs made for bad advertising vehicles had something to do with it. More important, however, was the reluctance on the part of the networks and large stations to enter the news field, for if radio could co-operate with and even supplement motion pictures, it had the potential to cripple the press, and both media knew it. Yet there would soon be a contest between the two for opinion-making power that still goes on, one that is sometimes muted and often uncertain but is there nonetheless. This too began in the early days of the New Deal.

7

The Making of a People's War

Public relations developed as both an art and a science during the interwar period, and Edward L. Bernays was one of the field's more important theoreticians and practitioners. Like others in the profession he was fascinated by radio, and constantly sought new means of exploiting its potential for his clients. "Radio is at present one of the most important tools of the propagandist," he wrote in 1928. "Its future development is uncertain," but surely it would soon become the dominant means of communication and method for influencing the public. As such, it would challenge and in the end defeat newspapers in the contest for advertising dollars. "Its ability to reach millions of people simultaneously naturally appeals to the advertiser. And since the average advertiser has a limited appropriation for advertising, money spent on the radio will tend to be withdrawn from the newspaper."[1] This, of course, is what occurred in the 1930s.

But in addition to competing with newspapers for advertising, radio had the potential to challenge the journals in their basic function, that of news. Such a contest did not develop in the 1920s and early 1930s, however, though leaders of both media were aware of possibilities. Editor Karl Bickel, who in 1930 was head of United Press, understood the threat. "When radio goes out on its own to cover news and report it on its own responsibility—entirely independent of the press—then the radio directly invades the newspaper field and immediately becomes competitive with the newspaper." United Press originated in journalism, but had an interest in radio as well. "Once let the radio become directly and seriously competitive with the newspaper, as a news distributor as well as an important creator of advertising energy, the issue will be joined and the newspaper will fight bitterly with all its power and its varied resources to protect its very life."[2]

Others held differing opinions. Walter Strong, publisher of the Chicago *Daily News,* thought radio would challenge movies as entertainment, but would only supplement newspapers and not cause drops in circulation or advertising. Similarly, the publishers of the Detroit *News,* the Kansas City *Star,* the St. Louis *Post-Dispatch,* the Milwaukee *Journal,* and the San Francisco *Chronicle* had kind words for radio in 1930. This might have been anticipated, since all owned NBC-affiliated stations that year, as did the Atlanta *Journal,* the Chicago *Tribune,* the Chicago *American,* and the Louisville *Courier Journal.* Among the CBS affiliates were stations owned by the San Francisco *Call Bulletin,* the Washington *Star,* and Capper Publications. That year, ninety-one American newspapers either owned or co-operated in the management of radio stations, and of these, twenty-three were affiliated with NBC and sixteen with CBS.[3] Hearst owned radio stations, to go with his newspapers, motion picture studio, and the International News Service and newsreel operations. But no newspaper publisher, not even Hearst, could hope to dominate radio. They had come to the field too late, for one thing, and for another, there were the antitrust laws, which might be used to break up any communications and news empire that transcended the boundaries of a single medium. The larger newspapers might own no more than three stations if they were to remain clear of the government's antitrusters and husband their resources for their primary occupations. And in any case, Strong was incorrect in his assessment of radio as an advertising medium. A full-page advertisement in a weekday edition of the New York *Times* cost $2,109, while sponsorship of an hour in prime time on the NBC Red Network, which covered twenty large cities including New York, cost $4,890 in 1930. Even when radio time rates rose in the decade while those for newspapers declined, it was evident that for advertisers of national products, radio was a better buy.

News was another matter, and it was here that the newspapers could claim a large measure of superiority. Newspapers were configurational, while radio was linear, which is to say that the bundle of newsprint a person purchased could be perused, parts ignored, a story reread, an argument followed as slowly or as rapidly as desired. An event could be covered on the front page or on an interior one, and reports could be pictorialized or not, depending upon the views and inclinations of the editor. In the case of radio one story followed another, with the listener unable to hear the second until the first was completed. Although the importance of a story could be highlighted by its place in the newscast, the amount of time spent on its recitation did not necessarily correspond with its importance—an international crisis might be related in two minutes, and the entire stock market table in twenty minutes, to give an obvious example. One could not refer back to a radio news story, but rather had to wait until it was repeated. Certainly newspapers could offer fuller coverage; the script for a fifteen-minute news program would take up less than half the front page of the New York *Times* in 1933. Newspapers could also cater to the interests of minority groups—readers of society and sports pages, for example—better than the broadcasts. Finally, the newspaper could be read at the convenience of its owner, and not at a specified time set down by the station.

Radio, on the other hand, did have some advantages. First of all, radio news was free. In addition, it could be absorbed while the listener was working, or driving a car, or performing some other function. It did not require the concentration of reading, and through the use of special effects, the listener could receive the impression of being closer to the event than any newspaper could accomplish. Listening to a portion of a speech could give the radio news follower as good an impression of its meaning as reading the entire speech could do for the newspaper purchaser. Taken together, the two media could complement one another in this regard. But radio news could deliver information—about a war, a murder, an election—more quickly. In the past, this had been accomplished through the use of newspaper "extras." But now the voice of newsboys screaming, "Extra, extra, read all about it," was replaced by the radio voice saying, "We interrupt this regularly scheduled program for a special announcement."

Radio news was more susceptible to outside control than newspapers. Freedom of the press had been well established in the 1920s, guaranteed by the Constitution, tested in the courts, and developed over time. Advertisers might attempt to sway editorial policy and news content at some journals, but the leading American newspapers had sufficient power to withstand such pressures. Radio, of course, was still in the process of creating a tradition in the 1920s. Was radio news covered by the First Amendment to the Constitution? Would advertisers have control over content? Did a station have the right to refuse time sales to a sponsor who put together a news program containing deliberately warped, distorted, or false information? Was a sponsor or a station legally responsible for libel? And what was the government's role, since in theory the airwaves belonged to the nation as a whole? How could there be freedom of speech and government responsibility at the same time?

The immediacy of radio news compounded this difficult situation. The editor of a newspaper, and sometimes the publisher, could control the content of any story. But on live radio a station manager could only sit back and listen to an interview; precensorship and editing was impossible. If a radio reporter in a remote unit happened to come across a news story that went on the air, he alone would have control of content. Even in prepared newscasts in which the station manager approved a script, the newscaster could deviate from it, or through voice inflection give the bare words new and subtle meanings. While radio drama, music, and even quiz programs had elements of motion pictures about them, radio news had the potential to develop into a new form as well as content. More than a motion-picture writer, or even a reporter, the newscaster could become a force in his own right. Once he developed a following and learned to skirt the bounds of government and sponsor disapproval, his power and audience would be greater than that of any columnist.

THE KALTENBORN APPROACH

The problem had not existed in the early post-World War I period, when the industry's pioneers were still trying to develop both form and content for radio. Once again, David Sarnoff recognized the problem before others in the field. Knowing that radio could duplicate newspaper functions, and intrigued with the idea of a newspaper printout through radio receivers, he could not believe newspapers would do anything to assist commercial radio. For this reason, he urged the stations themselves to enter publishing by putting out weekly magazines containing listings of programs, descriptions, and radio news, as well as advertising.[4] He could not imagine newspapers publishing radio "logs," as a service to their readers.

But the newspapers in fact did publish such logs at first; and as they established their own local stations, they used the radio to advertise their own papers. Intermixed with musical programs would be news "flashes," a brief summary of the headlines, after which listeners were urged to purchase the newspaper to get the full story. By the mid-1920s, most stations offered news summaries, read from local newspapers, while the larger ones purchased wire services from United Press and Associated Press. For the most part, the material was read by announcers, who were also responsible for selecting the proper stories, allocating time, and organizing the bits in sequence. Only a handful of them could be characterized as professional newsmen, and these looked upon their radio duties as part-time jobs, often taken to supplement income. They were not supposed to comment upon the news, or analyze it; their short programs were to resemble news stories, not editorials or columns.[5]

H. V. Kaltenborn, then the associate editor of the Brooklyn *Eagle*, was one of the pioneers, offering a weekly talk that was sponsored by the *Eagle* over WEAF. Once, when Kaltenborn criticized a local judge who was presiding over a case involving AT&T, the mother company contacted its station and attempted to quiet the newscaster. On another occasion, Kaltenborn angered a union official who demanded he be removed from the air, hinting labor troubles would ensue if this were not done. When Kaltenborn criticized Secretary of State Charles Evans Hughes in a mild fashion, the Secretary called AT&T and protested that such a program should not be permitted on the company's station. Soon after, Kaltenborn's program was dropped, thus sparking a period of bitter relations between the newspaper and the station. Kaltenborn, of course, remained in radio, and for the next few years went from station to station, becoming one of the first full-time newsmen on the air.[6]

There appeared to be no major conflict between radio and newspapers in the early network period. At the time, there was enough advertising money for both, and in any case, radio advertising was concentrated in music, variety, drama, and quiz shows. Spot announcements were sold for the short newscasts, and for the most part, these interludes were on a sustaining basis. There was no regularly scheduled news series on NBC Red, while NBC Blue had only Lowell Thomas, and CBS programmed Edwin C. Hill's "The Human Side of the News" (which concentrated on human-interest stories) and Kaltenborn. As far as could be seen, radio would go no farther, if only because the networks lacked the facilities to compete with the newspapers. Given sponsor interests and allocations of funds, none of the networks or larger independents had the will or the money to assemble a major news-gathering operation. Should the networks give a sign of competing with newspapers, the press would withdraw permission to use the newspapers as sources for programs and pressure the wire services to do the same. That this could and would be done was understood by both radio and newspaper executives.

The coming of the depression precipitated the first struggle between the two media. Engaged in a contest for advertising dollars, several large newspaper chains insisted the networks drop all news programs. When this was not done, they instituted a suit in federal court to restrain the networks from using newspapers as sources for their shows. In 1931, the courts agreed that the papers had a proprietary right to the news printed on their pages; now the newspapers could challenge the radio stations to demonstrate convincingly that their news broadcasts did not utilize newspaper news. At the same time, many newspapers halted publication of radio logs as a service for their readers; if the stations wished, they could pay for their insertions at regular space rates.

The stations reacted slowly at first. During 1932, almost all of the news on radio came from the wire services; no station established its own news operation. As for newspaper radio logs, the large stations refused to purchase space, reasoning that reader protests would cause the newspapers to reverse the practice. A large volume of angry letters, combined with lower circulations and the appearance of several radio log magazines, led the major papers to restore the logs by midyear, a clear sign of radio's power. Then, as the presidential election approached, the networks arranged to have live pickups from campaign headquarters—the same source newspapers used for their information. Americans learned of the scope of the Roosevelt victory on radio, not from "election day special editions" hours later. The well-sponsored radiocasts of the election caused many publishers to conclude that a stronger attack against radio news had to be mounted.

It came in 1933, at the bottom of the depression. At its April meeting, the American Newspaper Publishers Association resolved no longer to publish program logs as a public service, and reiterated its intent to bring suits against stations that used newspapers as news sources. At the same time, the major publishers brought pressure to bear upon the wire services. Later that month, the Associated Press agreed not to provide news to the networks, and the United Press and Hearst's International News Service followed suit.

The networks had expected this series of actions, but did little at first. The NBC networks were content to broadcast news gathered from local stations, usually through telephone calls to people mentioned in newspaper stories. Since NBC was radio's leading organization, it saw little reason to do more. Then and through most of the 1930s, the Blue and Red networks concentrated upon entertainment functions and tried to steer clear of controversies with the press. The situation was different at CBS, still far behind NBC in terms of power and reach. Since it could not compete with the industry leader for talent, it would try to do a better job with news. With the backing of William Paley, former United Press editor Paul W. White hired correspondents in major American cities, most of them on a part-time basis. The makeshift news organization worked, and when the newspapers began to see its success, they tried to put pressure on CBS sponsors by initiating a news blackout for their products. When this failed, all forces in the field—newspapers, networks, and wire services—met to seek a compromise solution. Under the terms of the so-called "Biltmore Program," the wire services would once again sell news to the networks, through a press-radio bureau established by the stations. On their part, CBS and NBC would disband their young news-gathering operations. Two five-minute newscasts a day would be permitted—one in the early morning, the other late at night—and these would be noncommercial. Radio commentators would not use news that was less than twelve hours old, and would refrain from competing with newspapers (how this was to be enforced or accomplished was not spelled out).[7]

The Biltmore Program lasted only a few months. Non-network stations were able to attract listeners to longer news programs, and this led the networks to skirt the agreement. The wire services were approached by sponsors who wanted to put news programs on the air, and they broke ranks too. Finally, some of the newspapers found that while the agreements helped their printed operations, they harmed their radio stations, and so they let the agreement drop. But the press-radio bureau remained intact and operative, and so newscasts—usually by station announcers—tended to remain short, sketchy, and unimaginative.

The network news commentators, on the other hand, became significant personalities by mid-decade. Kaltenborn's two broadcasts a week for CBS, for which he received one hundred dollars (with no expense account), was considered high, a sign of his importance. Kaltenborn also worked for newspapers and magazines on a free-lance basis in order to cover expenses and earn a decent living, even when his was one of the most familiar voices in America. Kaltenborn's clipped style, rapid delivery, and journalistic bearing, and his constant reference to eyewitness reports and confidences from the key figures, led listeners to believe that he was not only competing with columnists for information and analysis, but also doing so under more trying conditions and in a superior fashion. Floyd Gibbons, a dramatic newspaper reporter who had made a reputation for daring before and during World War I, also took easily to radio, and affected the reporter rushing into the city room with a "scoop." "Hello, everybody," he might begin, breathlessly. "Bushels of news today, things popping up all over the map." And then he would read a script, put together from wire-service reports and newspapers, together with commentary and asides. Boake Carter, also a former newsman whose English accent grated on some, punctuated his commentaries with exclamations like "by jingo," "great Scott," and "by golly," and he usually ended with a hale "cheerio." Carter was strongly anti-New Deal, isolationist, and rarely in full command of his facts. Often he would throw away his script and deliver a lecture against Prohibition or, after repeal, organized crime. The programs were carried on a sustaining basis at CBS, and on occasion Carter would be suspended, but he always returned, buoyed by angry letters from listeners. Lowell Thomas was in the same mold, although he always hewed to his script, written by Prosper Buranelli. On occasion, however, Thomas would interrupt with a *sotto voce* "I'll be damned" or "I didn't know that." A world traveler and romantic figure, Thomas specialized in historical asides, often straying from the main point to tell an interesting story or two. And there were others—Gabriel Heatter, Edwin C. Hill, John B. Kennedy, and later on Walter Winchell. Most affected the newsroom, the air of immediacy and excitement, and folksiness. These were men trained in newspaper journalism, either on the tabloids or the more traditional journals. They would write—or have written for them—a news story or a column, and then read it on the air. Some of them—Heatter, Kaltenborn, and Carter in particular—were capable of sustained reporting without scripts, but the newsroom-cracker barrel atmosphere rarely was ignored, as though the commentator were a combination of Hearst and Will Rogers.

Network executives were aware of the situation. They were troubled about editorializing on the air—this might bring retaliation against sponsors from customers, and action by the FCC—but the form and format gave little reason for concern. Was this the best that radio news commentary could be—an oral newspaper column or the ramblings of an informed observer? There was some experimentation with a combination of entertainment and news: the dramatized story, in which actors were utilized to portray actual people, and in some cases read fictitious statements, and in others, heavily edited ones. "The March of Time," which utilized the resources and style of *Time* magazine, was the leader in this genre, as well as a pioneer, first appearing on CBS in 1931. The first announcer was Ted Husing, but he was replaced by Harry Von Zell and, finally, by Westbrook Van Voorhis, whose stentorian voice opened the program with "Time . . . marches on," and who spoke with "Timese," such phrases as "As it must to all men, death came this week to . . ." Art Carney imitated Franklin Roosevelt, Jeanette Nolan played Eleanor Roosevelt, and Peter Donald was Neville Chamberlain. Almost all the leading radio voices appeared on "The March of Time" at one point in their career, and their obvious acting, the studio quality of the sound, made it evident to the increasingly sophisticated audiences that it was a drama more than a news program. But not to all, and in its own fashion, the program was a key adjunct of the *Time* empire, a voice for *Time* opinions.

The blandness of newscasts, the imitative nature of commentaries, and the forays into dramatizations were indications that radio news was seeking both a form and content in the mid-1930s and falling short of the mark. Some of the reasons for this are obvious—the lack of interest in radio news at the networks, the desire to remain free of controversy, the limitations of commentators, and arrangements with the newspapers. But there were other, equally important considerations, which while not as obvious as the others, helped change the concept of radio news in the last years of the decade.

The major news stories of the first Roosevelt administration concerned the problems of domestic recovery and reform. These were covered by magazines and newspapers, and although radio could present information and analysis of bills passed and actions taken, these only supplemented the written word. Few Floyd Gibbons or Kaltenborn commentaries would have lost much impact if printed the following day in the New York *Times* or the New York Daily *News*. This was not the case with several major on-the-spot highlights of the early years of the 1930s, however, such as Heatter's coverage of the Lindbergh baby kidnaping trial, or other broadcasts that gave the feeling of immediacy and excitement. But a Kaltenborn broadcast from Washington might just as well have originated in New York, as far as the listener in Chicago was concerned, for even though the commentator was reporting on-the-scene actions, it lacked drama, coming as it was from a studio not unlike most others in the nation.

It became obvious that tension and immediacy—the real kind, not the manufactured *Time* variety—were the keys to successful newscasts and commentaries. Radio was often called the "theater of imagination," and the news programs of the early decade did not take this into consideration, while "the March of Time," successful though it was, did so in a patently false fashion. Yet "the March of Time" was more popular than the broadcasts of any commentator, and this offered clues the executives did not understand or appreciate at the time. Then, in 1936, Kaltenborn went to Spain—paying his own way—to cover the Civil War there. His broadcasts, containing the usual Kaltenborn references to his contacts with important foreign diplomats, were well received in America.

These were not the first transatlantic broadcasts; in 1930 the Five-power Conference in London was reported on NBC and CBS. Frederick Wile, the CBS broadcaster at the conference and Cesar Searchinger, the London correspondent for several newspapers who worked part-time for radio stations, sent news of the meetings to America. In 1935, CBS sent some 150 overseas broadcasts to American audiences. But most of these were bland reports of flower shows, visits by a royal family, sports events, and the like.[8] Kaltenborn's coverage of the war was another matter. One could hear—or imagine he had heard—gunfire in the background, there was static that in other contexts would have been annoying but in transatlantic news broadcasts was romantic and exciting; and Kaltenborn excelled in descriptions of battles he had seen that morning. Ten years before, listeners had been thrilled to pull in stations several hundreds of miles away, and by the mid-1930s they were used to this. Now they tuned in on a war and heard the actual sounds of combat. This was far more dramatic than anything found in the next day's newspaper. It gave the listener the idea that he knew at least as much as the eyewitness newspaper reporter, since he had been on the spot too, in a fashion. The reporting of a foreign war was an ideal subject for radio, and did as much for oral news as the discovery of plot did for early motion pictures.

How would foreign news, war news in particular, be covered? In middecade, it was assumed that when and if another major European struggle began, it would be a replay of World War I, complete with trench warfare, stabilized lines, and strategy and tactics out of the texts. The same would be true of reportage; the dashing war correspondent of 1914–17 was expected to emerge once more, in pretty much the same form. Thus newspapers, magazines, and the networks began seeking the services of retired officers, veteran newsmen, and others who resembled them in style and form, to report on foreign developments.

But the new war when it came differed substantially from the old in several major respects insofar as the media were concerned. In the first place, the path to war was longer and more easily traced. Few in Europe or America had expected a major conflict in 1914, while from 1937 to 1939 there were a series of crises in which newspapers, magazines, and radio could perfect their approaches. After the fall of France in 1940, reportage on radio was centered in London and several neutral capitals; there would be no "trench-line reporters" for this war, at least at that time. This was to be a radio war, just as the newspaper had been the main means of obtaining news for World War I and the Vietnam struggle would be reported as a televised event. From 1914–19, reporters had been free to manufacture "color" and "background," to use their imaginations, and to utilize the words and values of the Edwardian age to describe what they had seen. At the beginning of the war at least, the idea of armed conflict had been popular, and all nations involved had enthusiastic support on the home front. In contrast, World War II was a more somber event; it lacked romance, even though it was a more determined contest on both sides. Such a war required a different kind of prose, and in the case of radio, a new style and voice—or group of voices. The radio veterans simply could not adjust to the demands of wartime broadcast journalism, which required the commentator to discuss in a specific time span an event that might not be mentioned in the next day's newspaper, and do so in such a way as to illuminate the happening as well as report it. A spare prose, not a hyperactive one, would be required, and this meant that the World War I retreads, such as Gibbons and Carter, would not do. Several of the old newspapermen-radio commentators of the 1930s possessed this talent, or had come by it over the years, but invariably they were too old to take the rigors of continual bombings by the time the main struggle had begun. Kaltenborn, for example, was over sixty in 1939, and although he had been most vigorous in his reportage of the Spanish Civil War, he was considered too important to be sent to the war zone on a permanent basis. Instead, he would remain in the United States to comment on the fighting from a distance.

Then there was the matter of editorialization. This had been difficult enough during the New Deal, but the problem was compounded in the late 1930s, when almost every commentator was anti-Hitler. In early 1939, for example, Kaltenborn was sponsored by General Mills, which had promised him complete freedom of expression. Starting with the 1938 Munich crisis, Kaltenborn began to openly voice his anti-Nazi sentiments. He continued to do so even after his sponsor went back on its promise and asked him to cease. In the end, sponsorship was withdrawn.

More significant was the fact that the network did not back its correspondent. Its defenders thought the reason was fairness. CBS President William Paley had said, in 1937, that broadcasting "must forever be wholly, honestly, and militantly nonpartisan." CBS, he said, would never have an editorial policy; "We must never try to further either side of any debatable question." Critics noted that at that time the FCC was investigating the networks, in preparation for antitrust actions of one kind or another.[9] In addition, CBS was still rather shaky, and Paley would hardly do anything to lose sponsors. But Edward Klauber, Paley's closest associate and the network's executive vice president, had long felt the same way. The former night editor of the New York *Times*, Klauber had spoken out in favor of impartial news while at the paper and afterward.[10] Paul White, the CBS director of news, stated that the network believed in "letting the radio listener make up his mind rather than allowing news broadcasters to make it up for him." This, then, for whatever reason, was the CBS policy.

In early 1939, Paley strained to please all factions by drawing a distinction between "commentary" and "analysis." The network welcomed the former, he said, but would not tolerate the latter. By this he meant that Kaltenborn might discuss various aspects of the news, but could not offer his opinions, even though they were labeled as such. The commentator thought the difference was manufactured rather than real. Angry and unhappy, he left CBS in late 1939 to take a position at NBC. Two years later, the news commentators formed the Association of Radio News Analysts, and Kaltenborn was elected its first president. Through this organization, he continued the fight for the right to editorialize. But before the contest with the networks—and possibly the government—could begin, the United States entered the war. From that point on, editorialization was not only welcomed, but even encouraged.

The Kaltenborn episode was only one of many in the area of broadcasting opinion on radio. At the time of Munich, Raymond Swing conducted a weekly broadcast for the British Broadcasting System, on which he had the right to analyze and comment upon stories. Swing's hushed, dramatic delivery appealed to the British, and to those Americans who heard his transcriptions over the Mutual Broadcasting System, a minor force in radio. For a while he was considered for CBS, but both Klauber and Paley were disturbed by his editorializations, even though they agreed with them.[11] In 1943, CBS newsman Cecil Brown noted, on one broadcast, that "enthusiasm for this war is evaporating into thin air." White rebuked Brown for editorializing, after which Brown resigned. Kaltenborn criticized CBS, while FCC commissioner James Fly thought Brown had every right to say what he thought, even though it was contrary to what he deemed the nation's best interests. But White did not back down. The following year, in a manual issued to newsmen covering the D-Day landing, he wrote, "Keep an informative, unexcited demeanor at the microphone. Give sources for all reports. Don't risk accuracy for the sake of a beat. Use care in your choice of words. . . . When you don't know, say so. . . . Exaggeration and immoderate language breed dangerous optimism."[12]

Paley, Klauber, and White demanded a new kind of radio journalist—this was the term they used. He would have to be knowledgeable, possess a good radio voice and demeanor, and be capable of understatement. Such a person would be quite different from the best and most successful commentators of the time. In some fashion, he would have to combine the functions of reporter and columnist, and do so in such a way as to capitalize upon radio's strong points and minimize its deficiencies. Up to that time, this had been done through the use of theatrical, contrived devices, mimicking what the public thought a newsroom should be. Radio journalism was considered and viewed itself as an outgrowth of and even an adjunct to the newspaper. Clearly this would not be changed all at once, or completely. But the war would provide an arena in which radio journalism could develop new forms, and at CBS at least, the content would conform with the ideas of men like Klauber and White.

THE MURROW STAMP

In 1935, Klauber decided the network needed a director of talks, whose job it would be to develop educational and related programs. He offered the post to Raymond Swing, who declined it when he learned the director would not be permitted to broadcast. Soon after, Edward R. Murrow accepted the position. He was twenty-seven years old at the time.

Murrow had no real journalistic background or experience.[13] He had been born in a small South Carolina town, raised in the Northwest, and attended Washington State College, where he had excelled in oratory. In 1930, Murrow had taken a position as president of the National Student Federation, an organization devoted to international education. For a while he considered a career in college administration; in 1932 he was employed by the Institute of International Education, where he helped arrange for radio broadcasts by visiting educators and authors. On occasion, Murrow delivered radio talks of his own, but he had no special interest in the medium at the time.

As director of talks at CBS, Murrow set up radio lectures by foreign visitors and special programs on current events; the work was not very much different from what he had been doing at the IIE. But he did come into contact with leading radio executives. Murrow went to London to meet with Cesar Searchinger, then the CBS European director, who introduced him to newspaper correspondents and arranged for contacts with important government figures. But Searchinger had little interest in the position, and in 1937 he resigned to devote himself completely to newspaper work. Murrow was offered the post, and he accepted. By late 1937, he was established in London, with a mandate to organize the network's foreign operations on the eve of war.

Although not yet thirty years old, Murrow had more radio experience than most of the network's newsmen, and in addition possessed all of the attributes Klauber and White expected in their commentators. He was not supposed to devote himself to broadcasts, of course, but rather was an executive charged with hiring and firing newsmen and supervising the network's European operations. Since there was practically no organization at the time, and precedents for war broadcasting were few—Kaltenborn's was the only guide in 1938—Murrow was able to develop the organization in his own image, and this he did.

As has been indicated, most radio newsmen of the time had been trained at newspapers, and at one point or another in their training—either in the newsroom or the journalism school—they had learned specific rules about reporting. For example, the reader was supposed to learn the answers to "who, what, when, where, and how" in the first paragraph, preferably in the first sentence or two. The story would have a headline, large or small depending upon its importance. Whether consciously or not, many news commentators of the 1930s imitated this form. They would raise their voices for important stories, or even say, "This is *really* important" or some other such phrase. Rapid speech, including an almost indigestible array of facts and analysis, would be flung out over the air. This would have been fine for a newspaper story, where the reader could set his own pace. But radio listeners had to use a trained ear to get the full meaning of broadcasts by some leading commentators. This was changing in the late 1930s, and even without Murrow, radio journalism would have developed different, unique forms. But he was its leading exemplar, and he came by the new form gradually.

Murrow had not intended to become a commentator; he had been sent to Europe to find others for the job and to organize operations. But the coming of armed conflict changed matters, and in early 1938 he obtained permission to broadcast. At first, Murrow's talks had the sound of a newspaper story. The first of these took place on March 13, 1938, and began:

> This is Edward Murrow speaking from Vienna. It's now nearly two-thirty in the morning and Herr Hitler has not yet arrived. No one seems to know just when he will get here, but most people expect him sometime after ten o'clock tomorrow morning. It's, of course, obvious after one glance at Vienna that a tremendous reception is being prepared.

By March 9, 1941, the Murrow news commentaries were quite different.

> Soon it will be spring in England. Already there are flowers in the parks, although the parks aren't quite as well kept as they were this time last year. But there's good fighting weather ahead. In four days' time the moon will be full again, and there's a feeling in the air that big things will happen soon.[14]

Murrow spoke deliberately in his prepared talks, in a low voice and with almost perfect timing. These were really essays—they read as such a generation later. They were understated and calm, even morose at times. In a different period, Murrow might have become a college president or, had he gone into literary life, a novelist, essayist, or historian. His pieces might have appeared in journals of opinion, or as signed columns in leading newspapers. But he was not a "reporter" as the term was understood in newspapers of the period and earlier. To him the language was important in itself, and not only as a vehicle for the transmission of information. On occasion, Murrow would deliver impromptu talks over radio, such as one while on a bombing mission, and he would interview soldiers and politicians. These were competently done, but hardly as memorable as his prepared broadcasts.[15] After the war, Eric Sevareid characterized the Murrow talks:

> One can read his broadcasts now, years later, in the printed form for which they were never intended and find London all around—its sights and sounds, its very smells and feeling through the changing hours, all brought back. . . . It was not his perfect poise, his magnetic face, or even his compelling voice that made him the first great literary artist of a new medium of communication. No practice, training, or artifice made him the greatest broadcaster by far in the English language. He was simply born to the new art.[16]

Important though the early broadcasts were in their own right, they had an added significance as examples for those who Murrow hired for CBS. During his first years in London, he searched for able newspapermen who were talented essayists, with good speaking voices.[17] He preferred young men; the war would be strenuous, and probably long. He wanted people who could function independently while at the same time conforming to the criteria established by Klauber, Paley, and White. "I don't know very much about your experience," said Murrow to Sevareid—who was a reporter for the Paris *Herald* and the United Press, and had just been offered a new, important position, at the wire service—"but I like the way you write and I like your ideas." Sevareid was offered a job as a news reporter for CBS. "There won't be pressure on you to provide scoops or anything sensational. Just provide the honest news, and when there isn't any news, why, just say so. I have an idea people might like that."[18] Sevareid's voice was not "right" for radio at first, but in time he came around, perhaps unconsciously patterning his phrasing on Murrow's. Murrow also acquired Howard K. Smith, Larry LeSueur, Charles Collingwood, Richard C. Hottelet, Winston Burdett, Ned Calmer, and other young men, and helped train them—or at least direct their efforts. William Shirer, an experienced newsman, provided balance in Europe, and he too accepted Murrow's leadership. Kaltenborn helped create the format of the "World News Roundup" in 1938. When sitting at his desk in New York he would "call in" the European correspondents, headed by Murrow and Shirer, to report on the developing crisis. George Fielding Eliot was the CBS military expert. After Kaltenborn left, Elmer Davis acted as moderator—in television the term would have been "anchorman"—for what soon became one of the most popular news programs on the air. The real attractions were the new correspondents, however, and by 1941, most were more or less in the Murrow mold. He had not only helped create a new radio art form, but also had developed an organization capable of presenting it to the public. And it was commercial as well; the "Murrow men" clearly had points of view, but unlike Kaltenborn, Swing, and others like them, they did not insist upon presenting them on the air.

The National Broadcasting Corporation was slower in entering the foreign news field, and less imaginative than CBS. By its very size, however, it did set the pace for a while for other networks. Both the Red and Blue networks were doing well in entertainment, where CBS lagged, and so as late as 1939, the NBC leaders tended to ignore the news function. Still, in that year, when CBS had twenty-four foreign correspondents and Mutual six, the NBC staff employed forty-six correspondents, and when Murrow sought an initial model to follow, it was the one provided by the senior network.

NBC was quite content with its staff and philosophy. Dr. Max Jordan, a former German correspondent, headed the Euopean operation from the Continent. He had connections with leading Nazi officials and so was able to "scoop" other networks on happenings in Germany. Fred Bate, who broadcast from London, was his assistant. A former newspaperman, Bate assembled a staff of people with good journalism backgrounds as well as a handful of academics. Karl von Wiegand reported from Prague; he formerly had been with the International News Service. Walter Kerr, then a New York *Herald Tribune* reporter, was stationed in Berlin. Walter Duell of the Chicago *Daily News* and Gordon Lenox of the London *Daily Telegraph* complemented Bate in London. Although all were well qualified, few had any particular talent for the medium. NBC covered the war as completely as CBS, but was far less popular than its rival.[19] By 1944 it had begun imitating the Murrow approach, and even attempted to hire newsmen from CBS to do so. But by then, it had fallen too far behind to catch up with the leader.[20] This, too, was an indication of Murrow's great impact on radio journalism. Before the war had ended, Murrow was a national figure, whose voice was as recognizable as Roosevelt's or Churchill's to that generation of Americans; he was an authentic war hero, and had he possessed political ambitions, they might easily have been realized.

The enthusiastic support the nation gave the war effort masked the almost forgotten legacy of Kaltenborn, Brown, and Swing and the questions they had raised that still had not been answered. Did the radio commentator have the right and obligation to voice his opinion on controversial subjects, to editorialize and hope thereby to sway public opinion? Kaltenborn clearly thought they did. He believed that by claiming to be objective, Murrow and others like him were doing damage to the cause of truth. No less than Kaltenborn, Murrow favored the Allied cause. But the older man let the audience know how he felt directly, while Murrow's sentiments were hidden. The result was that listeners knew where Kaltenborn stood and could judge him accordingly; isolationists always took him with a grain of salt. Not so with Murrow; his was supposed to be the voice of objective truth, as claimed by Klauber and White. And since this was not the case, was the Murrow news fair to the listener? Was it safe to trust such power to any individual or news agency, no matter how honest and selfless it hoped to be?

There was yet another, even more serious problem in the Murrow approach. The man had a theatrical flair and appearance. Pictures of Murrow appeared in the newspapers and magazines. Invariably he was shown either in a raincoat on the London streets, his brow furrowed, watching the passing scene, or at the microphone in shirt sleeves, a cigarette in hand, ready to speak to the nation. He had a face and bearing to match his unmatchable voice. Murrow was as handsome as any Hollywood leading man, and indeed was at times mistaken for one of them. Speaking as he did on the radio from London, with shellbursts in the background providing effects, it was as though the whole thing were staged. To a generation reared on radio drama, the war as reported on radio appeared dramatic; the news broadcasts took on the sounds of a continuing story, with the next episode to be aired the following night. It was every bit as good as "The March of Time"—and to some, as real as that dramatized program. To a nation that confused Orson Welles' dramatization of *The War of the Worlds* with an actual invasion from outer space, Murrow's reports of the war might easily be confused with a semifictitious account. Whatever his faults, Kaltenborn was a newsman whose passions and flaws were ever on display. Murrow was a highly intelligent writer, blessed with a fine voice and appearance and a sense of style. There was an element of show business about the performer on radio which, in the early 1940s, was welcomed by the nation. Murrow and his men reshaped radio news, but was the product all that it appeared to be? In 1942 the question was more moot than real, but it was there nonetheless.

THE ELECTRICAL MEDIA AT WAR

In mid-December 1941, after the Japanese attack on Pearl Harbor, the National Association of Broadcasters met to discuss wartime restrictions on the news. Already there was talk of censorship. Congressman Emanuel Celler of New York asked, "What shall our attitude be anent radio commentators who make prophecies? Do their predictions aid the enemy? If disheartening predictions prove false, have they unnecessarily hurt home-front morale?" Others spoke of the need to stifle pro-Nazi sentiments, to remove Japanese Americans to detention camps, to initiate a widespread effort to root out subversion and un-American activities. National opinion would have to be mobilized, as well as military and industrial power. Was this necessary? Professor Max Lerner wrote, "There is something a little hypochondriac in our preoccupation with our own patriotic temperature," but there were few such voices that December. Still, the NAB came out against government censorship of radio. The organization did support self-regulation, however. Programs "that might unduly affect the listener's peace of mind," "livid news dramatizations," and "frenzied flashes and hysterical mannerisms" by commentators were to be banned. Weather forecasts were to be discontinued; they might give assistance to enemy bombers headed for the United States. Man-in-the-street interviews, popular on many local stations, were also discontinued, for fear that a military secret might be revealed by a worker in a defense plant.

The regulations on commentary were difficult to enforce, while most of the other rules were unnecessary. The coming of war in 1941 was quite different from Wilson's Declaration of War in 1917. America had been attacked and was defending itself against aggressors. In addition, World War II had a moral dimension that was more obvious than that of World War I. From 1917–19 German Americans and pro-German writers had organized to speak out against the war effort; there was little of this after Pearl Harbor, and what there was could safely be ignored. Finally, most Americans had become acclimated to the idea of war through newspapers, newsreels, and especially radio. Although the Japanese attack had come as a surprise, by December 1941 the question was not whether America would enter the war, but when and by what means. Senator Arthur Vandenberg of Michigan, acknowledged leader of the congressional isolationists, echoed the sentiments of many who had opposed the Roosevelt foreign policy since 1939. "We were no longer 'free agents' after the infamous Japanese attack and Japan's Declaration of War in America," he wrote in his diary on December 8. "There is nothing left to do but to answer in kind."

This was true for radio and motion pictures as well. Executives and artists in both businesses were eager to assist the war effort, to accept leadership from Washington as to the best means to do so. Criticism of government was rare from 1942 to 1944, and even when radio commentators and motion-picture stars spoke out for Democrat Roosevelt or Republican Thomas E. Dewey in the election campaign, debate centered on postwar problems, not the legitimacy of the American role in the conflict. There was one major exception to this unity: Opinion was divided on the matter of American-Soviet relations during the war. Some viewed the alliance as one with the devil, while others believed it a union of progressive forces against tyranny. The issue of communism was discussed, but was not considered as significant as the need for unity and support of the war. Those who criticized the legitimacy of the conflict were dealt with by the media themselves. On radio, for example, right-wing commentator Upton Close of the American Broadcasting Network was warned to stop speaking against the war. When he refused to do so, he was fired, as was once-popular Father Charles Coughlin. There was no reaction from the NAB or other broadcasting groups to the dismissals; even Kaltenborn was silent, perhaps believing that in time of war, some limitations on opinion were justifiable.

Just as Woodrow Wilson had felt it necessary to mobilize American opinion in 1917, so Franklin Roosevelt thought it wise to do the same in 1942. But the two men had different approaches to administration as well as different problems to meet. Wilson had been willing to delegate great authority to trusted individuals, even though this might mean the establishment of rival power centers. Bernard Baruch at the Council of National Defense and George Creel at the Committee of Public Information had known that the power of the presidency could be summoned to enforce their orders. Neither man had to contend for long with contradictory orders from other bureaucrats; when conflicts threatened, an appeal to the White House would result in a prompt ruling establishing limits of power.

Roosevelt, on the other hand, used a different approach. He seemed to delight in subtle shadings, both in content and responsibility. He often spoke and acted as though information, propaganda, psychological warfare, and espionage were of a piece. Some of his aides wanted to keep them separate, but Roosevelt constantly overruled their objections. After a while, however, the Administration created a distinction between "black" and "white" propaganda and psychological warfare activities. The former was to be created for use overseas, while "white" was for domestic consumption alone. But there also was a "gray" area, which overlapped the other two, and often the lines between foreign and domestic activities became blurred.[21]

To further complicate matters, Roosevelt delegated the same responsibilities to several different offices and executives, often without informing one of the existence of the others, or the limits of authority.[22] The Army and Navy each had intelligence, propaganda, education, and psychological warfare units. Then there was the Office of Facts and Figures, a catch-all agency headed by Archibald MacLeish, the librarian of Congress—no one seemed to know how he obtained the wartime post—which had some vague authority over radio and the press, and recruited intellectuals for government service in the first months of the war. Lowell Mellett, a former Scripps-Howard editor, was in charge of the Office of Government Reports, which had a variety of tasks. Mellett was shifted from job to job during the next two years, and was never certain of his position or responsibilities. The Divison of Information of the Office of Emergency Management was headed by Robert Horton. The OEM was soon merged into another agency, but the Horton operation remained intact, with no determinable tasks. And there were others.[23] John O'Donnell, a Roosevelt critic, referred to the proliferating informational agencies as "several hundred ex-reporters, jobless foreign correspondents, lyric poets, dramatists, and ordinary merchants of literary mush." Senator Robert Taft, equally critical, claimed that there were five thousand people engaged in publicity operations that cost more than thirty million dollars a year. "This country can neither scare its enemies nor further its own war by talk," he said, as he launched an attack against the new agencies. Wilson had purchased the services of intellectuals on a retail basis; Roosevelt did so on a wholesale level.

The Office of Co-ordinator of Information supposedly provided direction for all informational units while at the same time entering the field on its own. It was headed by Colonel William J. "Wild Bill" Donovan, a World War I hero who afterward became a conservative Republican lawyer and an influential Washington politician. Donovan, who had a flair for mystery and was primarily interested in intelligence work, paid little attention to the other agencies, and instead concentrated upon erecting a combination espionage-propaganda mechanism at the OCI. Playwright Robert Sherwood, in charge of the OCI Foreign Information Service as well as being a confidant of Roosevelt, established an efficient press operation after Pearl Harbor, which by early 1942 was sending over three hundred short-wave programs to Europe and preparing to take command of domestic operations as soon as permission was obtained from the White House.

Donovan opposed the creation of any powerful office headed by Sherwood, and at the time he had Roosevelt's ear. Holding that in time of war and national emergency the government had the right to manipulate truth and even lie, Donovan resented Sherwood's insistence upon a "clean" operation. The Foreign Information Service was staffed by former newsmen and writers, some of whom had worked with Creel at the CPI. These men were prepared to use information in the war effort, but not to the extent of creating fabrications. Since Sherwood's branch disseminated information abroad, and Donovan considered propaganda in that area vital to his over-all operation, the two men clashed, so that by early spring they were scarcely talking to one another.

Roosevelt resolved the matter in a typical fashion. In mid-June of 1942, while Donovan was in London, the President transferred the Sherwood office away from him. What remained would be called the Office of Strategic Services. The new organization would have wide powers. In addition to collecting and analyzing information, the OSS would plan and operate "special services . . . taken to enforce our will upon the enemy by means other than military action. . . ."[24] Using the Sherwood operation as a base, Roosevelt also created the Office of War Information, which would be charged with tasks in the area of domestic morale as well as provide informational services to newspapers, radio, and motion pictures. Elmer Davis, then at CBS, was named to head the OWI, with the understanding that Sherwood would remain at his old post and serve under him.

Davis was one of the best-known newsmen in the nation at the time, as well as being highly respected within the profession. He was fifty-two years old in 1942, and as a result of his programs at CBS, was viewed as a logical successor to Kaltenborn. It would be his task, thought Washington insiders, to accomplish for Roosevelt what Creel had done for Wilson. Davis would handle white propaganda, while Donovan's OSS would be charged with the black variety.

It seemed a good choice and a workable idea. Davis had been a free-lance journalist and a member of the New York *Times* staff between the wars. In 1940 he wrote that civil liberties need not be abandoned in wartime, and even though he opposed American entry into the struggle, he believed it would come. A middle-of-the-road figure as far as the New Deal was concerned, he would be able to work with leaders of both parties in Congress and, perhaps, smooth differences between Sherwood and Donovan. To do so, of course, he would need a great deal of power and authority. He received neither. The conflicts in the intelligence branches continued to fester, and even broadened as the war progressed.[25] Davis would complain to Roosevelt that his authority was being undercut, receive assurances of support, and the conflicts would continue. In despair, he wrote to Creel for advice, but the old CPI chief had little to offer. "You have a man in the White House who does not like to see anyone get the blue slip," wrote Creel. "The whole success of the CPI was due to the fact that neither the Army nor the Navy had the right to sit in arbitrary judgement on what should or should not be printed. Time after time they disputed my authority and I won out only because Woodrow Wilson hammered them down. . . ."[26] Roosevelt would not do the same for Davis, and so the organization often appeared inept and on occasion it foundered. Still, Davis remained at the job, when perhaps a scathing resignation might have cleared the air. But such kinds of things were not done in wartime, and so he did the best he could.

The job included the use of black propaganda and outright falsehoods. Creel had been known to twist and manipulate facts, but although he had been charged with fabricating news, evidence of this was never presented or uncovered later on. The CPI chief conceded that he had withheld information on occasion and slanted releases, but prided himself on his integrity. Perhaps this was self-deception, an unsophisticated view of the news function and the nature of truth, but it was held nonetheless.

Davis sounded a similar note on assuming office. "This is a people's war and to win it the people should know as much about it as they can," he told reporters. Soon after, he said he wanted to give "the people the news . . . the background information that will help them understand what the news is about." After dealing with and working within the bureaucracy for a while, the OWI director spoke differently. He did not deny that his office was engaged in propaganda work. "We are going to use the truth, and we are going to use it toward the end of winning the war, for we know what will happen to the American people if we lose it. 'Propaganda' is a word in bad odor in this country; but there is no public hostility to the idea of education, and we regard this part of our jobs as education."[27] Was this the same kind of operation that Creel had run a quarter of a century earlier? One former newsman saw the problems of the CPI and OWI as being quite similar, and was able to rationalize the manipulation of news in much the same fashion as did Davis. "Many of us in the OWI were strongly predisposed by our previous training in favor of a program of information," wrote Wallace Carroll. "Our inclination, too, was to put the facts of the war before the world." He hoped this would achieve the goals of psychological warfare, increase morale, and help the war effort. But there were troubles. "Our real difficulties came over a choice between giving the news and withholding it, between the practices of journalism and the dictates of war, between the urge to inform and the passion to save lives, between common honesty and plain humanity."[28]

Carroll and others had had trouble with understanding and accepting the language of psychological warfare. "The Strategy of Truth," one of the OWI mottos, did not mean that honesty was to be insisted upon. Instead, truth in this context meant the utilization of facts to achieve desired goals. Were men like Carroll naïve? When Roosevelt told him to "tell the British they must plug the leaks in their censorship," Carroll was confused. He was supposed to deal with psychological warfare, not censorship. "It was a curious fact," wrote Carroll later on, "that the President who had established the Office of War Information never knew what it was doing and sometimes, apparently, confused it with the Office of Censorship. He had been opposed to the creation of a propaganda service and had established the OWI with considerable reluctance under pressure from his advisors whose primary aim was to provide an adequate flow of information to the American public." Secretary of State Hull asked, "Why doesn't Elmer Davis stop all this criticism of the State Department?" Other Cabinet officers and White House bureaucrats expected much of the same from the OWI. Newsmen like Carroll were asked to choose between the national good—the war effort in this case—and all they had learned about the nature of journalism. Either they would accept their roles as government propagandists, psychological warriors, and even espionage agents, or they would leave government service. Most stayed for the duration. The willingness to utilize news in the national interest carried on into the postwar period, when the conflict with communism replaced the one against Nazi aggressions. Davis, Carroll, and others would protest then that truth must be served and honesty prized. Such was not the first order of business in 1942–45, however.[29]

HOLLYWOOD AT WAR

There were no significant loyalty investigations of the radio industry in the late 1930s. In part this was due to the nature of the programming, which continued to be dominated by music, drama, and comedy shows. Liberal and conservative, pro- and antiwar legislators grumbled that some commentators were wrongheaded or even disloyal, but they could hardly investigate men like Kaltenborn, Murrow, Elmer Davis, or even Upton Close, for to do so would be to invite charges of interference with the freedom of the press. Charges that one radio star or another was disloyal would imply that his sponsor was a dupe, foolish, or disloyal too, and this could lead to serious repercussions for the legislators who made such accusations. Too, radio broadcasts had an ephemeral quality about them; once aired, they could not be recalled, and even textual criticism of a drama program appeared somewhat useless. Finally, there was no coherent radio community as such. Although New York continued to lead in programming, Holly wood and Chicago were also important centers, and by its very nature, network radio and news programs were nationwide in reach. Whatever community there was consisted of network executives, advertising agencies, and sponsors—not artists. Given the nature of the nation in the late 1930s, men such as these would more likely be attacked by liberals than conservatives, and rarely on loyalty issues.

The motion pictures were different. The industry had had censorship problems from the first, and these continued in the 1930s. Freedom of the press was not an issue for movies, although it was argued that the medium came under freedom of speech. Important films required a far larger investment than popular radio shows, while movie stars were more easily recognizable and better paid—and more difficult to create—than their radio counterparts. And there was a motion-picture community, in Hollywood, which already had been investigated for radical influences.

In late 1940 Representative Martin Dies, by then a familiar Hollywood nemesis, joined with Senator D. Worth Clark of Idaho to charge that the motion-picture industry was attempting to "incite the American public to war." Given the nature of war films in the 1920s and 1930s, the accusation was rather strange. Like most of the rest of the country, the industry was antiwar in this period. *The Big Parade, What Price Glory?, The Last Command, Wings, All Quiet on the Western Front, A Farewell to Arms, They Gave Him a Gun, Merchants of Death, Dawn Patrol,* the French-made but American-distributed *The Grand Illusion,* and even comedies like *Duck Soup* were all antiwar in one way or another. Whatever prowar films were produced dealt with Indian uprisings and European conflicts, in particular the British colonial wars of the nineteenth century. Soldiers and sailors were heroes of many B films in the 1930s, but these dealt with the peacetime service, and were more love story-musical comedy than prowar propaganda. *Blockade,* which was released in 1939, contained an antifascist message, and Dies referred to it on several occasions when asked to specify prowar productions. But the major release that year was *Gone With the Wind,* which was certainly antiwar. *The Great Dictator,* released the following year, was anti-Nazi, as were several minor efforts that dealt with German espionage in America. By then most opinion polls indicated that Americans favored the British and French and opposed Germany in the war. Hollywood was hardly in advance of American public opinion in this area.

Dies and Clark listed 17 films as being prowar, and these included *Escape* and *Foreign Correspondent.* The former was anti-Nazi, while the second, in which the hero was an American newspaperman, ended with a warning that unless America woke up in time, it could be destroyed by the enemy—meaning the Germans.

Industry leaders were embarrassed and troubled. After reaching bottom in 1933, motion-picture theater attendance had risen steadily for two years before leveling off. It rose again in 1937, set a record in 1939, and continued to climb in 1940 and 1941. There was some fear that contention would cause a dropoff in box-office receipts. Should the executives disown and fire the "political activists"? Or should they be defended? Will Hays realized that Dies and Clark were members of a dwindling minority and that their accusations would not stand scrutiny. In addition, then as before he opposed outside control of the industry. In August 1941 he attacked Clark. "No more false and shameful accusation could be made," he said, and then Hays retained Wendell Willkie, the defeated Republican presidential candidate in 1940, to defend the industry before Clark's Senate Interstate Commerce Committee. Willkie appeared before the committee in September and October, when pro-Allied sentiment was rising. "If you charge that the motion-picture industry as a whole and its leading executives as individuals are opposed to the Nazi dictatorship in Germany, if this is the case, there need be no investigation. We abhor everything Hitler represents." Clark argued that controls over propaganda films were needed, and indicated that Hollywood was engaged in propaganda activities. Hays responded by denying the charge. A major production cost in excess of a million dollars, he said, and experience had shown that the public is bored with propaganda of any kind. Would the Hollywood tycoons, who after all were businessmen, risk so much money on such a product? Willkie opposed all efforts at censorship. "No legislative body of any kind has in this country a right to dictate, or seek to dictate, to this or any of the arts, except in the broadest terms of common decency. Further, there is no right even to suggest to the motion-picture exhibitor what kind of pictures he should buy and present."[30]

The debate ended on December 7. The hearings were postponed and then dropped entirely. There would be no censorship from men like Dies and Clark. Did the war and full mobilization mean control from Washington? Roosevelt assured Hollywood that such would not be the case. "The American motion picture is one of our most effective mediums in informing and entertaining our citizens," he said in mid-December. "The motion picture must remain free insofar as national security will permit. I want no censorship of the motion picture." Then, in a separate memorandum, the President suggested that Hollywood's services would be required to assist in the war effort. The following month he named Lowell Mellett to the new post of co-ordinator of motion pictures. He was to work with the War Activities Committee, organized by the studio executives to co-operate with the government. Mellett said that "freedom of the screen is as important as freedom of press or of speech." Hollywood stars and executives would be granted exemptions from the military draft; they would be needed on the home front to sustain morale and in other ways serve the government's requirements.[31] Mellett had some kind words to say about Hollywood's prewar films. "Whether it was foresight, intuition or instinct, you saw what was happening in the world. You couldn't have done more in your efforts to educate people. The government, of course, was pleased, but we were unable to advertise what you were doing. Some misguided people in the Senate advertised the job you did, however. . . . Now nobody is concerned if the government frankly engaged in such co-operation. Now we can help you in your work."[32]

In this way, Mellett implied that the motion-picture industry indeed had worked to create a prowar sentiment in America, that perhaps Clark and Dies were correct. Furthermore, he would make certain the industry continued such efforts. The co-ordinator reiterated his intention not to censor films, but at the same time indicated that he expected Hollywood to co-operate with the Administration. The meaning of this was not clear, but Mellett implied that he would run the office in much the same fashion as Creel had run the CPI during World War I. This meant that Hollywood would produce government-sponsored films for exhibition in theaters, and be aware that any new feature turned out by the studios would be subject to his review.

Before this or any other program could be started, Roosevelt restructured the office. The Bureau of Motion Pictures was created, to be under the OWI. Mellett was shifted back to Washington, where he would be in charge of government liaison. Sam Spewack and William Montegue, Jr., two Broadway and Hollywood writer-producers, took care of propaganda operations and films, while Nelson Poynter and Fred Polangin took Mellett's place in Hollywood. Other changes in structure and personnel followed in 1943 and 1944. The film industry co-operated with the government whenever possible, but at times it was difficult to ascertain which office and official spoke for Washington.

In a series of position papers and manuals, Poynter and Polangin set down their ideas as to what kind of films and "messages" should be presented to the American people. Co-operation with the war effort was to be stressed, along with national unity and expectation of victory. Films with "war content"—by the end of the fighting this included approximately a quarter of all Hollywood productions—were to stress the issues of the war, the evil nature of the enemy, comradeship with allies, sacrifice on the home front, and the dedication of the American fighting man. When this created problems, Poynter suggested that all films be sent to his office for review, and this was done by early 1943. But it was hardly necessary. Americans welcomed both the escapist musicals and the war movies from 1942–45; the industry recorded excellent profits, and prosperity was widespread. Hollywood did not have to turn the war into a patriotic crusade, but it did reflect and reinforce already existing sentiments. Films such as *Air Force, Winged Victory, Walk in the Sun, A Guy Named Joe, The Purple Heart, So Proudly We Hail, The Story of GI Joe, Pearl Harbor, God Is My Copilot,* and *Wake Island,* among others, portrayed the American soldier and sailor as pure, clean, honest, and virtuous, while the enemy was sneaky, fanatical, cruel, and often stupid. The nation's leaders were intelligent, warm, and dedicated. In *Yankee Doodle Dandy* an actor protrayed Franklin Roosevelt, but his face wasn't shown—in the past, this had been done only for Jesus. Late in the war British actor Godfrey Tearle portrayed Roosevelt in full face, and there was some debate as to whether or not this was disrespectful. When in 1944 Paramount released *The Miracle of Morgan's Creek,* which poked fun at pompous patriotism, there was some question as to whether such a film should be allowed to play.

The Bureau of Motion Pictures co-operated fully with the industry, making military facilities available for background shots and releasing actors from the service to take leads in films. Few of the major war productions would have been possible without the assistance of the Army and Navy. At a time when ordnance and shells were in short supply in the Pacific, there were enough for use in the filming of pictures portraying the war in that part of the world. There was no major criticism of this practice, however, since it was assumed that the films not only helped morale on the home front, but in the armed forces as well.

The war films certainly were propagandistic in tone, at least insofar as popularizing the war effort was concerned. Were they more than that? In 1944, Twentieth Century-Fox released *Wilson*, a lavish production by Darryl Zanuck, which glorified the World War I President. It appeared to have a specific message, or at least some Republican congressmen found in it an appeal for the re-election of Roosevelt. The year before, Senator Rufus Holman of Oregon charged that Frank Capra's *Prelude to War* was an obvious appeal for a fourth Roosevelt term. To make matters worse, films such as these were shown to American servicemen, all of whom could vote by absentee ballot. If the film propaganda did exist and worked, the resulting vote would be overwhelmingly for Roosevelt.

A coalition of conservative Democrats and Republicans managed to kill the Bureau of Motion Pictures in 1943. The bureaucrats were reassigned to other duties, with Mellett going on a special mission to the Middle East. Hollywood continued to turn out propagandistic films, however, and the Army and Navy did not end co-operation in their filming. Like radio and other information and entertainment media, motion pictures did not have to be coerced into co-operating in the war effort. All that was needed was direction and initial guidance, and both of these had been established by 1943.

Up to the time of America's entry into the war, some radio and motion-picture artists had indicated their beliefs that the nation had some role to play in the conflict and might soon be drawn into it in one way or another. These stances drew criticisms from various quarters, so that debates between government and the artists in the case of films, and between network executives and news commentators in radio, were precipitated. Had the struggle lasted for several years, some kind of definitive resolution might have been achieved; either the government and business would have controlled news on radio and content of films in Hollywood, or the commentators and writers, artists, and directors would have achieved a measure of independence from their employers and the government. But this did not occur. Instead, the United States entered the war, and what was deemed radio and motion-picture bias in 1940 became patriotic zeal in 1942. Artist-performers in both media were now encouraged to express opinions, to support political causes—to do otherwise would leave one open to charges of being unpatriotic, perhaps even of sympathizing with the enemy. With this, the debate ended, to be replaced by what were considered the more important matters of survival.

What might happen when the war ended? Would those radio executives and motion-picture leaders, those government officials who encouraged editorializing on radio and "message" films feel the same way if any artist-performers insisted upon this right in peacetime? By the mid-1940s both radio and motion pictures were mature industries. Each had an array of stars, a cadre of leading artists. As a result of the war, they had become more prominent than ever before. No longer were they merely performers; such people had been utilized as opinionmakers, their ideas were considered important, and their influence was enormous.[33] Afterward, some artists would attempt to utilize their positions to continue these roles, and in the process reopen the prewar contest in a different fashion and on different battlefields.

At the same time many radio, newspaper, and motion-picture figures had entered government service and had been called upon to sacrifice objectivity and truth for the duration of the war. At the OWI, Elmer Davis, Carroll, and others like them had to measure the lives of servicemen against the right of people to know about their government through conventional channels such as newspapers and radio news programs. They came down on the side of saving lives. In more than one war film, a soldier would ask another, "What would you say if I told you that this mission, if successful, could end the war a month sooner?" The answer was obvious and always the same: "Let's get on with the mission, at any cost."

The costs would be high, and part of it paid with a different coin than expected in 1944. For if media played a greater role in World War II than in any previous conflict, they would face greater and more complex problems than ever before when the fighting had ended, and these due in large part to the methods by which information and ideology were used and transmitted from 1941–45. The end of the war not only marked the conclusion of the greatest military and ideological struggle in modern times, it also signified the coming of a new stage in the use of ideological weapons in films and on radio.

8

The Film as Battleground

Although the Office of War Information had been centered in Washington, and some of its battles fought in Europe and Asia, Hollywood had been the wartime propaganda capital. Newspapers and radio had carried patriotic messages, but these were not serious rivals for the motion pictures. In addition to actually making films, the stars had engaged in war bond drives, supported rallies, and entertained troops overseas. Studio executives had been in close contact with Mellett and others at the Bureau of Motion Pictures, while OWI directives were followed promptly and in a patriotic spirit. The industry prospered; almost any film turned out made profits. The public spent $809 million on the movies in 1941; by 1945, the figure had risen to $1.5 billion. Americans still listened to their radios, but wartime prosperity, the desire for inexpensive entertainment away from the home, and the yearning for both war films and escapist musicals and comedies resulted in increased attendance at motion-picture theaters.[1]

Davis, Mellett, and other OWI leaders were delighted with the co-operation given them by Hollywood, and they scarcely had to interfere with operations once the main themes had been established. The OWI and other agencies did produce propaganda films of their own, just as Creel had done in World War I, but these were shown in theaters as added features, never main attractions. Director Frank Capra, a lieutenant colonel during the war, produced the *Why We Fight* series, while other Hollywood veterans worked with the armed forces to turn out battle films, including John Huston's *The Battle for San Pietro* and *Let There Be Light*, John Ford's *Battle of Midway*, and William Wyler's *Memphis Belle*, all done in documentary style, without stars, and in such a way as to combine Hollywood techniques with those of the "documentaries." They were not very popular, however, for the public appeared more willing to accept John Wayne, Van Johnson, Richard Conte, and Dana Andrews as war heroes than on-the-spot movies of real happenings.

Seldom during the war did Washington attempt to influence the production of commercial films; when it did, the results were either boring or blatant propaganda. *Mission to Moscow* was the most obvious example of this genre. Urged upon Jack Warner by Roosevelt and based upon the book by Ambassador Joseph E. Davies, who had represented the United States in the U.S.S.R. before the war, the picture was released in mid-1943 with a well-financed publicity campaign. It opened with a shot of Davies himself, an open-faced individual, telling the audience that it was about to witness "the truth as I saw it." The film had no true story line. It began in 1936, with Emperor Haile Selassie of Ethiopia asking for aid against Italian aggression. Soon after, Davies, a businessman, was called to Roosevelt's office. As had become the practice, the audience did not see the President's face; he remained a man in an armchair, speaking with an almost disembodied voice, as though to a huge multitude over radio. In the picture Davies, as played by Walter Huston, was a handsome, intelligent-looking person, with a homey midwestern air of truth about him. He has conversations with actors playing Churchill, Stalin, various Soviet leaders, and others—all of whom recite as though from texts, and in a fashion that resembled "the March of Time" radio shows. Toward the end of the picture, Davies appears at a large rally to explain Soviet practices to an American audience. He is asked many questions, including several about Soviet-Nazi co-operation before 1942 and one regarding the Soviet attack upon Finland, and in each case, Davies answers in a fashion geared to promote Soviet-American relations.

There was nothing subtle about the film. Liberal critic James Agee asked, "Is it a federally subsidized or Lend-Lease? Are the sacred treatment of the President and the adroit suggestion that all isolationists were Republicans parts of a deal or good will? We can only suspect, through rumor and internal inference, that the Stalinists here stole or were handed such a march that the film is almost describable as the first Soviet production to come from a major American studio." Yet Agee thought that both as a motion picture and as a wartime tool, *Mission to Moscow* was significant. "Not entirely without skill, it inaugurates for a great general audience a kind of pamphleteering and of at least nominal nonfiction whose responsibilities, whose powers for good or evil, enlightenment or deceit, are appalling; and of which we are likely to get a great deal from now on."[2] Others had harsher things to say about the film. Philosopher John Dewey thought it was "anti-British, anti-Congress, anti-Democratic, and anti-truth." Columnists Anne O'Hare McCormick and Dorothy Thompson criticized the film, as did philosopher Sidney Hook and Soviet expert Eugene Lyons, and their attacks were in turn criticized by others, including Senator Claude Pepper of Florida, writers Theodore Dreiser and Walter Duranty, and composer Fritz Mahler, as a "distinct disservice to the cause of American-Soviet unity during the war and afterward."

Agee was incorrect in believing that *Mission to Moscow* would be the first of many such films. In fact, it was the last. After the war, however, it would be cited repeatedly as an indication that Hollywood was dominated by Communists. The community had successfully withstood assaults from Congressman Dies and others before the war, in part because the earlier accusers could not specify films with pro-Soviet content. In *Mission to Moscow*, however, Warner Brothers provided congressional and other investigators with a prime exhibit.

In retrospect, it would appear that 1943 had marked the height of Allied unity, at least insofar as Hollywood was concerned. *The Moon Is Down, This Land Is Mine, Hangmen Also Die, The Commandos, Edge of Darkness, Cross of Lorraine, Song of Russia,* and *North Star* all presented the nation's allies in a favorable light. At the time and afterward, it would be charged that these and others—especially English war films—had been overt propaganda, urged upon Hollywood by Washington and political activists at the studios. In no case would these accusations be proved; these films merely reflected the general pro-Allied, one-world sentiment so popular at the time.

In 1944 and 1945, however, the stress turned away from foreigners and toward the American soldiers and sailors. *Air Force, Sahara, A Walk in the Sun, The Story of GI Joe,* and *The Purple Heart* were leading examples of such films. In these and others like them, the protagonists would engage in fighting but also talk about the reasons for the war and their hopes for the future. The scripts included references to "the right to boo the Dodgers" and the importance of the freedoms to differ with the government and "speak my mind out," but more often than not the phrases were personal; the fighting men, as seen by filmmakers, were more interested in a secure job, a decent home, "the girl next door," a promising future, and close family ties. It was a middle-class dream—one that might have been expected from the young men of a depression period who had entered the Army just as the nation was coming out of its economic slump. The talk was not revolutionary, but some sensed that the film warriors would be as intent upon "making a lasting and durable peace" as they were in killing the "Japs" and "Krauts" in their movies.

Unlike World War I, the second conflict did not produce a great war film, or even a great war novel; World War I's *The Big Parade* would not have a counterpart in the Hollywood of the late 1940s and early 1950s. *Battleground* (1949), *Command Decision* (1949), and *Twelve O'Clock High* (1950), among others, had a great measure of popularity, but even at the time of their release, they were not considered major efforts or "message films." Instead, Hollywood concentrated upon escapism once more, and although there were some films with social content, these were deemed of secondary importance, often produced on low budgets. One might have expected several major productions in 1946 celebrating the victory, but the big five studios were wary of the theme, in part because they didn't know how to handle it, but also as a result of a continued demand for more frivolous entertainment.

THE BEST YEARS OF OUR LIVES

There was one such production that year, *The Best Years of Our Lives,* and despite its anomalous position it was also one of the most significant films ever produced by Hollywood, and one of the most celebrated. *The Best Years* won the New York Film Critics' Award as the best film of 1946, and went on to all but sweep the Academy Awards. In 1947, it was released to the European market, and was enthusiastically received there—even in Germany. Some critics complained it was not a well-made film, that there was no central story, and that on occasion the acting was maudlin, the direction weak. "At its worst this story is very annoying in its patness, its timidity, its slithering attempts to pretend to face and by that pretense to dodge in the most shameful way possible its own fullest meanings and possibilities," wrote James Agee. It would be possible, he conceded, "to call the whole picture just one long pious piece of deceit and self-deceit, embarrassed by hot flashes of talent, conscience, truthfulness, and dignity. And it is anyhow more than possible, it is unhappily obligatory, to observe that a good deal which might have been very fine, even great, and which is handled mainly by people who could have done, and done perfectly, all the best that could have been developed out of the idea, is here either murdered in its cradle or reduced to manageable good citizenship in the early stages of grade school." Despite this, Agee recognized the film's power. "I can hardly expect that anyone who reads this will like the film as well as I do. . . . It is also a great pleasure, and equally true, to say that it shows what can be done in the factory by people of adequate talent when they get, or manage to make themselves, the chance."[3] Bosley Crowther of the New York *Times* thought the film was "cut . . . from the heart-wood of contemporary American life. . . . It gives off a warm glow of affection for everyday, down-to-earth folks." In his year-end review of 1946 films, veteran writer Terry Ramsaye said the picture "is entirely in the tried and long-proved pattern which has made the American screen product successful merchandise. Art has its little moments, but merchandising is in happy control."

So was ideology, for this was a message film of the highest order. While the nation awaited the great war novel and motion picture, Hollywood produced, instead, a major postwar epic.[4]

Americans had been instructed by films on how to react to and behave during the war. Servicemen had learned what was expected of them by watching Hollywood heroes in studio production. *The Best Years of Our Lives* was entertainment and art, but more important, it was a primer intended to spell out for civilians what they might anticipate from the homecoming, and for servicemen what the future might bring. If *Mission to Moscow* had demon-

strated how Hollywood and Washington could use the club to hammer home a propaganda message, *The Best Years* represented the way of the scalpel, for it lacked much of the awkwardness and sententiousness of most propaganda films. Furthermore, it was convincing because those involved in the production truly believed the message and did not have to be instructed in what to do or say by Washington.

Samuel Goldwyn, Robert Sherwood, and William Wyler were more responsible than anyone else for the production, message, and structure of the film. Their views, ideals, and backgrounds were quite dissimilar. Although Goldwyn and Wyler had collaborated often before the war, they were not close, while Sherwood always was more at home in New York than Hollywood. Of course, Goldwyn was one of the Hollywood pioneers, an immigrant Jew who had helped organize the industry and give it a direction. Like most of the immigrant founders, Goldwyn was intensely patriotic and optimistic. He believed strongly in middle-class values and the central role of the family. "My idea of making motion pictures, the idea that fascinated me originally, was that films are family entertainment, a place where everyone can go and not blush over what they see on the screen." In the 1930s, while associated with United Artists as an independent producer, he was noted for a series of musicals featuring the "Goldwyn Girls," but he also produced *Dodsworth, Dead End, These Three*, and *The Little Foxes*. He had not made a patriotic film during the war, even though one might have been expected from him. Instead, Goldwyn had produced *Up in Arms, Wonder Man*, and *The Kid from Brooklyn* (all musical comedies with Danny Kaye), and other light films. One reason for this was his belief that the public needed escapism during the war; but in addition, Goldwyn hadn't been able to locate a good property, and there were rumors that he was on the decline and could no longer count on his old financial backers.

William Wyler, who was forty-four years old in 1946, had come to America from Germany (with stops in France and Switzerland) after World War I. A nephew of Carl Laemmle, he worked for a while as an office boy at Universal before entering films as a director of two-reelers in 1925. During the next two years he made twenty-one films, none of them memorable. In the early talkie period, Wyler directed *Hell's Heroes, The Storm,*

Tom Brown of Culver, *The Good Fairy*, and other low-budget or skimpily produced efforts for Universal, emerging with a reputation as a hard worker but little else. In 1935 he made *The Gay Deception* for Twentieth Century-Fox, his first non-Universal film, and the following year he signed a three-picture contract with Goldwyn, with the understanding that the first film would be *These Three*, which was based upon the Lillian Hellman stage play about homosexuality. Later that year Wyler directed *Dodsworth* and *Come and Get It*, also for Goldwyn and released by United Artists. Wyler soon became one of the most prominent American directors, his films including *Dead End*, *Jezebel*, *Wuthering Heights*, *The Letter*, *The Little Foxes*, and, just before he entered the armed forces, *Mrs. Miniver*. While on duty with the Air Force, he directed *Memphis Belle*, which was about the final mission of a Flying Fortress of that name and concentrated upon the crew. On one flight, Wyler experienced ear trouble, and for a while he was deafened. Although his hearing gradually returned, he became sensitive to the problems of disabled veterans.

When Wyler left the service, he and several other directors planned to organize a new company, Liberty Films, which would produce socially aware dramas to reflect the values of the new kind of nation they hoped would come out of the war. Wyler, George Stevens, Frank Capra, and others worked out arrangements with RKO, which would distribute the films, and they were prepared to begin work in late 1945. But they needed money, which could only be earned through working for established producers; in addition, Wyler owed Goldwyn a picture under his prewar contract.

Born in New Rochelle, New York, in 1896, Robert Sherwood had served in World War I, having been gassed and wounded, and released from the armed forces in 1919. For a while he worked as a journalist, and in 1927 his first important play, *The Road to Rome*, was produced on Broadway. It was followed by several others, including *Waterloo Bridge*, *Reunion in Vienna*, *The Petrified Forest*, *Idiot's Delight*, and, in 1938, *Abe Lincoln in Illinois*, his most famous play. In addition, Sherwood wrote many screenplays, and for a while divided his efforts between Broadway and Hollywood. On the eve of World War II, he was considered one of the nation's leading playwrights and certainly its most success-

ful, having won two Pulitzer Prizes (a third would follow in 1941). In addition, he was well known as a wit and, upon occasion, wrote speeches for President Roosevelt.

During the war, Sherwood traveled between Washington, New York, and London in his function as executive at the Office of Co-ordinator of Information of the OWI. He saw espionage activities being planned, outright falsehoods being released by government agencies, and the United States striking deals with Italian and German fascists and Nazis. The experiences of this period disturbed Sherwood, who looked upon the war as a crusade for social justice. Although Roosevelt knew much of what was happening—and Sherwood must have realized that the President had initiated some of the programs he detested—the playwright continued to work on presidential speeches, always introducing elements of idealism and optimism into them. He hoped the compromises made during the war could be justified by the accomplishments of peace. In May 1944, just before leaving the OWI, Sherwood wrote an essay on the subject, "Joe Legion, Private First Class," which presented the enlisted man as a democratic, decent, humane, and idealistic individual who could be counted upon to preserve and extend democracy after the war.[5]

Before the war, Sherwood had sued Goldwyn for withholding his salary while he worked on the film *Roman Scandals*. But the two men had collaborated on other films, and although they were by no means close friends, they knew they could work with one another. Similarly, Wyler and Goldwyn, both rigid men with sharp tempers, had clashed in the 1930s, even while on the same film. In 1946, however, all were interested in making a motion picture about the meaning of the war. Each was quite emotional about the subject, as was much of the rest of the country. Goldwyn brought Wyler and Sherwood together, and for a while it appeared they would do a film together based on the life of General Eisenhower. This project was dropped, however, and Goldwyn gave Wyler a short story he had recently purchased, *Glory for Me*, by MacKinlay Kantor, thinking it might be an acceptable substitute. It involved the difficulties three veterans had in making adjustment to civilian life. Air Force Captain Fred Derry, a soda jerk before the war, almost turns to crime, but in the end goes into partnership with a friend and opens a drugstore. Infantry Sergeant Al Stephenson, a banker before the war, cannot adjust, insists upon giving loans to veterans who are bad credit risks, and finally leaves banking to become a farmer. Sailor Homer Parrish has been wounded and is a spastic. He cannot accept either the wounds or the attempts on the part of his friends and family to help him, and becomes an alcoholic. There were elements of hope and optimism in *Glory for Me*, but for the most part, it left readers with a pessimistic view of the future.

Wyler was interested in Kantor's idea and the basic structure of the story, but he rejected the bleak conclusions. Working with Sherwood, he decided to end each story on a note of hope, even triumph, and in addition weave them more closely together than they had been in the original version. Captain Derry takes his old job as soda jerk, falls in love with Sergeant Stephenson's daughter (and separates from his flashy wartime wife, who is no longer interested in him), and quits work in despair. At one point he wanders into a "graveyard" for World War II planes—the implication being that he, too, might be ready for the scrap heap. But he talks with a foreman there, who tells him that the planes will be broken down and used to help make homes. He takes a laborer's job—like the planes, he will be recycled—and the audience is left with the idea that in time he will become a successful builder, marry Peggy Stephenson, and live a comfortable upper-middle-class life.

Sergeant Stephenson does go back to the bank in the screen version, and he makes chancy loans to returning GIs—one in particular to a man who hopes to become a farmer. He is criticized for this, but mildly; his superiors note that the veteran lacks the proper collateral for the loan. One evening, while half drunk, he gives a speech at the local country club, in which he speaks of the sacrifices made by soldiers and sailors in the war—when they were not asked for collateral—and he charges that America is doomed unless it gives returning veterans a decent chance based upon their character and performance in war, and not upon net-worth statements. In the film Stephenson convinces the bank executives he is right, and he remains on the job, prepared to fight for those who will get ahead by helping themselves.

Wyler and Sherwood made the greatest alterations in the story of Homer Parrish. The role was played by a nonactor, Harold Russell, a sergeant who had lost both hands during maneuvers in North Carolina and who had learned to use artificial limbs with great dexterity. As in the Kantor story, Homer has troubles adjusting to his new status—this part of the film was clearly a primer for disabled veterans and even includes a statement about pensions and medical help available. His parents and friends also have to learn how to behave toward him, and his fiancée is presented as intelligent and understanding. Homer learns to accept his status, and in the end he marries, with Al and Fred at the wedding. All, so Sherwood, Wyler, and Goldwyn indicate, will live in "the best years of their lives."

The film was well made, on a large budget. Its key scenes—Al's banking dinner speech, Fred's despair at the airplane graveyard, and Homer's being helped by his fiancée in taking off his artificial arms—were applauded by critics throughout the world. By all accounts, American audiences found the film inspirational, and exhibitors reported that many customers would return to see the film several times. A decade later, some critics and filmmakers would find *The Best Years of Our Lives* exaggerated, sentimental, and trite, even while they applauded Wyler's cinematography and parts of Sherwood's script. These were so good, said John Howard Lawson, that they "conceal the fact that the story has no positive center, and that the four [three?] men trying to adjust themselves to civilian life find nothing which offers an answer to their search for dignity and hope."[6]

At the time, however, the opposite seemed true. The war had ended, and many Americans seemed uneasy and concerned. Would the nation re-enter the depression? Had anything been learned from the sacrifices? Would there be another major war in a generation or so? Already there were indications of economic and social dislocations at home and the first signs of the Cold War in Europe. Franklin Roosevelt was dead, and his successor, Harry Truman, seemed insecure and indecisive. There appeared to be no one capable of indicating the direction of the peace or of inspiring the nation the way Roosevelt had done in 1933.

The Best Years of Our Lives certainly did not answer these questions; none of those involved with its production even attempted to address himself to the leadership gap. The film did offer a morality and a philosophy, along with an interesting story, good writing, and direction. The characters were plausible. Drawing upon experiences with documentaries, it had been shot in such a way as to stress reality, even while it obviously was a Hollywood product. Before the war, motion pictures had been used to present ideas, but with this film, the medium was employed to reflect national aspirations as interpreted by its creators as never before; it was more successful than any of those involved in its production believed possible.

Film as government propaganda had become respectable during the war, even when as obvious and crude as *Mission to Moscow.* With the release and acceptance of *The Best Years of Our Lives,* it appeared that the propaganda aspect—for directors, producers, writers, and perhaps even for actors and actresses—might continue afterward as well, even within the studio structure. This film was a personal statement on the part of its creators. Did its success mean that films would be used in this fashion in the future? If so, it would indicate that Hollywood and the artists would dominate the industry, not New York and the financiers. This, too, was a significant aspect of the film, although it was not considered important or even especially noteworthy in 1946.

Goldwyn continued to produce pictures in the 1940s and 1950s. For the most part, these were musical comedies—*The Secret Life of Walter Mitty, Hans Christian Andersen, Guys and Dolls,* and *Porgy and Bess,* for example. Never again would Goldwyn attempt so ambitious a "message film"; nor, for that matter, would many other Hollywood leaders in the late 1940s and early 1950s.

Robert Sherwood went on to write the prize-winning history *Roosevelt and Hopkins,* and received many awards in the next few years. But there was little call for his services in Hollywood, and he remained in New York, working for the stage and, toward the end of his life, television.

Wyler joined Liberty Films. Alone of the three, he tried to emulate the independence and idealism portrayed by the heroes of *The Best Years of Our Lives.* Liberty hoped to produce contentious films, dealing with ethical and moral questions not ordinarily touched upon by Hollywood. Its first film, *It's a Wonderful Life,* was directed by Capra, and as with almost all of his films, stressed the importance of love and decency against selfishness and greed; in some respects, it resembled *Mr. Smith Goes to Washington* or *Mr. Deeds Goes to Town.* Liberty purchased rights to the political comedy *State of the Union,* and Jessamyn West's novel about conscientious objection in the Civil War, *Friendly Persuasion.* But the company foundered, especially when

State of the Union was charged with being Communist propaganda. In the end, Liberty Films collapsed, the remnants taken over by Paramount. The studio system had prevailed. Wyler's first film for Paramount—his first since *The Best Years*—was *The Heiress,* a dramatization of Henry James' novel *Washington Square.* It was followed by *Detective Story* (1951), *Carrie* (1952), *Roman Holiday* (1953), and *The Desperate Hours* (1955). Like Goldwyn and Sherwood, Wyler himself did not make contentious films, at least until the late 1950s. New York still dominated Hollywood; so, for that matter, did Washington.

Like most other industries, motion pictures faced problems of conversion to a peacetime economy in 1946. There were shortages of raw materials, as well as talk of economic recession and a wave of strikes. In February, the New York tugboat operators walked out, halting fuel deliveries, which forced motion-picture theaters to close. Despite this, attendance soared, with receipts reaching a record $1.7 billion. All the major studios showed higher earnings, and their stocks rose steadily in a rather indecisive market.

The American motion-picture industry released 252 features in 1946, more than 100 below the prewar level, but well above 1945's 234. Shortages of film stock resulted in fewer prints being made of each picture, and because of this and the growing demand, the producers were able to ask for and receive higher rental fees from the independent exhibitors. To add to the cheering outlook, the prewar leading men were being released from the services, and most were busily engaged in making comeback pictures.

There were some short-term problems and unanswered questions in the midst of this euphoria, some of which appeared serious at the time, but quickly proved minor. For example, would the public still want to see the old stars in their new pictures? Had the millions of dollars that had been invested promoting the careers of men like Clark Gable, James Stewart, Robert Taylor, and others been dissipated? Would these artists retain their prewar glamor? On these scores at least, the studios did well. If anything, the old stars were more popular than they had been before the war.

Then there was the matter of content. From 1942–45, the major studios had concentrated on war films. It seemed questionable that the public would still want to see such pictures, and yet the studios were uncertain as to their replacements. Would the next cycle be led by musicals, gangster epics, Westerns, or comedies? Or would the public insist upon new themes? Since a major production might require an investment of over $2 million, this was a serious matter for both Hollywood and the New York banks that controlled the studios. But this fear too proved exaggerated, as the varied Hollywood products of the late 1940s received wide acceptance.

Three additional long-term challenges would not be so easily faced or met. One involved television (some thought of it in terms of a wedding of movies and radio), which had been talked about for more than twenty years. Commercial television might have been introduced on a wide scale in the early 1940s, but the war intervened. Now the radio firms were tooling up for a major effort. Still, only 6,500 receivers were sold in 1946, and these at high prices with dubious reception and few programs to view. Clearly television would be a threat, but most motion-picture industry leaders seemed convinced that the public would not abandon the wide screen for the miniscule tube.

The second challenge was in the courts, where the antitrust litigations that had begun in the 1920s continued. The government allowed the Paramount case to lapse in the early stages of the war, but it was reactivated in August 1944, and several other cases were added in 1945 and 1946. Yet the final decision might be as much as a decade away, and the worst that might happen would be a divestiture of theaters by the studios. In 1946, slightly more than 17 per cent of all the nation's theaters were owned by the big five studios, with Paramount alone accounting for almost 8 per cent. More important, the studio theaters dominated the major urban markets. Divestiture would seriously damage the industry, but given time to prepare for all eventualities, even this might be overcome.

In time the television and antitrust issues would combine in such a way as to force major changes in Hollywood's structure, product, and philosophy, and in ways almost completely unexpected in 1946. In the immediate postwar period, however, a third problem became paramount—the challenge from Washington's congressional investigation.

THE MOVIE INDUSTRY ON TRIAL

Already there were signs that the Cold War was being born. Secretary of State James Byrnes and Soviet Foreign Minister V. M. Molotov were trading insults and could not agree upon a German peace treaty. In the United States, the great debate over foreign policy was commencing. The political left called for co-operation with the U.S.S.R. and disarmament, while the right wing demanded opposition to Soviet influence in Europe and Asia and a strong "fortress America." President Truman appeared indecisive, not knowing which way to turn or which policy to accept. This problem, added to those of conversion, inflation, shortages, labor unrest, and a general insecurity, resulted in a Republican victory in the 1946 congressional elections. For the first time since the early 1930s, the Democrats were in a minority position in Congress. Republicans, who for more than a decade had criticized the New Deal and the Roosevelt foreign policies, were now in positions to do something about them and seek symbolic as well as real victories in preparation for the 1948 presidential election.

In 1945 Representative John Rankin of Mississippi, a Democrat, almost single-handedly engineered the establishment of the Committee on Un-American Activities. A rabid anti-Semite, anti-Catholic, and anti-Negro, who was convinced that all three groups were conspiring to create a Communist tyranny in America, Rankin hoped this committee would expose the malefactors and prepare legislation not unlike the sedition and espionage laws of the World War I period. The Un-American Activities Committee conducted some indecisive hearings in 1945 and 1946, and although there was some talk that it would be discontinued in the new Eightieth Congress, its appropriation was renewed. Democratic Chairman John Wood of Georgia stepped down, and was succeeded by Republican J. Parnell Thomas of New Jersey, who immediately announced an eight-point program, one of which was an investigation of Communist influences in Hollywood.[7]

The inclusion of the Hollywood investigation was Rankin's

idea. In early 1945, while acting committee chairman, he told reporters that "one of the most dangerous plots ever instigated for the overthrow of this government has its headquarters in Hollywood. The information we get is that this is the greatest hotbed of subversive activities in the United States. We're on the trail of the tarantula now, and we're going to follow through. The best people in California are helping us." Rankin went on to talk about coded German messages being placed in films that were shown in England and other such charges, none of which he would detail or substantiate; nor would he name his sources for the information. Chairman Wood dissociated himself from the charges once he took over. "We are not going to waste time on small birds," he said. "The committee is not going to do any witch hunting." And for a while, it appeared the Hollywood investigation would be ignored, as Wood and his colleagues investigated labor unions and the Communist party.

In May 1947, a subcommittee headed by Thomas went to Hollywood to hear testimony from several witnesses at a closed session. Actors Adolphe Menjou and Robert Taylor appeared, as did studio head Jack Warner. On the basis of their testimony, Thomas planned a full-scale investigation in the fall. In his report he wrote, "Scores of screen writers who are Communists have infiltrated into the various studios and it has been through this medium that most of the Communist propaganda has been injected into the movies." He planned to subpoena "Communist actors, writers, directors, and producers and confront them in public session with the testimony and evidence against them."[8]

The investigations, then, were to deal with the impact of communism and Communists in Hollywood. This was the view presented to the general public, and given the enlarged scope of anti-Communist investigations in the late 1940s and early 1950s, especially those conducted by Senator Joseph McCarthy, it would appear that the inquiry into Communist infiltration of films was the first barrage in the battle. But there was far more to it than that. On the committee's side, Thomas and Rankin had other interests. The Republican chairman was intent on discrediting the New Deal, while Rankin continued to mount his personal campaign against sinister foreign influences against white Protestant America.

Many of Hollywood's leading producers, directors, and actors had been sympathetic to the New Deal and, of course, co-operated fully with the government during the war. Did enthusiastic support for Roosevelt the war leader imply total acceptance of his social and economic policies? And if this were the case, need they be defended now that the Republican reaction had begun? Such questions bothered Hollywood's leaders in 1946, as they did the New York bankers.

The motion-picture industry in California continued to be led by Jews, many of whom were foreign born. Anti-Semitism had remained strong in America in the 1930s, and although some film figures were willing to identify themselves as Jews, others tried to hide or play down their religion. This was understandable, perhaps, in an industry that tried to sell its products to the broad spectrum of Americans, many of whom might not be willing to accept Jews in leading roles. Thus the motion-picture industry's leaders had been unwilling to sponsor an appeal for the formation of a Jewish army in Palestine in the early years of the war. David Selznick told screenwriter Ben Hecht, who organized the appeal, "I don't want anything to do with your cause for the simple reason that it's a Jewish political cause. And I am not interested in Jewish political problems. I'm an American and not a Jew." This attitude was heightened when, in 1943 and 1944, some right-wing organizations claimed that the United States had been dragged into the war by American Jews interested in saving their German coreligionists. Then, in 1946, when Zionists maneuvered for the organization of a Jewish state in Palestine, anti-Semitism seemed once again on the rise—even after the disclosures of the mass killings in Germany. Now the Un-American Activities Committee, with John Rankin the leading Democrat, was threatening to expose communism in Hollywood. The film industry's Jewish leaders, fearful of what might occur and troubled about charges of radicalism, were susceptible to arguments that it would be wise to join the anti-Communist crusade.

To this was added the union difficulties of the immediate post-war period. During the war, the Hollywood labor unions had been racketeer-dominated, and some of the studio chiefs worked in harmony with them. But there was an opposition group, headed by Herb Sorrell, a former prize fighter, known as the Conference of Studio Unions. Industry leaders and the old established locals tried to attack the CSU as being controlled by Communists, and accused Sorrell of "following the party line." In 1945 Sorrell led a strike against Warner Brothers, at which Jack Warner—known as a New Dealer and a personal friend of Roosevelt—hired private police and strike breakers to attack the pickets. Violence erupted, at which time the National Labor Relations Board entered the picture and settled matters. But the troubles continued, so that by 1946 it appeared that the major studios might have to deal in the future with independent unions unwilling to enter into "sweetheart" contracts.[9] Thus it behooved the industry's leaders—some of them, at least—to raise the Communist issue and to co-operate with the House Un-American Activities Committee. By so acting they would not only affirm their pro-American sentiments, but also help rid Hollywood of what they considered to be troublemakers.

The Screen Actors' Guild and the Screen Writers' Guild maintained official neutrality during the strike, but this did not mean that their members were neutral as well. For the most part, the actors' organization had had fairly modest ambitions in the 1930s and early 1940s. The situation was different with the writers. In the mid-1930s, a left-wing faction headed by John Howard Lawson, attempted to organize the Guild along political lines, hoping that in this fashion the unified writers could challenge the studios not only economically, but also in the realm of ideas, thus obliging the industry to turn out more films dealing with social problems. Lawson and others of his group were challenged by a right-wing conservative faction led by Rupert Hughes and James K. McGuinness, who later charged that Lawson tried to make the Guild an "instrument of Communist power." Hughes formed the Screen Playwrights, a rival organization, which for a while battled the Guild for leadership of the organized writers. When the Guild won a National Labor Relations Board election, Hughes and McGuinness organized the Motion Picture Alliance for the Preservation of American Ideals, a small group that continued to charge the Guild with being Communist-dominated. In 1946, however, the Guild was headed by Emmet Lavery, a moderate, and the left-wing influence appeared on the wane. Hughes described Lavery as "a man whose views are Communist, whose friends are Communists, and whose work is communistic." But he would go no farther, realizing perhaps that among other things,

Lavery was a lawyer and might sue for slander and libel. In any case, the industry knew that Lavery was a mild liberal, who on occasion had criticized even the New Deal as being too advanced. But despite this, the Screen Writers' Guild and Sorrell's CSU troubled the studios, which would have liked to be rid of both.

Finally the studios were concerned about the growing independence of some of their artists. They had returned from the wars with heightened senses of idealism, and some desired to use films in the fight against social injustices. These people were by no stretch of the imagination Communists or even what later came to be known as "fellow travelers." Rather they had been moderate New Dealers or politically apathetic prior to the war. Some had worked with the OWI and other government agencies, turning out films that explained the reasons for the conflict, and the ideals for which the war was being fought. These included not only the destruction of fascism, but also the creation of a better world—words like "brotherhood," "toleration," and "justice" appeared in many screenplays considered for production in 1945 and 1946. Some of these were written by individuals considered radical, members of the left-wing faction of the Screen Writers' Guild. *The Best Years of Our Lives* led the way in 1946. It was followed in 1947 by *The Naked City* (a pioneer documentary effort), *Boomerang* (critical of the court system), and *Gentlemen's Agreement* and *Crossfire* (concerned with anti-Semitism). Then Hollywood released *Home of the Brave* and *Intruder in the Dust* (about racial bigotry), *All the King's Men* (critical of native fascism), *The Snake Pit* (about conditions in mental institutions), and *Pinky* (about racial relations in America). All had dramatic appeal and entertainment values as well as social content, but they clearly were "message films." In the first years of the postwar period, it appeared that the new wave for Hollywood would consist of documentary-style exposés and social criticisms. Such films dominated awards ceremonies, and all the studios had plans for additional ones.[10]

At the same time, some moviemakers revived the concept of independent producing units, which would release their products through established studios, but obtain financing on their own and also control talent on all levels. Goldwyn remained the leading example of how it might be done, while Liberty Films provided another model. If indeed the antitrust decision forced the studios to relinquish their theaters, then independent producers might proliferate and in the end force the studios into secondary roles. Even then it appeared that the New York banks would be interested in supporting lean, flexible units, which would shoot on location rather than in a studio, rent equipment when needed, and might lure established stars from their home bases with percentage contracts. In terms of the nature of the industry, especially in its internal structure, this was the most serious threat of them all.

By mid-1947, the Cold War was on in earnest. Already the Truman administration had begun to investigate suspected radicals in government, while Henry Wallace, the leading spokesman for those who still admired the U.S.S.R. and hoped for peacetime co-operation, had left the Administration and was planning to run for the presidency. As various anti-Communist forces gained power in the United States, the backing for the Un-American Activities Committee grew. Still, few at the time truly understood the dimensions of the situation and all of its ramifications. Hollywood's liberal forces—a majority at the time—resented the probe. In May 1947, the Association of Motion Picture Producers stated that "Hollywood is weary of being the national whipping boy for congressional committees," clearly referring to the old Dies investigations, and expecting that J. Parnell Thomas was in the same rather pathetic mold. "We are tired of having irresponsible charges made again and again and not sustained. If we have committed a crime we want to know it. If not, we should not be badgered by congressional committees." Shortly before the hearings began, *Life* magazine, then considered a conservative periodical, ran a report on the investigations and asked, "Congressional committee poses a question: Is it un-American to ask a man if he is a Communist—or un-American to refuse to answer?"

In the past, Will Hays had defended the film industry against Washington through the skillful use of political influence and a keen knowledge of tactics. Hays had retired as director of the Motion Picture Association of America in 1945 and had been succeeded by Eric Johnston, a tall, handsome, 48-year-old ex-businessman who was then in government service. Johnston had managed his family's appliance business in the 1930s and made a name for himself in the area of employee relations. A moderate Republican, he was elected president of the United States Chamber of Commerce and was able to heal the breach between that organization and the New Deal. Johnston ran for a Senate seat from Washington in 1940 and was hailed as one of the new breed of Republicans who would consolidate Democratic gains if elected. But he failed at the polls, and instead took several jobs with the Administration, most of them in the area of union-management relations. Johnston was responsible for organized labor's no-strike pledge in 1942, and he soon became one of Roosevelt's major links with the business community. By 1944, he had excellent connections in Washington, and was a well-recognized national figure. That year, just before taking the position in Hollywood, Johnston visited the Soviet Union and was most impressed with what he saw. "When peace is restored, Russia and the United States will possess the greater share of the world's military and industrial power," he said in 1945. "The destiny of the world in large measure will depend upon the understanding and co-operation that will exist between Russia and the United States."

Just as Will Hays had used his political influence to defend Hollywood against the would-be censors of the 1920s, so it was expected that Johnston would do the same against the anti-Communists of the 1940s. To accomplish these ends, he organized a powerful staff. Paul V. McNutt, a former governor of Indiana and high commissioner of the Philippines—who at one time was seriously mentioned as Roosevelt's successor—was retained as special counsel. Maurice Benjamin, one of the ablest attorneys in the nation, was to help him. In the wings was James Byrnes, the former governor of South Carolina, Supreme Court justice, and Secretary of State, retained to provide special assistance if and when needed. The industry had very big guns indeed, and this, bolstered by the belief that the Thomas committee had no real evidence of Communist infiltration, along with memories of past victories over Martin Dies, encouraged those who thought the hearings would be short and unimportant.

During the late spring and throughout the summer of 1947 dozens of major Hollywood stars, writers, directors, and producers issued statements condemning the committee. Twenty-eight familiar artists—including Humphrey Bogart, Richard Conte, Ira

Gershwin, Sterling Hayden, Paul Henreid, John Huston, Gene Kelly, Danny Kaye, and Marsha Hunt—signed a statement beginning with the words, "The investigative function of the Committee on Un-American Activities has been perverted from fair and impartial procedures to un-fair, partial and prejudiced methods." It went on to accuse the committee of illegal activities, smearing innocent people, and in general embarking upon a witch-hunt. Together with screen writer Phillip Dunne, Huston and Wyler organized the Committee for the First Amendment, which was designed to fight the HUAC and quickly was listed by the California Un-American Activities Committee as a Communist front organization. Later, Wyler would say "I wouldn't be allowed to make *The Best Years of Our Lives* in Hollywood today." At the time, however, he appeared to be in the vanguard of the motion-picture community, as Henry Fonda, Katharine Hepburn, Gregory Peck, Cornel Wilde, Billy Wilder, Van Heflin, and Ava Gardner joined the Committee for the First Amendment. Under Wyler and Huston, it placed advertisements in newspapers, helped organize rallies, and shortly before the hearings were to begin, it sent a delegation to Washington "to see whether they would be fair." Recalling the events of that autumn, Wyler told of briefing the group—headed by Bogart and Bacall—before it left. "I told them to stay away from the 'unfriendly' witnesses. I told them that the newspapers would say they were there to defend the Communists, but that they were going to Washington to attack the House Un-American Activities Committee and not to defend any Communists."[11]

The press gave the investigations front page-coverage.[12] In part this was due to the rising interest in anticommunism. But there was another aspect of the hearings that was far more interesting and, in the long run, more important. The witnesses included some of the most famous film artists in the nation. Their appearances had the air of a performance, and many of those who saw them in the newsreels the following week may have had difficulties separating show business from political events. When Robert Taylor appeared to offer testimony, the halls were filled with his admirers, hoping to catch a glimpse of their hero. The same was true for Gary Cooper and others; the public was given an opportunity to see what they were really like, and it took on the atmosphere of an impromptu performance. In the past, such celebrities had limited their nonshow-business activities to sponsorship of commercial products or, at the most, token appearances at political rallies, usually in subordinate roles. Now they were volunteering for or were being pushed into taking political stances.

What did these people know of complex political and philosophical matters? Adolphe Menjou, one of the first witnesses to be called, claimed to be an expert on world communism, having achieved this status through the reading of more than 100 books on the subject—at one point he claimed to have gone through 450 works—of Russia, "an oriental tyranny, a Kremlin-dominated conspiracy." To those who read the transcript, Menjou seemed an ignorant and bigoted crank. But what of those who remembered the man who played dapper men-about-town and successful businessmen in the movies? Did they confuse the image with the man and take him seriously? And what of Robert Taylor, a major matinee idol? He claimed to have been forced to make a pro-Soviet film, and that until he agreed to do so, the OWI held back his naval commission. Lowell Mellett denied the accusation, but his attempts to be heard before the committee were ignored. Would the public believe Taylor or the faceless Mellett? Clearly the actor had the advantage, in this case and in others that followed. And if Taylor was convincing and Menjou impressive, what of Gary Cooper and others of his type, men whom most Americans had trusted—in their fictional roles—for so many years? The committee's investigations of Hollywood communism were of some significance in 1947, but the emergence of the actor as politician would have even greater impact.

The first session was held on October 20, and in the week that preceded it the newspapers indicated that there would be "friendly" and "unfriendly" witnesses to offer testimony. In the former group would be those who had asked for the investigation in May. With the exception of a few minor figures, all the rest would be lumped together as "unfriendly." It was a designation that no one of importance bothered to challenge in October.

But there were differences within the "unfriendly" group. First of all, there was a small handful of writers who had already determined to challenge the legitimacy of the committee. Most had been Communists in the past, and some still belonged to the party. They hoped to use the hearings as a stage upon which to attack the investigators, to open a debate on the nature of political repression in the United States. How many fell into this group? Some claimed Hollywood was filled with radical writers; others conceded they didn't know how to classify most of them. By the end of the first week of hearings, it appeared that some of them might be isolated from the rest—there was talk of the "unfriendly nineteen" at this point. Later on, the number dwindled, until the group came to be known as the "Hollywood Ten."[13]

Few of the other anticommittee figures were or had been Communists, while those who were, hurriedly left the party and disclaimed affiliation. Although some had toyed with communism in the 1930s and during the war, when it had been fashionable, almost all had done so with little knowledge or forethought. To them, it was a variety of reformism that offered a measure of political excitement; to a later generation, this flirtation in a time of war and economic disturbance would be known as "radical chic." It was changing with the advance of the Cold War, and toward the end of 1947, Hollywood's anticommunism was accelerating.

The film industry's leaders, represented by Eric Johnston, had little interest in defending the radical writers, even though some of them were highly talented. The stars and directors were another matter; under the proper circumstances, they would be protected, especially if by so doing the industry as a whole would be benefited.

On the evening of October 19, just before the first session, Johnston, McNutt, and Benjamin met with the attorneys for the writers—among them Bartley C. Crum, Robert Kenny, Martin Popper, and Charles Katz. This latter group included civil libertarians and radicals, who like their clients were convinced the committee had overstepped its bounds. Kenny told Johnston that his clients were prepared to challenge the committee in the courts by refusing to co-operate and thus inviting a charge of contempt. But he feared that while the case was pending, Hollywood would blacklist those who brought the case. Thomas had implied that Johnston had agreed to co-operate in such a blacklist. Was it true? Johnston denied the rumors vehemently. "As long as I live I will never be a party to anything as un-American as a blacklist, and any statement purporting to quote me as agreeing to a blacklist is a libel upon me as a good American." The writers' lawyers were relieved. "Tell the boys not to worry," added Johnston. "There'll never be a blacklist. We're not going totalitarian to please the committee."[14]

Thus, as the House committee prepared to call its first witnesses, the radical writers believed they had the support of the industry and in addition were prepared to test the committee's constitutionality in the courts—they were anxious to have a show trial, and the leading congressmen were prepared to oblige them.

The hearings began with accusations and apologies from the friendly witnesses—Jack Warner, Louis B. Mayer, and Walt Disney for the studios; directors Sam Wood and Leo McCarey; writers Rupert Hughes and Morrie Ryskind; and actors Menjou, Taylor, and Cooper. In addition, writer Ayn Rand and Lela Rogers, mother of and agent for Ginger Rogers, gave testimony. These witnesses were a varied lot; McCarey was humorous, Rogers was befuddled, Menjou theatrical, and Warner philosophical though troubled. "If making *Mission to Moscow* in 1942 was a subversive activity," said Warner with much justification, "then the American Liberty ships which carried food and guns to Russian allies and the American naval vessels which convoyed them were likewise engaged in subversive activities. The picture was made only to help a desperate war effort and not for posterity." Likewise, Mayer defending having made *Song of Russia* with Taylor on the same grounds. Ayn Rand thought the film highly propagandistic in that it showed Russians smiling. "They don't smile?" asked the committee counsel. "Not quite that way, no. If they do, it is privately and accidentally. Certainly it is not social. They don't smile in approval of their system."

Although the hearings produced headlines, nothing of substance regarding Communist infiltration of the studios had been demonstrated. Even Menjou had been obliged to back down on several statements. At that point, too, there had been no questions regarding the propriety of the hearings. Witnesses were allowed to read statements into the record, enter upon digressions, and even joke with counsels and representatives. The hearings were attracting more attention than the Dies investigations of the prewar period, but this was due to the Cold War and not to the substance of the testimony.

Eric Johnston was called to testify on October 27, and on the same day the Committee for the First Amendment sent a large delegation to Washington to protest the investigation. Practiced in the arts of such matters, Johnston performed well, defending Hollywood against charges of communism and rejecting suggestions that the industry accept government dictation in the future. He conceded that one of his former aides had been a Communist, but with this exception, Johnston had placed the House committee on the defensive. In part because of this, Thomas dismissed Johnston with thanks and called the next witness, John Howard Lawson, considered the leader of the Hollywood Ten.

The choice was a good one from the House committee's point of view. There was little doubt that Lawson was a Communist—writing in a left-wing journal before the hearings, he had said, "As for myself, I do not hesitate to say that it is my aim to present the Communist position and to do so in the most specific manner." He had propagandized in the studios during the 1930s, and was well known for his hot temper and doctrinaire views. Lawson was sworn in, and immediately asked for permission to read a statement into the record—others had been granted this right before him. Thomas asked to see the statement, and when he looked it over, he refused permission. Then began a shouting match between Lawson and members of the committee and counsels. "I am not on trial here, Mr. Chairman. This committee is on trial before the American people. Let us get that straight," said Lawson. On several occasions, Lawson was asked, "Are you now, or have you ever been a member of the Communist party of the United States?" Lawson refused to answer, at least in the fashion the committee demanded. In the end, he was taken from the stand and cited for contempt of Congress.

Lawson set the pattern that the others followed—all were cited for contempt, preparing the way for their trials. The committee had its headlines; the Hollywood Ten had achieved the kind of notoriety and provoked the debate they had desired. All this had been accomplished in less than a week. The House committee, which had been on the defensive in mid-October, now appeared vindicated; the performances of the Hollywood Ten convinced many that they were Communists, part of a large network that included key artists in all the major studios. The search to ferret them out accelerated.

Had the writers answered the questions put before them—had they even conceded or proudly proclaimed their membership—little might have been done, and the hearings might have concluded with evidence presented of a handful of Communist writers, no more. At the time the Communist party was a legal entity, and membership by itself no crime. This was observed by Emmet Lavery, president of the Screen Writers' Guild, whom Rupert Hughes had accused of having Communist views. "Let me break the suspense immediately and tell you that I am not a Communist," said Lavery, before the committee could ask its question. He went on to defend Hollywood and dared the legislators to present evidence that wrongdoing existed. "If any individual members are guilty of indictable offenses, that are clearly sedition or treason, let a proper complaint be brought to the FBI and an indictment sought by a federal grand jury and action taken accordingly." This did not occur; instead, the Hollywood Ten were tried on contempt of Congress charges. Similarly, Ronald Reagan, then president of the Screen Actors' Guild, conceded that there were Communists in Hollywood, but warned against a witch-hunt; the vast majority of artists and businessmen were anti-Communist, he told the committee, and prepared to cleanse their ranks, but they would not tolerate a blanket indictment.

The activities of the Hollywood Ten confused and even frightened leaders of the Committee for the First Amendment, which was now accused of being a Communist-front organization. "There may have been some Communists in the group," conceded Wyler, "but then there are probably Communists in any organization. The point is, they did not run the committee, and a Communist-front organization is one that is run by Communists. *We* ran the committee and we were not Communists." In the atmosphere of late 1947 and early 1948, this did not suffice. Wyler went to see some of the accused writers to implore them "to go before a judge, or the press, or something, and answer the questions." Recalling that time he added, "We were naïve, and of course they wouldn't do it." Humphrey Bogart said that his anticommittee activities had been a mistake. "Roosevelt was a good politician. He could handle those babies in Washington, but they're too smart for guys like me. Hell, I'm no politician. That's what I meant when I said our Washington trip was a mistake." The sentiment was echoed by others, as the Committee for the First Amendment melted and disappeared. Fearful of being placed on a blacklist and confused by what had occurred, the motion-picture artists vied with one another to proclaim their anticommunism, and some, called before the House committee later on, presented it with the names of associates who they said were members of the Communist party.

Shortly before Larson took the stand, Johnston had written, "Too often, individuals and institutions have been condemned without a hearing or chance to speak in self-defense; slandered and libeled by hostile witnesses not subject to cross-examination and immune from subsequent suit or prosecution," while McNutt charged Thomas with trying "to dictate and control through the device of the hearings, what goes on in the screens of America. It does not require a law to cripple the right of free speech. Intimidation and coercion will do it."[15] Such talk ended after the Hollywood Ten made appearances before the House Committee. By mid-November it appeared that further investigations would follow, ending with legislation to control the film industry, perhaps even to censor content.

CAPITULATION

After two weeks of hearings, the House committee suddenly adjourned; other suspected Communists had been scheduled to give testimony, but these never appeared. The Hollywood Ten claimed to have routed the opposition, and expected to return to their jobs in triumph.[16] In fact, though, their support had rapidly eroded, and even those who remained sympathetic to their arguments withdrew, fearing retribution. Johnston was silent after the adjournment, consulting with studio heads and the New York bankers who really controlled the industry. Fearing for the safety of their investments, these men indicated a desire to capitulate to Thomas—at least in part. At their direction, Johnston called a conference at the Waldorf-Astoria Hotel in New York for November 24, where he met with leading Hollywood figures. At that time he spoke of the need to placate the committee. When asked to explain this stand in the light of his previous boldness, Johnston replied that he was "only a messenger."

The so-called Waldorf Declaration, released after two days of deliberation, began by stating disagreements with the actions of the Hollywood Ten. "We do not desire to prejudge their legal rights, but their actions have been a disservice to their employers and have impaired their usefulness to the industry. We will forthwith discharge or suspend without compensation those in our employ and we will not re-employ any of the ten until such time as he is acquitted or has purged himself of contempt and declares under oath that he is not a Communist." The Declaration went on to urge the industry to rid itself of subversive elements through self-policing and co-operation with other agencies and the government. "The absence of a national policy, established by Congress, with respect to the employment of Communists in private industry, makes our task difficult. Ours is a nation of laws. We request Congress to enact legislation to assist American industry to rid itself of subversive, disloyal elements." Along with others, Johnston insisted that "nothing subversive or unAmerican has appeared on the screen."

This was of key importance, and was never successfully challenged by the committee and its allies. The belief existed that somehow writers and directors dictated content, and this was far from being true. Rather, most were assigned to films, and even independent producers had to mold their products to fit the desires of studio heads and New York bankers. None of the Hollywood Ten had been involved with the making of such pro-Soviet films as *Mission to Moscow*, *North Star*, *Song of Russia*, and *Days of Glory*. Nor was the committee able to prove they had inserted pro-Soviet messages in the films they did create. In the immediate postwar period, Scott and Dmytryk worked on two films, *Crossfire* and *Till the End of Time*, which contained eloquent statements against racial and religious bigotry, but none on the committee singled these out as being Communist ideas. At the same time, Hollywood Ten writers worked on such nonideological productions as *Fiesta*, *Smash-up*, *New Orleans*, *The Romance of Rosy Ridge*, *Forever Amber*, and *Smart Women*. Whatever their activities outside the studios, the Hollywood Ten were highly paid but uninfluential artists during working hours; they were, in the views of their employers, laborers for hire, without real power or influence.[17]

Nonetheless, all were willing to co-operate in this strange charade, and they accepted their martyrdom with proper revolutionary rhetoric. As for Thomas, he called the Waldorf Declaration "a constructive step," indicating that more would be expected in the future. He was not disappointed. An informal, and later formal, blacklist was created. Moderate artists hastened to swing over into the anti-Communist camp. Known conservatives became "clearances" for those who had affiliated with the Committee for the First Amendment. Veteran actors admitted past sins, offered to co-operate with the Un-American Activities Committee, and in this way hoped for clearance. At parties rumors about forthcoming pictures and deals were replaced by those regarding actors and actresses suspected of being Communists. Throughout this period, however, the essential power structure remained intact. Writers and character actors who could be replaced easily remained on blacklists, and their careers were destroyed. Should a studio want a particular blacklisted writer to work on a script, he would do so, under a pseudonym, and all involved would co-operate in the deception. Careers of major stars were protected, either by covering up old radical connections or arranging for forgiveness through the proper clearances.[18]

Why had Hollywood co-operated so fully with the House committee and its allies? Clearly the temper of the times, the rapid jelling of Cold War attitudes, had much to do with it. The 1948 presidential election—when the Hollywood Ten strongly supported the Progressive party candidacy of Henry Wallace and almost all others took pains to remain aloof from it—provided a seal of sorts for the development. Various patriotic groups, led by the American Legion, picketed films made by or starring suspected or acknowledged radicals, and this too had a major impact upon studio attitudes. Without anticommunism of the Cold War variety, none of this—the capitulation or the blacklist—would have occurred.

Other factors having nothing to do with the investigations heightened Hollywood's fears and resulted in more severe reactions than might otherwise have been the case. The industry was in a slump toward the end of the decade, as television began to make inroads into paid admissions. In 1946, 6,500 receivers had been sold, by 1949, sales were over 3 million, with more than 4 million in use nationwide. That year, one out of every eight electrified homes had a television set, and the 50 per cent mark was passed in 1952. The familiar motion-picture theater was being bypassed for the novel television set, which in addition to everything else offered free entertainment. For the moment at least, the motion-picture industry had no idea of how to meet the challenge.

The MGM staff had been cut by 25 per cent in 1947, and Columbia had done the same the following year. Budgets for major productions had been slashed, while several were canceled. Motion-picture attendance began to slip in 1947, and would continue to do so for a decade. In 1946 there had been 80 million paid admissions per week, and in 1949, 62 million. Little wonder, then, that the studio chiefs and their bankers were skittish over anything that might further threaten solvency—such as charges of being infiltrated by Communists.

As Hollywood foundered, seeking to find a way to meet these challenges, a portion of the public rediscovered foreign films. To be sure, many had been top hits during the silent era, but they had done poorly when sound arrived. Now again, in the post-World War II period, they became popular with urban audiences. From 1945 to 1946 such films as *Open City*, *Shoeshine*, *Paisan*, and other realistic Italian features were becoming hits in small "art theaters," where exhibitors were delighted to find alternatives to the block-booked products of the Hollywood studios. These were followed by *The Bicycle Thief*, *Les Amants de Verone*, *Jour de Fête*, *Manon*, *Le Silence de la Mer*, and several British features released outside the Anglo-American agreements on distribution. Most of the successful foreign films were made in the semidocumentary styles similar to those of the American pictures of the same period. As Hollywood swung away from social commentary in the late 1940s, the Europeans continued to turn them out, and in this way retained their audiences and won new ones. This, too, troubled the American producers.

Moreover, in 1948, just when Hollywood was organizing its

blacklisting operations and attempting to come to terms with anticommunism, the U. S. Supreme Court upheld lower-court decisions on the illegality of trade practices within the industry. Several appeals were filed, but the following year all were rejected, and the cases concluded. Henceforth, block booking would be illegal, as would other, related practices. Furthermore, each major studio would have to divest itself of its theaters. Appeals followed, with the last of them, from Loew's, being rejected in 1952.

The motion-picture industry might have survived the anti-Communist crusade intact. Artists might be successfully blacklisted by the executives, and motion-picture theater operators punished if they transgressed rules. The Supreme Court decision, however, altered the situation drastically, although its implications were barely noted at the time, given the more dramatic news of the blacklist and communism in the motion-picture industry. The studio system, the quasimonopoly held by the big five, and the subordination of the artists to the businessmen and bankers—all would be ended or severely changed once the restructuring was completed and when a new generation of artists, without the memories and fears of the old ways, appeared on the scene.

This would take time. Not until the early 1960s would the old system collapse and a new one take its place. It was the most important structural change in Hollywood since the motion-picture industry had settled there a half century before. Now the artist would be supreme, not the studio or even the New York bankers. The Un-American Activities Committee hearings and the Waldorf Declaration captured the headlines, and even space in the works of historians. The blacklist was a major victory for the business of motion pictures over the artists. But it would be the last, given the smashing of the studio-theater nexus. The Hollywood Ten were the symbol of a moment, their defeat a sign that the old regime still had power.[19] A generation later their descendants in the arts would occupy central positions in motion pictures. But that was in the future. At the time, in the late 1940s and early 1950s, change seemed to be emanating from the committee hearings rooms on Capitol Hill. Now it can be seen that still more significant changes were being created by the Supreme Court.

9

The Genesis of the Multiversity

As one of the first witnesses called before the Committee on Un-American Activities, Jack Warner had felt obliged to defend the industry against charges of being dominated by Communists. At that time, Warner Brothers was in a particularly vulnerable position. Throughout the 1930s it had been the most socially conscious studio in Hollywood, and Warner himself a leading figure in liberal Democratic circles. Like some of the other immigrant tycoons, he often played the role of an innocent in public. But those who had survived in the industry through its many twists and turns since before World War I were among the most sophisticated businessmen in the nation. Pressed by the New York bankers, artists, unions, competition, and would-be censors, they had learned to adjust when necessary and to fight only when certain of victory. Those artists who had joined the Committee for the First Amendment believed they could defeat the congressional investigators. The studio heads knew better. They would stay on the sidelines until victory for one side or the other was assured, and then they would move; or, like Warner, they would appear as friendly witnesses while at the same time claiming to defend the rights of artists to engage in political activities. Warner had named dozens of writers and directors as radicals during the closed sessions in May, and on the first day of the October hearings, he said, "Ideological termites have burrowed into many American industries, organizations, and societies. Wherever they may be, I say let us dig them out and get rid of them." But he also told Chairman Thomas, "I can't, for the life of me, figure where men could get together and try in any form, shape, or manner to deprive a man of a livelihood because of his political beliefs."

Warner was in a sensitive position due to his production of *Mission to Moscow*. He understood this, as did the investigators. And Warner was prepared to admit his errors. "How did I, you, or anyone else know in 1942 what the conditions were going to be in 1947?" he asked committee counsel Robert Stripling. "I stated in my testimony our reason for making the picture, which was to aid the war effort—anticipating what would happen." This satisfied Stripling and the others, but freshman Representative Richard Nixon pressed on. He could understand Warner's reasons and even sympathize with him. Nixon led Warner into a discussion of the anti-Nazi films the studio had made during the war. "Under those circumstances, I would like to know whether or not Warner Brothers has made, or is making at the present time, any pictures pointing out the methods and the evils of totalitarian communism, as you so effectively have pointed out the evils of the totalitarian Nazis." To this, Jack Warner happily replied: "Under the circumstances, I think this committee is glad to hear that Warner Brothers is contemplating for the first time now making a motion picture in which they point out to the American people the dangers of totalitarian communism as well as fascism."

In fact during the decade following the House committee's 1947 investigations, the Hollywood studio turned out a series of anti-Communist films. Few were economic successes and many were more blatently propagandistic than any picture of the war years; they served to satisfy congressional investigators, however, that the motion-picture industry had indeed joined the struggle against the U.S.S.R. As Warner had indicated, the movement began immediately. Joseph Losey's *The Boy with Green Hair*, directed by Adrian Scott at RKO, was to have been an allegory about racism. Then Scott refused to testify about his alleged membership in the Communist party, and Losey was blacklisted. The film underwent several changes. When finally completed, it contained little of the original message, and was instead a mild antiwar picture, with even a few anti-Communist touches. *Monsieur Verdoux*, a Charlie Chaplin film that combined comedy with a series of strong statements against war in general, was picketed by patriotic organizations that considered Chaplin a Communist, while many independent theater owners and small chains refused to show it.

In November, Louis B. Mayer told Chairman Thomas that MGM had begun work on its first anti-Communist film. But the studio hesitated, as Mayer understood such pictures would probably fail at the box offices. *The Red Danube*, released by MGM in late 1949, dealt with Communist intrigues in Central Europe, and was an artistic and financial failure. Mayer later produced *The Conspirator*, *The Hoaxters*, and several other minor anti-Communist films, all of which had the marks of B pictures. It was as though MGM offered them as tokens of goodwill, and little more. Meanwhile, the studio turned to musicals, comedies, and escapist films, which became its staple product in the 1950s.

The first of the postwar anti-Communist films had come from Twentieth Century-Fox. *The Iron Curtain*, released in mid-1948, concerned Igor Gouzenko, a Red Army soldier sent to Canada as a code clerk. He and his wife soon realized that all they had been told about the West was false. They abandoned communism and sought Canadian citizenship. Much of the film is concerned with Gouzenko's awakening and the attempts of Soviet agents to track him down. The portrayals of the Canadians and those of the Soviet agents were throwbacks to the World War II caricatures of Americans and Nazis, and in fact it was received as a war film. The National Council of American-Soviet Friendship and the Progressive Citizens of America picketed the picture, just as the American Legion and similar groups had picketed what they considered to be pro-Communist films. If a war of ideas was developing in the aftermath of the Hollywood hearings, it was one in which each side was determined to silence the other. *The Iron Curtain* was financially successful, and thus encouraged, Twentieth Century-Fox scheduled others of the genre. But the studio quickly realized that there was a limited market for such films, and like MGM, turned to escapist fare instead.

A similar situation prevailed at RKO and Warner Brothers. The former studio produced only two anti-Communist films, *The Woman on Pier 13* and *Whip Hand,* both on small budgets, and offered them to exhibitors at low rates as second features. Jack Warner joined patriotic organizations but would not risk funds on anti-Communist films the public clearly was not buying. Not until 1951 did he release his first such picture, *I Was a Communist for the FBI,* which did poorly at the box office in large cities but drew well in rural areas. *Big Jim McLain,* which played the following year, made money, but this may have been more the result of star John Wayne's drawing power than the picture's merits.

Paramount produced more anti-Communist films than any other major studio. *Peking Express* was released in 1951, and the following year Paramount's *My Son John,* the most ambitious of the propaganda pictures, played large downtown theaters. It concerned a middle-class family, one of whose members joined the Communist party. The father and mother—played by Dean Jagger and Helen Hayes—were decent, religious, hard-working people, whose two older sons were bold, clean-cut, and patriotic. John was the outsider, a dark, brooding person. The role was played by Robert Walker, who at the time had come to specialize in portraying deranged criminals. John lies and cheats for his comrades, but toward the end he sees the light, and is about to cooperate with an FBI man (played by Van Heflin) when he is gunned down by Communist agents on the steps of the Lincoln Memorial.

Paramount was disappointed with the box-office receipts for the picture, as well as negative reviews. *My Son John* played at the height of the anti-Communist movement, when Senator Joseph McCarthy was considered the most powerful person in the nation. It was suggested that the reviewers were either Communists or fellow travelers, since they seemed to dislike all the anti-Communist films. But this did not change the reviews. Not a single such picture received any of the major awards or made a substantial amount of money for the studios. A majority of the anti-Communist films were potboilers from the minor studios, turned out at little cost with the realization that while they would not become hits, they would offer a fair return on investments of money and talent. Republic released *Rose of the Yukon, The Red Menace,* and *Bells of Coronado.* Film Classics had *Project X* and *The Flying Saucer,* and Monogram produced *The Steel Fist* and *Arctic Flight.* All were melodramas, often rewrites of low-budget anti-Nazi films of World War II.

For the most part, despite pressures to prove their allegiances, the major studios were more interested in escapism than social commentary in the posthearings period. A movie about anti-Semitism or one that dealt with poverty in America might be suspected of having a radical message, while a light comedy or a musical would be considered beyond politics. In 1948, before the studios could retool for new pictures in the aftermath of the hearings, one of every five Hollywood features was concerned with social and psychological problems; by 1953, the figure was one in ten. In this same period the percentage of musicals, biblical films, biographies, and romances rose steadily. Among the major serious films of 1948 were *The Treasure of Sierra Madre, The Snake Pit, Call Northside 777,* and *The Naked City,* all of which, directly or indirectly, dealt with provoking social themes. The important films of 1953 included *The Moon Is Blue* (considered contentious because the word "virgin" was used in it, and released without approval of the Hollywood censors), *The Robe* (a biblical spectacle in CinemaScope, a new wide-screen process), *Mogambo* (a remake of *Red Dust,* starring Clark Gable and Ava Gardner), *Lili* (a musical), and *Shane* (a highly regarded western). In addition, there was *Stalag 17* (a comedy about a Nazi prison camp—an unthinkable theme in 1947), and *From Here to Eternity* (about Army life just prior to the Japanese attack on Pearl Harbor). There was unpunished adultery in *From Here to Eternity,* talk about sex in *The Moon Is Blue,* and simplified morality in *The Robe.* Those who strained might have found anti-Communism in *Shane,* in which the forces of good confront and defeat those of evil, but this would have required more than a bit of imagination.

Reluctant to produce films with anything resembling social commentary, the major studios went so far as to scrutinize scripts to make certain they contained nothing that might anger the anti-Communist groups. Movies portraying Soviet-American co-operation during World War II were out of the question, and the war films that appeared in the late 1940s and early 1950s—*Command Decision, Yellow Sky, Battleground, Sands of Iwo Jima, Task Force, Twelve O'Clock High, Halls of Montezuma, Operation Pacific,* and *Decision Before Dawn* among them—were either about the fighting in the Pacific or, if they did portray events in Europe, avoided mentioning the Soviet contribution.[1] It was also taboo to dwell upon themes that might appear critical of conditions in America, since to do so might open the studio to charges of "fellow traveling." Thus there were no additional productions dealing with racial problems in America or economic injustices, or even referring to them in some past era. Moral uplift pictures were on the borderline, accepted so long as they clearly weren't too serious.

Miracle on Thirty-fourth Street, directed by George Seaton, was one such film. It concerns an elderly man, played by Edmund Gwenn, who insists he is the real Santa Claus while working at Macy's as a store Santa during the Christmas season. He is supposed to encourage children to ask for toys and games, naturally to be purchased at Macy's, but rather tells them of sales at other stores, including Macy's across-the-street rival, Gimbel's. Interwoven with this main story are a love story and some minor subplots, but the stress is on the meaning of the Christmas spirit. In the end a court rules that Gwenn is indeed Santa Claus, and he leads the executives at Macy's and Gimbel's to agree that honesty is the best policy. From now on, they will tell children and their parents where the best buys are to be found—in effect, removing part of the commercialism from Christmas.

Could *Miracle on Thirty-fourth Street* be viewed as Communist propaganda? It did present a narrow view of capitalism, indicating that the nation's business leaders could not tolerate a man who insisted upon telling the truth about inferior services and an economic system that prized profits above all. In its way, the film did call for reforms, along Christian if not Communist lines. The message was similar to those of the Capra movies of the late 1930s, especially *Mr. Deeds Goes to Town.* But Seaton's film lacked the moral fervor of Capra's film; Seaton kept the tone light throughout, whereas Capra had insisted upon several direct assaults upon his audiences' consciences. Furthermore, Seaton's films portrayed middle-class people, or at least those who had middle-class values, while Capra had chosen to depict the poor of the land and how they were suffering under the contemporary political and economic system of the thirties. Were it not for these factors, in addition to the film's love interest and upbeat ending, *Miracle on Thirty-fourth Street* might have been seen as social commentary, and so listed as such by the House investigators. Such was not the case. Instead, the film was a great financial success and was revived occasionally in the next decade.

The studios did not understand the meaning of this phenomenon, or if they did, chose to ignore it. Social commentary could be introduced into motion pictures, even at the height of the McCarthy period, so long as it was encased in comedies that had happy endings.

In October 1948, when Hollywood and the rest of the nation were adjusting to the anti-Communist crusade, Seaton's next film, *Apartment for Peggy*, opened at the Roxy in New York. Once again Seaton used Gwenn, this time as a retired philosophy professor, a widower living alone in his Victorian house near his old university. The school, clearly located in a small New England or midwestern town, is trying to adjust to the influx of veterans, attending under the GI Bill of Rights program. Many students are obliged to live in temporary quarters, and some cannot find accommodations of any kind. One of these is Jason Taylor and his nineteen-year-old pregnant wife, Peggy (played by William Holden and Jeanne Crain). The professor is considering suicide, seeing no further reason for living, and Jason is discouraged, and wants to abandon his plans for a teaching career. The young couple moves into the professor's attic—against his will at first—and despite her miscarriage, Peggy remains optimistic about the future. When Jason leaves school to take a job selling used cars, she chides him, while the professor talks him into returning to college. Peggy shows both men they have important work to do. The professor teaches classes consisting of students' wives, while Jason will continue in his studies, and in the end become a teacher.

Seaton had taken his story from a novel by Faith Baldwin, who at that time was one of the favorite writers of stories for women's magazines. The picture was produced by William Perlberg, who was nonpolitical and had no role in any of the Hollywood investigations. Yet *Apartment for Peggy* was an important social documentary, as much in its way as *The Best Years of Our Lives*. New York *Times* critic Bosley Crowther devoted two reviews to the film. In the first he complimented Seaton on having "a tender and genuine comprehension of a real slice of modern life." A few days later Crowther wrote that "He [Seaton] makes you understand the determination of this new generation of the dispossessed to emerge from the cheap and the rootless, both in living and in thinking, that events have imposed."

Perhaps there was less to the film than Crowther saw, for there is no indication that either Peggy or Jason have emerged from poverty. Indeed, their attitudes, speech, and behavior are middle-class throughout, as are those of their friends and members of the university faculty. When Jason leaves school it is for a job that will pay more than any he might have obtained in education. Peggy is angered because she views teaching as a special calling, unlike selling autos, an occupation that she belittles on several occasions. Throughout the film the value of education, the importance of learning, and the central role of the teacher in society are stressed. As in other postwar films, the message seems to be that the returning veterans will make America a bright new land, transforming it with their idealism and energies. Never again will the country suffer through depression and war; the ex-GIs will make certain this will not recur.

These ideas can be found in *The Best Years of Our Lives*, but the people there are quite different from those in *Apartment for Peggy*. Fred Derry enters the construction business—he does not go to college to become an architect. Al Stephenson confronts his banker colleagues over loans to veterans who want to become farmers or small businessmen; the GI bill for education is not mentioned in this segment. Homer Parrish will marry his childhood sweetheart and settle down, perhaps enter business. He is told about educational possibilities, but does not appear interested. Why did Sherwood and Wyler omit college from their film? The obvious reason would appear to be that Kantor did not mention it in his short story, but Sherwood had changed other parts of the story. Why not this one too? The most plausible answer appears to be that he simply did not believe college would be an important part of "the best years" of the returning veterans' lives. In 1945, when he adapted the Kantor story, there were only eighty-eight thousand veterans in the nation's institutions of higher education, slightly more than 5 per cent of total enrollment. In 1947, when Seaton began work on *Apartment for Peggy*, almost half or all the nation's college students were veterans, who also accounted for seven out of every ten male students. That year, one out of every eight ex-GIs was a college student. Much had been expected of the former servicemen, but not this. The crowding of former soldiers and sailors into the nation's schools came as a surprise, even to those who drew up the GI Bill of Rights. Almost overnight, education became the major American industry, and learning—not work—the aspiration of the nation's young people.

COLLEGE LIFE BETWEEN THE WARS

If one were to accept the caricatures presented in motion pictures and on radio, the prewar colleges and universities had been inhabited by absentminded professors, football players, co-eds seeking proper husbands, and a handful of grinds. The schools themselves had been depicted as either high-priced playgrounds for the wealthy or the spawning ground for urban revolutionaries and preprofessionals. These outworn and in any case much exaggerated beliefs would soon be dispelled. Other American institutions were obliged to convert from a wartime to a peacetime society, and so were the schools. Institutions of higher learning had additional problems, for a return to the prewar forms would not do, if only because of the press of numbers. Instead, they would have to create new structures, with contents somewhat different from those that were desirable in the 1920s and 1930s. The academics themselves would have to adjust to the idea of their central role in society and learn to use their new prestige and power.[2] This would require the efforts of more than a generation, but the start was made in the late 1940s, when college and university administrators and faculty attempted to construct a new system upon the foundations of the old.

The nation's population had risen by 16 per cent in the 1920s, while that of the college-age population had increased by 23 per cent. Enrollments almost doubled in that prosperous period, rising from 531,000 to well over 1.1 million. Fewer than 49,000 bachelor's degrees had been awarded in 1920, when less than 8 per cent of all individuals between the ages of 18 and 21 attended college. By 1930 there were 122,000, and by that time, 12 per cent of the cohort attended colleges and universities.

The nation experienced a sharp decline in population growth during the 1930s, due to the continuation of the falloff of the late 1920s aggravated by the depression. But though the population increase fell by 7 per cent, the college-age group still rose by 8 per cent. Despite economic hardships, there were 1.5 million college students in 1940, an increase of almost 40 per cent over 1930. During each year but one of the Great Depression—1934—enrollment expanded, as did the number of degrees awarded. Over 186,000 bachelor's degrees were conferred in 1940, while the numbers of advanced degrees kept pace. So did the expansion of institutions of higher education—there were 1,041 of them in 1920, 1,409 in 1930, and 1,709 in 1940. Total expenditures for colleges and universities went from $216 million in 1920 to $432 million in 1930, and in 1940, when financial pressures were still strong, $758 million. Other statistics were equally impressive—library expenditures, often the first to be cut in bad times, rose from $9.6 million in 1930 to $19.5 million in 1940.[3] Only state and local payments for new plant declined during the depression, indicating that the collegiate experience of 1940 was somewhat more threadbare and cramped than had been that of the 1920s. Yet college sports, especially football, remained important. The major games continued to attract sellout crowds at the bottom of the depression, while basketball, a minor sport in 1920, became significant in this period. In 1940, despite poverty and unemployment, more than 15 per cent of the cohort were in colleges and universities.

The population explosion in higher education during the 1920s and 1930s was as impressive, at least in a quantitative sense, as the far more famous one that followed World War II, and an appreciation of the latter is impossible without an understanding of the former. What caused this tremendous upsurge of interest in higher education, which continued during bad times as well as good? In what ways were the students of the interwar period similar to and different from those who had preceded them? What did they hope to obtain from their educations, and were they disappointed with the results? In the past the colleges tried to mold young men and women, and they continued to do so in the 1920s and 1930s. At the same time, however, the students helped change the nature of their institutions, to a greater degree than ever before in the nation's history. More studies were published on the inner workings of colleges and universities, the rationales of education, and the nature of curriculum than in any previous period. Yet when the expansion was ended by the coming of war, higher education lacked the rationale it had had at the turn of the century, when it was assumed that colleges prepared the collegian for gentlemanly pursuits, offered a cultural background to those who wished one, and initiated the new professionals—the grinds of 1900—into the processes of their crafts. Rather, by 1940 the colleges filled a multitude of tasks, with each institution not quite certain it was performing as well as it might, or in the way that it should. The old forms were still there, as were the accepted patterns of behavior, but the spirit had changed. The college student of 1900 was asked, "What will you do for the old school?" His grandchild was apt to ask, silently perhaps, "What can this place do for me?"

As with most major changes, there was no single reason for the increase in college and university enrollments in the 1920s and 1930s. The sons and daughters of the collegians continued to attend the older institutions, to an extent impelled to do so by their parents. At the time, a developing economy that required trained or at least trainable personnel was attracting more and more students to higher education. An increasingly technological society, in which managerial skills were in demand, offered employment to college-trained personnel. The apprenticeship system would not suffice—the nation's industries and professions no longer had the time or even the expertise to take young men and women and, over a period of time, turn out qualified workers. Institutions of higher learning would accomplish the task for them. Rather than hire a person for a low wage and then spend many hours in teaching him the craft, industry could obtain a certified graduate, theoretically prepared for the main job, and in many fields equipped with the latest ideas and techniques. This could be done at no cost to the employer, for the college graduate, entering his first job, often received the same salary as an apprentice might after four or more years of training, during which time he was not fully productive. American businessmen could praise the colleges and support private ones through donations and public institutions through taxes, realizing that they were assisting them in their work.

From 1920 to 1940, the employed labor force increased by only 18 per cent—a result of the Great Depression. But the professional and managerial categories showed far greater advances, rising by 72 per cent for professionals and by a third for managers. There were 118,000 accountants in America in 1920, and by 1940, 238,000. In the same period the numbers of librarians rose from 15,000 to 22,000, engineers from 134,000 to 297,000, chemists from 28,000 to 57,000, and architects from 17,000 to 22,000. Due to more stringent standards at medical schools, the physician population had a smaller increase, from 146,000 to 168,000, but the dentists went from 56,000 to 71,000, and lawyers from 123,000 to 182,000. The demands upon higher education were felt in the colleges too. The number of faculty rose from 49,000 to 82,000 in the 1920s, but the increase was even more dramatic in the next decade, for despite the depression, there were 147,000 faculty members in 1940.[4]

The situation was more complicated in the elementary and secondary schools, and this too had its effect upon the colleges and universities. There were some 680,000 teachers in 1920, when graduation from a normal school—the two-year training institutions of the period—was considered ample preparation for the position. Teachers with only a few courses at a local normal school had little trouble finding employment in rural areas, while those with college degrees were usually found only in the prestigious private schools. In the 1920s teaching careers were attractive alternatives to manual labor, especially for women, and salaries were rising as well—they averaged $871 a year in 1920, $1,420 in 1930. By the end of the decade there were 854,000 teachers, and the college-educated public-school teacher was no longer a rarity, especially in the major cities, where salaries tended to be higher than they were in rural areas and small towns.[5]

Local school boards cut budgets in the depression, while the sharply reduced elementary and high school populations created intense competition for available posts. Would-be teachers now sought bachelor's degrees rather than the less well regarded normal school certificates. On their part the normal schools upgraded their faculties, and some petitioned their states to become four-year teachers' colleges. A new symbiotic relationship developed between institutions that trained teachers and their students. Higher standards in elementary and secondary schools drove teacher candidates to better-qualified institutions of higher learning and graduate schools, and the increased demand there, coupled with a plenitude of applicants for positions, enabled these to raise faculty standards. This is turn obliged potential faculty to seek advanced degrees, which added to the demand in that area.

Education underwent a major transformation in the 1930s, in the large part the result of a new mix of teachers and students. Many talented individuals turned to teaching in the 1930s, in the hope of finding positions in the public schools—with safe and regular paychecks. Then they would go on to take advanced degrees, which could lead to higher salaries and status. Thus the liberal arts and teachers colleges received a major infusion of intelligent students, who in other times would have been vocationalists seeking prelaw or premedical courses to be followed by additional years in professional school. The student who no longer could afford the eight years needed to obtain an M.D. would spend four in acquiring a B.A. in Education, get a job as a biology teacher (if he was fortunate), and then go on for advanced degrees, while receiving a good salary for the times. In differing ways, the prosperous 1920s and the depression 1930s saw the emergence of teaching as a respected and desirable occupation, and there was a new awareness of the importance of education.

These talented teachers-in-training attend colleges with students who were there as a result of New Deal measures that supported education. By 1939, the National Youth Administration, through grants to individuals and institutions, enabled some 750,000 to attend institutions of higher education. Many of these students must have hoped that their additional training would help them find jobs, but given the tight situation of the times, this was questionable.[6] So they went to college instead of participating in other federal programs—the Civilian Conservation Corps, among others—or vegetating at home. Once in schools they made the most of their opportunities, learning for the sake of learning, perhaps because they knew that to be dropped would mean the end of aid.

The depression was supposed to have accelerated the movement away from private and toward public higher education. At the turn of the century, 62 per cent of the students attended private colleges and universities. By 1920 the figure was 43 per cent, but in the prosperous decade that followed the private colleges staged a recovery—graduation from the proper school was considered the means by which the children of immigrants could mingle with the elite.[7] By 1930, the private and public colleges divided the students equally. The depression that followed impelled many to seek lower-cost public education, but in 1940, 47 per cent of students were in the private schools—a higher percentage than had been there in 1920. In part this was due to the shortage of space in public institutions, and the ability of private schools to lower tuition and standards.

The depression-era students were strikingly different from those who had preceded them, even though they became sports enthusiasts, pledged for prestigious fraternities and sororities, and generally exuded "college spirit." Underneath all of this most had a strong practical streak. They were there for trainings in particular areas, and so were more akin to the grinds than to the collegians. They attended colleges in order to obtain certification; they accepted the institutions as they were, and tended to look upon college as a way station to higher status and salary. As for the students who wanted to be educated, for them the college was a bastion of free thought and expression; they would criticize the economic and political system as it existed, but view the colleges as one of the more enlightened areas of American life.

What of the old collegians? Their counterparts were still there. In this period they were known as BMOC's—Big Men on the Campus—although by the late 1930s this term was also used to describe the grinds who had become editors of school newspapers as well as the leaders of fraternities. They remained the ideal, even though they were no longer widely imitated. The gentleman's C was out of tune with the sentiments of college youth in the depression decade, when aggressive competition for places was more common. Hints of this might be found in the college musical films, usually made on low budgets, which for a while enjoyed a vogue. The football player was still a hero, but more often than not he was also a comic figure—played by Jack Oakie or Joe E. Brown—or shown as big, strong, but dumb. The love interest was provided by a cheerleader, who in the end falls in love with the editor of the school newspaper, the team's manager, or a youthful member of the faculty. Brains and accomplishment did count. Given the intense competition for jobs, little else might have been expected.

Most of the nation's colleges and universities experienced sharp and sudden drops in enrollment during World War II, as young men entered the armed forces and many college-age women either found jobs in defense plants or entered the services themselves. Throughout the war it seemed somehow unpatriotic to remain in school—where "business as usual" went on. The nation was urged to sacrifice, and attending college hardly seemed a proper response to the call. Thus the number of bachelor's degrees granted fell from 216,000 in 1940 to 142,000 in 1944, the last full year of the war. Some schools, especially those that in the past had specialized in those areas relating to the war effort—languages, some branches of engineering, science, and foreign relations, among others—received federal grants for their work, and students majoring in these subjects were urged to continue on and graduate. Many served as training areas for officers; in 1944, the federal government reimbursed the nation's colleges and universities by close to $100 million for contract courses alone.

The large research-oriented institutions were able to attract federal contracts during the war, and some actually expanded operations in the face of declining enrollments.[8] It was different at the colleges, especially those that depended almost wholly upon tuition to meet expenses. Many were in desperate shape—seventy closed down from 1943 to 1944. Research and specialization, not general education, appeared to be in vogue while the war was being waged; there were few collegians in the colleges in this period, as the grinds and professionals came to the fore. But what of the future? By the end of the war, most leading educators were demoralized, cautious, confused, and uncertain as to what might happen next. During the past four years they had become accustomed to looking to Washington for guidance. They continued to do so in 1944.

A NATION OF STUDENTS

In 1942, President Roosevelt had established the Postwar Manpower Conference, charging it with the development of a demobilization program to be put into effect once hostilities were ended. Roosevelt and the conference members did so with two thoughts in mind. The first was a fear of the mood of the returning veterans. At the time it was believed the nation might sink back into the depression after the war, as it had in 1920. What would be the reactions of men who had risked their lives for several years to such a situation? General Frank Hines of the Veterans' Administration thought "the greatest danger was that of having idle veterans drifting aimlessly about the country." Such men, in the Germany of the 1920s, had become the backbone for the Nazi movement. Already some prewar demagogues were thinking along such lines. Gerald L. K. Smith, who had inherited part of Huey Long's following, said that he had little hope for victory in the 1944 presidential election, but was certain the nation would go his way in 1948, when expected to support a disgruntled former soldier for the presidency.

Aware of the situation, the Administration moved to make certain the veterans would not pose such a threat. Jobs were one response, and education was another. In 1919, the Wisconsin legislature had provided each returning veteran with thirty dollars a month for four years at any nonprofit educational institution in the state. Although there had been no federal educational benefits after World War I, the conference considered them vital for the Second World War's veterans. So did Republican politicians looking ahead to the 1944 elections, and several bills were introduced in 1943, both by the Administration and the opposition. In November, Roosevelt addressed Congress, saying he was certain it would agree "that this time, we must have plans and legislation ready for our returning veterans instead of waiting until the last moment. It will give notice to our armed forces that the people back home do not propose to let them down.[9]

The second motivating factor behind the legislation was idealism. Roosevelt had spoken loftily of war aims that included freedom from fear and want. It had been a patriotic war, and the President hoped to maintain the spirit during the peace. The men in the armed forces had been promised a better world for their efforts, and the nation's political leaders felt obliged to deliver on that pledge. Ample veterans' benefits, aimed at preparing the former soldiers and sailors for jobs, would be one way to accomplish this.

The so-called "GI Bill of Rights" was signed into law on June 22, 1944. Among its provisions was one year of schooling for veterans who were not over the age of twenty-five at their time of entry into the service, with additional time based upon their period of active duty. It included the payment of all fees, tuition, and supplies as well as a monthly subsistance allowance of fifty dollars for a single person and seventy-five dollars for a married veteran. These provisions were liberalized under the Truman administration, especially after General Omar Bradley became head of the Veterans' Administration late in 1945. But the essential outline remained the same, as did the purpose of the provision: The federal government was prepared to underwrite the educations of those veterans who wished to attend college.

Would many utilize the educational sections of the GI Bill? Most commentators thought they would not. Several veterans' organizations, lobbying for increased aid for disabled soldiers and sailors, were willing to to relinquish educational assistance for job guarantees, additional insurance, and apprenticeship programs. Roosevelt himself was not favorable to the idea, and planned a form of CCC for veterans should the depression return. None of the major books on the subject of returning veterans, written to ease the adjustment problems, gave education a major role, and a few even omitted analysis of these benefits. And they had reason to do so. The average age of the returning veteran would be twenty-eight, and he would have a good deal of lost time to make up. One of the more influential commentators on the subject thought he "will be interested only in education to help him vocationally, preferring mechanical, business, or mathematical subjects; will want to go into a trade, technical occupation or business. . . . Any government program for his benefit must roughly be based upon this norm, with enough flexibility to meet the deserving special case."[10]

Educational leaders did not anticipate a flood of veterans to their colleges and universities, but even so, they feared the impact of the GI Bill. A. J. Brumbaugh, dean at the University of Chicago, said the schools would not be able to accommodate married veterans with families. President James Conant of Harvard thought "we may find the least capable among the war generation . . . flooding the facilities for advanced education." One of the nation's most prestigious educators, Robert Hutchins, called the GI Bill "a threat to American education" and "unworkable." Presidents and deans of marginal colleges were more enthusiastic about the measure, for in it they saw the salvation of their institutions and the preservation of jobs. Yet most of them, too, believed relatively few would take advantage of the provisions. They remained convinced that the late 1940s and early 1950s would be among the worst periods in history for American higher education.

These comments and conclusions may appear exaggerated and remarkably shortsighted today, but they seemed prudent at the time. In 1940, there had been 9.7 million Americans in the college-age cohort. Due to the low birthrates of the late 1920s and the 1930s, the size of the cohort was shrinking rapidly. According to most projections, it would be only 8.6 million in 1950, a decline of 1.1 million in a decade. According to one calculation, World War II had prevented some half a million individuals from achieving bachelor's status, and a like amount from attending college without graduating.[11] In 1945, it appeared that most of these would never return, and given the smaller cohort, the colleges seemed destined for a long period of belt-tightening. In such a situation, standards might be lowered in order to attract students—especially the veterans. This troubled Hutchins, Conant, and others, and at the time their fears appeared to be justified.

There was an alternate argument, however. After all, if the colleges had done fairly well in terms of enrollments in the 1930s, why should anyone doubt that they would survive in the late

1940s, when the government was offering scholarships to some 10 million veterans? The administrators might have considered that some of those whose educations had been interrupted by the war would return, while others, given the GI Bill, might be lured to the campuses. Then there were the high school graduates of 1945–46 and after, who would not be entering the armed forces, and instead attend college. Even without the veterans, this group would have filled the institutions. Too, there was the widespread prediction of a new depression, and if this occurred, federal aid to students—nonveterans as well as veterans—might come about. Still, those who took cognizance of the positive elements in the picture were unable to visualize the boom that did develop.

There had been close to 1.5 million college and university students in 1940, slightly less than 16 per cent of the cohort. Excluding military personnel, the student population was slightly above 1 million in 1944, less than 13 per cent. The following year, as the veterans began to arrive along with an enlarged high school graduating class, there were some 1.7 million students; the GI Bill recipients accounted for 5 per cent of the total registration and close to twice that of the male student population. In 1946, the first full year of demobilization, there were well over 2 million students, over 1 million of whom were veterans. The institutions registered 1.1 million veterans in 1947, when the total registration was 2.3 million.[12] That year, close to 20 per cent of the college-age cohort was in the schools, almost twice that of 1940. The figure held for the remainder of the decade. The great education boom was on, which would alter the faces of the nation's colleges and universities, both in a qualitative and a quantitative fashion.

While it is difficult to generalize about so large a group, clearly the returning servicemen were older than the high school graduates of 1945–46. According to the Veterans' Administration, about half of them were married, and of these, half had children. Given their age, experience, and status, they were quite different from the kinds of students the faculties and administrations had been accustomed to in the past. Although they mixed with the high school graduates in class, few did so afterward—they joined veterans' clubs on the campus, and not fraternities. It was difficult for the old collegians to thrive on campuses where so many of the male students were older, married men, uninterested in hazing, ancient traditions, and sports. There was a serious mood in that period, and the veterans reinforced it. As a group they were grinds, seeking educations as passports to the better lives for which they had fought. The situation varied from campus to campus, but on the whole it appeared that the veterans were more interested in engineering programs than were the other students, and also gravitated toward the social sciences, psychology in particular. In the immediate postwar years fewer than might have been expected majored in commercial subjects, and *Apartment for Peggy* notwithstanding, there was no unusual increase in enrollments for education programs.

By the end of the decade, newspapers and magazines were carrying stories about the impact of the veterans upon the colleges. Almost all agreed that it was beneficial. According to administrators, the veterans were a hard-working group, serious about their pursuits, and, as such, an inspiration to the high school graduates. Professor George MacFarland of the University of Pennsylvania wrote that "the veteran is acknowledged to be serious, time conscious, industrious, and capable." Professor Clifton Hall of George Peabody College for Teachers thought they "contributed a steadying influence to college life." In a special study of the group, *Fortune* concluded that the class of 1949 was "the best . . . the most mature . . . the most responsible . . . and the most self-disciplined group" of students in history. Conant of Harvard conceded he had been in error in 1945; the GI Bill students were "the most mature and promising . . . Harvard has ever had," he told reporters the following year.[13]

The colleges were obliged to change in order to meet the needs and demands of these new students. Deans who in 1939 had admonished students not to drink and smoke could hardly do the same in 1949, when half their charges might be men who had spent several years in combat, were married, and had children. There was a general relaxation of rules in the late 1940s, and the schools became more informal than they had been before the war. The veterans had helped crack the shell of tradition, for better or worse, and educational leaders were inclined to accept the changes. This was particularly true for the newer faculties who came to the colleges and universities in this period.

In 1944 there had been 106,000 faculty members; because of

the boom, there were 186,000 by 1950, and the figure was increasing rapidly. This sudden demand for college teachers caused the schools to accept individuals with lower and fewer credentials than might otherwise have been the case, and obliged them to increase salaries so as to become more competitive with other professions. As a result, many faculties, especially those at the large universities, became far less homogeneous than they had been before the war. On the one hand there were the marginal faculty members, including a growing army of part-time teachers, expanding at a rapid rate, while on the other were the "hotshots," star faculty members attracted from industry and government, usually with special expertise about both. In the middle were the old professors, who had ruled in the more sedate pre-World War II period. As far as they could see, their world had melted. In the place of the structured faculty of the 1920s and 1930s, with the tradition of genteel poverty and subservience inherited from an even earlier period, was the chaotic scene of the late 1940s, when new teachers streamed into the schools, with novel ideas, backgrounds, traditions, and desires.

The old professors had been able to adjust to the influx of new students in the 1920s and 1930s, for although many came from different backgrounds than had the old collegians, at least they accepted the values and traditions of their academic ancestors. This was not so with the veterans and the high school graduates of the postwar world. They chaffed at some required courses—classical languages, for example—and argued for programs that stressed present problems and possible solutions. In many schools, especially the larger ones, students petitioned administrations and faculties and discussed matters in conferences and student newspapers. The schools bent with the wind; requirements were dropped, electives expanded, and new programs proliferated. All the while, standards remained high, given the maturity of the student bodies and the traditions of many of the old professors, who still dominated their schools.

But the tone was different. No longer did male students wear jackets and ties to class—increasingly, faded Army clothes were seen, and accepted. By the end of the 1940s, informality was the rule at the public colleges and universities, and change was being felt at even the Ivy League schools. And if the appearance of students had changed, that of the campus was altered still more radically. College Gothic, the ideal of the first half of the century, was expensive and took years to construct. To meet the influx of students, the schools erected temporary structures, often Quonset huts or frame buildings, and later on contracted for plain brick classroom and office quarters rather than the ornate structures of the prewar period. Woodrow Wilson had boasted that by utilizing College Gothic, Princeton had pushed back its history a millennium. His university, and other prestigious ones of the period, did look somewhat like Oxford and Cambridge, or other old European universities, and the less prestigious schools imitated them. The colleges of the late 1940s and early 1950s, however, rejected this, and if their newer buildings appeared somewhat temporary, they were more efficient and serviceable. Here too, the break with tradition was important. The enlarged colleges and universities of the postwar period had been constructed upon the foundations established before the war, but the result surprised and dismayed many who had been raised in the old ways.

The invasion of the campuses by veterans was only the first of the waves to transform the colleges and universities in the postwar period. Contrary to expectations, there was no depression in the late 1940s or early 1950s. Instead, the American economy expanded rapidly, quickly becoming the dominant force in the non-Communist world. Business and government demanded trained and trainable personnel, to a greater extent than even they had in the 1920s, and once again the institutions of higher learning were called upon to provide them. Furthermore, the wartime experience of universities as research arms of various federal agencies continued in the Cold War, while the commercial enterprises too utilized the talents of faculty members. This had been done before; the academic in government service had his roots in La-Follette's University of Wisconsin, Wilson's New Freedom, and Roosevelt's New Deal, while corporations had utilized academic scientists since the turn of the century. What was different, however, was the magnitude of the situation during the Cold War, when academic "think tanks" existed at several major universities, manned by professors who had little contact with any students except a handful of graduate assistants.

The quantitative changes of the early 1950s may have been

more significant, and this was derived in part from the veterans, often the same people who had sparked the initial expansion of the colleges and universities. As has been indicated, the birthrate had dropped sharply in the late 1920s and early 1930s; in 1936, there were 18.4 live births per thousand population (in contrast, there had been more than 50 per thousand just prior to the Civil War, and as recently as 1910, 30 per thousand). The rate had risen somewhat during World War II, a phenomenon explained by wartime marriages, looser sexual morality, and the end of the depression. In 1945, when the rate was 20.4 per thousand, most demographers anticipated a leveling off after a slight jump, this the result of the return of servicemen. Such had been the case after the Civil War, and again after World War I. The rate did jump to 24.1 in 1945, and then to 26.6 in 1946. Toward the end of the year it appeared a decline would be in order—again, following the pattern after past wars.

The rate did not decline. It was 24.9 in 1951, a minor dip given the unusually large amount of babies in the late 1940s, and the prediction that the new mothers would wait several more years before they had additional children. Then it rose to 25.1 in 1952, a level that was maintained until the end of the decade. By then *Cosmopolitan* magazine and the popular press, recognizing the phenomenon, indicated that large families had become "fashionable," while polls showed that newlyweds hoped to have at least three children, preferably before the wife reached the age of 30. And all the while the average married age for females was dropping, going from 20.5 in 1946 to 20.1 in 1956. After a sudden upsurge after the war, the divorce rate stabilized, while the rate of marriages rose steadily. *Cosmopolitan* gave the fashion a name: "togetherness." It implied life in the suburbs, a two-car garage, white-collar employment—and many children. Other periodicals, concentrating upon this last item, dubbed it the "baby boom."

The phenomenon continued throughout the early 1950s, declining slightly toward the end of that decade. Not until 1965 was there a return to the 1945 reproduction rate, while there were fewer marriages than anticipated in the 1950s and far more divorces. Thus the baby boom of 1946–55 was like a huge, undigested, statistical anomaly on the demographic charts. The babies born in this period would upset the nation for the rest of their lives, creating new problems and shortages whenever they entered the next stage in their development. Characteristically, the nation would respond by a hurried effort to accommodate them and then, just when this was accomplished, the population of that age group would decline, leaving an overbuilt and underutilized sector of the economy. First there was a shortage of maternity hospitals and doctors with various child-related specialties after the war, and then came a housing boom, as parents sought additional living space for their children (the rapid growth of suburbia may in part be accounted for by the large numbers of babies). The next shortage, of course, was in the elementary schools, and when this occurred, the colleges and universities experienced their second major postwar shock.

There had been 19.4 million elementary school students in 1920, and 21.3 million in 1939. In 1940, once again as a result of the declining birthrate during the depression, only 18.8 million children were in the nation's elementary schools, or approximately as many as had been in attendance in 1916, when there were 30 million fewer Americans. Yet at that time, 76 per cent of the school-age children were in elementary schools, while in 1940, the amount was more than 85 per cent. Clearly, the nation was growing older, and the low birthrate appeared to indicate a general stagnation in the elementary school cohort.

In 1948, when some of the babies born toward the end of the war came to the elementary schools, there were 18.3 million in attendance. Two years later, when the leading edge of the baby boom arrived in kindergarten, the figure was 19.4 million. At mid-decade, some 25 million children were in the elementary schools, which were expanding as rapidly as possible to meet the demands made upon them. This had an immediate and dramatic effect upon finances. In 1944, Americans spent only $2.5 billion on all aspects of public elementary and secondary education. This figure was doubled by 1950, and doubled again in 1956. By then expenditures for new plant, only $54 million in the last year of the war, had reached $2.4 billion, as the nation engaged in a massive drive to upgrade its schools and create classrooms for the new students.

This had an immediate effect upon the teaching profession. Prior to the war, teachers were considered fortunate in that they had safe jobs with fairly descent salaries. But there was a labor shortage during the war, and in 1944 there were only 828,000 classroom teachers; many had entered the armed forces or had taken work in defense areas. It was believed that once the war ended—and the depression resumed—the old glut would reappear. Such was not the case. Instead, the demands for teachers increased as the schools came to appreciate the dimensions of the baby boom. In 1956 there were 1.2 million teachers, and there would have been more were it not for a general shortage of trained personnel—for the first time in American history, there were many more positions than people to fill them. Salaries rose sharply. In 1944, the average annual income for American teachers had been $1,728. Twelve years later the salary reached $4,156 and was rising rapidly, as school districts bid against one another for recent graduates.

The veterans had spearheaded the first postwar college and university expansion, but this had petered out by the early 1950s—in 1953, only 138,000 veterans were in attendance, and by 1955 only 42,000.[14] By then, however, teachers-in-training—in part for the children of veterans—had taken their places. For all intents and purposes, many liberal arts colleges and universities had become teacher-training institutions. Furthermore, almost all the normal schools were gone, replaced by four-year teachers' colleges, while those students hoping to obtain positions in the secondary schools were obliged to take many courses in the liberal arts area, this too part of the general upgrading of programs. In time, the secondary-education students would take virtually the same programs as those in the liberal arts, and in addition, some would have to complete their master's degrees before receiving full certification in their states.

As a result, there was no major decline in the number of college students in the 1950s, as many educators had feared would be the case when the veterans graduated. Instead, the college population expanded once the pressures upon the teacher-training institutions were felt. In 1949, there were 2.4 million students enrolled in the nation's institutions of higher learning. As the veteran wave receded and the effects of the Korean War were felt, the figure declined to 2.1 million in 1951.[15] There was a slight increase in the student population in 1952, and in 1953, attendance was 2.2 million. In 1957, over 3 million students were in the colleges and universities, with various education programs among the most popular in the nation. To serve them college faculties expanded; there were 247,000 such teachers and researchers in 1950, and more than 300,000 in 1957.

There were major differences between the veterans' effects upon higher education and those of the new educationalists of the 1950s. Because of the way the GI Bill had been written, it made little difference whether the student attended a public or a private institution. In either case, the government would pay full tuition. But the teacher candidates of the 1950s who were not veterans had to pay their own way, and so many hoped to enter public institutions rather than the more expensive private ones. A student anticipating employment in the private sector might wish an Ivy League degree as a door-opener at the more prestigious firms. Positions in public school teaching, however, were usually determined by civil service requirements and state regulations, which might be satisfied just as easily at the mass institutions run by the state. So the teacher candidates crowded their ways into these places, obliging their states to construct additional facilities, and in the process to upgrade their colleges and universities. In 1950, half the nation's college and university students attend public institutions. By the end of the decade, six out of ten of them were enrolled in state and municipal colleges and universities.[16]

By then, many college and university administrators and faculty members had come to understand the meaning of the demographic charts. The baby boom cohort would begin knocking on their doors in the early 1960s, at which time an even greater expansion would be required. In what had become an almost traditional aspect of such extrapolations, those who made them underestimated the numbers, desires, and nature of their next group of students.

THE PROLIFERATION OF THE MASS INTELLECTUAL

The nation's colleges and universities had responded to the needs of their students in the late 1940s and the 1950s. In so doing, they had been obliged to change, often radically, and only in the late 1950s had leading educators begun to assess the meaning of these transformations and consider their implications for the future. The students themselves had changed; they were markedly different from their predecessors. In the first place, there were more of them. Almost 4.5 million students received bachelor's degrees from 1948 to 1960. Approximately the same amount had received the degree from the end of the Civil War to the close of World War II, eighty years later. The age of mass higher education, financed in large part by local, state, and federal agencies, had begun.

Before World War I, the collegians had been the dominant force, and while the professors were beginning to achieve some power, especially at the state universities of the Midwest, the stereotype of the absentminded professor continued as the image of the profession. The grinds of this period might have dominated the graduate schools, but they held little sway over the undergraduate imagination; individuals attending college simply to get a good education were rare. In the 1920s and 1930s those students seeking professional training of one kind or another—the lineal descendants of the grinds—grew in number, but while they pursued their studies more avidly than the collegians, that latter group was still a dominant force and ideal, surviving even the Great Depression. The postwar veterans too were concerned with professionalism, and their presence on the campus killed the last vestiges of collegian influence at all but the older and often out-of-the-way institutions, and perhaps in some of the southern universities as well. But even while the postwar veterans set the tone in the late 1940s, it was evident that it would not last—when the veterans departed, they would be replaced by the high school graduates of the late 1940s and early 1950s.

The college student of 1949 had been born in the depression—the freshman of that year, if he or she was 17, had been born in 1932, the last year of the Hoover administration. The student's childhood had been spent in hard times, followed by a major war. Despite the Korean War and the Cold War, such a student had not known a major conflict in his adolescence, and there had been no new depression. The anxieties were present, to be sure, but the reality was not.

The demand for college graduates was real enough, however, and the students understood this and meant to profit therefrom.

Many followed the examples set by the veterans; although they were much younger and lacked some of the veterans' drive and seriousness, they were equally ambitious. Those who hoped to obtain positions as teachers were required to enroll in liberal arts courses—in effect become what society considered "educated people," for that was what elementary and secondary school officials said they wanted. At the same time businessmen spoke highly of "well-rounded inviduals" and encouraged potential trainees to take a variety of liberal arts courses, not merely those in their specialty. Thus was wedded the attitude of professionalism and the content of liberal education.

Learning for its own sake as well as for the purpose of obtaining jobs became respectable. Those professors at liberal arts colleges who long had spoken of the need for an educated citizenry—but rarely encountered classes of young people who agreed with them—now found their audiences. Gone was the stereotype of the absentminded professor, and in its place the image of a person of knowledge who was accorded prestige—and rewards as well, for due to the rapid expansion of colleges and universities and a shortage of teachers, salaries rose, going from an average of $4,354 in 1950 to $6,810 a decade later.

It was an age of mass education. And its products, as might have been expected, were the mass intellectuals—large groups of people conversant in liberal arts, literate, and accustomed to dealing with abstractions. This was a new force and class, one not quite understood at the time. The collegian had emerged from the old colleges, and the professionals from the graduate schools. The mass intellectuals found their homes and places of incubation in a new structure that, in the early 1960s, was known as the multiversity.

10

Television: The New Reality

Harvard economist Seymour Harris spoke out against the GI Bill's educational benefits program in 1944, and continued to do so for the next five years. In itself, this was not unusual, for many leading academics had doubts about the measure. Harris seemed unconcerned about the veterans' abilities at adjusting to college life, and in fact remarked that the schools might be enriched by the new students. Rather, he saw the program as part of a far larger and more important movement, the broadening of the college and university population to include all who wished to attend. He considered this dangerous to an extreme.

In the past, said Harris, the institutions had demanded that their students measure up to certain requirements. Although these had been breached on occasion, for the most part the system had succeeded. Newcomers had learned the ways of the older students, accepted them, conformed, and so left the schools with at least the semblance of an education. Now this could change. Might not the enlarged student bodies, swollen by veterans and a far larger percentage of high school graduates than previously had gone on to college, effect a watering down of standards? Already the President's Commission on Higher Education, reporting in 1947, had indicated that such might be desirable. "If the colleges are to educate the great body of American youth, they must provide programs for the development of other abilities than those involved in academic aptitude, and they cannot continue to concentrate on students with one type of intelligence to the neglect of youth with other talents."

Extrapolating the student enrollments of the 1920s and 1930s into the next generation, Harris envisaged a nation in which more than a third of all high school graduates would go on to college, to the great detriment of standards. While this might be deplorable for the colleges, he wrote, it would be disastrous for the economy. Potentially fine skilled workers would be diverted into liberal arts programs, from which they would emerge four years later as rather mediocre graduates, unwilling to accept manual jobs, insisting upon professional or at the very least managerial positions. These positions would not exist, and so even the best of the graduates would be hard-pressed to locate themselves in the labor force. While others spoke and wrote of the possible fascistic tendencies of veterans, Harris painted a picture of tens of thousands of graduates, their expectations raised by their experiences, finding themselves a permanent glut on the market. To make matters worse, he saw no way by which this could be avoided. As did many other economists, Harris feared a postwar depression, in some ways more dangerous than that of the 1930s. A frustrated cadre of mass intellectuals might not accept a warmed-over version of the WPA, and insist instead upon power and status. Such people would be fine targets for some demagogue; their reactions would be unpredictable, for the situation would be unique.

Harris presented his conclusions regarding the problems in higher education before a limited public in the Autumn 1948 issue of the *Harvard Educational Review*. His article, entitled "The Future of Higher Education," held that academics were doing many students a disservice by encouraging them to seek degrees. Then, on January 2, 1949, a second article, "Millions of A.B.'s and No Jobs," appeared in the New York *Times*, and it was then that he argued that the nation would soon have a permanent jobless corps of college graduates. Long considered a political liberal, Harris was now critized for holding elitist views. In order to explain his position more fully, he wrote a short book, which was published later that year. In his preface, Harris attempted to sum up his findings. "I must also add that we are being unfair to the country's youth if we encourage them in further education, with-

out at the same time warning them that a large proportion, after graduation, may not enter the professions or occupations of their choice."

Harris illustrated his points with precision and clarity, and from the available statistics and simple logic, his conclusions appeared unassailable. For example, he noted that about one third of the "professional outlets" for graduates was in teaching. Should the colleges enroll from 2.5 million to 4.6 million, as he thought they would, the required number of openings for teachers in schools and colleges by 1968 would have to expand by about 3.3 to 4.5 times the numbers in 1940 to provide jobs for all who wanted them. Clearly this would not occur. Given the current growth rate, "there is going to be a surplus of potential teachers. . . ." Harris was gloomier than ever. "I see no easy remedy for the surfeit of college graduates."[1]

The remedy was there, however; Harris's projections proved inaccurate. In 1968, there were close to 7 million college and university students, far more than anyone had anticipated. Throughout much of the decade there was a shortage of teachers, and not a glut. In 1949, there were some 1.5 million teachers on all levels, from kindergarten to graduate and professional schools. Twenty years later, there were 2.5 million of them.

How could so distinguished and respected an economist be so wrong? It might be argued that he could not have foreseen the implications of the civil rights movement in the education area, or the great demands of a surprisingly vigorous economy. Nor could he have imagined the reactions of some young people to the Vietnam War, when they sought deferments by enrolling in schools. But he did know of the baby boom in 1949, and yet ignored it. Nowhere in his writings is there a discussion of demography, and in fact, Harris extrapolated the 1940 birthrate rather than that of the late 1940s. He believed there would be 175 million Americans by 1975; instead, there were more than 220 million.[2]

THE IDEA OF MULTIVERSITY

As Harris wrote in Cambridge, Clark Kerr, a professor at the Berkeley campus of the University of California, was making a reputation for himself in several areas. As a member of the faculty

at the Institute of Industrial Relations, Kerr was considered a pioneering thinker in the sociology and politics of work—what would later be known as interpersonal relations. In addition, his thoughts on what the future might bring were attracting attention, and Kerr was in great demand as speaker and panelist throughout the country. But his home base remained at Berkeley, one of the fastest-growing institutions in the nation, both in terms of population and reputation. The world of academia appeared far more promising from Berkeley than it did from Harvard, and the future seemed brighter to the young political scientist than it did to the older economist.

If Harris was troubled about the quantity of students, Kerr was concerned about the quality of academic life. The internal subversion issue, which had shaken Hollywood in 1947, hit the colleges and universities two years later. Throughout the nation, professors and administrators debated matters of academic freedom in the face of assaults from outside. Were the colleges part of a network of communism? Few believed this to be the case, and only a handful of national figures made the charge, but faculty members, sensitive to such matters, entered into the debate, and this, perhaps, helped stimulate additional interest in the matter. For some faculty members and some schools, attacks from anti-Communists were real enough, especially after Senator Joseph McCarthy emerged as the leader of the movement in 1950. State legislators demanded investigations of public colleges, more often than not to obtain political advantage or to please constituents rather than in reaction to actual evidence of subversion. In many states, professors were singled out, as a group, to take loyalty oaths, as though their positions somehow placed them under suspicion. In addition, trustees at private colleges and universities fell into line. Due to real or suspected pro-Communist leanings, teachers were fired or were unable to find employment.

Faculties rallied in defense of academic freedom at many campuses, while at others, teachers remained still, hoping the movement would pass them by. How strong were the anti-Communists? How much influence did they have, and how far would they go in using it? The answers were not readily available; the depth and breadth of anticommunism in academia could not be gauged. But on some campuses, where the dangers of "witch-hunts" were minor, faculties behaved as though the stakes were

prepared and the faggots readied. Anti-anticommunism was also a product of the times, and just as Senator McCarthy's supporters rallied to combat nonexistent Communists on some campuses, on others defenders of academic freedom saw witch-hunters where none existed. In this somewhat paranoid atmosphere, tempers ran high and the potential for confrontation was great. It had been that way in Hollywood after the House Committee on Un-American Activities ended its investigation—suspected Communists were placed on one blacklist, while some of those who had been friendly witnesses before the investigators went on another. So it was at the colleges in the late 1940s and early 1950s. To oppose the loyalty oaths placed one under attack from one group, while to favor it might mean ostracism from another. The issue polarized faculties, but more important, isolated them in the face of real or suspected "outside influences," and encouraged them to band together to prevent deeper penetrations of academic freedom than had already been made. The concept of the college as both citadel and fortress emerged from the anti-Communist crusade of this period, with the liberal or radical professor at the barricades, leading his troops with words and deeds. The institutions of higher learning were not only places at which students could prepare for their roles in society and professors conduct research to be utilized "on the outside," but also the essence of reality; not only part of the world, but also its center. It was this, too, that interested and intrigued Clark Kerr in late 1949.

Berkeley was one of those campuses involved with both anti-communism and anti-anticommunism. Politically ambitious Lieutenant Governor Goodwin Knight more often than not sided with the anti-Communists, as did a majority of the trustees, while Governor Pat Brown usually spoke out for the anti-anti-Communists.[3] A large majority of the faculty opposed outside interference with campus affairs. The national American Association of University Professors, founded to provide economic security for professors as well as to safeguard their academic freedom, supported the faculty and censured those who acted against them. Later on, the AAUP condemned the loyalty oaths, but there were no calls for strikes or political actions; the support was moral and intellectual instead.

Kerr was at the center of this struggle, one of those entrusted by the faculty with gathering support throughout the academic community. Later on, he negotiated with the regents, and showed an adeptness at the art. In 1950, when faculty members who refused to sign the loyalty oath were dismissed, Kerr emerged as one of the leaders of the antiregents camp, and more important perhaps, a symbol of academic freedom to the intellectual community, which only a few months before had not known of his existence.

Although the Kerr forces lost several battles, they won the war, and a leading indication of this was the advancing career of Clark Kerr. In 1952 he became chancellor at Berkeley. Seven years later, he was named president of the entire seven-campus University of California system. The loyalty oath was dropped; the fired professors were, where possible, rehabilitated and rehired; the campuses were opened to dissident political organizations, many of which had been banned in the late 1940s and early 1950s. For these and other similar actions, Kerr was awarded the Alexander Meiklejohn Prize, given by the AAUP to those who had done most to preserve and extend academic freedom. But defense of civil liberties was only one aspect of Kerr's career, and not the most important. In the early 1960s, Kerr was better known as the proclaimer of a new entity, which he called the "multiversity."

In the spring of 1963, Kerr went to Harvard to deliver the Godkin lectures. As was the custom, these were collected and published, and in Kerr's case, were given the title *The Uses of the University*. There were three lectures in all, "The Idea of Multiversity," "The Realities of the Federal Grant University," and "The Future of the City of Intellect." It was the last talk that attracted the most attention, for in it Kerr developed the idea of multiversity and indicated where the nation's academic communities appeared to be heading. Earlier he had defined the multiversity as "not one community but several—the community of the undergraduate and the community of the graduate; the community of the humanist, the community of the social scientist, and the community of the scientist; the communities of the professional schools; the community of all the nonacademic personnel; the community of the administrators." It would appear that the multiversity was merely an enlarged university, but this was not so. According to Kerr, the university of the past had prided itself on serving the needs of the students and faculties. The multiversity, on the other hand, is "a prime instrument of national purpose.

This is new. This is the essence of the transformation now engulfing our universities." What the railroads accomplished for the second half of the nineteenth century and the automobile for the first half of the twentieth century "may be done for the second half of this century by the knowledge industry: that is, to serve as the focal point for national growth. And the university is at the center of the knowledge process." The metropolis was giving way to the "ideopolis," the community of scholars. "One such plateau runs from Boston to Washington. At the universities and laboratories situated along this range are found 46 per cent of the American Nobel Prize winners in the sciences and 40 per cent of the members of the National Academy of Sciences. A second range with its peaks runs along the California coast." These leading intellectuals were bound to one another by ties of interest, not through the institutions of which they were members. Doubtless the numbers of students would grow in the 1960s, and calls upon the talents of such individuals would increase. They would travel from school to school and divide their time among academia, private corporations, and government service—with international service a distinct possibility for some at least. The graduate schools would take care of intellectuals-to-be, while the colleges and junior colleges would cater to the needs of the others. The most desirable faculty members would no longer see undergraduates. "Teaching loads will be competitively reduced, sometimes to zero," he thought, even while recognizing there would be problems. "Although more teachers are needed and students complaining about lack of attention," the needs of society at large would have to be served. Kerr concluded with a vision of "cities of intellect," and asked, "Will it be the salvation of our society?" He gave little doubt of his belief that it would.[4]

What of the undergraduates? Clearly their needs would become less important at the multiversity, where the graduate schools were central. "The best graduate students prefer fellowships and research assistantships to teaching assistantships," he said. "Postdoctoral fellows who might fill the gap usually do not teach. Average class size has been increasing." Whatever else it was, then, the multiversity became, for the undergraduates, a knowledge factory, in which the student became a faceless number, one of the mob of would-be intellectuals, at a campus where monetary and status awards went to those who knew little of the inside of the classroom. Such was the case at institutions that served society, not students. "How to escape the cruel paradox that a superior faculty results in an inferior concern for undergraduate teaching is one of our more pressing problems." Kerr did not offer a solution in the Godkin lectures, or anywhere else; for this was not, by his own definition of the term, a major concern for multiversity.

Others were investigating the problem, and indeed had done so for the past decade, for Kerr was not only offering a blueprint for the future but also mapping the contours of the present. The "free-lance professor" was becoming more familiar in the 1950s, offering advice to corporations and government, flying to Washington or New York "on assignment," and receiving the applause and envy of their more academically inclined colleagues on their return. With the advent of the Kennedy administration in 1961, intellectualism became fashionable, and the status of the Ivy League professor reached a new high. And one measure of this status was "teaching load." Generally speaking, the fewer hours one spent in contact with students on almost any level, the greater was one's prestige. At the university, the ambitious faculty member might hope to rise to deanship, perhaps a presidency. But the teaching aspect remained central to the integrity of the institution. Not so at the multiversity, where faculty members aspired to consultantships, positions in government, places on foundation panels—almost anything that would take them away from the campus. The problem, then, was how to retain the services of the prestigious faculty member while at the same time accepting his new status and work habits. The answer was to be found in several techniques—the use of graduate assistants and large lectures were most common. More interesting, in the 1950s at least, was television teaching.

Even before World War II there had been talk of a "television school of the air," this at a time when the industry barely existed. Television would not replace teachers, said the experts, but merely supplement their work. This was an important consideration, for there was a surplus of teachers who could hardly be expected to co-operate in making themselves technologically redundant. Surgical operations might be televised to medical students; astronomy classes throughout the nation might witness the workings of Mount Wilson Observatory; law schools would benefit from seeing Congress in action. "Only a rash person would venture to set any limit to the future usefulness of television in the classroom," said James Angell, president emeritus of Yale and educational counselor to NBC in the early 1940s. "The most unimaginative person can at once foresee many possible developments of outstanding value and interest."[5]

Even more possibilities presented themselves in the late 1950s, when the teacher shortage at the college level was beginning to be felt. Instead of having a professor lecture to a large class, numbering in the hundreds, would it not be better to disperse the students throughout the campus, in small rooms each with a television set, and have them watch in this fashion? The professor might put his lecture on film or tape, and it might be played while he was in Washington, consulting the President. Or a two-way telephone arrangement might be developed, so that students miles from the studio could ask questions and have them answered. For a while, television teaching was considered a vital aspect of the multiversity, even though Clark Kerr had his doubts about it. Studios and camera setups were installed at several large universities, and some small colleges indicated their interest in making television an integral part of most classes—this in an attempt to be modern and progressive.

Despite high hopes, intense efforts, and much foundation support, televised teaching never became an important feature of higher education. Some argued that the experiments hadn't been given sufficient chance, that they had been aborted by student unrest and disruption in the late 1960s. Advocates might point to a handful of programs deemed successful by their initiators. But more noted that students didn't respond well to television in the classrooms, even while they remained glued to sets at home. Television served to intensify the coldness and lack of human contact at large schools, and in any case, could not hold student interest, as did the more conventional lectures and seminars. Students seemed to respond differently to the teacher in front of them than to the same person on the TV screen. They might pay attention to the human being in flesh and blood, but would become restless when only viewing his or her image.

A somewhat different situation existed when programs labeled as "educational" were presented on the home screen. New York University's "Sunrise Semester," which featured faculty members delivering lectures to home viewers who might take the course for credit, had some success, as did other programs on public television channels, especially a series on American history by Professor James Shenton of Columbia University. But most were failures, perhaps because they were dull. In the early 1950s it was common to train a camera on the lecturer, who might be standing in front of a desk or at a blackboard and talked as though in a classroom. Some faculty were frightened by the technology, or at least behaved as though they were. Others did not know how to pace their talks, and some overprepared. The large majority, while usually leading teachers at their institutions, were failures on television—at least as far as their audiences were concerned.

There were exceptions, notably Professor Frank Baxter of the University of Southern California, a Shakespeare expert who in the mid-1950s became a television celebrity, in part the result of his enthusiasm for his subject, great natural abilities, sense of humor, and stage presence. The most effective educational force on network television in this period was Alistair Cooke, an English-born journalist who hosted the network program "Omnibus" with ease and panache. Others, with greater learning and success on the lecture circuit, were unable to attract audiences. Educational television failed, as had educational radio before it. Whatever else it became, commercial and public television did not become media for public education in the strict sense of the term; Clark Kerr's troubled conscience regarding the undergraduates would not be assuaged by the electronic medium. Television, which along with the automobile was a key technological invention and social influence in the twentieth century, came to influence almost every aspect of national life. But not education.

Why?

TELEVISION AS INVENTION AND BUSINESS

Radio had its Marconi and motion pictures its Edison, men who could be singled out as "fathers of the industry," even while recognizing that each had a long series of progenitors. These technicians had been followed by businessmen—Sarnoff and the corporate leaders at AT&T, Westinghouse, General Electric, and RCA in the case of radio, Zukor and the other immigrant tycoons for movies—who helped organize the industry and give it a form.

In turn the businessmen had been challenged by and in some cases obliged to share power with the artists. Thus there had been a continual tension between form and content, dictated by the demands of the audience, the nature of technology, and the personalities of key individuals—as well as occasional governmental regulation, and competition with rival media.

This situation did not exist in television. No single individual could be credited with inventing the technology, although two, Vladimir Zworykin and Philo Farnsworth, were more important than the others. But they were more akin to DeForest than to Marconi—they produced inventions and perfected techniques that made the work of others practical; neither man was responsible for the keystone effort. Furthermore, television developed within a pre-existent business structure and did not have to create one of its own. The same was true for the art, at least for the first few years. In effect, television was the child of radio, motion pictures, and the press, and in its early days adapted the forms and contents of these to suit its own technology and requirements.

This was to have been expected; after all, radio had borrowed from the concert hall and vaudeville, motion pictures from the stage, and newspapers had evolved over hundreds of years, continually incorporating new technologies and concepts. It was different with television, even though it became a more powerful medium than its predecessors. To this day it has not produced its own essential structure, either artistically or commercially. There was no early period of trial and error among a group of pioneers, as there had been in the other media. Instead, from the first, television was an arena for giants. Nor was there a period of relatively free enterprise, for the government was there at creation. Each of the other media experienced some measure of this; there was little in the evolution of the television industry.

The position of the artists (performers, writers, directors) was not as clear in television as in other "idea industries." This was due in large part to the nature of the business and the presence of government, but each might have been overcome had the artists themselves some clear idea of what they wanted. Just as there was no single technological genius for television—no Marconi or Edison—there was no pioneering businessman, such as Zukor or the young David Sarnoff. Instead, television was the product of corporate intelligence, and not even the contribution of Sarnoff, important though it was, was indispensable. The industry lacked a "father," a recognized founder, and this, too, is an indication of the essentially derivative nature of the medium and industry.

European technicians explored the possibility of transmitting pictures over wire and though the air a century ago. In 1862 an Italian priest, Abbé Caselli, devised a crude method of sending images over telegraph wires. Twenty-two years later a German engineer, Paul Nipkow, invented an "electrical telescope," really a crude transmitter and receiver. Lazare Weiller conducted experiments with the "Nipkow disc" in the 1890s, and later on Julius Elster, Hans Geitel, Ferdinand Braun, William Crookes, and Boris Rosing added to the technology. On the eve of World War I a British scientist, A. Campbell Swinton, developed a cathode tube capable of electronic scanning, and his papers on the subject were well known to researchers. J. L. Baird, another Englishman, actually constructed receivers and transmitters, and by 1930 was sending test signals over BBC to individuals who had purchased his sets for $130. But the work was not commercialized. Television remained a laboratory curiosity, and these men are memorialized in a handful of histories of technology and in few other places.

American inventors had a more commercial view of television. Alexander Graham Bell considered wedding sight and sound in his telephone, and in 1880 he took out patents for television devices. Forty years later Herbert Ives of Bell Laboratories was assigned the task of perfecting "telephoto" transmission, and in 1927 he sent a "pictorialized broadcast" of a Herbert Hoover speech from New York to Washington. By the end of the decade Ives and others at Bell had developed a color receiver, and an experimental system was established in New York, where it was witnessed by several thousand people. Bell Laboratories continued to experiment with the device, considering it the kind of telephone Alexander Graham Bell had dreamed about. In time such a telephone was perfected, but in the meanwhile, others pioneered in commercial television.

In order to finance his television experiments, Boris Rosing took a position at the St. Petersburg Institute of Technology, where among other duties he instructed students in electrical subjects.

Zworykin was one of these, and just before World War I he became Rosing's assistant. While working for the Russian Wireless Telegraph and Telephone Company in 1917, Zworykin conducted his own experiments. Two years later, Zworykin immigrated to the United States, and after failing to find backing for his own company, he joined Westinghouse as a radio researcher. Unable to convince that company of the importance of television, he left in 1921 to work for a small electrical manufacturing firm in Kansas, only to return to Westinghouse in 1923, when its leaders had a change of heart. Toward the end of the year, Zworykin had perfected the iconoscope, a practical photoelectric tube for television transmission. Although the Westinghouse leadership was pleased with the result and helped Zworykin obtain his patent, the company did nothing to commercialize it, and for the next five years the scientist worked in his laboratory, developing new television tubes, none of which were given commercial application.

At the time of Zworykin's invention, RCA was still owned by other companies, Westinghouse among them. Radio was becoming popular, and all efforts were geared to the increased production of receivers, the development of new transmission apparatus, and the creation of stations. David Sarnoff, who earlier had spoken of the commercial possibilities of the "radio music box," was charged with developing both the art and the commerce of that invention. Like others, he knew of television, of Ives' experiments at Bell Laboratories, and of Zworykin's work at Westinghouse. In a memorandum to the RCA directors early in 1923, he wrote, "I believe that television, which is the technical name for seeing instead of hearing by radio, will come to pass in due course. . . . I also believe that transmission and reception of motion pictures by radio will be worked out within the next decade." In a speech at the University of Missouri the following year, Sarnoff said, "Let us think of every farmhouse equipped not only with a sound-receiving device but with a screen that would mirror the sights of life."[6] He continued to write and talk of television throughout the rest of the decade, but could do nothing more so long as the radio boom continued, RCA remained under the control of other companies, and he lacked authority within the firm. The situation had changed by 1929. Early that year, Sarnoff and Zworykin held a series of meetings, at the conclusion of which the inventor asked for $100,000 to perfect a system of commercial television. Sarnoff agreed to the request, and with this, the company became the leader of the yet-to-be-born industry.

While Zworykin met with Sarnoff, the second American pioneer, Philo Farnsworth, was seeking backing for his inventions. A farmboy from Rigby, Idaho, who became interested in radio through the reading of popular magazines, Farnsworth attended Brigham Young University in Utah, working his way through by repairing radios. In his spare time, he conducted several crude experiments with television. Shortly before graduating, Farnsworth met George Everson, a San Francisco businessman, who agreed to raise money to back further experiments in the field. From 1926 to 1929, Farnsworth spent some $140,000 of his backers' money, with spotty results. He needed additional funds, and headed East to find them. New York's investment banks weren't interested, but some of the directors of Philco Radio were, and they offered to finance Farnsworth's experiments provided they were geared to the creation of a commercial product. The inventor agreed, and in 1930 he took out his first patent. Others followed, along with a visit by Zworykin to the California laboratory to check them out. For a while it appeared that RCA might offer to purchase his patents, or give the inventor a position, but nothing came of this.

Farnsworth had little interest in business, and almost no talent in the board room. His operation was close to bankruptcy in 1938; to salvage it, he offered to sell patents to RCA and was rebuffed. Then he approached Paramount, and talked of the potential in a marriage of motion pictures and television. Once again, he had no success. Obliged either to give up or continue on his own, he organized Farnsworth Television and Radio Corporation, scraped up enough money to purchase the manufacturing facilities of the Capehart Corporation, and began turning out radio receivers. The World War II boom enabled the company to prosper, and Farnsworth became fairly wealthy, but he remained far from the board rooms, in his laboratory, working on television. Due to his efforts, the company owned many key patents, which it licensed to others, RCA in particular.

The same situation existed at Hazeltine Electronics and Allen B. DuMont Laboratories, each headed by a television pioneer. Neither of these had the financial power or the managerial experience to challenge RCA, and so they left the field to others. Columbia Broadcasting, while not as large as RCA, had become its leading competitor in programming, and was interested in entering television. In 1936 it acquired the services of Peter Goldmark, a young Hungarian engineer who led the CBS technological efforts, and three years later the company erected a television transmitter on top of the Chrysler Building at a cost of $650,000. Still, it lacked the funds and the will to make a major drive in the early 1940s, so that RCA continued to lead the others when the war ended.

Need television have become the child of radio? There were other possibilities. The leading newspapers might have taken an interest in the medium, as they had in radio, so that by the early 1950s, several key stations, even networks, might have been owned and managed by newspaper publishers. Under such a system the news function could have taken on primary importance, resulting in a radically different relationship between the stations and the Federal Communications Commission. With the exception of the Hearst organization, however, no publisher had the funds and depth for such an undertaking, and the elderly, ailing William Randolph Hearst showed no interest in the medium. Later on some newspapers did purchase stations, usually unaffiliated ones serving local markets, but few were significant factors by the mid-1950s.

Had the motion picture companies entered television, the development of both industries might also have been quite different. In 1938, when Farnsworth held his conversations with Paramount, the affinity between the two was quite evident, at least as much as that between radio and television. The exhibition of television at the 1939–40 New York World's Fair was geared to such a marriage, as guides told visitors that one day, through the use of the tube, they would be able to see movies at home. During World War II there had been some talk of mass television, with large-screen projectors, piping new movies into hundreds of theaters simultaneously, thus saving fortunes on print costs. Technology militated against this plan, and in any case, home television offered even more interesting possibilities.

Before these could be acted upon, however, one had to consider the anatomy of the new medium. Was television radio with pictures? Or could it be considered as a motion picture set for the home? These were key questions, for the industry might have gone either way. The motion-picture link would have required the development of some system of collecting admissions, either through subscriptions or coin-activated screens. In the 1950s several companies, Zenith and Skiatron among them, experimented with such systems, and although nothing came of it, the idea would have been developed had the motion-picture companies entered a relationship with Farnsworth. For while RCA and other radio-oriented firms possessed capital, management, and even talent, they lacked experience in programming visual shows; in the early days, they tended to point their cameras at radio programs performed on sets. The radio networks had the electronic structure for home television—the form—while the motion picture companies possessed ready-made programs, their films—the content. Either the radio networks would have to develop programs, or the motion-picture firms would have to acquire stations. These appeared to be the prime alternatives in the immediate postwar period.

Some motion-picture firms recognized the situation and began to explore the potential of television. Paramount established an experimental studio, while Columbia had a study group look into the matter. But the other major studios, led by MGM, were not interested in the "small screen," even after the postwar boom began. Most Hollywood executives could not believe the public would reject their superior products for the inferior programming then available on television. Paid admissions had been high during the war, and with the return of the old stars, might soon be better. The motion-picture industry leaders hoped that television would prove a fad, and a high-priced one at that. After a while, audiences would return to the theaters, tired of puppet shows, wrestling, and antique educational films. Even if television persisted, the networks would have to knock on Hollywood's door in the end, and television might become a good dumping ground for old B movies, a source of additional profits for the studios.

There was some talk of network films, low-priced shows produced for television. The threat was more apparent than real in the mid-1940s; the studios had the major stars under contract, as well as the best directors and cameramen, and any who dared offer their services to television would suffer Hollywood's retribution. In addition, new talent was informed that too close an identity with television would mean an end to hopes for a Hollywood career.

Hollywood was in no position to destroy the new medium, but the stations did need programs, especially after the initial novelty began to pall. The leading shows in 1947 were in the area of sports (especially the roller derby and wrestling), some live drama ("Kraft Theater"), and childrens' shows (led by "Howdy Doody"). In most parts of the country, programming was limited to a few hours a day, usually in the late afternoon and evening. Radio was still booming, offering superior dramas, expanded sports programs, rapid and complete news, and many variety and situation comedies. Why should the consumer pay some $350 for a miniscule television set, when for a tenth of that figure he could obtain a fine radio? Sarnoff understood this, for more than any other firm RCA had committed itself to television. The company was busily constructing the NBC television network, manufacturing receivers, and trying to organize presentations. The last problem was the most difficult to overcome, for without content, financial and technological expertise would lead nowhere. The motion-picture companies appreciated the situation, and in 1947 rejected feelers from the networks for old movies.

This changed quickly in 1948, when the combination of anti-Communist sentiment and the U. S. Supreme Court's decision in *United States* v. *Paramount et al.* frightened all the executives. The red scare could lead to a decline in paid admissions; the Court decision meant that the long-awaited breakup of studios and distribution facilities was about to take place. Shortly thereafter, Twentieth Century-Fox made an offer to purchase the American Broadcasting Company (formed from the old NBC Blue Network in 1943), which was rejected, and in case was not very serious. The production company's strategy was obvious; it would have entered television through ABC and played its old films on the air. Some Paramount executives, acting even before the divestiture was completed, held conversations with ABC. These continued from 1948 into 1950, when Paramount Pictures was separated from United Paramount Theaters. Industry journals predicted a merger between Paramount Pictures and the television company.

But Paramount was unwilling to enter into such a combination. Instead, in 1951, the theater chain joined with ABC to form ABC-Paramount. This combination was surprising, for the new company still lacked films. Still, United Paramount was able to contribute cash and managerial talent to the industry, and it was an important step in the formation of a television-motion-picture nexus.

Meanwhile, several small motion-picture studios, emboldened by the divestiture, began producing half-hour dramatic and Western films for television, and some of the majors sold a few old movies for viewing. Clearly the new medium was no mere fad, and Hollywood needed a new approach in order to retain audiences. This came in 1949. The studios stopped turning out B movies, and instead began making "blockbusters," spectacles that cost a great deal of money, had many stars, and were filmed in color—the kind of picture one could not adequately see on television's small tube. Big films were booked into many theaters at once, and this saturation policy was supposed to help recoup costs rapidly while drawing the public to the neighborhood movie houses.

The gamble failed. Theater receipts, which were $1.6 billion in 1947, fell to $1.2 billion in 1953 before leveling off and rising somewhat. By then, too, Hollywood had all but capitulated to the new industry, and film sales to television rose rapidly. The surrender was highlighted when in 1955 Mutual Broadcasting (owned by General Tire and Rubber) purchased RKO Pictures. Mutual was not interested in RKO's studios, but rather its film library of 740 features and over 1,000 shorts. These were shown over WOR-TV in New York and stations in other cities under the program title of "Million Dollar Movie" and attracted large enough audiences to repay the purchase price in the first year. The RKO sale opened the floodgates. By mid-1956, more than 1,500 old features had been sold to the networks, while MGM announced it intended to sell an additional 770 movies produced prior to 1949.

Part of the money obtained from film sales went into the conversion of motion-picture sound stages to television operations. Either directly or through affiliates, the large studios became important factors in the production of television films, on occasion producing "packages" of them for the major networks. Columbia

Broadcasting took over the old Republic Studios in Hollywood for its productions, while the Music Corporation of America (MCA) purchased Universal Studios, relinquished its talent agency business under government edict, and concentrated upon television programs and low-cost features for theaters (to be sold to television after completing their runs). At the same time television production firms went to Hollywood, either to purchase their own studios or to erect new ones. Mergers, buy-outs, and transformations followed. Within a decade the old Hollywood was gone, its back lots closed down or geared to the needs of television. Theater films continued to be made, but the theaters themselves were closing or converting to other uses, as television became the central American amusement medium. The studio system was rapidly becoming an institution of the past.

The network executives, however, could not await the resolution of their struggle with Hollywood. In the late 1940s they tried to develop their own shows. Given their backgrounds and experience, their early attempts were based on radio models. They utilized radio artists and technical personnel, drew upon the theater and old vaudeville talent, and searched for new ideas and people. As had been the case with radio, the shows were broadcast live, usually from New York, and sent out to affiliates. The radio structure persisted in sponsorship, too. Just as the radio practice had been to have sponsors take or even create their own shows, so it was in early television. The first to do this was "Kraft Theater," in 1947, but the best known was "Texaco Star Theater," starring Milton Berle, which appeared the following year. There were also the "Philco Television Theater," the "General Electric Theater," and the "Ford Theater," as well as the "Colgate Comedy Hour" and the "Camel News Caravan." Almost all such sponsor-identified shows were short-lived, the victims of changing tastes, new film technologies, and just as important, the economics of a new philosophy of advertising.

Simply stated, television shows cost more to produce than did their radio counterparts; in this respect, they were more akin to films than to radio. Talent costs were not high, even though artists in television dramas had to memorize most of their lines, a labor not required for radio dramas. But cameras and sets had to be amortized, costumes rented, makeup artists hired, and many other problems dealt with. Even the electricity bills were higher, the result of the many lights used on the sets. In 1948, "Texaco Star Theater" cost $15,000 a show, and this included Milton Berle's fee. Ten years later, network specials could run well over $100,000 for an hour; by the 1970s, weekly dramatic programs were being budgeted at well over twice that figure. Major advertisers increased their expenditures during the period, but most of them saw little to be gained in placing most of it in one show. Instead, they would purchase "spots" on popular programs, whose prices were geared to their rating in the polls. In the great days of radio, the person who put together the package for the sponsor was a key individual; in television, he was replaced by the time buyer, the executive capable of judging the merits of new shows before they appeared on the tube, paying low rates on the gamble the programs would be a hit.

This structure enabled small production companies to obtain a great deal of power in the late 1950s and early 1960s. Backed by risk capital and often centered around a single artist or businessman, they would rent equipment and studios, hire actors and actresses, and make a pilot film for a series. This would then be presented to the networks, in the hope that it would find approval. Should the network see merit in the show, it would take an option and try to interest advertisers. If all went well, the sponsored programs would appear on the tube, and further success resulted in new and better contracts. Some production companies expanded and became major forces within the industry—Desilu, organized by Lucille Ball and Desi Arñaz, was one of the first. Failure could result in the company's dissolution, after which its members would join other units.[7]

Such production units, the logical response to the omnivorous demands of television, were also products of a technological development that affected the medium as profoundly as sound had the motion picture.

The sensible way to prepare a pilot was through the use of films, which would be sent to the networks and agencies. The alternative was a separate live performance for each interested party, and this was not only unbearable financially but also unrealistic in that the purchasers were interested in the show on the tube, not live. Films had other advantages. Unlike live shows, they could be edited, replayed several times on the network, or rented to local stations, thus spreading the costs over several performances.[8] But there were drawbacks, too. They were expensive to produce, while those who knew best how to make them were still bound to the motion-picture industry. Some pilot films were made, but most were technically unsatisfactory; unlike the Hollywood products, they appeared on the screen like amateur performances. The matter of replays also presented a problem. Television engineers developed "kinescoping," a simple process by which a motion-picture camera was aimed at the televised image to make the film. These tended to be harsh, grainy, and lacking in contrast; kinescopes could be no better than the televised image, and in the early days they left much to be desired.

At the time most companies involved with tape were interested in sound rather than sight; they predicted that within a decade, the tape recorder would replace the phonograph. Zworykin and others at RCA began experimenting with videotape shortly after the war, and demonstrated a camera in 1953. Several new firms pioneered in this field, and one of them, Ampex Corporation, entered videotape research as well. In 1956 one of its scientists, Charles Ginsburg, perfected a videotape camera and recorder, and Ampex won several basic patents. Within less than a year the first Ampex recorders and cameras, selling for over $50,000, were being installed at the studios, and by the end of the 1960s, the videotape revolution had been completed. Unlike motion pictures and radio, this was not a case of a technology seeking utilization but rather the development of technology to fill recognized requirements.

Videotape had almost all the advantages of film and none of the drawbacks. The tape itself was inexpensive and compact. Unlike film, the completed videotape did not have to be processed, but instead could be played back immediately. With film, the director would shoot his scene but not be able to see it for a day or so. With tape, he could have an instantaneous view of what had been produced. The quality of tape was superior to that of film, especially when the latter was used by newcomers. Tape could be reused many times, and this added to its economies. In fact, the technology had only one drawback, in that tape was difficult to edit, since there were none of the familiar "frames" of film. Rather videotape was opaque, not unlike recording tape, and it could be edited only through the use of special viewing machines. These were expensive and, in the early days, difficult to obtain. More often than not the directors would not edit, but instead tape the program live and play it back over the air, hoping for the best. In this way, videotape preserved the illusion of live performances but combined it with the advantages of the canned ones.

Videotape was the bridge between films and live performances; in effect, it enabled producers to combine the best features of both.[9] By the mid-1960s, almost all network drama, variety, comedy, and late-night programs were either taped before live audiences, or in a studio with audience reactions dubbed in afterward. Tape was particularly well suited to sports events. Given the "instant replay," the director was able to show the audience dramatic moments in a contest—umpire or referee calls included, complete with close-ups and in slow motion. Thus the viewer of a dull game might ignore the action, knowing that the truly important plays would be reshown and analyzed. In effect, this afforded the viewer an advantage over those in the stadium or arena. Sports contests became shows, stadiums were stages, and those in the stands were akin to the crowds of extras in motion pictures, in that they provided a touch of reality for the home viewer. But audiences at sports events were not required for any other purpose, since television receipts were becoming more important each year. Owners of baseball and football teams feared poor attendance, since it might indicate to viewers that the contest was somehow not worth watching, and television receipts were becoming increasingly important. Given the higher rates charged the networks with each new contract, baseball team owners could afford to keep the prices of their tickets low, in the hope of luring the "audience" to the "show."

Until the development of videotape, television had developed along lines that were familiar to old radio hands. Just as in the early 1920s, radio stations had relied upon a pre-existing medium, the phonograph, for its programs, so the television networks tried to utilize films. They turned to live programming only after failing to crack the studio film libraries. Then, as films became available, they were used to complement existing programs. The old movies could be replayed many times, and the audiences for them hardly declined. Given the choice between such a movie whose cost had been amortized, and two hours of comedy and variety programs, which might require over $150,000 to produce, station and network executives naturally preferred films. This situation did not change drastically with the advent of videotape, but at least this new technology encouraged the showing of "live on tape shows," which could be edited for content, and syndicated later on. In some cases the reruns were almost as popular as the original shows, and even attracted larger audiences than well-considered fresh programs.[10] Radio had progressed from a recorded content to a live one, but television, given videotape, went in the opposite direction. Those involved in producing and directing shows welcomed tape, though some actors and actresses professed to prefer the live performance. As for the audiences, after a short time they too accepted videotape and gave the matter little thought. One picture was not that different from the other. By the early 1970s, Americans were being shown news shows in the early evening that appeared up-to-date and live, but in reality had been taped an hour or so earlier so as to take advantage of the medium in programming for different time zones. To further complicate matters, most of the news shows utilized films and other tape to illustrate stories, and so the home viewer really witnessed tape on tape on tube, or film on tape on tube. This, too, he took in his stride.

ILLUSION AND THE TUBE

More than any other medium, television was involved with illusions. This is not to say that those in control were deceptive, or in some way involved in a sinister operation. Rather, it was their task to create impressions, to amuse and entertain, to capture an audience and hold it, and they utilized the technology toward that end. The same was true for motion pictures, but there was an important difference. Films were presented as fiction, and the audiences learned to accept them as such, realizing that actors and actresses were playing roles. In addition, one "went to the movies," watched and listened in a theater, a place that was designed for illusion and amusement, not fact. At the fringes of the medium—for some subjects and some artists—fact and fiction blended. During World War II more Americans received stronger impressions of their enemies from fictional films than from live radio and newspapers. In addition, some artists became typecast, and part of the public came to believe they were truly as good, bad, sexy, or honest as their roles indicated. Still, at their core, films were entertainment, and were accepted as such by those who went to the movies two or three times a week to escape from their "real lives."

The situation at the newspapers was more complicated. There the division between fact and opinion was always unclear, and the desirability of each changed over time and distance, and was not the same at any two newspapers or chains. Still, most claimed to provide both, whether labeled as such or not. Regular readers of the same newspaper quickly learned the editorial biases of their journal and those of its columnists—perhaps they selected the paper for them. Likewise, they came to understand, and even to appreciate, the differences between "hard news" and opinion. Also, one might read a paper at leisure, reread an interesting section, clip out articles, and refer to them later on. If so moved, the reader might write a letter to the editor, and it could be published. In this way, newspapers could be talked back to, held to account by their readers, and for this reason each had to consider the nature of its particular audience carefully. Newspapers might become popular because of the content of editorials and columns, but they were judged more rigorously by the speed and accuracy of hard news. One could not compare the opinions of a Hearst and a Pulitzer on an impartial basis, but the veracity of their news stories and their "beats" on one another could be measured.

What is news? How did an editor decide which stories to print and which to discard? No matter how fair and impartial the editor, how value-free the reporter and rewrite man, they found themselves in the business of illusion. Even the New York *Times*, through much of its history considered the "newspaper of record," could not avoid this, and neither could the lesser journals. Since 1897, the *Times*' motto has been "All the News That's Fit to Print," and this implies that someone at the newspaper is the judge of "fitness" as well as space assigned and placement. Important stories went to the front page, the headline size indicating the degree of significance. But what would happen if there were several stories considered pressing, all breaking at the same time? One or more might be shoved into the second page, or even a different section of the newspaper. On the other hand, there have been times when little of note has happened; still, the front page had to be printed, and so it was, with the readers assuming that these stories were somehow as significant as others that appeared in that position. It was possible for a newspaper editor to create an illusion in the minds of his readers—of panic, fear, admiration, love—and to impel action through manipulation of news. In fact, it was impossible to avoid at least some of this, for to do so would be to become a moral and even a mental eunuch. Whatever the motivation, the newspaper created illusions, though for the most part these were more transparent than those found in motion pictures.

Radio was more suited to illusion than either newspapers or motion pictures, due to both form and content. The printed word could be used to convey abstract ideas, and newspapers prided themselves on veracity. The spoken word, over radio, rarely dealt with abstractions, but rather with recitations that had at least the illusion of action. Radio stations had experimented with academic and other lectures in the early 1920s and found that they bored listeners. Later on, informational programs were cast in the mold of a quiz, or a debate, with the tensions as responsible for listener interest as the content. Kaltenborn, Murrow, and others learned that the newspaper columnist and reporter and his radio counterpart were quite different. The former had to possess a good mind and an ability with words, while in addition to these, the radio commentator had to add a stage presence and a dramatic voice. They were newsmen, but in addition had to be "personalities" as well, and dramatic ones at that. Intonation, inflection, stress, excitement, and other emotions were of paramount importance to radio newsmen, while they could be ignored by columnists and reporters at the newspapers. As they did with drama and comedy shows, listeners to Eric Sevareid, Howard K. Smith, Raymond Swing, and men like them placed the radio newsman in a "theater of the mind." When Murrow described a London air raid from the top of a building, he tried to create an illusion for the listener, to make him feel as though he were there too, and the sound of the bombs bursting heightened the atmosphere and helped it along, in a way that no newspaperman of World War I could have duplicated.

But there were dangers too—the line between fact and fiction could be crossed without the listener realizing it. The most famous case of illusion on radio was the Orson Welles dramatization of H. G. Wells' *The War of the Worlds* in 1938. Despite a clear statement that the show was fiction, Welles managed to frighten a large number of listeners through sound effects, fine writing, and excellent acting. Nor could some listeners distinguish between fact and fiction while listening to "the March of Time." In addition, unlike motion pictures and newspapers, radio presented both, often within seconds of one another on the same station. Thus a listener might hear the end of a drama and then, after station identification, news from Europe. He would have to make the "switch" in his brain on his own, and if the drama was realistic and the news commentator dramatic, this might be somewhat difficult.

Television compounded the problem, especially after videotape was perfected. Unlike motion pictures, television was seen in the home, in a familiar surrounding, one that was "real" and not theatrical. If one assigned a definite personality to a motion-picture actor after seeing him in a half-dozen roles, what might be the opinion of an actor in a continuing weekly television series, complete with taped reruns? James Stewart and John Wayne developed their screen personalities over a period of many years. After only one season in popular series, in which they portrayed lawyers, actors Raymond Burr and E. G. Marshall were addressing bar associations; they were more profoundly typecast than any Hollywood personality of the 1930s or 1940s, and had to remain away from the tube for a season or so before emerging in their new personae, Burr as a detective, Marshall as a doctor. On the other hand, James Cagney could create the illusion of a gangster, and quickly move, in his next picture, into musical comedy, alternating between these and other roles for three decades without too much difficulty. Motion-picture actor Robert Young could portray villains as well as heroes. Not so television actor Young, who as Marcus Welby created the definitive illusion of a modern general practitioner. To cast Young as a murderer today would be impossible, unless he went into seclusion for a season or two.

At least the Marcus Welby and other such shows are filmed as though motion pictures. What of those programs taped live? In the late 1960s one might see them on the tube, and not knowing of the technology involved, assumed they were being telecast live. By then, the differences between taped and live shows, at least insofar as the viewer was concerned, were negligible. Thus one might see a comedy program in which several principals had died, and yet assume they were still alive. This was true in the case of reruns of old movies, of course, but in these the illusion of immediacy was not present. The situation was different for taped audience shows. Once again, the line between fact and fiction was blurred, and audiences adjusted to this, too.

What was real, and what was not? Should one's physician behave more like Marcus Welby, or should Marcus Welby reflect reality more than he did? As more Americans entered the television dream world in the 1960s, the lines were increasingly unclear. For some Americans, reality consisted as much of television drama and comedy as day-to-day existence; Archie Bunker was as real as most politicians, or even friends and neighbors. Just as the newspaper editor and reporter dictated what was fit to print, so the three major networks held sway over what would be telecast. Television combined the most powerful elements of radio, motion pictures, and newspapers, but still lacked a form and content of its own. Yet the technology was so powerful that its controllers could determine national tastes, attitudes, and even positions on political and economic matters in the "real world." But what was this world, for the person who spent five or six hours a day in front of his set, or his child who learned more from television than from any other source? If indeed television brought the world into the living room, as was claimed in the 1950s, who determined what parts of the world would enter, in what order, and how presented? The matter of control was vital, and yet this, too, was determined in a haphazard fashion, based more upon the traditions of the past and other media than the requirements of the new, dominant one.

MATURATION

11

Television and Truth

Wendell Willkie was born in the farming community of Rushville, Indiana, and attended the local schools, graduating from Indiana Law School near the top of his class. He was a big, rugged-looking man, who spoke with a midwestern accent, whose suits were generally rumpled and tie askew. Willkie had a direct way about him, and yet was genial; he exuded integrity and decency. In 1940 he captured the Republican presidential nomination and ran a strong campaign against Roosevelt. For the next four years Willkie remained a major force in American politics. Yet he never held elective office. During the campaign, Secretary of the Interior Harold Ickes called Willkie "the barefoot boy from Wall Street," knowing all the while that Willkie was far more than that. Still, the characterization was perceptive, for Willkie was the first media-created personality of the electronic age to be nominated by a major party for the presidency.

After graduation and a brief Army tour, Wilkie joined the Firestone Rubber Company at its Akron headquarters. Soon after he entered an Akron law firm that specialized in defending utilities against regulatory bodies. This was the great age of electric company expansion, and Willkie soon became well known for his forceful representations. In 1929 he moved to New York, handling cases for the most prestigious companies, receiving large fees for his efforts. As the representative for a holding company, Commonwealth and Southern, he clashed with the Tennessee Valley

Authority, and in the process became known as a defender of free enterprise against "Roosevelt socialism." In the end, Commonwealth and Southern bowed before the TVA and was liquidated, but in the process Willkie's reputation spread throughout the country.

In January 1938 Willkie was invited to debate Assistant Attorney General Robert Jackson on the issue of government regulation of the economy on the popular radio program "Town Hall Meeting of the Air." Jackson was believed a potential Democratic presidential nominee for 1940, while Willkie was still unknown to the general public. The following day, those stations that carried the program reported a record volume of mail, most of it favorable to Willkie. Even those who disagreed with him indicated they liked the man, who was compared to Will Rogers. The debate all but ended the short Jackson boom, and one was started soon after for Willkie. Other radio appearances followed; when a director or producer needed a liberal anti-New Deal speaker, Willkie's name and voice came to mind. At the same time, he attracted favorable mention in the Republican press. Then he appeared on "Information Please," an intellectual quiz program featuring such regulars as John Kiernan, Franklin P. Adams, Oscar Levant, and George S. Kaufman, and moderated by Clifton Fadiman. Each week the show would have a guest panelist, who was required not only to compete with the regulars but also match quips with them. Willkie's appearance went off well; again, listeners were attracted by his warmth, knowledge, and voice. The leading Republicans in the nomination race—Robert Taft, Thomas Dewey, and Arthur Vandenberg—lacked the proper personality or approach for radio.

In April 1940 Willkie's article "We the People" appeared in *Fortune* magazine. Soon after, that journal's managing editor, Russell Davenport, took a leave of absence to manage the Willkie pre-election campaign. Davenport recruited others in the Henry Luce magazine group, as well as several leading newspapermen. Then Davenport brought advertising men from Young & Rubicam, Pedlar & Ryan, and Selvage & Smith into the organization. A New York lawyer, Oren Root, helped mobilize the financial community for the candidate. Willkie was given the kind of treatment that would later become so familiar during the television age. He was required to lose thirty pounds and submit to cosmetic dentistry. A "spontaneous grass-roots movement" was organized and set into operation, the goal being to make the candidate familar to the nation prior to the Republican Convention in June. Willkie's public-relations men presented him as a small-town lawyer, friendly, somewhat shy, careless about his appearance but careful with his morals, in opposition to Roosevelt, the aristocrat in the White House. "Neither Willkie's personality, nor the weight of his ideals, could conceivably have produced even a fraction of the phenomenon that we lived through," said Fred Smith of Selvage & Smith, shortly after Willkie's nomination. "It should never be forgotten that the 'Willkie boom' was one of the best engineered jobs in history."[1] Willkie lost the election, but did far better against Roosevelt than had Hoover or Landon. The media had nominated a presidential candidate in 1940, a man who had virtually no professional political support prior to the convention. However, the imagemakers could not yet put such a person in the White House; that would come later on.[2]

As had been the case in both 1932 and 1936, most of the nation's newspapers supported the Republican nominee in 1940; over 80 per cent came out in favor of Willkie. And for the first time, several radio stations, controlled by the Republican press, did the same, through editorials and commentaries by staff newsmen. Roosevelt could do nothing to curb the press without inviting a storm of disapproval, such as that which had greeted his attempt to pack the Supreme Court. Radio was another matter, for the Federal Communications Commission had jurisdiction over the stations, and the White House need not interfere directly.

The Administration's position surfaced in 1941, when Station WAAB in Boston, part of the Mayflower Broadcasting Corporation, applied for a license renewal. Earlier the station manager had been reprimanded for scheduling anti-Roosevelt editorials, and he had agreed to drop them. Still, the FCC took the opportunity to issue a new warning, this one to the entire industry. The station had "revealed a serious misconception of its duties and functions under the law," said the commission. "A truly free radio cannot be used to advocate the causes of the licensee. It cannot be used to support the candidacies of his friends. It cannot be devoted to the support of principles he happens to regard most favorably. In brief, the broadcaster cannot be an advocate."

This view, which came to be known as the "Mayflower Doctrine," was not unlike a position taken two years before by the

National Association of Broadcasters. According to that organization's 1939 code, editorials were not to be aired, and the "elucidation of the news should be free of bias." But World War II changed the minds of some broadcasters, who had taken sides in the struggle between Kaltenborn and Paul White at CBS. Frank Stanton, president of CBS and a man who defended the White position against editorialization, nevertheless spoke out against the Mayflower Doctrine, claiming that it abridged free speech and suppressed public discussion of vital issues. More to the point, Stanton claimed that "radio should have all the rights of other media," newspapers included. In other words, radio should be covered by the First Amendment guarantees of freedom of the press, even though it was a government-regulated industry; the airwaves, theoretically at least, belonged to the people. Defenders of the Administration rejected this position. This was a time when the public view of newspapers was that they were controlled by businessmen, while liberals believed the press was the handmaiden of antiprogressive, even fascistic, forces in the nation. They urged the FCC to remain firm in its determination to prevent editorials on the air. Given the nature of the ownerships of stations, they said, and the press-radio nexus, these editorials were bound to be anti-Administration. "The group interests of the press barons are reflected in the overwhelmingly conservative if not reactionary tone of their editorial columns," said Charles Siepman, a leading student of the FCC and the regulatory process. "We can expect a similar trend in radio."

The debate continued for several months, and was ended by the Japanese attack on Pearl Harbor. Considerations of free speech came to be viewed as relatively unimportant as the nation united for war—the matter could be considered after victory. Radio commentators now expressed their opinions openly—urging total victory, supporting the United Nations, calling for Allied unity—and the FCC said nothing. Still, the Mayflower Doctrine had been promulgated and the battle lines drawn. A liberal Administration had attempted to prevent or at least control the open expression of opinion by broadcasters, and had been met with industry opposition and referrals to the First Amendment, while liberal spokesmen criticized newsmen and accused the networks of bias. In time the actors would change, but the positions and rhetoric would not.

THE FCC AND TELEVISION

The FCC had no policy toward television during World War II, and one was not deemed necessary. Programming was sparse and erratic; there were only five thousand or so receivers in the New York area, for example, and only a handful of programs on WNBT, which was the NBC station in the city. In 1941, there were six stations nationwide, and four of them hadn't bothered to initiate programming. In 1942 the FCC halted the expansion of commercial stations and the production of sets, but this was a meaningless edict, since no company indicated a desire to enter broadcasting. On the other hand, the major radio firms continued their work during the war, preparing for the time when the fighting and freeze would both end. Several manufacturers of electrical and electronic equipment also explored television, and as an Allied victory seemed more assured, independent firms applied for broadcasting licenses. The FCC had over a hundred such applications in late 1944, and fifty more came in before the end of the war. American business was prepared for a television boom, even though the FCC still lacked a doctrine or strategy as how best to deal with the medium.

RCA was the dominant company in the field. It owned key patents and had spent more money and time on television than had any other firm. Under Sarnoff's direction, RCA produced receivers, established stations (and filed for additional ones), concluded agreements with talent, and was prepared to manufacture transmission equipment. Just as RCA had managed to obtain a strong beachhead in radio and hold it against competitors, so it appeared to be doing the same in television. But there was a difference, for unlike the situation in the early 1920s, there were strong rivals in the fields of technology and manufacture. Still, most of them lacked the capacities and head start Sarnoff had provided for RCA, and so they fell in behind the leader. Philco, Dumont, Magnavox, Motorola, Admiral, Crosley, Arvin, and most other radio manufacturers appeared content to utilize RCA licenses to produce receivers, though some of them thought to compete in transmission equipment. Even the giants, General Electric and Westinghouse, conceded RCA's dominance, and while they hoped to operate stations as well, indicated they would co-operate with RCA in most other areas.

Only two companies rejected the policy of co-operation. Zenith Radio had been a minor manufacturer of quality receivers before the war, and had expanded its base by producing military equipment. The company's president, Eugene McDonald, hoped to challenge RCA in the production of both radios and television sets. Realizing he could not hope to compete directly against the industry giant, he decided upon a flanking strategy. Sarnoff was determined that television would resemble radio in that the individual would purchase a set for his home and then receive programs without charge, the costs being born by advertisers. This was to have been expected from RCA, given its wide experience in radio programming. Zenith was solely a manufacturer of equipment, and so McDonald developed a plan that would maximize its advantages. Under his concept, television would resemble motion pictures, the main difference being the location of the receiver. A family might own a set and pay a fee to see programs, the money going to the station, which would use it to purchase and develop talent. Although McDonald said little about the commercialization of programs, he clearly thought sponsors would not be required. In 1951, he obtained FCC permission to test the Zenith creation, "phonevision," in approximately three hundred homes. The company would transmit first-run movies, which would appear on ordinary television sets as a scrambled pattern. If the customer wished to see the film, he could call the local telephone company, which would make the connection that normalized the picture. The price for the film would then be added to the customer's telephone bill. The phonevision test was inconclusive, and others followed, by Zenith and allied firms, while all the time RCA attempted to block progress in the field. The larger company won the struggle; by the late 1960s, all of the pay television programs had either been abandoned or suspended.

While working on phonevision, Zenith co-operated with CBS in another flanking operation. In 1945, CBS was a major network, but did not produce radio or television sets, and had only a marginal interest in equipment. Hoping to challenge RCA across the board, and realizing that its rival owned most of the key patents in the field, CBS attempted to "re-invent" television. William

Paley of CBS decided that the best approach would be through the perfection of a new method of color telecasting and receiving. RCA was working in the field, but thus far had succeeded only in demonstrating that satisfactory colorcasts were extremely difficult.

In mid-1947, when there were some fifty thousand receivers in use, Paley petitioned the FCC for permission to continue work on a new color system, one whose picture was superior to RCA's but could not be received on sets then in use. As might have been anticipated, Sarnoff opposed the application, pointing out that acceptance and success might require the viewer to purchase two sets. There was more at stake than that. Had the CBS system triumphed, RCA would have had to scrap most of its licenses and purchase technology from its chief rival. Supported by Zenith, CBS would have entered all aspects of the industry, and the allied companies might have taken television leadership from RCA. Already CBS had applied for many new stations, was aggressively seeking new affiliates, and planned to produce receivers, while Zenith was challenging RCA for domination in the latter field.

The FCC rejected the CBS application, and Paley prepared to reopen the struggle at a higher level; the FCC response had been weak, hastily prepared, and somewhat contradictory. This was not unexpected, for the commission was in shambles. Faced by a flood of applications for new stations, the need for decisions on color, pay television, cable systems, explorations into ultrahigh-frequency technology, and other problems, the FCC was paralyzed. Unable to continue, the commission announced that it would stop processing applications in September 1948, thus freezing the industry as it had been during the war. The freeze remained in effect for three and a half years, while the FCC attorneys tried to process applications and develop programs. Meanwhile, Paley persisted in his efforts, and in 1949, the commission agreed to hold hearings on the CBS and RCA color systems. Holding that the CBS system was superior, the FCC announced that commercial color television on the CBS model could commence in late 1950.

The decision startled the industry and angered the nation. There were some 4 million television families in early 1950, whose sets would be unable to receive the CBS colorcasts. They had paid over $300 for their black-and-white receivers; now they would have to purchase color sets as well, at prices ranging upward of $400.

The government and CBS argued that the new technology was worth the cost, but the public seemed to feel otherwise. By the spring of 1950 it had become evident that the FCC has miscalculated public sentiment; some congressmen talked about an investigation of the commission.

The Korean War intervened. The FCC announced—with evident relief—that it was suspending all decisions for the duration. RCA took advantage of this to step up research on an improved, compatible color system, lobby in Washington, and organize its allies against CBS. All of this was accomplished effectively. A new system was developed, and together with General Electric, Sylvania, Hazeltine, and others, RCA organized the National Television Systems Committee, which lobbied for it within the industry and in Congress. Court cases were initiated as well, and all the while Sarnoff orchestrated the anti-CBS campaign with skill. In the end, RCA had its victory; in December 1953, the FCC reversed its earlier decision and gave the NTSC color system its approval. Earlier it had lifted its freeze against new stations, and RCA had emerged the leader there too.

In 1951, over 10 million American families had television sets, and there were 107 commercial stations. Five years later, there were 35 million television families and almost 500 stations. Radio revenues rose from $450 million to $518 million in this period; television revenues went from $235 million to just below $1 billion in the same span. It had become the dominant medium in the nation by most statistical measurements; Americans were reorganizing their lives to watch favorite programs, and even reruns. But even then, the industry lacked a common rationale, the technology a controlling influence, the government a clear role.

Zenith had been defeated in phonevision and CBS lost its battle for noncompatible color. Television would resemble radio, as David Sarnoff had expected it would. But RCA would not dominate the industry, despite its successes. Zenith rallied to take the lead in sales of black-and-white sets. Other firms, many of them quite small, challenged RCA in technology. The company didn't even try to make an effort in cameras, entered tape late, and generally did poorly in research and development. As for programming, CBS and ABC proved strong competitors, while old movies on local stations often outdrew the big three networks. By the 1960s, RCA had turned to nontelevision areas—computers, automobile rentals, publishing, and later on, carpets—and became a conglomerate. Television lacked clear leadership, in any of the areas; a system had evolved, but had not been created by a company with a plan, as had been the case with radio.

This was not due to a lack of talent or imagination on the part of the pioneers, but rather to the complexity of the medium; for television was not radio with pictures, or motion pictures at home, as it had been described in the late 1940s. As for the content, it couldn't be described as fiction interspersed with fact, or fact with touches of fiction—fantasy and reality merged in programming and, more importantly, in perception by viewers. Few thought to ask about the role truth played on television in the 1950s and early 1960s, even though later on it would become the central question in a major, deep, and long-lasting debate.

TELEVISION AND THE NEWS

"We have no models to follow, no traditions to accept or reject, and so we have haltingly and fitfully taken what flimsy traditions there were in the media that gave us birth—from the marriage that may have been illegal and certainly was immoral." This complaint of a television newsman might appear to have been written in the mid-1940s, when like all other aspects of programming, news forms had to be created. Certainly the use of tense would indicate this to have been the case. But the speaker was not Douglas Edwards of CBS or John Cameron Swayze of NBC, two of the pioneers of that early period. Instead, it was David Brinkley, who with Chet Huntley is identified with the creation of the modern newscast. And he was addressing an audience in 1966, not two decades earlier.[3]

Brinkley went on to say that television news had a diverse parentage, "of Fox Movietone Newsreels covering beauty contests and radio commentary by such diverse personalities as Raymond Swing and Fulton Lewis, as Ed Murrow and Gabriel Heatter, and as Elmer Davis and Father Coughlin." While there were elements of newsreel and commentary in early television news, far more important was the tradition of the newscast, in which a staff announcer would read from wire service releases, throwing in a few public-interest stories at the end so as to close the program on a light note. FCC doctrine and technology militated against reliance upon the sources Brinkley cited. Radio still functioned under the Mayflower Doctrine, and while Murrow and Swing might appear to have editorialized during the war, their phrases had been subdued and in favor of an Allied victory, and so were not criticized. Networks news directors would have liked to have utilized newsreel techniques; just as the entertainment aspect of television tried to employ movies, so the news departments wanted to imitate newsreels.

This presented problems, both technical and editorial. During the 1930s and 1940s, some of the leading newsreel producers had utilized their product for propaganda purposes. Hearst Metrotone News, owned by the newspaper empire, was strongly anti-New Deal, opposed organized labor, and for a while reported favorably on Mussolini and Hitler. Pathé News, also affiliated with newspaper interests, was not much different; Paramount News, alone of the "big three," at least appeared to seek objectivity in its reports. The typical newsreel, whether of these companies or others in the field, consisted of several national and international reports, each no longer than a minute, plus two or three human-interest stories. All emulated "the March of Time" approach, complete with dramatic musical accompaniments and the voices of well-known newscasters.

Critics complained that most newsreels were inaccurate and often misleading, and while the companies denied the charges, they also responded that the viewers in theaters had alternate sources of news, especially radio and newspapers. In addition, foreign film stories appeared in newsreels days after they occurred; the film would have to be sent to America, developed, edited, and fitted into a forthcoming newsreel. Domestic stories could be processed more rapidly, but even these could hardly be up-to-date. Thus newsreels were supplements to the main sources of information, and were considered as such by most viewers.[4] Still, the newsreel techniques might have served television newscasts well were it not for the technological problems involved. The network news show of 1946 could not obtain foreign film footage each night, and Washington film could not be utilized, since it would take several hours to process and ship the cans of film. Even local stories could not be pictorialized, unless the studio had at least two or three hours to work on the product. The major technical problems arose from film and transmission, and before these were overcome, television news had to imitate its radio counterpart.

The typical news program of the immediate postwar period consisted of a radio announcer sitting at his desk, reading the wire stories, either from a script in his hands or cue cards held beyond the camera's range. Behind him might be a screen, on which would be projected still photos of people and places being discussed, or charts of the points being made by the newscaster. Each newscast would feature films rushed to the studio and processed as rapidly as possible, or stock footage purchased or leased from newsreel companies. The key was visualization; directors preferred to run stories that could be pictorialized to those that required the camera to remain focused on the newscaster. Thus analysis was considered of little importance, or even desirable; the newscasters of this period were more akin to the voice-over commentators of the newsreels than to the major radio personalities of wartime network news. Swayze, the best known of the early telecasters, had been a minor figure during the war, and was chosen for his voice and appearance. He was a good-looking individual, cheerful, and possessed of an easygoing personality. Swayze won several awards as the best-dressed male on the tube, and his garb was at least as important as what he had to say. His "Camel News Caravan" would conclude with a selection of short items, introduced with, "Now let's go hopscotching the world for headlines."

This was the tone and content of the early newscasts. Those who wanted to learn what was happening in the locality, nation, and world still relied upon radio. Television was a novelty; viewers tuned in to Swayze to witness the phenomenon rather than to be informed. This was a time when owners of sets might watch test patterns, or old government films on subjects that did not interest them. In this period the magnet was the technology, not the program, and the newscasters did not have to be more than visual.

As much as possible, the networks and local stations leaned upon newsreel techniques, even companies. Telenews, which was purchased by Hearst in the early days, turned out a daily package of films for its clients, which included the major networks. United Press Movietone (an outgrowth of Fox Movietone) was its major competitor. Together these two firms operated for television as the wire services did for the newspapers—they provided filler material and, on occasion, lead stories as well. Given the audience demands and expectations of the early years, a station could easily put the entire package on the air, do little rewriting, and add local items when needed. NBC, ABC, Mutual, and the Dumont networks relied upon these and other services. CBS, which from the first made a strong effort in news, formed CBS Newsfilm, but also subscribed to other agencies, leaning heavily upon Telenews. Considering the nature of the technology of the time and the available sources of material, it was inevitable that the newscasts would appear light, frivolous, and out-of-date—not unlike the newsreels upon which they had been patterned.

Few in the industry seriously believed that television news would remain wedded to newsreels and offered in so haphazard a fashion, no more than they considered "Howdy Doody" and the "Texaco Star Theater" the height of the art. In the late 1940s local stations and networks experimented with the existing technology, creating programs of topical interest, which would later be known as documentaries. For the most part these were bland and innocuous, more experiments with form than art. Most relied heavily upon stock footage, and owed more to the vogue for cinema realism after the war than to new television techniques. At the same time, the National Association of Broadcasters and other industry groups continued their battle against the Mayflower Doctrine, more in order to free radio than to affect television. In 1949 they won their contest, as the FCC reversed itself, ruling that a station might take a stand on a particular issue, so long as it provided opportunities for those with differing views to be heard. This view, which soon became known as the "Fairness Doctrine," was elaborated upon in the next few years, and created more problems than it solved. For the moment, however, it freed radio commentators from one of their restraints.

Two other safeguards, created by the industry itself, were more difficult to overcome. The first of these was the tradition of radio news as developed by Murrow and CBS—the unwritten law that newsmen could comment upon events but not editorialize about them. Murrow had stamped his personality upon the profession, for with the exception of local, idiosyncratic, and old-time reporters (including Gabriel Heatter, Walter Winchell, Lowell Thomas, and H. V. Kaltenborn), his style and approach were becoming the norm; just as serious columnists attempted to imitate or emulate Walter Lippmann, so radio newsmen looked up to Murrow. His serious, almost funereal voice, his dispassionate demeanor, and his understated eloquence was copied faithfully by a generation of radio commentators, even when the approach, which had been so well suited to war news, was applied to frivolous subjects. This heritage—derived in part from journalism, in part from academia—would fade over the years, but buttressed by the Fairness Doctrine, would always be present.

The second of the internal safeguards, longer lasting than the first, was station and network pressure. While head of CBS News, Paul White had insisted upon objectivity. "Ideally, in the case of controversial issues, the audience should be left with no impression as to which side the analyst himself actually favors," said White in 1943, and the CBS approach was a combination of his and Murrow's philosophies. But even had this approach not existed, the network executives would have created a similar one, if only to avoid contention with the FCC and retaliation from sponsors. As long as this remained the case, television news and documentaries would be bland, safe, and—more often than not—dull. The last point was important, for as Pulitzer and Hearst, and before them Greeley and Bennett had known, dull news did not sell papers. Still, the networks weren't too concerned with this, for they were not in the business of news, but rather of entertainment, of delivering audiences to sponsors. Situation comedies and quiz programs did this admirably, while news shows consistently received low ratings and sponsor interest.

Murrow and his producer, Fred Friendly, were the first to attempt to create a television news tradition. They were fortunate in being at CBS, for that network lagged behind NBC, and was amenable to experimentation. In addition, Murrow's reputation and power at the network—he became a vice president there after the war—were such that it would have been difficult to stand in his way.

In late 1950, he hosted a radio documentary series, "Hear It Now," which was transferred to television the following year as "See It Now." Murrow opened the first show by saying, "Good evening. This is an old team trying to learn a new trade," and as though to illustrate the potentials of television, he showed viewers simultaneous images of the Atlantic and Pacific oceans, made possible by the completion of the AT&T coaxial cable a few months earlier. Then followed "photo essays" concerning Winston Churchill and Anthony Eden, two American senators, and a study of an Army division. None of this was "hard news," in the sense that the stories were not of the kind that newspapers printed on their front pages or were featured on radio newscasts. Rather, the early "See It Now" programs, though frankly experimental, were based more upon Herbert Hoover's ideas about a "magazine of the air," discussed in the early 1920s. Murrow borrowed techniques from "The March of Time" and added the content of World War II film documentaries, in the hope of evolving a new form. This went on for two years, during which time another program—"Omnibus," hosted by Alistair Cooke—expanded upon the approach, while other networks and independents did little work in the field.

Murrow changed the format late in 1953, with two quite different shows. In "The Case Against Milo Radulovich, A0589839" he explored injustices committed against an Air Force officer who had been forced to resign his commission when accused of having radical leanings. The show, which was put on the air on October 20, created a sensation. In it Murrow showed how faceless accusers could destroy a person's career, making his points through interviews and stock film. As always, Murrow attempted to stand above the battle, to be impartial, and he offered the Air Force facilities and air time for a response. "Whatever happens in this whole area of the relationship between the individual and the state, we will do ourselves; it cannot be blamed upon Malenkov, Mao Tse-tung, or even our allies. It seems to us—that is, to Fred Friendly and myself—that it is a subject that should be argued about endlessly. . . .[5] Shortly thereafter, the Air Force announced that the action against Radulovich had been reversed. Needless to say, this would not have happened had it not been for the "See It Now" telecast.

"The Case Against Milo Radulovich" demonstrated the powers of both television and Murrow, and so was significant. Even more so was a second program that year, "Christmas in Korea," in which an attempt was made to show Americans the nature of the war there. Of course, Murrow had a great deal of experience in this field, and his work with Friendly in the past two years had given him a good grasp of the medium. He led a film crew to Korea, where they took shots of the terrain, the fighting, and most important, the soldiers themselves, several of whom were interviewed. The completed, edited film illustrated Murrow's contention that the war was tedious and that American soldiers were not quite certain what it was all about. "Christmas in Korea" was a television landmark, more important even than the Radulovich program that had preceded it. Murrow had combined elements of newsreel and film documentary and newspaper column, to which he added his own abilities and experiences, to produce a program that appeared unbiased and accurate, but in fact had a strong editorial message for the audience.

The content of the Radulovich show and the format of "Christmas in Korea" were combined in the next contentious "See It Now" presentation, which dealt with the actions and beliefs of Senator Joseph McCarthy, who at the time was considered even more powerful than the President. In addition to his attacks on various agencies of government and accusations of Communist activity in the private sector, McCarthy had indicated that the news and entertainment mediums were Communist-infiltrated and influenced. *Red Channels,* an anti-Communist publication that gathered the names and backgrounds of radio and television artists and newsmen purported to be Communists or their sympathizers, was utilized by McCarthy's followers as a check on the networks. Just as a blacklist had developed in Hollywood, so there was one in New York. Among the newsmen listed in *Red Channels* were several at CBS, including Howard K. Smith and Alexander Kendrick. Both said the network had placed them under no pressures at all, either to slant their news or to resign. Kendrick attributed this to Murrow's influence, quoting him as saying, "If you're in trouble, we're all in trouble." Yet Murrow and other network news leaders said little about the subject on the air and were circumspect in public. In fact, a group formed to combat McCarthyism, called the Voice of Freedom, criticized Murrow, calling his Korean report "a moldy dish of red-baiting rhetoric."[6]

The networks tried to remain aloof from the controversy. The anti-Communist movement was news, and was reported as such, while a good deal of air time was devoted to McCarthy himself. Public officials appeared on network interview programs to present their points of view, and at all times the stations made certain their questioners interviewed individuals on both sides of the issue. The policy seemed sensible; to do otherwise might be to invite sponsor disapproval and viewer criticism. FCC investigations, even given the Fairness Doctrine, were also possible.

Murrow's report on McCarthy, aired on March 9, 1954, must be considered against this background. For more than two years he and Friendly had been perfecting their television techniques and were now masters of the technology and medium. During 1953 the CBS staff had gathered McCarthy films, and under Murrow's direction, had begun preparing for the program. Murrow had broken the ideological ice with the Radulovich program, and "Christmas in Korea" demonstrated that he knew how to utilize the faces and voices of others to make his points. "See It Now's" sponsor, Alcoa, had allowed Murrow a wide degree of latitude in the past, and indicated a willingness to continue to do so.

The McCarthy program consisted of an introduction by Murrow, who also did a voice-over to explain actions and tie them together. Most of the show, however, was of McCarthy himself, in action in Congress and before public audiences. The program showed inconsistencies in statements, and the films made the senator appear more than a little sinister, and a demagogue. To individuals who were used to seeing old movies on television, he seemed like the villain in an old Warner Brothers epic—a fact that could not have eluded the CBS staff. The contrast between the cool, dispassionate Murrow and the heated, often wild senator was striking. Murrow did not take an ideological or extreme position in his conclusion. "No one familiar with the history of this country can deny that congressional committees are useful," he said. "It is necessary to investigate before legislating. But the line between investigation and persecution is a very fine one, and the junior senator from Wisconsin has stepped over it repeatedly." Murrow went on to charge that McCarthy had confused the public over the internal and external threats of communism, finding a ready audience for his accusations. He did not call for action as much as for introspection. "The actions of the junior senator from Wisconsin have caused alarm and dismay amongst our allies abroad and given considerable comfort to our enemies. And whose fault is that? Not really his; he didn't create this situation of fear, but merely exploited it and rather successfully." As Murrow saw it, "Cassius was right. 'The fault, dear Brutus, is not in our stars but in ourselves.'"

In order to comply with the Fairness Doctrine—in line with his earlier practice, as demonstrated in the Radulovich program—Murrow offered McCarthy equal time to respond. The senator accepted, and with the aid of newspaper columnist George Sokolsky and a crew from Fox Movietone, readied his own program, which was aired on April 6. The McCarthy response was weak, and in comparison with Murrow's, inept. This was to have been expected. Murrow's program had been prepared for months, by the most experienced staff in the industry, and delivered by its most talented practitioner, a man who knew how to appear fair and unbiased while actually presenting a strong message. Although McCarthy was a talented speaker and at the height of his popularity, his telecast showed little preparation, and that by comparative amateurs. As a leading critic of the medium noted, the two programs proved that the idea of equal time was a sham—that there was no way for an outsider to compete with or reply to a person in command of the medium.[7] This held true even in the matter of costs. Most of the "See It Now" programs cost over twenty-five thousand dollars to produce, while the McCarthy response, which was paid for by CBS, came to less than seven thousand dollars. Yet McCarthy had not lost the encounter. An audience survey indicated that 59 per cent of those questioned had either seen the program or had heard of it, and of these, a third believed that the senator had raised questions regarding Murrow's loyalty, or had proved him to be pro-Communist.[8]

The Murrow-McCarthy interchange was a true watershed in television, for more reasons than were believed at the time. Murrow had demonstrated that television journalism could be as powerful as that of radio or newspaper, and have an even greater impact. Those attacked by Pulitzer and Hearst could respond with words, and even individuals criticized by radio personalities might make an effective response. Countering an Edward R. Murrow, however, was another issue, especially when he had the resources of the network at his disposal and could call upon a lifetime of training as well as his unusual gifts.

"See It Now" continued as an important force in television news and commentary, and its style was imitated by other programs later in the decade—"CBS Reports," "NBC White Paper," and "ABC Close-up!" among them. More important, Murrow made it respectable for newsmen to present their views, and even offered the form and technique by which it could be accomplished.[9] But Murrow never again took on an opponent the way he had McCarthy in 1954, perhaps because he understood the power of the medium and the responsibility that went with that power. In effect, he had countered fire with fire. McCarthy had become a master of innuendo, taking statements out of context and drawing inaccurate juxtapositions. Murrow had done the same, using the rapier and not the bludgeon, but doing it, nonetheless. McCarthy had been a success in his medium—politics—and Murrow was as well practiced in his, television. When McCarthy tried to invade Murrow's domain, he foundered, just as Murrow did poorly during the Kennedy years, when he served as head of the United States Information Agency.

Later on, Murrow was hailed as the man who had helped bring McCarthy to his knees, and the program as a signal act of courage. This view is exaggerated. In the first place, Murrow's program was seen long after McCarthy and McCarthyism had become subjects of criticism. Newspaper journalists, among them Bill Lawrence and Clark Mollenhoff, spoke out and wrote against McCarthy at a time when to do so endangered one's career. At some newspapers—the New York *Post*, for example—anti-McCarthyism was a house doctrine, to be transgressed at risk. Indeed, it might be argued that without the publicity given him by his enemies, McCarthy might have been far less powerful and influential. Furthermore, even after Murrow's broadcast, McCarthy continued his activities, undeterred, only to be halted by the Senate's reaction to his conduct during the Army-McCarthy hearings and the censure movement that followed. Murrow never claimed credit for defeating McCarthy, or indeed argued that his was an act of bravery, but the credit was bestowed nonetheless, a tribute to the man, to be sure, but even more so, perhaps, to the medium; for Murrow could not have accomplished what he did without sight as well as sound—he purported to show the audience McCarthy in action, to convict him not only of his own words but also by his actions and demeanor.

Demeanor was important. In late 1953—that seminal season for Murrow—CBS released a new show, "Person to Person," which featured Murrow's "visits" to the homes of famous people, during which he and the audience were taken on a tour of the house accompanied by conversation. It was a light, even frivolous program, for although Murrow was comfortable with politicians, philosophers, scholars, and scientists, he had little to say to celebrities, and was almost inept when he attempted to joke with them. "To do the show I want to do, I have to do the show I don't want to do," he explained. But dislike of format and content was not the only reason for the clumsiness of "Person to Person." Murrow, a product of war and postwar conflict, was thought of as a serious man. Although he had a good sense of humor, which was displayed off microphone and camera, the public heard and saw a different voice and face—that of a deadly serious person, what one commentator called "the voice of doom." The voice had been perfect for radio, reporting on a war, and its intelligence and training carried over to television, especially in areas of contention. But television was not necessarily a medium for controversy, witness the disinterest with news programs and documentaries, few of which did better than old movies and quiz programs that played opposite them on other channels. The public watched television to be entertained, not to be informed, and would be drawn to news programs only if presented in an entertaining fashion. For all of his gifts, Murrow was not amusing, on "See It Now" or on "Person to Person." Nor did he want to be. He had not been an entertainer—a personality—when reporting the war on radio from London, and he did not intend to change for the new medium. His shows were talked about within the profession, and made an object of discussion in the newspapers and news magazines. They were referred to in textbooks and in congressional committees. But they did not draw high ratings, and hardly paid their way. While Murrow dominated CBS News, such considerations were of secondary importance.

THE DEVELOPMENT OF FORMAT

Although NBC had won most of television's technological and political battles, the network was unable to dominate programming. It was about even with CBS, more often than not slightly behind in the over-all ratings, with ABC a distant third. But there was no contest in news; there CBS had a clear lead in the early days, both in audience ratings and reputation within the profession. This was particularly evident in the fifteen-minute network evening report, where "Douglas Edwards with the News," produced and directed by Don Hewett, was the most popular program of its type. The show moved quickly, with the imaginative use of film and tape. In addition, there was an analysis portion, labeled as such, featuring comments by Howard K. Smith, Eric Sevareid, and other men brought to the network by Murrow. ABC's counterpart, "John Daly and the News," tried to imitate CBS techniques, but the program had neither the staff nor the personnel to carry it off. On the other hand, the Daly program was more popular than NBC's "Camel News Caravan," due in large part to the fact that Daly was also host of the quiz program "What's My Line?" and so was recognized not only as a newsman but also as a celebrity and public personality in his own right. Viewers who liked the popular Sunday night quiz and admired Daly, watched him loyally during the week as well. A radio war correspondent, Daly had a Murrow-like voice, but was not considered particularly distinctive before making his television debut. There he showed a ready smile and a fine wit, and his work on "What's My Line?" earned Daly several awards. By the mid-1950s he was no longer considered a newsman, but rather an entertainer, who was valued more for his show-business qualities than for his abilities at news and analysis.

NBC's Sylvester Weaver, who in the early 1950s had developed the "Today" and "Tonight" shows, turned his attention to straight news in 1955. Clearly his magazine concept could not be applied to the fifteen-minute nightly news programs, and NBC lacked the recognized and experienced staffs of CBS and the celebrity of John Daly stature. Whether by accident or design, Weaver decided to meld the two concepts, and add other show-business aspects to the revamped NBC news. To accomplish this, he brought together two veteran newsmen, Chet Huntley and David Brinkley, and made them "co-anchor men," with Brinkley reporting from Washington, and Huntley from New York. Huntley, who in 1957 was forty-six years old, had been a radio newsman, stationed on the West Coast, who had been brought to New York the year before to narrate specials. He was a tall, handsome, somewhat stern man, with a deep voice and a commanding presence. He looked like a newsman, and indeed had played the role as a bit player in several movies. As for his abilities and reputation, they were considered good if not outstanding. Huntley was interested in conservation, was given to philosophical statements about the nature of the world, and in the early 1950s, he made several anti-McCarthy reports on local and network radio. Brinkley, a North Carolinian, was thirty-six years old in 1957, and had started at NBC in 1943 as a radio news writer in Washington. That year he also made one of the first newscasts on television, to only a hundred or so homes, and appeared occasionally on local television after the war, as well as filling a staff position on radio news. "I had a chance to learn when nobody was watching," he later said. Brinkley was a youthful-looking man with a drawl and a fine sense of humor. Like Huntley he was considered a liberal, but with a more indirect style.

The two men were united as a team in 1956, when they covered the presidential election. They received favorable notices and attracted a larger audience than either CBS or ABC. Noting this, Weaver asked one of his associates, Reuven Frank, to try to put them together in a nightly news program. Show-business concepts, not news, provided the guide. The Huntley-Brinkley team was handled and created in much the same way as Abbott and Costello or Martin and Lewis. Huntley was to be the more conservative of the two, the defender of the Establishment, the wise older man with the broad view of affairs, who would on occasion smile at one of the humorous comments made by the brasher, more liberal Brinkley. "Image" was an important consideration, even where it clashed with reality, for Huntley was no conservative, while the Brinkley of 1957 was not as liberal and open as he appeared to be. For the sake of contrast, however, they played their roles and took care to preserve appearances. Both men felt uneasy at their positions, and continued to write much of their own material, insisting upon this fact being made public. Brinkley in particular appeared to resent his celebrity status. "A lot of people tend to assume that everyone on TV is an entertainer or celebrity, sombody to ask for autographs," he complained. Yet at the same time he must have realized that he was an entertainer; even if he didn't, his salary would have told him as much. In 1959, Brinkley was paid $75,000 a year, and Huntley, $100,000 a year. Newscasters of that period did not receive such payments, but entertainers did. By that time, "the Huntley-Brinkley Report" led in the polls, with John Daly in second place, while Douglas Edwards at CBS fell to third position.

CBS responded to the Huntley-Brinkley challenge by replacing Douglas Edwards with Walter Cronkite. That CBS did not imitate the successful NBC format was due in large part to Murrow, who insisted the program be given to an experienced newsman and remain as free from entertainment considerations as possible. Yet Cronkite was different from Smith, Sevareid, and other CBS veterans. As a student at the University of Texas he had dabbled in acting as well as journalism, and possessed a fine, deep voice and sense of timing. Then he had obtained a job at the United Press, and after meeting Murrow early in the war, became a CBS radio stringer as well. Cronkite went to CBS radio in 1950, and soon after also appeared on television. He was more dynamic than Edwards, and far more conventional than Huntley or Brinkley. By the early 1960s he functioned as head of a network editorial staff, and tended to put together his program as he might a newspaper.

Cronkite was not a great success in his early days as Edwards' replacement. A May 1961 poll conducted by *Television Quarterly*, which attempted to measure the popularity and familiarity of commentators, awarded Brinkley a rating of 89, and Huntley, 88. Edwards, no longer a key man at CBS, received 85, while Cronkite had a score of 83. Cronkite had been the CBS anchor man for the 1960 presidential election, and was so badly beaten by Huntley and Brinkley that he was replaced by a team for the 1964 election, Roger Mudd and Robert Trout, the latter a veteran whose sense of humor rivaled Brinkley's. Soon after, however, Cronkite's popularity began to rise, and by the end of the decade he was not only secure, but voted the "most trusted American" in several polls.

Cronkite's eventual acceptance resulted from familiarity and trust rather than format and style. He was consistent, appeared fair and impartial, and as time went on, projected a fatherly image. His writing showed the Murrow influence, and was not as somber as Huntley's or as light as Brinkley's. Despite this, he too became a performer, as much because of the nature of the industry as anything else.

Television in the early 1960s was becoming show business as

much as news. The program was run by a producer, not an editor, and was called a show. The newscasters had to be good-looking, and they were made up before each appearance as were any other performers. Newsmen hired agents and personal representatives, and some even advertised commercial products and delivered commercials on the air. They had contracts, much the same as actors and actresses. During one industry strike, Chet Huntley protested that performers and crews might be in one union, and newsmen in another, while Cronkite wondered whether such strikes violated freedom of the press. But the situation did not change; television newsmen still belonged to performers' unions, appeared on sets, not newsrooms, although in the early 1970s some sets were made to appear like newspaper offices. Huntley, Brinkley, and Cronkite were stars, and were paid and treated as such.

The leaders at ABC understood the situation and acted to incorporate features of both CBS and NBC news in their program. Without adequate talent of its own, the network hired Howard K. Smith (who had been dropped at CBS for his courageous news programs, on which he took stands opposed by sponsors) and teamed him with Frank Reynolds, in the hope they would become a new Huntley-Brinkley team. The experiment failed, and so Reynolds was replaced by another CBS veteran, Harry Reasoner. Smith reported in from Washington, and Reasoner from New York. Smith took the Huntley role, and Reasoner became the ABC version of David Brinkley. Of course, both were experienced newsmen, and personalities in their own right, but even there, format dictated content.

In the early 1970s, several "media consultant" firms began to advise stations and networks as how best to make their news programs commercial. Frank N. Magid Associates, a leader in the field, pioneered in the concept of "action news," which featured "news teams" who reported on the scene—on tape, to be sure—and reported on "what people *want* to know" rather than "what is news" or "what people *should* know." In other words, action news, and its later hybrid, eyewitness news, was geared more to ratings and consumer appeal than to older ideas of the nature of news. Although the concept was applied primarily to local news programs, its success affected the networks as well, and marked the culmination of the evolution from John Cameron Swayze's newsreel on television to Huntley and Brinkley's attempt to combine entertainment format with news content to a pure show-business approach. The divorce from the newspaper was complete. In the mid-1970s, the New York *Times* continued to proclaim that it published "all the news that's fit to print," while the popular local news program "ABC Eyewitness News" advertised that viewers would like the performers because they liked one another. Technology had dictated content and approach. "TV news is like getting socked in the belly by a ghost," wrote Robert Daly in his assessment of the medium. "You look back to see what hit you and it's not there any more. You can't even be sure if it was a substantial punch or not. Newspaper headlines have impact all day, and sometimes for years afterward, whereas TV news is vapor. It is as if print has a closer working hookup with the brain, and registers in a different place—the cortex rather than the retina, perhaps."[10]

THE POWER OF THE TV NEWSCASTER

Popular journalists of the nineteenth century might reach a million or so readers; syndicated columnists of the 1920s had audiences in the tens of millions, while the radio newscasters of World War II spoke to the nation. But they were newscasters and commentators, little more, with the possible exception of Murrow. Huntley, Brinkley, and Cronkite were of a different order; they were newspapermen, television commentators, and personalities, all of which gave them great power. An influential motion-picture actor or actress appeared before a large audience once a year, perhaps a trifle more often in some cases. Tens of millions of Americans watched Cronkite nightly, hanging onto his every word, trusting what he had to say. To them he, and not an unknown executive at CBS headquarters, was the network news. He not only reported upon the happenings of the day, but also selected stories he considered important, and determined how much time each story would receive. With the aid of his staff and the camera, Cronkite could show the public what he wanted them to see, thus illustrating his points as he went. A large portion of the nation saw the news through his eyes; by the late 1960s, more Americans received their news from television than from the newspapers or radio.

In 1868, New York *Tribune* publisher and editor Horace Greeley, the most powerful newsman of his day, fought for and received the Democratic nomination for the presidency, and failed miserably in the popular canvass. At the turn of the century, William Randolph Hearst, by then the nation's best-known and most influential publisher, was disappointed in several attempts to win nomination and election for high office. Radio had helped create political careers for several figures, among them Father Charles Coughlin, but none were seriously considered for national office. In 1972, someone at candidate George McGovern's headquarters suggested that Cronkite would make a fine running mate. They didn't know whether or not he was a Democrat, but his popularity was such that he merited such talk. The offer was never made, and a year later, Cronkite indicated that had he been asked to run, he would have refused to do so. He was not interested in a political career. (Some of his colleagues noted that the vice presidency would be a downward step for him; Cronkite exercised more power over the nation at CBS that he could in ruling over the Senate.) But the suggestion had been made, and it seemed sensible enough at the time. Cronkite was considered for high office not for his knowledge of the world or administrative abilities, though both were considerable, according to television executives. Rather, it was because he had the right image.

In the nineteenth century, newspapers had opened their columns to a wide variety of cranks and extremists, who reflected both the idiosyncracies of publishers and the tastes of specialized audiences. This tradition continued into the next century, especially for local audiences. But the wider the reach, the more homogeneous the product. By the 1950s news magazines offered a generally bland product, and took care not to offend too deeply, balancing one set of beliefs against the other; the public, not the government, imposed a fairness doctrine. The same was true of syndicated columnists. Those with the widest audiences fell within a fairly narrow spectrum, from moderate conservative to old-line liberal. A similar situation had developed in radio in the 1920s and 1930s; network radio did present extremists in the early years, but as time went on, the more radical and unusual individuals left the airwaves. In the late 1930s and early 1940s, some news commentators who held strong beliefs were fired, but no attempt was made to fit them into a mold. This was done, however, in a more subtle fashion. Edward R. Murrow stamped his personality upon news projection, not only at CBS, but the other networks as well. Fairness, impartiality, and decency were to be the rule, with the commentator rarely stepping out of his role to take an editorial stance.

The combination of the heritage of radio journalism, the presence of a national audience, and the nature of the technology obliged television news to take on the appearance of homogenization even before the advent of action news. The appearance—the haircuts, clothing, and even the figures—had to be middle American, and so were the voices. The words had to be carefully chosen, as free of passion as possible, and direct editorialization was a taboo. The political spectrum had to be narrow, at least for the major figures, running from David Brinkley on the left to Howard K. Smith on the right. The configuration of the band may best be appreciated by recalling that earlier in the decade, Brinkley had been classified as a moderate while Smith had been named as a Communist sympathizer in *Red Channels* and had been in constant trouble at CBS for his liberal stands on major issues. Dan Rather of CBS was considered a liberal maverick, and this reputation may have harmed his career, yet when appearing as a newsman on a regular news show, his reports were value-free, and might have been interchanged with Smith's or those of any other reporter considered conservative. As several critics remarked, opinion on network news ran the gamut from A to B.

Yet this was only the superficial appearance. As Murrow had demonstrated, it was possible to editorialize through the skillful use of videotape and film, by the selection of topics and coverage, and even through a raised eyebrow or a meaningful pause. "Ed never pushes his liberalism beyond a carefully calculated safety point," said one of the newsman's friends, Charles Wertenbaker. It was this awareness of a safety point that made him place a governor on his activities, to refuse to make strong statements either on or off the air, and most important, to reject strong advocacy positions. This was the heritage of 1940s radio. Even Murrow, for all his celebrity, was still primarily a newsman.

The leading newsmen of the 1960s understood the problems and possibilities of the television medium, and while on the tube—as performers—they strove to *appear* fair and objective. Whether due to frustration, the nature of the men, or the problems of the times, they dropped this façade off camera—as though actors leaving their roles in the studios. They were willing to admit biases, and even expound upon them. "News is what I say it is," said Brinkley in a published interview. "It's something worth knowing by my standards." On another occasion he said as much on camera—but on a program that appeared on poorly watched National Educational Television. "Objectivity is impossible to a normal human being." As Brinkley saw it, to be objective was to be a "vegetable." Brinkley made no secret of his dislike for President Nixon. Chet Huntley told reporters, "The shallowness of the man [Nixon] overwhelms me; the fact that he is President frightens me." Yet at the time, Huntley and Brinkley were reporting upon Nixon's activities, in an apparently dispassionate fashion.

Was it possible to separate fact and opinion? Did their opinions lead to distortions? Quincy Howe, the old radio commentator, thought the two aspects were by necessity intertwined, and should be viewed as such. "All news presented on radio and TV editorializes. The newscaster editorializes in what he emphasizes and what he plays down, in what he omits and what he includes." How far might this go? In the CBS special "Hunger in America," reporter Charles Kuralt held a frail child in his arms. "Hunger is easy to recognize when it looks like this. The baby was dying of starvation. He was an American. Now he is dead." It was a dramatic and moving picture, one that was easily etched on the mind. Viewers could believe it, for they had seen the baby with their own eyes, and had heard Kuralt speak of him with both tenderness and authority. Yet the baby, though dead, had not expired due to malnutrition or hunger; rather it was a premature child who had little chance of survival. A government probe of the program indicated that other, similarly false statements had been made in the special broadcast. CBS had tried to obtain statements from doctors that hunger had been the cause of death, but was unable to do so. In the end, the network claimed that although in this particular case some staging had been necessary, there was indeed hunger in America. In effect, the network had sacrificed what would normally be considered the "facts" for a larger truth. Or at least, this was the claim. And in any case, Kuralt was considered by viewers to be a far more plausible person than those who uncovered the deception. The public knew him, and he was trusted. Viewers had never heard of Dr. Luis Ray Montemayer, the baby's doctor, who denied death by hunger.

Newspapers had been instruments of communication, of ideas and facts. To a lesser extent, so had been radio. But television was and is an art form, best utilized for entertainment, for the presentation of celebrities. Had the medium emerged from motion pictures instead of from radio, this might have become its principal purpose. It also presented news and news-oriented programs that purported to be factual. At first this was a small part of network programming, but in the mid-1950s and after such news became far more important, even more so than it had been on radio, at least in terms of impact. But it was not true news, but rather a different form of entertainment, bearing as much relationship to fact as the documentary motion pictures of the late 1940s did to actual occurrences. The network newsmen desperately clung to the belief that they were reporters and journalists, even as they applied their makeup and took to wearing blue shirts, and shaving before being seen on the tube. They were in the business of creating images, not in imparting information and bandying about ideas. On a typical night, they would be seen after the rerun of a situation comedy and before a variety program. Entertainment, news, and public affairs were melting one into the rest. The seams were still visible in the late 1950s. Soon they would be gone, and all would be of a piece.

12

A Different Reality

The news industry has had a triple function ever since the early days of the penny press. To some extent it has entertained and amused, a role some editors, reporters, and publishers deplored, but that existed nonetheless. More important, they claimed, was the responsibility of newspapers, and later on news magazines and radio and television news programs, to inform and then comment upon events—to serve both as a source of information and a guide to opinion formation. These last two functions often clashed. On the one hand, the journalist was supposed to observe and report, while on the other he was to issue an interpretation.

Should the journalist report the news or create it? Are both roles proper? Can they be separated, and if so, would such a divorce be desirable? These questions, asked and never really answered in the newsrooms of the 1840s and in television studios in the early 1970s, have also interested readers and critics of written and electronic journalism. In practice, all newspapers contained both information and commentary, as did radio and television reports, if only in the selection of facts and the methods of presentation. The real questions are involved with the necessity of separating and labeling each function, and the method by which it might be accomplished. In the late nineteenth century, it was supposed to be done through the mediums of the unsigned news story and the editorial. The former was supposed to be factual, and was presented as such, while the latter contained the avowed opinions of editors and publishers. Thus, noneditorial newspapermen were to provide the grist for the mills of editors and publishers, and do so anonymously. Newspapers were businesses, and the reporters were employees who happened to write rather than set type. They were not to make news, unless ordered to do so by an activist publisher or editor.

Beginning in the 1880s, however, some Chicago newspapers began running signed articles, usually by the same person and in the same page location each day. These were written by reporters, but an occasional poet or magazine writer would become a "columnist." All of the early columns were humorous, and were usually comments upon individuals and events. Burt Leston Taylor, Eugene Fields, and S. E. Kiser were among the first Chicago columnists, while Finley Peter Dunne's "Mr. Dooley" was the most famous and influential. Franklin P. Adams began his career in Chicago before moving to the New York *Tribune* in 1914, by which time the New York *Sun* featured Don Marquis' "Sun Dial."

It was a strange occupation; the columnist was not a reporter, and not an editorial writer, but a cross between both as well as an entertainer. The columns were popular, and some of the more famous of them were syndicated. Almost all the columnists received higher wages than reporters, even though the latter sneered at them for not being true newspapermen. The columnists were becoming celebrities in their own right, men whose names were recognized while the reporter remained anonymous. At the center of reportage was news, but the personality of the columnist often was more significant than the events upon which he commented. The columnist, then, was coming to have an importance that was independent of his newspaper.

The popularity of humor columns created a demand for features that had the same form but a different content, and the political columns made their appearance shortly before World War I, and became a major part of the industry after the war. David Lawrence, Frank Kent, and Mark Sullivan, all of whom were syndicated, reported from Washington, and each had an influential column. Editors of afternoon papers in particular were interested in running such columns. Unable to compete with the morning press for news, the afternoon and evening newspapers turned to columns, in which the reader could find interpretations of that news.[1] Under the editorial leadership of Walter Lippmann, the New York *World* developed a full page of such columns, which ran on the page opposite the editorials, and this "op ed page" attracted additional readers and gave the columnists greater power than before. When the *World* merged with the *Telegram* in 1931, Lippmann himself became a columnist, and soon was the most influential in the nation.

By that time the reporter had acquired a greater degree of influence than he had had in the late nineteenth century. Important reporters were given bylines, and although weeks might pass without such a signed story appearing on the front page, their names too were becoming known. On occasion, reporters would achieve columnist status, but still the separation of functions remained. The reporter was supposed to do just that—report—while the columnist looked through the other end of the telescope, took a broad view, and was supposed to interpret.

Some newsmen were able to combine the two functions in a new fashion. In the 1930s, Drew Pearson, Robert S. Allen, and Paul Mallon published revelations of wrongdoing, and uncovered secrets and commented upon them. Thus they not only explored the nature of events, but also, in a way not unlike that of Hearst, affected the course of events. What a later generation would call "investigative reporting" emerged out of this marriage of reporter and columnist. But what was fact, and what was interpretation? In the 1930s and afterward, this question was asked and not answered. As syndications grew, columnists like Lippmann, Raymond Clapper, Westbrook Pegler, Pearson, and Dorothy Thompson became better known than most editors and publishers, and in some cases, had more influence upon readers. Each had his or her own personality, and the public came to view them as forces in their own rights.

Reporters had a different image; they were lumped together in the public view, considered as representatives of their papers and profession. What were they like, and what did they do? Few studies of the profession were made before World War II, and those that remain are partial, crude, and often impressionistic. Much of their work was dull and routine, and their writing bland and homogenized. Leo Rosten, who conducted a study of the Washington press corps in 1937, thought them simple individuals, who "evidence a marked insecurity in the presence of social theories or political conceptualization." Yet they were well educated. In the early 1970s, when less than half of all Americans their age had high school diplomas, half the 127 Washington newsmen had graduated from college, and only eight lacked a high school diploma.[2] These were middle-class people, thought Rosten, who had middle-class values and aspirations.

Many Americans thought otherwise, for their ideas of the lives of newspapermen were derived not from the reality of the newspaper, but from the fiction of the motion picture and radio. In 1928 Ben Hecht and Charles MacArthur's play *The Front Page* appeared on Broadway, and three years later it appeared as a film. In it reporters and editors were portrayed as living exciting lives. More important, perhaps, they appeared as amoral opportunists, hard-hearted, calculating, willing to lie, cheat, and steal in order to get a "scoop" on rivals. The picture was successful, and since Hecht and MacArthur had both been journalists, was assumed to be realistic. Other, similar films followed. In *Blessed Event* the reporter-columnist, clearly modeled after Walter Winchell, destroyed his enemies. *Front Page Woman* and *His Girl Friday* (a remake of *The Front Page*) indicated that women, too, were of the type. Radio made an even greater contribution, since stories of newsmen appeared as weekly series. Listeners to radio dramas came away with the idea that reporters usually were hot on the trail of corruption. The motion-picture reporter drank heavily and had a cigarette in the corner of his mouth; his radio counterpart would get his story, grab the telephone, and then, after contacting his paper, scream, "Gimme rewrite, and make it snappy." Soon after, the harried but grateful editor would shout, "Hold the presses. We're coming out with an extra." Both motion picture and radio portrayed the reporter as a tough individual, usually Irish in extraction, but on the screen he might use corrupt means to expose the villain, while on the air he became a reformer.[3] Such programs as "Big Town," "Casey, Crime Photographer," and "Front Page Farrell" were among the most popular of their time, and had many imitators.

Thus the public received the image of the cynic, scornful of middle-class values—including education and religion—from the motion pictures, while radio presented the crusading journalist who exposed wrongdoing when even the police were baffled. More often than not, the real reporter was a middle-aged, middle-class scribe, whose life contained more or less the same amounts of danger and excitement as those of teachers, dentists, and accountants. But the images were at least as powerful as the reality, and just as many young people who saw the motion picture *Goodbye, Mr. Chips* decided to become teachers, and received their impressions of the lives of doctors in hospitals from the popular Dr. Kildare series, so young men and women were first attracted to journalism as a career by the movies and radio dramas of the 1930s. And as with all such things, image and reality merged, but in the public eye, the image remained the more powerful of the two.

What was the newspaperman to the public of the 1950s and 1960s? Some thought of him as a courageous exposer of evil; others believed reporters were capable of falsehoods, who indeed could be bought off by corrupt politicians and businessmen, and used their positions to propagandize for points of view. Perhaps most thought reporters had elements of both in their makeups; when readers agreed with a story, the reporter was brave and forthright, and when they disagreed, the assumption was that he was corrupt or worse.

In 1973 reporter James Perry, a respected moderate employed by the *National Observer*, wrote that "the Middle Political Journalist is a 45-year-old white male reared in the suburbs of Peoria, Illinois, whose wife is a member of the PTA," and he went on to note that most reporters attended public high schools and state universities. Those covering national politics earned between fifteen thousand dollars and thirty thousand dollars a year, with some stars and syndicated reporters doing much better. "He is not very liberal," wrote Perry, "and not very conservative . . . he is not an intellectual but surely not an ignoramus."[4] These were the men of the "faceless press," faceless at least as most newspaper readers were concerned. Perry named some of them—Paul Hope, Martin Nolan, Loye Miller, Thomas Ottenad, Godfrey Sperling, and James Dickenson—and noted that they are respected within the profession but not well known to readers. The same could be said of Perry himself.

As had been the case before, the columnists were a different breed. David Broder, Rowland Evans, Robert Novak, Joseph and Stewart Alsop, Walter Lippmann, Arthur Krock, and David

Lawrence, among others, were familiar names, whose signed columns carried much weight and who were considered the leading lights of newspaper journalism. In the early 1970s a major syndicated columnist might earn in excess of a hundred thousand dollars a year from his newspaper work alone. Many also wrote for magazines and authored books.

Television brought a major change to their status, however. An Arthur Krock or a Walter Lippmann might dominate his profession in the 1930s, be considered major forces by Presidents and legislators, and still walk down the streets of big cities unrecognized. Even an Elmer Davis, Edward R. Murrow, and H. V. Kaltenborn could do the same in the 1940s, and not be known until they spoke. Such men could retain a measure of detachment from the political scene, could observe events without becoming the object of undue interest. Their successors in the 1960s, however, appeared on television interview programs and, on occasion, were guests on late-night talk shows, while some had shows of their own. In the process they became celebrities in their own rights, not reporters, columnists, or commentators—they were the objects of attention rather than the recorders and interpreters of events.

Merriman Smith, who arrived at the White House in 1941 as a United Press correspondent, understood this. Although Smith was a Pulitzer Prize winner, his name was familiar only to those within the industry and to readers who noted his byline over Washington reports in their newspapers. His face and voice were known to the Washington community and some others throughout the nation, but otherwise, Merriman Smith might have been John Smith, an ordinary middle-class individual. Then he began to appear on late-night talk shows, to tell anecdotes about the Presidents and offer opinions on the news. His status quickly changed. Smith found he no longer could walk behind the Presidents with the rest of the newsmen, watching and reporting. Instead, some onlookers would recognize him, call out his name, and even ask for autographs. It was even more difficult for a television newsman to achieve any sort of anonymity. Tom Brokaw and Dan Rather would be spotted by many in a crowd. As for stars on the magnitude of Walter Cronkite and Chet Huntley, such men could no longer appear in public without receiving the kind of attention usually reserved for motion-picture artists. Their salaries reflected this; in the mid-1970s a network television newsman might have a starting salary of $35,000, while famous anchor men earned an annual salary in excess of $250,000 for their nightly half-hour stints alone. With the emergence of individuals such as these, the media of radio-television and newspapers came together, as did fiction and fact, illusion and reality.

And there was more to come. In late 1972, two Washington *Post* reporters, Bob Woodward and Carl Bernstein, began investigating the Watergate break-in, uncovering evidence of wrongdoing which, ultimately, helped topple President Nixon. For their work—careful, straightforward stories—the newspaper received the Pulitzer Prize. Then they wrote a book about their experience, *All the President's Men,* which was advertised, among other things, as "the greatest mystery story of the century." Unlike their newspaper reports, the book was written in a highly dramatic style, as indeed a mystery might. The presentation was akin to a working sketch for a motion picture. So it was. When Woodward and Bernstein appeared on television talk shows, they seemed pleasant, bright, but somewhat uncomfortable young men. But in the magazine stories written about them they emerged as a "crack news team," tough and dedicated, with Woodward as an "establishment type" while Bernstein was "street-wise." They were dramatized as a team—a version of Clark Gable-Spencer Tracy or Paul Newman-Robert Redford, or more to the point, a newspaper analog of Huntley and Brinkley. Then Redford purchased the film rights to the book, announcing that he would play Woodward. Later Dustin Hoffman was cast as Bernstein. The motion picture—a medium still considered fictional at base—would be used to present a factual story, but in an even more highly dramatized form than the book. Thus the unity of radio-television and newspapers with motion pictures. In *The Front Page,* Hildy Johnson was a fictional character. When Robert Redford played Bob Woodward, would the audience separate fact from fiction? More to the point, did the audience care to know, or for that matter, need to understand the difference?

THE MEDIA AND POLITICIANS

Politicians have attempted to utilize and manipulate the press from Washington's time to the present. Lincoln was an avid reader of newspapers, not only to digest their contents, but also to calculate the impacts of men like Greeley and Bennett. Theodore Roosevelt wooed the Washington press corps, hoping that reporters would become enthusiastic for his projects. In his own unique fashion, Coolidge was a master of the reporters who covered his activities. Franklin Roosevelt and Woodrow Wilson before him enlisted the motion-picture industry in a war effort. Roosevelt also became a master of radio, a medium that enabled him to speak directly to the American people without the intercession of reporters and editors. But he, like all of his predecessors, had achieved office through the mastery of the political process, by dealing directly with local and national leaders in order to win nomination and then election. Local politicians were of great use at such times, since a candidate from New York could use them to reach constituencies in other parts of the country. Roosevelt would utilize radio, but neither he nor any on his staff developed a rationale for the medium, nor seemed to understand how it might be used to alter the political process.

The beginnings of change came with the 1940 campaigns of Wendell Willkie and Thomas E. Dewey. Newspaper publicity enabled Dewey, while still only the New York district attorney, to make a serious bid for the Republican nomination, while Willkie, who defeated him at the convention, was a product of public relations and radio. Willkie faltered in 1944, when he attempted to obtain the nomination through conventional methods, and Dewey, by then governor of New York, was selected by use of the conventional channels.[5]

Harry Truman recognized the importance of the electronic media but was unable to employ them effectively. His flat, nasal Missouri twang and rapid delivery came over poorly on radio, and he was uneasy on television. The White House hired a media coach, Leonard Reinsch, who tried to fit Truman into a more dramatic mold, but the attempts failed. Truman did utilize radio and television to make important announcements, but was often compared unfavorably with his predecessor. Still, he continued making efforts in that direction. He presided over a televised Cabinet meeting, and in 1951 permitted newsmen to tape-record press conferences in order to check their notes. After a while, he allowed portions of the tapes to be played on radio. But Truman was not a man for the media; he not only refused to be altered by it or alter himself to make an impression, but also bridled at the idea, and was angered when changes were suggested.[6]

Truman's successor, Dwight Eisenhower, was not created by the media, though he learned to use it effectively and even daringly. The Eisenhower legend was so powerful by 1952 that it needed no embellishment; his reputation alone insured election. Eisenhower lacked Roosevelt's fine, dramatic voice—a decided asset in a radio age—but he was more telegenic than FDR; by chance, Eisenhower happened to be ideal for a visual medium. His smile alone was worth hundreds of thousands of votes, and his firm, direct stare was additionally impressive. His managers moved quickly to capitalize upon them. Robert Montgomery, an actor, was taken on to coach Eisenhower in the use of visual media, while an advertising agency, Batten, Barton, Durstine, and Osborne, was charged with developing new ideas in the area. James Hagerty, an experienced reporter who became Eisenhower's press secretary, understood the power of television. "We are in a day of a new medium—television," he told the press corps. "I would like to work out with television representatives . . . a system whereby the President could give talks to the people of the country—possibly press conferences. . . ." But there were to be no televised press conferences for the first three years, although Eisenhower did appear occasionally to deliver addresses, and of course his activities were covered by the news programs.

Then, in 1955, the President had a heart attack, and he delivered a television address soon after, more in order to assure the nation that he was physically and mentally capable of continuing in office than anything else. In early 1956 Hagerty scheduled a press conference at which cameras were permitted, with the understanding that films would be made, submitted to the White House for possible editing, and then released on the networks. The same practice was followed at a second news conference following Eiesnhower's abdominal surgery. Both press conferences were seen by large audiences, which were not so much interested in what the President had to say—this would be covered in the news programs and in the next day's newspapers—but to see if Eisenhower could "handle himself" well, and how he looked. Thus the press conference became a performance, almost a contest—and was used by Eisenhower for his purposes, not those of the press. But the press corps benefited too, though in a different fashion. By exchanges with the President, they became celebrities, their faces and voices known to a larger public than might have been reached by the printed word. Like Eisenhower, they had to perform well, appear proper, and impress those who watched.

In 1953, a member of the Administration had conceded, "We all suddenly realized we were busy manufacturing a product down here, but nobody was selling it." The selling began in earnest the following year—not that Eisenhower needed merchandising, but that the technology existed, and so would be utilized. Press Secretary Hagerty quickly became a key man in the Administration, with more power than any of his predecessors. In part this was due to Hagerty's native abilities and experience, but here too, the media transformed the role. The term "press secretary," coined during the newspaper age, was a misnomer in the television era. Hagerty was a director, a man who moved the main actors into positions, who attempted to manipulate the press corps, where earlier secretaries had just cajoled and insinuated. He thought his main task to be the orchestration of the Eisenhower White House; Charles Ross and Joseph Short, the Truman press secretaries, had considered their job the translation of presidential ideas to the press. Hagerty wanted to influence reader's attitudes; Ross and Short performed before and for the press corps.

Television critic Jack Gould noted that the Administration could "turn television on or off as it deems expedient," that this gave Hagerty "potentially a most awesome power."[7] Yet Hagerty had no need to create an image for Eisenhower, nor could television remold the man. This had been done prior to 1952, during World War II. The tube could enhance or highlight in his case, but no more. If Truman was the last of the pretelevision Presidents, Eisenhower was the last who did not need the tube to make his initial political impact. When the Republicans nominated Richard Nixon and the Democrats John Kennedy in 1960, it became evident that both were products of the media, not conventional politics as practiced prior to the mid-1950s.

This was not as obvious in the case of Nixon as it was with Kennedy. Nixon had been selected for the vice presidency in 1952 in an attempt to balance the ticket. He was a hard campaigner in the conventional fashion, and if not considered particularly telegenic at the time of nomination, he was at least at ease before the camera. His televised appeal for support in 1952, after it appeared he would be dropped from the ticket, was the highlight of the campaign. The content of the so-called "Checkers Speech" is so familiar as not to require analysis or commentary. Overlooked by most at the time, however, was its form. While the press critics of Nixon concentrated upon the substance of the speech, Walter Lippmann for one was disturbed by the very fact of its having been delivered. The question of whether or not Nixon should have remained on the ticket was at base judicial and moral, to be decided by reference to basic principles, not a plebiscite. "What the television audience should have been given was not Senator Nixon's personal defense. That should have been made first before General Eisenhower. What the television audience should have been given was General Eisenhower's decision, backed by a full and objective account of the facts and of the points of law and morals which are involved." This did not occur. Instead, thought Lippmann, the nation experienced "mob rule by modern electronics."

As Roosevelt had done on radio, Nixon appealed to the people directly, without the intercession of the political process. He understood this, and although not impressive in his television appearances while Vice President, he refined his techniques during the next eight years.

Kennedy had arrived in the House of Representatives in 1947, the same year as Nixon, and went on to the Senate in 1953, when Nixon became Vice President. Kennedy was not a distinguished legislator; his name was not associated with major legislation, he lacked power within the Senate, and his absentee rate was high. Nor was Kennedy well considered within the Democratic party. As a Catholic whose father was believed anti-Semitic and isolationist as well as an admirer of Joseph McCarthy, Kennedy did not offer a plausible foundation for a presidential bid. Yet he was interested in the presidency, and planned to achieve it in a new fashion—through the media. In 1956, when Edward Murrow was preparing a film to be shown at the convention, he recommended Kennedy as its narrator, recognizing his fine vocal qualities. Kennedy did narrate the film, and made an attempt to win the vice-presidential nomination as well, on this occasion working through the conventional channels. As a result of his 1956 experience, Kennedy was better known, but still hardly considered a serious challenger for 1960.

From 1956 to 1959, Kennedy appeared regularly on television interview programs, while his staff worked diligently to keep his name and face before the public through newspaper interviews and magazine stories. Given the choice, Kennedy would bypass Senate business in order to accept an invitation to speak before reporters or appear on television. In the process he won the envy of other presidential hopefuls and became a national figure, even though identified with no major issue. In the autumn of 1959—before the campaign had begun—he was recognized by approximately 70 per cent of the electorate, a remarkable showing. Having achieved this, he went on to announce his candidacy for the presidency.

Though better organized and financed than the campaigns of other candidates, the form of the Kennedy effort to win the nomination was not unique. He attempted to win the party professionals through private conferences and arrangements, while at the same time entering primaries, hoping to win enough of them to enter the convention a leader. The content of the Kennedy campaign was different, however. He utilized volunteers effectively, not only to address envelopes and ring doorbells, but also to attract the attention of television newsmen. As a result, his campaign attracted considerably more interest than those of his opponents. The clear opposition of some leading party regulars, including Harry Truman and Eleanor Roosevelt, may actually have helped his cause, for at this stage of his career, Kennedy liked to portray himself as functioning independently of the "old politics."

In the past, candidates had sought to obtain support through the utilization of the political establishment. Kennedy bypassed it, creating his own constituency through the careful use of television and volunteers. Of course, his cause was greatly assisted by "style" and "image." Long after audiences forgot the substance of a Kennedy speech, they recalled his appearance—he was so young, so vital, so attractive. Rivals claimed Kennedy lacked depth, that he was just a handsome dilettante, and that a Kennedy victory would be the result of packaging, not experience and intelligence. This may have been so, but it was hardly new; ever since the first half of the nineteenth century, image had been of prime importance in political campaigns, even though it went under different names. Still, the Kennedy image was different. Presidents were supposed to have gray hair, be somewhat portly, and exude an air of quiet confidence—the picture of statesmanship was painted in dark tones. When Franklin Roosevelt and Dwight Eisenhower posed beside show-business people, they seemed properly presidential. This was not the case with Kennedy, who looked as much like a motion-picture star as most of the Hollywood contingent that later supported his campaign.

Kennedy achieved nomination through primary victories and a skillful effort at the convention. Then he moved quickly to come to terms with the rest of the party, through the selection of Lyndon Johnson for the vice presidency and assurances of co-operation with the regulars. Meanwhile, the Republican team of Nixon and UN Ambassador Henry Cabot Lodge began to plan for the campaign.

In a poll taken in early 1960, approximately 60 per cent of respondents indicated that television was their major source for political information. This was up from the 40 per cent of 1956 and the 31 per cent of 1952. Media blitz campaigns would increase that figure, and the candidates, both of whom had confidence in their abilities on the tube, planned to utilize it as much as possible. Kennedy told reporters he would campaign throughout the nation, while Nixon pledged to visit every state. This meant little, except that the candidates did fulfill promises and made public appearances. More important, in the early stages at least, were "guest shots" on such television programs as "Meet the Press," "Face the Nation," "Person to Person," and the Jack Paar "Tonight Show," the last perhaps the most important of all, certainly the one with the largest audience. To those who followed the campaign closely on television, it appeared more an audition than a political contest. Both candidates understood and accepted this. Kennedy welcomed the opportunities to address the largest audiences possible, since he was at a disadvantage compared with the more familiar Vice President. As for Nixon, he distrusted the press, the result of bad experiences, and so he sought to eliminate the reporter middleman by taking his case directly to the electorate.

There were serious issues in the campaign—domestic priorities, the recession, the Cuban situation, and America's defense posture, as well as the unspoken issue of Kennedy's religion. In addition, there was the issue of experience and maturity, which was considered Nixon's strong point, and he hammered away at it. Only four years younger than the Vice President, Kennedy seemed far more youthful. This was an advantage insofar as attracting those who sought glamor for the office, but on the other hand, it raised questions of whether Kennedy was truly well prepared for the job.

Afterward, most observers wrote that the "great debates" were the keys to the election. But these were not debates, in that the two men did not respond to each other's arguments. Rather, they stood at lecterns in a studio, while a moderator asked questions, to which each responded. In format, it resembled the familiar quiz programs, and in part the programs were viewed as such—more akin to "stump the candidate" than "issues and answers." There were four debates in all, with the television critics and political commentators keeping score as to who was ahead. It was generally agreed that Nixon won the second debate after losing the first, and that the last two were draws. Reporters noted that he was haggard and drawn, the result of a recent illness, and that his makeup man was not very skillful.

But what of the substance of the debate? Shortly after they had ended, the public had forgotten about this. What remained was far more important. Kennedy had overcome the fears of many that he was not sufficiently experienced for the presidency—it was as though the heavyweight champion had accepted a challenge from an unranked contender, who then fought him to a draw. The debates were seen in that light—as more sporting events-entertainments than serious discussions of national and world problems. Nixon's error was in "stepping into the ring" with his opponent, for he had far more to lose than had Kennedy in such a contest. The debates were important in the context of the election, but they also had an impact that continued long after it was over. They insured that the next Administration, no matter who was elected, would contain important elements of show business, and that future presidential races would be media events, to be orchestrated by directors, rather than political contests to be managed by professionals.

The merger of politics and show business was obvious to all

who attended the movies in the early 1960s. In 1959 Stanley Kramer's film *On the Beach* warned Americans of the consequences of an atomic war. *The Manchurian Candidate,* released in 1962, concerned political fanaticism and the danger of thought control. *Advise and Consent,* filmed on location in Washington, was a political movie based on the best-selling novel of a former reporter. In late 1963, *Seven Days in May, Fail-Safe,* and *Dr. Strangelove* were being prepared for release, while *Panic in Year Zero, Ladybug, Ladybug,* and *The Best Man* were in various stages of readiness. Hollywood was creating—perhaps re-creating—the political motion picture, which contained elements of fantasy combined with the visual impact of reality. Moviegoers could leave the theater after seeing *On the Beach,* turn on their television sets, and learn of the Berlin crisis, with President Kennedy telling the public of the dangers of atomic war. Or they could watch the United Nations debate during the Cuban missile crisis, and afterward see *Dr. Strangelove.* They could see Presidents portrayed on the screen by Henry Fonda, Franchot Tone, and Fredric March, and then see Kennedy on television. As was so common in this period, reality and fiction intertwined, assisted as always by the nature of the media, and the conscious and unconscious utilization of it by the practitioners.

Kennedy understood the value of media, and he used it more effectively than any public figure since Roosevelt. In addition, he had a healthy respect for those who made their livings by interpreting events, as well as a liking for some of Washington's leading analysts. He knew how to deal with the new kinds of reporters and columnists—the young, college-bred intellectuals who were taking their places at the news services and major newspapers—and he wooed them assiduously. David Broder, Ben Bradlee, Robert Novak, Rowland Evans, Mary McGrory, Russell Baker, and others were courted by the Kennedys before and after the election.[8] The family, especially Jacqueline Kennedy, made good copy and even better pictures. The White House staff, led by Press Secretary Pierre Salinger, had excellent relations with the working press, and this continued throughout the Administration.[9] At the same time, however, Kennedy preferred to continue his prepresidential practice of also speaking to the public directly after he was elected. At Salinger's suggestion, the President decided to conduct live press conferences. New York *Times* columnist James Reston thought it "the goofiest idea since the hula hoop," and other veterans wrote gravely of possible dangers. But as with the debates, Kennedy had far more to gain than to lose. In the first place, he could utilize the questions to put forth his ideas on a variety of subjects, not really answering at all. Thus these would not be news conferences as much as public briefings, even pep rallies. The reporters would be part of the audience, as it were, at a performance, asking questions on cue, properly deferring to Kennedy, never having a chance to retort. In addition, the live conferences would be broadcast at a time of the President's selection; unlike the Eisenhower filmed conferences, they could not be retained and shown for the first time on the nightly news shows. Salinger understood this completely, and as he wrote in his memoirs, "There was . . . no question that TV was willing to preempt millions of dollars in commercial time to carry the press conferences." There was a bonus: Since they were news conferences, the appearances did not fall under the FCC's equal-time provisions; there would be no right of reply. But if they constituted news, they were also show business. White House adviser and resident intellectual Arthur Schlesinger, Jr., observed, perhaps unwittingly, that a Kennedy appearance was a "superb show, always gay, often exciting, relished by the reporters and the television audience." All benefited—the President by reaching his audience; the audience by hearing what he had to say; and the reporters, who by being seen on the tube achieved enhanced individual and collective status.

Enjoyment of such drama might have been heightened through a reading of *The Making of the President, 1960*, by Theodore White (a former classmate of Schlesinger's at Harvard). The book remained on the best-seller list for a year and then sold well in paperback. White was a veteran political reporter who had a fine dramatic sense—he had also written two novels. In *The Making of the President, 1960*, he combined the substance of fact with the format and drama of the novel, so that the reader was both entertained and informed. This was not familiar academic history, but rather a journalistic account in the form of a factual novel. It excited and entertained, offered the reader inside views of the political process, and left them with the sense of having participated vicariously in the campaign. The book opened with the sentence-paragraph, "it was invisible, as always," and concluded with "This perhaps is what he had best learned in 1960—even though he called his own victory a 'miracle.' This is what he would have to cherish alone in the White House, on which an impatient world waited for miracles." These were the words of an artist, not an academic historian, of a man of poetry rather than one of prose. As academic history became more scientific—and lost readers among the general public—journalists like White entered the field of history and achieved huge successes, by selling their products to the millions of B.A.s turned out by the colleges in the postwar period. It coincided with the coming to power of an Administration that would later be characterized as "Camelot."

The Kennedy Inaugural was to have begun with a recitation by Robert Frost. The sun glared off the snow that day, so the poet could not see to read his words. He did speak of the appropriateness of having artists to celebrate "the august occasions of the state." The events, he thought, presaged "the glory of a next Augustan age." Frost saw in the Kennedy accession the beginning of "a golden age of poetry and power." The public witnessed the drama and heard the poetry—on television sets and radios. The power was there too, but could not be discerned. It didn't really matter. Electronics enabled Americans to witness a historic event, one that was staged so as to be memorable in that fashion. The screen, not what went on behind it, was the true reality; form became substance.

A little more than three years later, Walter Lippmann was interviewed on television, and asked to assess the Kennedy impact. "Well, my feeling about that is this: When President Kennedy was murdered, the situation abroad and at home was in a state of —I think you could fairly call it crisis. His own policies were blocked at home, and they were frustrated abroad, and the country was very deeply and bitterly divided about him. There was sectional feeling. There was class feeling. There was racial feeling."[10] This was not the view held by most Americans. The media presidency had ended—tragically, with a media event, the funeral. Millions watched and listened for hours, as the network commentators —Cronkite, Huntley and Brinkley, and others—described the coffin, the moods of onlookers, the plans for ceremonies, and whatever else they could find to fill the time between developments. Camera crews followed the cortege every step of the way, showing the audience all that was happening in a minute fashion. Those who missed the assassination of Kennedy's killer, Lee Harvey Oswald, were able to see replays on the late-night news, and on special broadcasts shown during the next few days. There had been periods of national mourning following the deaths of other Presidents, but none could match the Kennedy funeral and its aftermath for drama and vicarious participation.

Was this news? Perhaps not, but to cover the funeral in any other way would have been unthinkable. Certainly the networks could not have continued on their old schedules—comedies, movies, reruns, and the like—and they could hardly have left the air. Thus the public watched and listened to the somber events, as they might the launching of a space vehicle. David Brinkley had said on several occasions that he decided what was news and what was not. This time the networks made the decision, and no other could have been made. Were the names of those who attended the funeral the stuff of news? Did it demand this kind of coverage? And was it necessary for the nation to remain riveted to receivers? These questions and others like them could not be answered in social science terms, or with a discussion of the relationship between technology and society. Rather the nation came together via television to attend a funeral; the event created the mood, with the technology making the event possible—and creating strong images in the minds of a nation. The funeral, not the assassination, became annealed in the public consciousness—and the unconscious as well. The assassination had been of a President, while the funeral was that of a man. Thus television technology helped enhance and etch the memories of the man, just as earlier it had focused attention upon style rather than substance.

Within a dozen years the Kennedy legend had achieved a measure of permanence. The record, as discussed by Lippmann, no longer mattered as much. Whether or not the transfer of power to Lyndon Johnson resulted in major alterations in domestic and foreign policies can be debated, but the matter cannot be resolved. In any event, the transfer went smoothly. Johnson was able to push the Kennedy program through Congress, while continuing the old policies overseas, retaining both personnel and ideologies. Memories of Kennedy persisted, of a youthful, vigorous, attractive, and charming man, not of a powerful Chief Executive. When pressed to list his accomplishments, Kennedy supporters more often than not spoke of plans interrupted by tragedy, the promise of the future, and the grace of the man. But Kennedy had been in the White House for close to three years, and in that long a period every other modern Chief Executive had put together a long list of accomplishments, both positive and negative. The Kennedy years may have been laden with promise, but they were relatively barren of accomplishment.

The difference between the memories and the record is easily explained, and rested in the coming together of the man and the media, and their symbiosis. If Kennedy had used the media well, he was also its subject and object, perhaps its victim. Not since the days of Franklin Roosevelt had the White House provided such good copy for reporters, or been so amenable to ideas from journalists. Kennedy could be counted upon to provide an excellent television performance, one that was pleasing, informative, and entertaining. After a press conference, one asked whether the President had handled himself well, not necessarily what he had said. The overseas trips were news in themselves, even though little of importance was accomplished on them. These, too, were media events.

The flawed and failed Johnson administration and the Nixon disaster made Camelot seem all the more alluring. Some critics, on both the political left and right, noted that the roots of much of the discontent of the mid-1960s and after had been planted during the previous administrations, and that Kennedy, no less than Johnson and Nixon, had been guilty of what came to be known as "the arrogance of power." This too could not be discerned in the continuing popularity of the young President. The texture of life during that period was ignored, perhaps because memories of what truly happened might have been stirred. In the 1970s a minor nostalgia boom developed, and this concentrated upon the Eisenhower years, not those of John Kennedy. Still, the image remained untarnished, and Kennedy continued to occupy a unique position in the presidential pantheon. Several polls indicated that Americans considered him to be among the nation's greatest Presidents, and even scholars gave him "good grades." Few examined the reasons for his uniqueness, however.

THE NEW PERCEPTION

Beyond accomplishments and the lack of them, the Kennedy years constituted an important watershed in the national life. In this period, the various arts and businesses of communications, entertainment, and information reached a new level of maturity and power; some united, or at least appeared to come together to form the skeleton for an altered civilization and consciousness. This is not to say that some of the major events of the period and after would not have taken place or not have become significant were it not for the framework. The Vietnam War, the civil rights movement, the various aspects of the youth culture, and the women's rights movement may be traced to events and decisions of the 1950s, and in some cases even earlier than that. The increased use of drugs and the campus disturbances, the ecology movement and the crusade against pollution, were strongly influenced by developments in the media, but were not created by newspapers and television. Rather, the media acted as a catalyst in some cases, and served to accelerate the pace of change and sharpen interest. The forces that had controlled and even created the media lost control of their vehicles, which were now taken over by a different element, individuals who had been employees and subjects in the past, when they possessed good salaries and expectations but little in the way of power within their industries and occupations. To some, the changes appeared to have been caused by a "generation gap," an alluring concept since so many of the more prominent individuals involved in the movements were young or affected youthful poses, while those who opposed them were middle-aged or elderly. But later studies indicated that the young radicals were very much like their parents, who supported their ideas and efforts —there was little in the way of a generation gap within the families. Still, the concept of a conflict of young against middle-aged is useful, though not necessarily because the young people of the 1960s were by nature more revolutionary than their parents.

More to the point, it was an upheaval within the civilization, which appeared at times to break out of its confines and become a rebellion, even a revolution. It never achieved that status and, upon reflection, never really was meant to do so. The movements could not be explained by conventional Marxist analysis, though at the time and afterward attempts were made to do so, both by supporters and critics of change. The middle class and the wealthy spearheaded the movements for reform and revolt, while among their opponents were poor and lower-middle-class individuals, the very ones who were supposed to benefit from the changes. The situation was dramatized by the juxtaposition of the wealthy Harvard radical and the lower-middle-class "hard hat," who was conservative on most issues. These two had differing concepts of reality, and in essence were products of quite different kinds of civilizations, even though they lived within miles of one another. The differences were not so much the result of class and status, however, as they were of experiences with the media in the postwar period. In other words, educational institutions, radio and television, motion pictures, and newspapers molded consciousness then, as they had with their parents. These media of information and entertainment both developed and changed, and did so in such a way as to create separate realities for different people.

Higher education provided some of the greatest surprises. In 1960, there were some 3.8 million students enrolled in the nation's colleges and universities. By then, most educators were aware of the implications of the baby boom of the late 1940s, and were preparing to meet it by expanding facilities and hiring additional faculty. It appeared then that the crest of enrollments would take place in the mid-1960s and then level off. At the same time, it seemed certain that larger numbers of minority-group students would attend colleges than did so in the past, and they too would swell enrollments. Still, the educators were unprepared for the dimensions of the new college classes of the 1960s. In 1965 there were 5.9 million students, quite higher than projections had indicated. And there was no slaking the demand; in 1967 the figure was 6.9 million, and by 1970, more than 8.5 million college students were in attendance. In less than ten years, the college population had doubled.

At the time, it was common to attribute the increased enrollments to those males who wanted to avoid the military draft. But the female college population rose more rapidly than that of the males through the decade. It also was claimed that the new students, unlike their predecessors during the "silent 1950s," were more interested in "pure education," as distinct from vocational training. Yet, the largest group of students on the nation's campuses were those majoring in education, and three out of every ten graduate students were interested in teaching or school administrative careers. In the graduate areas as a whole, the largest increases came in library science, foreign languages, and business. The university as a vocational training center, the college degree as a passport to the upper middle class, seemed as valid in the early Kennedy years as it had been during the Eisenhower era.

But there were important qualitative differences between the college students of the early 1960s and those who had preceded them. The freshman who learned of Kennedy's assassination between classes in 1963 had been born in 1945. He had no direct experience with the Great Depression, and might not have noticed the minor dips of the 1950s. Instead, he had been raised during one of the great upward economic sweeps, a time when college-educated and -trained individuals were at a premium. The young graduate of this period could select from many positions; the future was brighter for him than it had been for any previous generation. Some were eager to grasp the chance, but others, usually of the middle class, could afford to ignore it for a while. Fears of joblessness and deprivation were unknown, or at the very most, something obtained from history textbooks and old movies. The better students—those who read current nonfiction books—might have learned of the persistence of poverty in parts of the land, while all knew of racism, the civil rights movement, and the Cold War through watching television news programs and reading newspapers. Aware of problems within the society and economically secure enough to forgo self-interest, they could become involved in various reform movements. Their older brothers and sisters, who had attended colleges a decade earlier, might have held back—due to desires for jobs and fear of being labeled a Communist during the McCarthy period. The students of the 1950s, with some recollections of World War II, might have retained some of the intense patriotism of that period, which called upon the individual to support his country against all attackers and critics. College freshmen of 1963, born after the war, had no such memories, no such period of indoctrination, either in the schools or through the media.

The processes of education itself had changed by the 1960s. Some social scientists estimated that the average ten-year-old

American child had spent more time in front of a television set than in school, and concluded that a generation was being raised on old movies, quiz programs, situation comedies, and half-hour dramas. Debatable though such figures might be, and however much one might question the conclusions drawn from them, television did become a major preoccupation for the nation's youth. Most surveys indicated that viewing tended to replace reading, at least in the early 1950s, although the effects were moderated as the novelty wore off. Still, book sales rose steadily, and while several major magazines failed, the circulations of those that remained increased. Did the programs help inculcate an acceptance of violence among the young, along with a disrespect for property, as was later charged? One could watch television almost any night and see uninterrupted mayhem. Did television tend to oversimplify? All outstanding problems were resolved, either in a half hour or an hour. Sociologist Marshall McLuhan claimed the visual image on the tube was replacing the printed word, and to him this meant the substitution of emotion for logic, the withering away of abstract thought among the young. The young person of the early 1960s was supposed to have been the product of such forces, which influenced him more than the schools and the family or church. And this was offered in partial explanation for the college uprisings of the decade.

The conclusion is seductive but highly questionable. After all, the young man of the early 1930s had been reared on radio, which offered much the same message, and yet he accepted the values of the society and fought in World War II. Like radio, television stressed the virtues of obeying the law, and taught the conventional morality, both in programming and commercials. Why should the father have accepted it in the 1930s and the son reject the values in the 1950s and 1960s?[11]

Still, television did teach some young people a lesson, and this was in the matter of news. As was the case with radio, news consisted of the unusual, the bizarre, the unexpected. Given a quarter of an hour, the stations looked for those stories that lent themselves to taping and could be shown on the evening news. Demonstrations and rallies of one kind or another might be broadcast if the demonstrators facilitated the work of newsmen, made themselves interesting and "videogenic." Articulate individuals who said atrocious things might appear on a news broadcast, which would ignore dull, conventional people who had even more important information or ideas to present. Television interview programs sought out those who had achieved or desired celebrity status, and in the process often helped make them still better known. Later on, it would be claimed that without television coverage, many campus demonstrations would not have taken place, and indeed, the entire student revolt of the late 1960s had been one huge television spectacular. Doubtless many students learned to use the media, just as the media used them. But the noncollege youth did not revolt, and their parents learned the same lessons, and they too tended to remain passive. Television may have enhanced student activism, but the cameras did not create it.

A more plausible source for the student rebellions might be found within the individual universities themselves. In the early 1960s most of the nation's colleges were still considered institutions where students came to learn or be trained, where teachers did the tutorial jobs and administrators oversaw the entire process. By then, however, the large universities of World War II, which had accepted government contracts in order to help win the war, had begun to develop into Clark Kerr's multiversities. Some had important institutes where foreign-policy problems were discussed, alternates developed, and close contacts with the State Department maintained. Similarly, institutes for defense programs, for the development of various means of warfare, and even the production of knowledge to be used in the creation of weapons, had come into existence in major schools. These institutes served the needs of the faculties and a handful of graduate students, but for the most part, were divorced from the rest of the school. Also, universities were accepting grants from private industry and serving as research arms for major corporations. The old "publish or perish syndrome" still existed, but increasingly, professors sought status and satisfaction through grants and release time —and participation in off-campus projects. In the multiversity, high-powered faculty members seldom conversed with students, especially undergraduates.

For the mass of multiversity students, education was becoming a homogeneous, undifferentiated process. Freshmen and sophomores often had little contact with the professoriate, and none with administrators, while upperclassmen might hear lectures given by professors in large halls, attended by hundreds of their fellow students. More often than not, most of their teachers were assistants and young instructors, themselves only a few years away from the undergraduate experience. There was little mixing of generations or of coming into contact with people of different backgrounds. Instead of functioning as a training ground, some of the large universities were evolving into places where young people, most with middle-class backgrounds, could meet and mix for four years, obtain a degree, and then, perhaps, find their places in society.

In this respect, they were somewhat like the smaller colleges and universities at the turn of the century, where the collegian ruled. But there were important differences. The collegians were of an elite; they were self-confident and assured of places in society, not merely jobs. The mass students of the early 1960s often were the first of their families to attend college, had few models upon which to base their behaviors, and sought status in education. Too, the collegians had a set of values, inculcated by their society and social group, which was reinforced by the faculties and administrations. The mass students, coming to maturity and leaving their homes at the same time, to live in large dormatories with hundreds of others their same age and in their same circumstances, were often left to their own devices, to develop values and interests and create what came to be known as a "counterculture." The high-powered faculty members were divorced from the campus, and administrators planned for the further enhancement of the multiversity. Teaching assistants either worked on their own research in the hope of joining the leading faculties, or failing this or lacking such an interest, came to identify themselves with their students.

Although most students remained vocationalists, hoping their educations would provide certification in one form or another, some attended colleges for other reasons, or none at all. The desire to avoid military service was one; the simple lack of having anything better to do was another, for affluent students at least. Boredom was a third, while a yearning for excitement was a fourth. At a time when psychology was a glamor discipline, many came in the hope of "finding themselves." Parental pressure was clearly a major consideration as well. Many of these students hoped to find identities through membership in a mass movement —not unlike the collegians who had attended football rallies three quarters of a century earlier. Like the collegians, the students of the 1960s viewed the campus as a place where things more important than training took place: It was an arena for molding character, for communication with one's peers, for preparation for life rather than passing tests and accumulating credits.

They had a disdain for the grinds. The Gentleman's C had been a status sign at the turn of the century; in the late 1960s, militant students demanded an end to the grading system and charged that marks were unimportant indicators of learning and certainly not a valid method of determining worth. The collegians had admired the football coach and the stadium; the militants emulated the radicalized young faculty members, often better known for political activism than academic accomplishment. The collegians had shared ideas at bull sessions while drinking beer; the militants organized free universities that offered noncredit courses in esoteric subjects, while smoking pot. In both cases, the emotion and sentiments of comradeship were deemed more important than intellect, and for both groups action was regarded more highly than contemplation. A leg broken in a football game was a badge of honor in 1890; a head cracked by the police (the other team?) during a demonstration served the same purpose for 1968. Football players had been the big men on the campus in the 1890s, admired and envied by others, the object of news stories, while non-Ivy League schools hoped that through their football programs they could become part of the academic elite. Similarly, the campus activists of 1968 often were among the best-known figures at their institutions, appeared on television, and rarely attended classes. The media concentrated upon them and helped forge a symbiotic relationship, a union of higher education and other media-entertainment industries. Each served the needs of the other.

As a result, for some students it became a badge of shame to be at a school not mentioned among the closed institutions during major demonstrations. And just as the grinds had been portrayed as somehow out of place in their day, so the vocationalists of the late 1960s were presented as not being representative of students as a whole. The grinds had not attended football games and either refused to join fraternities or were barred from them. They majored in business or technical subjects, sought certification, and went on to graduate and professional schools for advanced degrees. Their counterparts existed in the late 1960s—again, usually among the business and technical students or in the professional or graduate schools. But the media largely ignored them, as the media had the grinds of the turn-of-the-century period. Just as the general public viewed the students of the 1890s as beer-drinking privileged football players, somewhat irresponsible but at the same time romantic, so the students of the late 1960s were presented as bearded revolutionaries who took various illegal drugs and were engaged in turning the society on its ear. Both stereotypes were created by the media. Neither was accurate. But the image was stronger than the reality.

Years after having graduated, the collegians had attended reunions. They visited their fraternity houses and the stadiums, and compared notes with contemporaries who like them had settled down into middle-class, often dull lives. They recalled past glories and ignored the absentminded professors. Similarly, in the mid-1970s, some militants returned to the scenes of old demonstrations, inquired about those who had "sold out," and relived their moment of glory, while continuing to view professors who had remained in their classrooms throughout the turbulent years as "irrelevant."

Education, training, and socialization—these had been the functions of American colleges for more than a century, and so they remained in the 1960s. Those undergraduates who had been reared on television in an affluent society, relatively free and economically and socially secure, became the new collegians. In the early part of the decade they lacked a proper arena for their energies—just as their counterparts in the 1870s had searched for one before the great age of football. Then, with the arrival of the Vietnam War and related social programs, they found their vehicles. In both periods training was concentrated among the students bound for the professions, and later on in the graduate and professional schools at major universities. Education—such as it was in the huge universities of the 1960s—languished and often went unrecognized and unrewarded. The media indicated that action and excitement, not reflection and contemplation, were desired, desirable, and rewarded. President Kennedy, whose cool style was admired on many campuses, was often described as "vigorous," and vigor was another ideal. Those faculty members considered "stars" were accomplishing things, creating change, and not merely thinking about problems. All the pressures for a new kind of student society were there—the multiversity helped hatch it. The traditional moorings of college students were being cut and discarded; direct action and initiative were not only accepted, but also encouraged and admired. And it began to jell in the early early 1960s.

A somewhat analogous situation had developed in the motion-picture industry, where the studios and artists were in similar positions as the faculties and students. The Supreme Court's decision in the Paramount case, the divestitures of the early 1950s, and finally the crippling effect on movies caused by television all contributed to the creation of a different kind of industry. In the past the studio had been central to the business, controlling the artists through a quasimonopolistic situation, which included domination of distribution and exhibition. Now the artist was set free from the studio, to form his own company, obtain backing from banks or private sources, arrange for distribution, and help publicize the product, often through television appearances. The studios continued to turn out films, but increasingly they concentrated on renting space to independents, producing television shows, and working out arrangements for ancillary activities. In time, Paramount was taken over by Gulf & Western, a conglomerate that had begun as an auto parts company. Kinney National, involved in funeral parlors and parking lots, acquired Warner Brothers. Metro-Goldwyn-Mayer and Twentieth Century-Fox ended direct production for a while, re-entering only when an especially interesting deal could be arranged. New, rather unusual forces entered the industry. Quaker Oats, Kellogg, Mattel, and similar nonmovie companies backed independents in productions. Burt Lancaster, Kirk Douglas, John Wayne, and other established stars organized their own firms, on an individual-picture basis or in package deals. By the 1970s a few individuals, such as Francis Ford Copolla, were able to construct personal empires, which included production, distribution, and exhibition functions, and were on their ways to becoming self-financing.

For decades, critics had written of the hatred that existed between the moneymen and the artists, the former supposedly lacking sensitivity to art, the latter lacking a business sense. When movies were businesses, the product often was safe, sensible, and above all, salable. This had been the case in the 1920s after the creation of the Hays Office, and remained so into the late 1940s, when the studios bowed to the House Un-American Activities Committee and accepted the blacklist. That period was ended, for the artist-businessman now functioned without such controls; the product became more daring, more scornful of the kind of morality so prized by the old tycoons. Films like *Easy Rider*, *Panic in Needle Park*, *Medium Cool*, *The Revolutionary*, and *Bonnie and Clyde* were financial and artistic successes. All came from the independents, and while some were released by studios, the old guard had no control over content. These films and others like them were not produced with older audiences in mind—in some cases, the slang was so current as to be unintelligible to many older moviegoers, while the morality and values presented approvingly were even more alien to them.

A different reality was being molded in the early 1960s. The organization of the motion-picture business, the nature of television, the power structure at newspapers were all undergoing major alterations; in all, the artist was becoming more independent, even divorced from the businessman who formerly had controlled him. As for the situation in the colleges, the students were creating their own communities, separating in many ways from their professors and administrators. It was happening in politics too. John Kennedy, the hero and symbol for the age, had himself broken the old political rules, utilizing television, artists, newsmen, and students to create new constituencies and methods of achieving power and holding it. The old forces were still there, to be sure, not aware of the changes that had taken place, or of the role that media opportunities would play in the life of the nation. Indeed, the term was hardly known in this period, even when it had already become the battleground for a struggle between two value systems, ways of life, and moralities.

13

Of Poetry and Power

The term "media opportunity" gained currency in Washington and New York during the Kennedy period, even though it was well known and utilized earlier. It signified a happening, often of no real importance, which had been staged for the media, in the hope it would appear on the evening news and on the front pages of newspapers. The press corps would be notified well in advance; the television and still cameras would be in place, and the reporters and commentators would be at their stations. Then the President or some other high official would appear, usually with a retinue, to greet a visitor, cut a ribbon, make a statement, or engage in some other ceremonial function.

Almost all Presidents had been concerned with favorable press coverage. They would try to engage in newsworthy activities, court publishers and editors, and banter with reporters, all with the goal of receiving the front page in leading newspapers. The media opportunity did not evolve from this kind of performance, however, even though there were similarities. The Presidents wanted publicity and the newspapers needed stories, so each worked with the other. Still, the smaller newspapers of the nineteenth century, which lacked headlines and photographs, might ignore a President for weeks.

The media opportunity derived, rather, from the pictorial press, which was perfected in the 1920s. Warren Harding understood that much of his popularity was based upon his presidential bearing, and he happily posed for photographers. Calvin Coolidge, that master of image who wooed the press in a unique fashion, donned Indian feathers for reporters, stood beside anyone the photographers brought to Washington, and patiently waited for the cameramen to adjust their lenses or the sun to break through the clouds. Coolidge appeared regularly in the newsreels, dressed in cowboy garb on a horse, always appearing somewhat bored and dour—knowing that this was part of the game and that the public expected it. The newsreels of this period and afterward were based, to a large extent, upon media opportunities, in politics, sports, fashion, and other fields. Motion-picture audiences, which received news from papers and radio, understood this. The newsreel was always more entertainment and pose than news and "real."

The early television news programs, based upon newsreel techniques, carried the same kinds of stories. But as the art evolved—and especially after the perfection of videotape—the media opportunity became more widespread. President Kennedy appreciated this, and he utilized the media to suit his ends. During his Administration the techniques of the media opportunity and the content of significant news were combined. Reporters complained about this manipulation, but there was little they could do about it. The imperial presidency had arrived, and whatever the President did was news by definition.

At the same time, the media learned that they could create personalities, and make the personalities appear far more important than they were. The Black Muslims, a small religious sect, appeared interesting at a time when the civil rights movement was gathering steam. It was a colorful, unusual group, and one of its spokesmen, Malcolm X, was a forceful speaker and highly telegenic. Thus he and the movement were given national audiences, and in a short period of time made to seem far larger and more significant than they really were. Similarly, the Free Speech Movement at Berkeley, based upon local discontents and, in the beginning at least, a small, unrepresentative group, was bizarre, while one of its leaders, Mario Savio, appeared well on television. The movement, its demands and makeup, were publicized on television news programs, with commentators hinting that it, too, was representative of a far larger group throughout the nation. A decade later, artist Andy Warhol would say that in the future, everyone would become a famous celebrity for fifteen minutes. There was a beginning for this in the development of the media opportunity in the early 1960s.

This is not to say that all or even most of the events displayed on television and featured in the newspapers resulted from media opportunities. Rather, significant occurrences could be made to appear more important than they were if pictorialization in one form or another was possible. If this were not the case, then the story might be relegated to the back pages and never appear on television. There was a competition for space, which became hectic in the mid-1960s and after. Just as the Kennedy-Nixon debates had resembled quiz programs in format, so the scramble for television and newspaper time and space came to appear somewhat like the popular daytime program "Let's Make a Deal," where oddly dressed individuals hoped to catch the master of ceremonies eye and be chosen as a contestant. So it became with the news. The odd, the strange, the unusual, the visual could at least hope for celebrity, while truly important individuals and causes had to learn the techniques of the media opportunity in order to insure media interest and attention.

In August 1963, the Southern Christian Leadership Conference, headed by the Reverend Martin Luther King, Jr., called for a March on Washington in support of pending civil rights legislation. King had been a national figure for seven years, ever since leading a successful bus boycott in Montgomery, Alabama. He had appeared on television regularly, both on news and interview programs, and gradually had taken leadership of the civil rights movement, in part as a result of his telegenic qualities. As much as any figure in American life in 1963, Kennedy included, King understood and appreciated the power of the media. The President attempted to dissuade King from leading the demonstration; now that Kennedy was in power, he no longer needed media events, and instead was trying to push the legislation through Congress in the more conventional ways. But King, without elective power, needed the media, and he was certain a mass demonstration would attract the kind of attention required. Those who came to Washington would not do so in order to demonstrate support as much as to provide an audience for King's speech, and, even more important, a solid human mass for the home television audiences that evening.

The demonstration went off without a major hitch; even the weather was good that day. There was no violence—this would have been counterproductive in 1963—and instead some two hundred thousand people were at the Lincoln Memorial to hear King deliver an eloquent address, the backdrop being the giant seated figure of Lincoln. By itself the meeting was of importance, but as a media opportunity, it was perfect.

Up to that time, major media events had been indoors, staged to a certain degree, with the cameras stable, the directors in relative control of format if not content. This had been the case with the Kefauver crime investigations, the McCarthy investigations, and the Kennedy-Nixon debates. The August 28 March on Washington demonstrated that large-scale mass events could also be covered—indeed, it insured that such events would receive coverage, and so helped encourage them to take place. However, more than was the case with the previous media events, the mass occurrences would be beyond the control of the media—the television crews were being used by those the cameras were directed upon. Later on, the news staffs of the major networks would be accused of bias and manipulation, and there was some merit to this charge. More to the point, however, was the fact that those politicians and other public figures who understood the nature of the media were now able to manipulate it to their advantage, often without the directors and newsmen knowing what was happening —on occasion, without the manipulator understanding completely how well or how badly he was performing.

This happened on November 27—after the spectacular Kennedy funeral, when the nation was still in a highly emotional state —when President Johnson appeared before Congress to deliver his first address, which was aimed more at the nation than the legislators. It was to be Johnson's finest moment. "All that I have, I would have given gladly not to be here today," he began, and from there he went on to pledge himself to the continuation of the Kennedy programs. In particular, Johnson asked for rapid passage of the civil rights legislation then before Congress. The speech was effective, in terms of both content and delivery, and might have been even more so on radio, since even at his best Johnson was not telegenic.

On this occasion, however, television served the purpose better, though not through design. While in the Senate, Johnson had suffered a severe heart attack, and there were some fears regarding his health. Seated behind the President as he spoke, in full view during most of the talk, was feeble, seventy-two-year-old Speaker of the House John McCormack, who that day looked rather ill, and next to McCormack was Senate President pro Tempore Carl Hayden, eighty-six years old. According to the presidential succession act then in force, McCormack was next in line for the presidency should anything happen to Johnson, and in the absence of a new Speaker, Hayden would succeed if McCormack died. The provisions of the succession act had been discussed earlier on several television shows and in the newspapers. Given this knowledge, viewers could only feel even more dependent upon Johnson, and wish him well, than might otherwise have been the case.

JOHNSON'S MEDIA FAILURES

Johnson's first months in office were impressive, both in substance and image. Most of the Kennedy legislative proposals were signed into law, and by early 1964 reporters were writing that Johnson was still the master of the Congress, that he had accomplished what Kennedy had only discussed. The nation's involvement in Vietnam deepened, especially after Johnson reported attacks on American ships in the Bay of Tonkin, and the Senate passed a resolution authorizing him to counter threats in the area. The President utilized television widely in order to publicize his views and establish contact with the nation; in one week, in early March, he appeared before the cameras on three occasions, and then and later pressured television executives into allocating time for Cabinet members as well. In order to meet presidential requests of this and related natures, the networks established a small theater in the east wing of the White House—a television theater—to be used whenever Johnson or any of his successors asked for time. In this respect at least, Johnson enlarged upon

Kennedy's use of media to address the public directly without the intercession of the press.

Johnson was wary of the press, even though he was on good terms with some reporters. Like many from his region, he felt the nation's media were dominated by eastern intellectuals who had contempt for practical people from other parts of the country. Too, he was aware that reporters often compared him, unfavorably, with Kennedy, who was much better attuned to the values of the press corps. For a while, Salinger remained as press secretary, but then he resigned to enter politics and was replaced by George Reedy, a former United Press International correspondent who had later become a staff official at the Democratic Policy Committee. While remaining friendly with the press corps, Reedy often appeared overly cautious, fumbling, and unaware of what was happening in the White House. In large part this was the result of Johnson's unwillingness to include Reedy in important conversations and apprise him of key decisions, but the result was that press relations deteriorated, although this was not evident in 1964.

Johnson's political reputation had been based upon his abilities within the Senate, where he functioned as a major leader among a hundred professional politicians. He was particularly effective in making deals, arranging compromises, and pressuring senators into voting for measures he supported. Of course, he had to be elected by the people of his state, but at the time there was no effective Republican party in Texas, and more often than not, nominations were won through arrangements with party leaders. Thus Lyndon Johnson, considered one of the most effective politicians in American history, had had less experience in manipulating public opinion than any president since William Howard Taft. It is doubtful that a person with his experience could have achieved the nomination of his party and then gone on to victory against a strong opponent. In the age of media, men with the talents of a Lyndon Johnson could achieve the presidency only by accident or default.

The Republicans defaulted in 1964. New York's Governor Nelson Rockefeller, the party's strongest candidate, had utilized television effectively, and was better attuned to the mechanisms of the media age than any other party leader. As had been the case with Kennedy in 1960, Rockefeller had a small power base within the national party, and hoped to appeal to the electorate directly. But there were differences too. Due to what conservatives considered his lack of loyalty and his ideological positions, they united against him, and stood behind the candidacy of Arizona Senator Barry Goldwater. In addition, Rockefeller had recently been divorced and remarried, and this hurt him among Republicans more than Kennedy's Catholicism had harmed him among Democrats. Rockefeller refused to leave the race and so no other moderate-to-liberal Republican—such as Henry Cabot Lodge, George Romney, or William Scranton—was able to make a strong national appeal. Former President Eisenhower either refused to mediate disputes or was unable to do so. In addition, there was no compromise candidate available. Richard Nixon, who might have filled that description, had lost the gubernatorial race in California two years earlier, and so was for the time being on the sidelines.

Goldwater was an unusual candidate, neither a product of the media age nor a politician of the previous period. One has to go back to the 1896 campaign, when the Democrats selected William Jennings Bryan, to find a comparable national figure. Bryan had been able to utilize the political structure of his time better than Goldwater did in 1964, but by dominating the Republican right wing while the left and center were in disarray, by collecting on political debts, and after a close victory in the California primary, Goldwater was able to capture the nomination. Even in the best of times for Republicans, he probably would have lost—Americans rarely oust sitting Presidents who run for reelection, and Johnson was at the height of his popularity in 1964—but the Goldwater campaign was conducted in such a way, especially on the media, as to insure a landslide Democratic victory.

Like Kennedy in 1960, Goldwater attracted many volunteers, who appeared on television as a backdrop for the candidate. But the Kennedy workers often were young, attractive, and usually smiling, while the Goldwater people seemed older and often grim. On television, this came over as fanaticism. When Rockefeller was booed down at the Republican convention, the cameras played on the faces of the Goldwaterites who were shouting, and to many moderates who watched the event on television, it appeared frightening—and unfair. There was little doubt the Republicans distrusted television. Many at the 1960 convention had jeered at reporters, and this was repeated in 1964. Some of the more fanatical Goldwaterites claimed the media were Communist-dominated, and for a while it seemed that an outright conflict between media and politics was in the making.

The candidate himself was a handsome, well-spoken person, transparently honest and forthright. In films of Goldwater on horseback or at the controls of an airplane he was as telegenic as Kennedy. Pictorially at least, Goldwater was far superior than Johnson. On the other hand, Goldwater was unwilling to compromise his beliefs, often spoke off the cuff, contradicted himself, and didn't appear to care whether or not he won votes—later he would claim that he knew from the first he could not win, and so had embarked upon an educational campaign. The Republicans outspent the Democrats for television time—$3.8 million to $2.1 million—but as President, Johnson appeared more often than did Goldwater. The Republicans challenged Johnson to a debate on the 1960 model, but he refused, the reasoning being that while debates between candidates were desirable, they should not take place if one were an incumbent, since the national security might be compromised by an impromptu reply to a question. Republican commercials warned against Democratic radicalism and fiscal irresponsibility. On their part, the Democrats implied that Goldwater could not be trusted with the atomic bomb.

Afterward, some reporters and television commentators who had been charged with unfairness toward Goldwater claimed they only reported what he said and did, to which the response was that this, in itself, was unfair. The free-wheeling candidate made no visible attempt to manipulate the press and cared little about his image. Some of the more wary columnists claimed this was the ultimate in image creation, but Goldwater's apparent lack of guile appeared an indication he was not qualified for the presidency—given the experience of the recent past. Reporters and crews traveling with the Republicans in 1964 may have opposed Goldwater's views and doubtless most voted against him in November, but he was popular with the press on a personal basis. Some reporters, aware that Goldwater was making a poor appearance with his confusing statements, tried to help him out, to little avail.[1] If this did occur, was it not an indication that the press was playing a greater role than that of reporting and commenting?

The Democrats won an immense victory in 1964. Johnson received 61.1 per cent of the popular vote, more than any candidate before or since. Goldwater's 27.2 million votes were 7 million below Nixon's total in 1960—and slightly below Adlai Stevenson's 1952 vote, when far fewer individuals had cast ballots. Johnson seemed to have a great mandate, one that rivaled those he had received in the Texas elections. However, commentators noted that many voters had opted for the incumbent against the challenger, and not for Johnson as a man or personality. In addition, there was much to be said for the argument that Goldwater, not Johnson, had been the issue in 1964, and that the public rejected him, and in the process had not actually given Johnson a vote of confidence. In other words, Johnson's support may have been broad, but it was not deep. Furthermore, in essence it was not a media election or event; the result was never in doubt, merely the dimensions of the victory, and so television and newspapers did not have a decisive impact in 1964.

Social critic Michael Novak recently wrote that "the American people have seemed to love eight qualities in Presidents, at least until the present"—action, honesty, goodness, self-control, genuine emotion, decisiveness, administrative control, and finally, an instinct for ends and means that are "characteristically American." Novak wrote with the Nixon failure in mind, but claimed that other Presidents had succeeded or failed due to their possessing or lacking some or all of these qualities.[2] All are symbols, and each can be projected through the media. A President does not need reporters or editors in order to speak directly to the American people, and in his personal performances can show evidence of the first six qualities. For the other two, he will need the press and the goodwill of television newsmen. All modern Presidents have known this, but until the 1960s, they lacked either the technology or the need to manipulate the public's emotions. Given the means of manipulation and the public sophistication of the media era, political leaders now must either learn to create images or fail to accomplish their ends.

Lyndon Johnson understood this. He dieted, attempted to wear contact lenses, dyed his hair, took elocution lessons, tested various electronic prompters, and had a professional makeup man at his call—all in an attempt to project a favorable image. There were many media opportunities in the Johnson years: the weddings of his daughters, coverage of Mrs. Johnson's speeches on the need to beautify America, and ceremonial occasions such as the presidential presence at space launches. The President tried to woo the press—at times flattering reporters, on other occasions threatening them—and did what he could to make their professional lives more comfortable. None of this, however, seemed to work. Throughout most of his full term in office, Johnson's popularity declined.

In part, Johnson was the victim of forces and circumstance he did not create and could not check. During his Administration the civil rights movement accelerated and changed. There was large-scale urban violence in 1964—the first of the "long, hot summers"—and street mobs burned and looted, while those who had led the civil rights movement in the late 1950s and early 1960s could not control them. The President had been responsible for more civil rights legislation than any other Chief Executive in history; while in the Senate he had introduced and voted for such measures, often the only senator from his section to do so. Still, he could do nothing to stem the violence, and because he would not condone radical activities, he was accused of racism.

Similarly, Johnson could have done little to end student discontent. The movement had its roots in the late 1950s, in the multiversity and reactions to it. Campus demonstrations were rare in the early 1960s, but all the elements for trouble were present, awaiting ignition.

The Vietnam War, of course, proved Johnson's undoing. Already in 1965 there were rumors that the Administration had been less than candid in reporting on the Bay of Tonkin attack. That year the American forces intervened in the Dominican Republic, and once again the White House was caught in several misstatements. Throughout 1965, 1966, and 1967 there were promises that the Vietnam War would soon be over, that we could see "the light at the end of the tunnel." The successful conclusion of the fighting was to be accomplished either through negotiations or a massive military attack. Both were tried and failed, and repeatedly Johnson and others were caught in falsehoods and misrepresentations. Thus was born the "credibility gap."

These three movements—the civil rights crusade, the campus activism, and opposition to the war—came together from 1965 to 1966, and Johnson was unable to deal effectively with the domestic unrest.

Given his policies, could Johnson have countered his critics or disarmed his opponents? Unlike his predecessor, he lacked the personality to inspire a mass following and the abilities to command enthusiasm among nonprofessionals. Kennedy had been viewed as a strong advocate of civil rights, even though he had done far less in this area than Johnson; Kennedy had established a rapport with the campus youth, more the result of appearance than philosophy; and although Kennedy had spoken of the need for the Vietnamese to fight their own war, he had introduced American troops into the area and had given no indication of removing them or allowing a Communist victory. A hawk, a moderate, and an aristocrat, Kennedy knew how to deal with doves, activists, and the poor, and lead them to believe he was with them, at least, in spirit.

In essence, Johnson lacked the Kennedy touch—in contrast, he appeared devious and insincere. Most Presidents had on occasion misled the press and public, but Johnson's reputation as a Senate "wheeler-dealer" followed him into the White House, and he could not shake it. He did not know how to treat the press, in the process losing the confidence and trust of the White House corps. Later it would be claimed that the press had a vendetta against Johnson, based in large part on their dislike of a Southerner in the White House. Yet some of Johnson's major critics were from the Midwest and South, and the same people who were supposed to dislike Johnson for his cowboy antics were quite friendly with Goldwater, who often had demonstrated an even more exaggerated view of the western code. Utilizing Novak's criteria, by late 1967, Johnson seemed to lack goodness, self-control, and honesty, while his instincts for means and ends were coming under question by an ever-larger portion of the electorate. Eventually, the President was considered a prisoner of the White House, afraid to venture forth, knowing that demonstrators would follow wherever he went, shouting, "Hey, hey, LBJ. How many kids did you kill today?"

THE TWO SOCIETIES

On January 3, 1964, Minnesota Senator Eugene McCarthy announced that he would challenge Johnson in the New Hampshire primary. At the time it was considered a quixotic move by an erratic legislator who was more interested in poetry than politics. Any serious challenge to the President would have to come from New York Senator Robert Kennedy, and at the time he showed little interest in the task of unseating Johnson. Later that month, however, the Vietcong and North Vietnamese launched what came to be known at the Tet offensive. The attack was unexpected, at least in its intensity, for it was carried into the streets of Saigon itself. In time the attack was repulsed, with the Communists suffering heavy losses—in effect, it became a victory for the South Vietnamese and Americans. But for the North Vietnamese, military victory may not have been the most important goal. The Tet offensive was, in essence, a media opportunity, to be covered by American newsmen and television cameras and shown in American homes. The North Vietnamese too understood the impact of media in America, especially in an election year. And they had calculated well. Scenes of street fighting in Saigon caused Johnson to lose much of his remaining credibility. New demonstrations in the cities and on the campuses began, despite warnings from remaining Johnson supporters that the Vietnamese Communists were trying to win in America what they could not accomplish in Asia.

McCarthy did far better in the New Hampshire primary than anticipated, even though he had not defeated the President on the Democratic line. His young volunteers had attracted considerable press and television coverage; the McCarthy "children's crusade" was now being taken seriously. The senator was becoming a rallying point for many campus dissidents, who were considering working for him in future campaigns, even shaving and wearing suits. The motto of the day was "Come Clean for Gene." Still, it did not appear that he could win the nomination at the convention.

The McCarthy challenge and the Tet offensive were given full television coverage. The medium was geared to report on surprising events, and viewers who had been raised on television drama looked for the unusual and exciting on the tube, turning off when they didn't get it. McCarthy's low-keyed talks, often delivered in unusual settings, came over well—the handsome senator, surrounded by shining young faces, appeared like the crusading hero of a drama program, especially when contrasted with Johnson. As for the Tet offensive, the scenes of bloodshed were captured by the cameras and relayed immediately by Telstar communications satellite. They were as exciting as any World War II movie. In most years, these stories would have been considered media highlights. But 1968 was one of the most unusual in American history, and as it happened, most of the important events lent themselves to television.

Robert Kennedy announced his candidacy in mid-March, in the same room his brother had used for the purpose. Like McCarthy, he opposed the Vietnam War and favored broad internal reforms—in fact, there seemed little to choose between their programs. But there were differences, in media image above all. McCarthy appealed to middle-class white college students and intellectuals—he had inherited the mantle and image of Adlai Stevenson. As for Kennedy, he often spoke of his brother's unfinished work, appeared as an activist, and directed major efforts at the poor and minorities. Stereotype and image, not program, determined the makeup of their followings, even while each tried to capture the support of the other's constituency.

For the moment, Johnson's activities were relegated to the inside pages of newspapers and minor television items. Then on the evening of Sunday, March 31, the President addressed the nation on television in what was advertised as a report on foreign affairs. The talk began at nine o'clock, and contained nothing of major importance on Vietnam. Many viewers tuned out before the conclusion, while others awaited the end so as to catch the nine-thirty programs. But the President continued on, beyond that time, and so more of the audience left their sets. At the end of the speech,

Johnson announced he would not run for re-election. This was a political bombshell, reported as such the following day. Once again, however, the President had misused the medium. The following day, he addressed a meeting of the National Association of Broadcasters. "I understand, far better than some of my severe and perhaps intolerant critics would admit, my own shortcomings as a communicator."

The Johnson abdication was the first of a series of shocks the nation was to undergo that spring and summer, all of which were fully reported on television, which highlighted and dramatized them. On Thursday, April 4—four days after the Johnson speech—Martin Luther King was assassinated, and as the police searched for his killer, riots erupted in the nation's major cities. For the next few days television viewers saw looting and arson, and clashes between police and blacks in Chicago, San Francisco, Philadelphia, Detroit, and other cities. In New York Mayor John Lindsay walked through the Harlem streets, television cameras capturing his every move and statement, and the attractive politician—who seemed more a motion-picture star than ever—received additional national coverage. That the murder and the racial violence were serious could not be denied, but the television coverage, by its very nature, gave the impression the country was about to collapse, which was certainly not the case. This sentiment was heightened by interviews with inflammatory individuals, who made dire predictions and, in some cases, promised additional violence.

In May, when the racial violence in the cities had subsided, the student movement dominated the evening news. The Students for a Democratic Society and other militant groups at Columbia University were protesting the presence of federally sponsored defense work on the campus, and in addition opposed plans for constructing a new gymnasium on Morningside Heights. Student demonstrations and takeovers of buildings followed, and television cameras were there to report on all that occurred. Unlike the events following the King assassination, this was a true, almost pure, media opportunity. Without television there might have been protests and even demonstrations, but students raised on the tube, many of whom had seen how other dramatic events had been covered, were able to transform protests into a national movement. It was ideal for television, and the students understood this. On occasion they would delay a speech or an attack until the cameras appeared, and schedule "spontaneous" protests for the newsmen.[3] Opportunities for clashes with police were exploited fully—the bloodied students being taken into police vans became a common sight on evening news programs in late April and early May. And the movement spread to other campuses, even those where there were no outstanding complaints against administrations. There were hundreds of "teach-ins" that spring, and individuals who were not acquainted with the situation at the nation's colleges and universities, and learned of them through television, came away with the idea that an entire generation had turned revolutionary, and that each college was a hotbed of anarchism, a center for the drug culture.

In the early morning of June 5, after he won the California Democratic primary, Robert Kennedy was assassinated. Most Americans learned of his death when they tuned in their radios or read the headlines in their newspapers, but that evening there were television pictures of the event, including a still shot of the dying man on the floor. Once again there was a Kennedy funeral—and the nation became still more numb, even more inured to this kind of violence. But more was to come—a kind of climax. Demonstrators arrived in Chicago in August, many of whom announced their intention to disrupt the Democratic convention. Mayor Richard Daley seemed eager for a confrontation, and one took place, in which television once again played a crucial role.

From the first the demonstrators taunted the police, shouting obscenities at them and hoping to provoke assaults. The cameramen gave the confrontation blanket coverage—not only was it exciting, but also the demonstrators wore colorful clothing, were unusual and somewhat exotic, and provided a clear contrast to the stolid police. It was a motion-picture director's dream, and indeed, some of the scenes had a cinematic quality. The cameras did catch the action—police brutality, riots, and general mayhem. Later on, it was learned that some of the confrontations had been staged for television, that uninjured demonstrators had rolled over in feigned agony when the television crews came their way. The police were seen to behave in a savage fashion, but the home viewers did not see the provocations, even though they were reported upon in the press and by television commentators. Meanwhile, in the hall, the Democrats argued among themselves, and tempers ran high. Though ostensibly at the convention to report upon the happenings, the press soon became part of the action. Several reporters were roughed up by the special police, and Dan Rather of CBS was struck on the head while on camera, prompting Walter Cronkite to speak angrily of "thugs." At NBC, Chet Huntley said "Chicago police are going out of their way to injure newsmen, and prevent them from filming or gathering information on what was going on. The news profession in this city is now under attack by the Chicago police."[4]

Yet every important poll indicated that a large majority of viewers sympathized with the police and opposed the demonstrators—and the press in particular was singled out for distrust. Was this innate conservatism, a feeling of being manipulated, or a lack of trust in individual newsmen? Whatever the reason, a new kind of credibility gap appeared during the Democratic convention. The long road from the attempted impartiality of the early 1940s to the use of film cuts to create impressions of the 1950s and the media opportunities of the early 1960s had come to rest with the newsman and television commentator as participant. A literary contingent, headed by Norman Mailer, was at Chicago, to report on the happenings in a semifictitious manner. So were actors and actresses working for McCarthy, along with others attached to Senator George McGovern, who was trying to rally the Kennedy forces. Given the choice of believing what television was showing them or the old yearning for law and order inculcated in their youth, a sizable number of middle-aged, middle-class Americans indicated their anger at the press. In the end, the Establishment Democrats nominated Vice President Hubert Humphrey for President and Senator Edmund Muskie for Vice President. The dissidents—the McCarthy and Kennedy people—indicated they would never accept Humphrey, and instead would sit out the election.

At the time it appeared that this would doom the Humphrey candidacy to failure, and the ticket tried to heal the wounds by making gestures to the left wing of the party. Later analysis indicated, however, that one of the reasons Humphrey did as well as he did was because most Democrats saw him as opposed to the demonstrators. In other words, identification with what many newsmen and intellectuals were calling the wave of the future could spell defeat in a national canvass. This dislike of the media men could be seen in other ways. Governor George Wallace, running as the candidate of the American Independent Party, did well in the public-opinion polls, and eventually received almost 10 million popular votes, after a poorly organized campaign. Wallace concentrated his attack upon intellectuals and the media. At the time, it was assumed that the Wallace vote was racist, but his strength in all parts of the country, among groups not usually identified with race issues, indicated that his appeal was deeper than that.

While intellectuals talked of a generation gap, a more significant division was developing. Indeed, a cultural division was deepening, with many intellectuals and prominent media figures on the one side, and the so-called middle Americans, nonactivists, and what appeared to be a majority of blue-collar workers on the other. The two groups differed on many issues, but in some respects they were similar, and this served to confuse matters somewhat. Young people of both persuasions mixed at rock concerts, even though some might use drugs and others alcohol, openly as though they were campaign badges and signs to others of their persuasion. Despite attempts to paint middle Americans and blue-collar workers as bigots, most polls indicated that their attitudes on race relations were not substantially different from those of intellectuals. By the mid-1970s, it appeared clear that working-class youth trailed college students in attitudes and beliefs by only a few years, and that the time lag was narrowing. Still, the former were more concerned with immediate needs—jobs, salaries, living conditions, and the like—while the mass intellectuals in the colleges had a broader scope—they debated foreign policy, the future of civilization, and the meaning of life itself. The workers saw in the mass intellectuals individuals who cared little about their values and wanted them to pay for social experiments they didn't want or need, while the latter considered relatively unschooled workers as short-sighted and narrow in interests.

The mass intellectuals in the colleges would go to see *Easy Rider* and cheer its message, while the workers saw in it a couple of drug pushers who disdained real work and were parasites. The workers were attracted by *Walking Tall*, which to the intellectuals was the story of a simpleminded individual incapable of genuine thought, who gloried in violence for its own sake. Both might watch "All in the Family" on television, but some considered Archie Bunker a bigot, while others called him a hero. Each group was intrigued by violence, even while deploring it in others. Action—especially violent action—was attention-grabbing, while ideas for their own sake often were dull and boring; the student Marxists of the late 1960s did not read Marx, but instead turned to works like the collected sayings of Chairman Mao, which were short, pithy, and easily digested. Both seemed to confuse fact and fiction, and tried to fit complex events into simple philosophies. Thus the Vietnam War was good or evil, segregation right or wrong, young people depraved or "the best generation in history." Some radical leaders, who had little difficulty in being invited to appear on television talk shows, told viewers not to trust anyone over the age of thirty—did this mean that continued thought stultified the brain and emotions? Other guests spoke with despair of anyone with long hair. Age and appearance could be seen; ideas could not be pictorialized. Image was what counted in this period, and image was what was transmitted.

The public seemed to know it was being manipulated, and the process created cynicism, which reinforced the despair caused by national and international events at the time. This was quickly translated into distrust of media figures, especially those in the business of news. Apocalypse was in the air in the late 1960s, and the temptations to use media pulpits to preach and exhort was greater than at most periods in American history.

The vehicles were there to be used, and so they were. Increasingly, reporters and columnists were becoming participants, unable or unwilling to stand above the battle. Some welcomed activist roles, indicating that impartiality was impossible, and if a virtue, one that was highly overrated. Others complained that viewers and readers confused the message with the messenger, and they deplored the change. Whatever the reasons, it appeared that many of those involved in the transmission of ideas and sensations had lost portions of their objectivity, and with it, segments of the general audience. The former had traded trust for virtue, and seemed satisfied with the situation. But there was an additional price. While public-opinion polls showed that Americans had little confidence in politicians, the same people did not trust the media's ability to report honestly on events and people.

NIXON AND THE MEDIA

Richard Nixon understood this, and in 1968 conducted his presidential campaign accordingly. He would use the media as best he could. Candidates could not purchase news columns in major papers, but they could buy television time and, within wide limits, use it as they desired. Nixon was pleasant enough with reporters and columnists, but it was no secret that he distrusted most of them and that few journalists had any affection for the man. That candidate and press would attempt to manipulate one another was not new—it had been the rule rather than the exception in American presidential politics. In 1968, however, Nixon spent little time in courting the press. Rather, he tended to ignore reporters, perhaps because he was convinced he couldn't obtain a fair deal from them, but more probably because he considered their goodwill relatively unimportant.

In the past, candidates and Presidents had hoped for media support. It was different in 1968 and throughout the Nixon presidency. Nixon's personality favored aloofness from journalists, and public opinion led him to believe that such separation was desirable; in addition, electronic technology and public-relations techniques made it feasible for the President to report directly to the public and ignore the press.

Nixon was a complicated individual, more difficult to understand than Kennedy or Johnson. With the exception of Franklin Roosevelt, no American in history had been nominated by a major party for national office as often as he. On his record, Nixon was better prepared for the presidency than any other person in this century. That he was intelligent and even sophisticated was conceded by even his most bitter opponents. He had appeared at the dawn of the new age of media and developed along with it. On occasion Nixon had used television skillfully, the most obvious example being the Checkers Speech. More to the point, he understood media, and many of his closest advisers came out of media-based industries. Despite the fact he lacked Kennedy's personality and dashing appearance, Nixon took office at a time when this didn't seem too important—indeed, to some Americans such qualities as youth, dash, and vigor were anathema. He struck the proper note in his Inaugural Address when he said that "Greatness comes in simple trappings," adding that "to lower our voices would be a simple thing."

Perhaps it was no accident that psychohistory emerged as a subbranch of both psychology and history at the same time Nixon became President, or that the best books and articles on the new President delved into his psychological makeup. No Chief Executive of recent years had lent himself so badly to conventional analysis as did Richard Nixon. His use of media and his reaction to it were particularly unusual.

The first sign of this came shortly after the election, when Nixon announced that Herbert Klein, an old friend and a former newspaperman, would be his "director of communications." The title was deceptive, for it seemed to indicate that Klein would have far-ranging powers, when actually he did not. Klein was a good choice for the post. He was one of the few Nixon men who were liked and trusted by reporters, and he could be counted upon to act as a soothing force between them and the incoming Administration. But then it was announced that Klein would confine his dealings to department heads, and that Ronald Ziegler, a young former advertising man who had no journalistic experience, would handle day-to-day press relations and briefings and, in effect, be the press secretary. Ziegler proved stiff, awkward, and unable to establish the proper rapport with reporters. More important, he demonstrated little evidence of wanting to do so. Within a few months he was using his position to punish enemies and reward those who wrote favorable articles about the President —much to their embarrassment. Other press secretaries before him had taken an adversary position against the press, but always there had been a measure of civility and good humor between them. Whatever remained of this eroded away rapidly during the first Nixon term; by 1972, the reporters took delight in noting Ziegler's errors and misstatements, while Ziegler openly criticized the press in interviews.

Nixon's selection of Ziegler and his subsequent performance indicated a certain contempt for the press on his part. Had he let it go at this, he would have been criticized by newspapermen but no more. But Nixon went farther, developing his own brand of public relations, one that not only overlooked the reporters, but also considered them unimportant.

Whenever the President wanted to speak to the public, he would do so on television in prepared addresses, thus not only establishing direct contact in a context over which he had complete control, but also preventing misinterpretations as far as was possible. During his first nineteen months in office, Nixon made fourteen appearances on prime-time television. In contrast, Johnson had appeared half as many times in his first nineteen months, and Kennedy only four. Nixon showed little interest in the established press conferences. He had five of them in his first four months in office. Then he turned to a different technique. From November 1969 to July 1970, there were only four press conferences, but on seven other occasions the President pre-empted prime network time for talks on domestic legislation and the Vietnam War. The Democrats complained that Nixon was taking advantage of his position to dominate the media, but Republicans noted that Kennedy and Johnson had done the same in their days. Given his almost unlimited access to television and the continued distrust of the press, Nixon might have gone on to ignore the reporters and in time create a new form of communication between Presidents and public. The press conference might have been scrapped, and in its place there could have been regular speeches on a variety of issues. The newspapermen would complain, to be sure, but there would have been nothing they could have done about such a situation.

Nixon was not content with such a subtle victory; instead, he aggressively attacked the press, and in the process, blundered. One indication of this was the assault on the media by Vice President Spiro Agnew. Ever since taking office, Agnew had complained about the unfairness of reporters, touching upon a sensitive nerve on several occasions. On November 13, 1969, he spoke on network television at length regarding the fashion by which President Nixon's activities had been covered on television. Agnew hit out against "this little group of men who not only enjoy a right of instant rebuttal to every presidential address, but more importantly, wield a free hand in selecting, presenting, and interpreting the great issues in our nation. . . ." As he saw it, television news was controlled by a small group of eastern-oriented intellectuals who were out of touch with the rest of the nation and were attempting to manipulate public opinion to their own ends. "Now, my friends, we'd never trust such power, as I've described, over public opinion in the hands of an elected government. It's time we questioned it in the hands of a small and unelected elite."

The networks were stung to the quick—and further shocked when the mail the following week indicated that a vast majority of viewers supported Agnew's stance. Public-opinion polls confirmed his popularity as a spokesman for the "silent majority" and indicated the increasing distrust of newsmen. Columnists and commentators opposed to Agnew wrote of how a powerful government was attempting to stifle free speech, but there was no act of evidence of a Nixon vendetta against the networks; stations did not lose licenses due to unfair reporting. Agnew had merely asked for a review of the media, exercising his own freedom to say what he believed. Apparently many agreed with him, for his popularity rose sharply. In early 1970 he was looked upon as the man who would bring the George Wallace supporters into the Republican party and assume leadership after Nixon's retirement. Republicans who were fairly unenthusiastic about the President rallied to Agnew, who at the time seemed the most potent political force in the nation—and a symbol of a continuing Administration attack on the media.[5]

Another sign of the rising attack was the emergence of Charles Colson, a special counsel to the President, as a White House power in his own right. A lawyer and a former lobbyist, Colson had been known as Nixon's "hatchetman" in 1969. Now he assumed additional powers and responsibilities, most of them on a public-relations level. Colson was supposed to rally the hard hats to Nixon's Vietnam positions, and he did so well that his powers soon rivaled those of Klein and Ziegler. Unlike them, however, Colson was also concerned with undercover work, including preparation for media activities during the 1972 campaign. Part of his assignment was to encourage further criticism of the press, and if possible, discredit the media so as to make it a minor force in the election.

The Nixon-Agnew contest with the media continued throughout the rest of the first term. The President did continue to utilize television whenever he saw fit to do so, in speeches, special addresses, and at ceremonial functions. With the exception of November and December 1971, he appeared at least once a month, and of course was covered on a daily basis on the evening news. But he rarely scheduled press conferences; there were only four in 1971, and none after June 1, and he indicated that such appearances would not play an important role in his re-election campaign. Some reporters said this was surprising, since Nixon usually came off well at such confrontations. The reasons, however, were no secret to the White House press corps. Peter Lisagor, a veteran newsman, spoke openly of them at a late 1971 convention. "I do think the President regards the press as hostile to him and I think he has some reason for that. I believe he's slightly fearful of the press because of some past experiences, some episodes I could mention but won't, because they too are subjective. I think really . . . that the President would just rather do business without us."[6]

At the same time, the White House hit out at the press in different ways. Some reporters had their telephones tapped, and others were investigated for possible wrongdoing. When the President took his trip to China early in 1972, some reporters and representatives of newspapers that had been critical of him were excluded from the press plane and had to rely upon others for reports. All the while, the Agnew attacks on media irresponsibility continued, and were well received by the public. At the same time, however, the White House sought to utilize the media in underhanded dealings. For example, there was an attempt to forge documents so as to implicate the Kennedy administration in the assassination of Vietnam's President Diem, and "leak" information about them to selected reporters. On other occasions, when Nixon and others wished favorable columns to be written, they thought it could be done by passing the word to a handful of newsmen, William F. Buckley among them. These and similar efforts were unmasked and failed. The press itself caught the Administration in misstatements—such as when, in 1971, it was learned that a section of pipeline Secretary of Defense Melvin Laird showed reporters and claimed had been run down the Ho Chi Minh Trail was shown not to have originated there. That same year the Washington *Post* and New York *Times* began printing stolen documents—the Pentagon Papers—which seemed to indicate that the Kennedy and Johnson administrations had engaged in deception during the war. The White House went to the courts to end publication, asserting a right of prior censorship. The press claimed freedom to act as it did under the Constitution, while Administration spokesmen talked about national security and charged the newspapers with putting sensationalism and circulation above the national interest. In a country already badly polarized, the Nixon-press contest served to exacerbate already existing difficulties. Increasingly the newsmen found themselves supported by Administration critics who were not so much interested in freedom of the press as with attacking Nixon and Agnew.

Each side lost in this contest. By late 1971 the polls showed that President Nixon's credibility was below that of Johnson in 1967, and while Agnew was personally popular with Republicans, he was intensely disliked by much of the rest of the American people. The reporters, on the other hand, were both admired and despised, not for their professional work, but for what the public had come to see as their new role as Administration critics. Some newsmen helped reinforce this impression by claiming that the responsibility to inform the public was a vital part of the constitutional process—speaking as though the press were indeed a branch of government, somewhat akin to the Congress. The press conference, they said, was the American equivalent of the question period in the British House of Commons, when members of the political opposition were given an opportunity to examine government policies. In the absence of a strong legislature—Congress had decayed considerably since the end of World War II—they claimed that the press was obliged to fill the role of opposition. This was a dubious argument, and in any case, had little public appeal.

This was the situation in late 1971, as the nation prepared for the upcoming presidential election. Like those of the 1960s, it would in large part be a media event, one in which those who controlled and appeared on the media would exercise a great influence. But many Americans who had been raised on television, understood manipulation better than ever before, while the Administration had instructed all on biases and prejudices. Many in the nation no longer trusted the press and television to report fairly. This troubled editors and publishers as well as many reporters and commentators, who took special pains to appear unbiased. But the legacy of the past four years, in which newsmen had often taken adversary roles, could not be eradicated. The impression affixed upon the public mind by Agnew—of the newsman as a liberal Easterner prepared to distort news in order to achieve his ends—remained. As for President Nixon, his popularity rose as a result of his foreign travels, but the Vietnam War still raged, and his many switches in the area of domestic policy were confusing. Thus, while a large number of Americans did not believe reporters and columnists, they were equally suspicious of the Administration.

As a result of the role of media in American life, reporters and columnists were still looked upon as experts of a kind, and expected to predict elections in much the same way as handicappers performed at racetracks. The comparison is not as bizarre as it may appear, for from the start, the newsmen called the race, noting who was ahead, the order of the others, the meaning of new entries, and the like. Newsmen would inform the public that unless a particular candidate received a certain percentage of the vote in one or another primary, he would suffer a major setback. They would assess the image of candidate A as compared with that of candidate B, as though examining their withers. And while their independence was challenged, the public, in the age of the expert, took such confident judgments seriously. So for that matter did most of the candidates, who vied with one another for media coverage and the goodwill of influential reporters and commentators.

According to polls and news stories, Senator Edmund Muskie was a certain choice for the Democratic presidential nomination. Politically he was considered a centrist, one who might be able to unite the two feuding wings of the party. Actually, Muskie had taken few stands on major issues, in part because he hoped for the nomination, but also because on many occasions throughout his career he had been indecisive. More important, however, was the fact that Muskie had what newsmen and commentators called "a Lincoln quality," presumably meaning that he was tall, and was somewhat soft-spoken in prepared speeches. Muskie did not excite the country late in 1971, but on the other hand he was considered a clear choice over Nixon, then at a low point in popularity. Muskie himself understood the situation, and the power of the media. On a flight to Washington in August, he spoke with reporters. "You can make me or break me," he said.

So they could and did, but not necessarily because they wanted to. Convinced Muskie would win, reporters covered his actions intensively, and he suffered from overexposure while being obliged to take stands before it was wise to do so. Then leading columnists suggested that unless Muskie had a major victory in New Hampshire, his candidacy would wane. Reporters were there when Muskie stood in front of the offices of the Manchester *Union Leader* and hit out, tearfully, at publisher William Loeb, who had attacked his wife. The newsmen said the tears would harm Muskie's image, but how they came to this conclusion is unknown—in fact, one might consider that such a personal reaction would please those who disliked the cold, mechanical Nixon and Agnew. After Muskie won the primary—but with only 46 per cent of the Democratic vote, less than many reporters said he would need to demonstrate his hold over the nation—the candidate held a press conference at which he was asked how the results would affect his future chances. "I can't tell you that," said Muskie in anger. "You'll tell me and you'll tell the rest of the country because you interpret this victory. This press conference today is my only chance to interpret it, but you'll probably even misinterpret that."

Later, the Senator apologized to reporters, who accepted his regrets as a matter of course. He understood their power, the fact that many newspapermen and television commentators had come to view themselves as surrogates for the general public, seeing things the way most people did, doing much of the thinking and reacting for the readers and viewers. Without the goodwill of such people, Muskie could not hope to reach the voters and present a favorable image. Presidents could use the media when and how they wished, undercutting reporters and commentators; in 1972, nonincumbent candidates could not do the same. The media could help create a candidate and then assist in his destruction. The media could not do the same for a President—yet.

Nor could the media create a candidate when there was little with which to begin. Mayor John Lindsay of New York had many drawbacks as a candidate—he had only recently switched parties to become a Democrat (in 1968 he had nominated Spiro Agnew for the vice presidency at the Republican convention) and was unpopular in his own city, where many observers had said he was not up to the job. (One of those in the Muskie camp suggested that the slogan "He'll do for America what he did for New York" would kill a Lindsay candidacy.) Lindsay had a quick wit, was tall, handsome, and most telegenic—a reporter opened a Lindsay story with, "A casting director's dream of a television-era politician . . ."

But this was not the case. Reporters and commentators were as much victims of the media as were the candidates; the reporters and commentators did not consciously set out to create a President, but instead used the media to report on stories they thought would interest the public. Although many reporters agreed with Lindsay's stands on issues, they appreciated the essentially tinsel quality of the candidacy, and perhaps recognized he had image without substance. He blundered in the Florida primary, and some newsmen seemed to take pleasure in the blunders. Newspaper and television commentators knew that media candidates were here to stay, that primaries and campaigns were media opportunities, and that these gave the candidates national audiences that could enhance their careers. But at the same time the newsmen and television commentators resented this, and some newsmen may have overreacted in Lindsay's case.[7]

Each of the other candidates had drawbacks. Representative Shirley Chisholm, Mayor Sam Yorty, Senator Birch Bayh, and Senator Vance Hartke—as well as many other legislators—were not truly serious candidates. Governor George Wallace consistently misinterpreted the scope of his support throughout the country. He had struck several sensitive nerves, one of which was a deep criticism of and distrust for reporters, but had never been able to capitalize upon his instincts with organization and intellectual comprehension of the situation. As for Hubert Humphrey, he was old and familiar, a condition that had been useful in a previous period, but that was a drawback in the media age—Humphrey appeared like a summer rerun on television, one you might have enjoyed the first time around but switched off during the second and third showings. Senator Henry Jackson of Washington had the organization and financial backing for a major campaign, but lacked proper press relations and did poorly on television. Senator Edward Kennedy, who possessed all that the others lacked (but still suffered from memories of Chappaquiddick), was not interested in the nomination.

Finally, there was Senator George McGovern, a candidate with great strengths and greater drawbacks, at least as far as the media were concerned. McGovern had the volunteers, young people who appeared well on television and impressed reporters. He created a good organization adept in the use of media—part of it had been inherited from Robert Kennedy and Eugene McCarthy. McGovern had active support from a large segment of the show-business community. Marlo Thomas, Dennis Weaver, and other celebrities came aboard early, and dozens of others followed. Shirley MacLaine was a McGovern delegate, and with her brother, Warren Beatty, helped organize several major rallies that attracted television time and contributions. The McGovern people wooed the press assiduously, and in some cases in an adept fashion.

But the candidate himself was badly flawed. For all his good qualities, McGovern was stiff and awkward on television, had a poor voice, and looked bland. In addition, he lacked a natural sense of politics, a joy for the art, the kind possessed by most of the other candidates. Most important, he was trapped by his own image. Nixon could back and fill, for this was expected of "Tricky Dick." But Honest George could not do the same. Thus the many mistakes and miscalculations, the obvious compromises and changes—shown full on television—seemed out of character. The image age was in full swing in 1972. Richard Nixon was busily playing the role of a brave, unpopular man intent on doing the right thing even in the face of united opposition from well-meaning but misinformed people. McGovern had assumed the role of the honest, decent reformer. His actions subsequent to obtaining the nomination—his overtures to the Democratic center and right as well as the independents—in addition to his switches on policy and the Thomas Eagleton affair—caused him to lose support. It was as though John Wayne tried to play the role of a homosexual dress designer: The public would not buy it.

Reporters and commentators recognized the sham, and they reported on the disarray and amateurish nature of the Democratic campaign. McGovern's own managers realized they had created a campaign without a candidate worthy of it, and one of them, Bill Dougherty, reflected upon this in a moment of weakness. "I'd like to lock up the candidate," he told a reporter, implying that the campaign would have been far better without McGovern.[8]

For each asset was also a liability. The organization that had been geared to win primaries and appeal to segments of the population was the same that had alienated a majority of Americans at the 1968 Democratic convention. The organization was fine at image creation. The show-business people had lent his campaign an aura of unreality and even glamor—but the homely and homey George McGovern simply did not fit into it. John Kennedy might have done so, but McGovern was no Kennedy.

Finally, how worthwhile was an endorsement from this show-business contingent? Unfair though it was, Shirley MacLaine had become identified with roles of good-natured prostitutes, while Dennis Weaver was Marshal Dillon's limping sidekick Chester. To sell a man like McGovern would have required endorsements from people who were somewhat like him—at least in terms of image—and who had won public confidence and trust. This meant less of a focus on the inflammatory younger Hollywood liberals and more from the established former boys-next-door, such as Henry Fonda, James Stewart, Robert Young, and the like. But these men, trusted and familiar, were either not available or had little interest in the McGovern campaign. A minute on television with Gregory Peck might had enhanced the campaign; interviews with Shirley MacLaine probably lost votes for this candidate.

There was intense but narrow support for McGovern in 1972, while that for Nixon was wide and shallow—in this respect at least, it was a rerun of 1964. The larger public reacted with indifference—despite the importance of the election, heightened by continued negotiations for a truce in Vietnam—and there was little enthusiasm and excitement outside those with a direct emotional or political stake in the race. An overwhelming majority of the newspapers supported Nixon in their editorials; those relative few that came out for McGovern usually did so out of dislike for the President or because of their support of some planks of the Democratic platform, rarely out of enthusiasm for the candidate himself. The Nixon people continued to criticize electronic and print journalists for their supposed biases; the McGovern supporters were bitter when the same people noted flaws in their candidate's performance, with some going so far as to suggest that the press should unite in the campaign against the President. The reporters, then, were being attacked by both sides.

That there would be a Nixon victory in November was never really in doubt. But the magnitude of the victory was stunning. McGovern captured Massachusetts and the District of Columbia, nothing else. The rejection of the Democratic "radicals" was complete.

Scarcely had the election results been tabulated than the Vietnam War came to an end for Americans. Almost simultaneously the nation learned more about the Watergate break-in, considered a minor episode during the campaign, but now shown to have far wider implications than originally thought.

The events of the next year and a half were among the most dramatic in the nation's history, and still have to be fully digested. It was a different reality from that which most midle-aged Americans had known. Indeed, the struggle was so intense, dramatic, and convoluted that the resignation of Vice President Agnew, who only a year before had been considered a certain victor in a 1976 presidential election, was only a footnote. At times many Americans thought they were living in a novel, and a poor one at that, for the events were so unbelievable.[9]

All of it was covered on television and commented upon widely in the press. The images of Senators Sam Ervin and Howard Baker, the members of the House special committee considering impeachment, and Judge John Sirica, Attorney General Elliot Richardson, and Special Prosecutor Archibald Cox were contrasted sharply with those of the White House staff, to the detriment of the latter. Considered a master of media only a few months before, Nixon blundered badly in this period, misjudging the popular temper, misusing the media, and in the end contributing to his own downfall. The President had few supporters in the press or television, and so it appeared at times as though he was fighting the media. To a degree this was so; some men and women of the media had uncovered wrongdoing, and comments on talk shows and the like were hardly favorable to the President. Would Nixon have been forced to resign without the intervention of the media? Perhaps, for long before newspapermen discovered the complications behind the break-in, the matter was in the courts. On the other hand, it would have been carried out quite differently in the premedia age.

Upon assuming office, President Ford said that the long national nightmare had drawn to a close. It was a proper tone to set for a new beginning as well as a good assessment; the last weeks of the Nixon presidency had been nightmarish in tone. The clashes with the press, the televised resignation preceded by network interruptions of scheduled programs for bulletins, the tearful farewell, the postmortems by commentators—some of whom had been major actors in the drama—had an air of unreality, different from but comparable to the atmosphere of the Kennedy funeral. "The system works," wrote the major news magazines, just as they had done after Lyndon Johnson's speech to Congress and the nation in November 1963. In 1974, however, many were unsure what that meant, or how the system had been changed by recent events.

By 1976 the media had become an integral part of that system, the vehicles through which power might be obtained and perpetuated. This was not wholly unexpected. Without really understanding the implications of his actions on and in the media, Theodore Roosevelt had engaged in manipulation through the press. Woodrow Wilson, not John Kennedy, had been the first media President, the first to rally informational and educational industries to perform his will. Other Presidents after him added their own touches, and as media became further developed and new techniques appeared, this manipulation became more obvious. Today the substance of an act and the way it is packaged are taken together; they have merged. A similar change has taken place with the men and women of the media industries. They are powers in their own rights—Dan Rather is as much an adversary of the White House as any congressman, while the Washington *Post* is a greater check on presidential powers than is the Senate.

The beginnings of this could be seen in the age of yellow journalism, of Pulitzer and Hearst; later on the free-wheeling columnist added his touches. But the final merging of newsmaker and news reporter was left for our time.

What might occur if a person of the media, or one who understood it and possessed those attributes needed for manipulation, appeared on the national scene? Certainly such an individual would be a popular choice for the presidency, and might achieve it without the intermediation of a major political party. That a Walter Cronkite or Chet Huntley of the future might aspire to the White House is not considered so wild a thought today. The possibility that a politican like Sam Ervin or Barbara Jordan might achieve national prominence through appearances in Watergate-like spectaculars of the future is almost taken for granted. What stands would such people have to take on other issues? What would they do if elected to the presidency? Cronkite and Ervin were admired and respected by millions who had no idea of their philosophies—their images were far more important. The same will be true in the future, only in a more obvious and significant fashion.

Of all the major national figures of the past decade and a half, only John Kennedy possessed both the poetry and the power, and he lacked the time and inclination to utilize them fully, in such a way as to create a presidency based upon the use of media, not the more conventional channels through which power had been exercised in the past. Clearly Johnson, Nixon, and Ford have shown that we may, at one time in the future, have a plebiscitary presidency. Though each of these men, in a different way, lacked the ingredients to make it possible, there is little doubt that such a presidency is possible, and perhaps inevitable. Every indication is that the old political structures are crumbling, though the shapes of new parties and interest groups cannot be fully seen. The reason for this may be that the structure itself, at least in the way it has been perceived in the past, is becoming obsolete. In its place stands the popularity poll, with those participating obtaining information through media, often unable to separate fact from fiction, image from reality. Thus our postwar Presidents may be seen as having functioned in a time of transition, with the future belonging to the men of media. This accounts for a large part of the current popularity of Truman and Eisenhower. Even those who believed them to have been poor Presidents are aware that they were not creatures spawned by electronics. Due to training, inclination, indifference—and the state of the art and technology—neither man used television and the techniques of fiction as fully as those who followed. In retrospect they seem men of iron and concrete; they were followed by Presidents concocted of plastic, cardboard, film, and videotape.

Perhaps there is no way to reverse the tendency to elevate image and fantasy over reality. The future of American politics appears to be in the hands of those individuals capable of swaying the public's emotions, playing upon love and fear rather than intellect and even self-interest. And it is a two-way street, for just as politicians have come to ape show-business personalities, so the artists have become intrigued with politics, especially elections. John Lindsay makes a foray into motion-picture productions—playing a senator in a melodrama—while Robert Redford announces that his greatest thrill came from playing a candidate for the Senate, for then he caught a glimpse of the excitement of the race and its innate drama.

Indications are that the next President—or at the very most, the one after him—will be the first Chief Executive of the coming high media age, a period in which the lines between reality and fiction are all but obliterated. Television and motion pictures have accomplished what no other forces could have done—they have helped shatter the American political process and cripple the party system, replacing them with a plebiscitary democracy, run more by polls than elections. It began with the 1960 canvass. There is no way of telling where it will end.

"I'd prefer to ignore the various media, but they won't go away, and neither will I." So wrote author and occasional politician-watcher Mark Harris late in 1974. He reflected upon the Watergate experience and how it affected the nation. For months it was virtually impossible to avoid hearing of it on radio, seeing hearings and watching discussions on television, and reading about Watergate in newspapers and news magazines. Rumors filled the air as the nation turned into one huge whispering gallery. It was grand drama, building to a spectacular climax.

But was all of it news, he asked? Harris wasn't sure of the answer. "Watergate was the ultimate in entertainment. The media are not only business but show business, featuring hard plots, clear conflicts, games, a star system. The principles of news coverage are identical with the principles of dramatic entertainment: Give the people what they want; follow the trends, keep sacred the customer's expectations." The Senate had become the political equivalent of the motion-picture studio of the 1930s, with one hundred actors struggling to get top billing in blockbuster productions, which would end in superstar status in the White House. Was that Ervin and Baker on the television tube, or actors playing roles —perhaps Lionel Barrymore and James Stewart? Several columnists wrote semihumorous articles on how they would cast the story—in most of them, the actor selected to play Nixon was Humphrey Bogart (recalling his role as Captain Queeg in *The Caine Mutiny*).

Such talk would have been dismissed as fanciful in the 1930s. It seemed quite plausible in 1974.

Of course, Watergate was more than that, but on the other hand it was high drama, of the kind that previewed with the 1960 election, ran through the Kennedy administration and into the first televised war in American history, the spectacular events of 1968, and the media struggles of the Nixon years. What would be done for an encore? Can a people grown accustomed to high drama and intense if short-lived emotions adjust psychologically to a more placid period, one that is not orchestrated by the media or filtered through the eyes, ears, and minds of those who control the cultural technology of our times? We have become akin to sleepwalkers at the circus, moving to the prodding of the electronic whip. "The drama of one period can never be suited to the following age," wrote Tocqueville a century and a half ago, "if in the interval an important revolution has changed the manners and laws of the nation."

We are in the midst of that revolution today, and drama has been transformed into manners.

Notes

Chapter 1

1. Meyer Berger, *The Story of the New York* Times, *1851–1951* (New York: Simon & Schuster, 1951), p. 114.
2. Three of the best of these are James Melvin Lee, *History of American Journalism* (Boston: Houghton Mifflin, 1917), Edwin Emery and Henry Ladd Smith, *The Press in America* (Englewood Cliffs, N.J.: Prentice-Hall, 1954), and Frank Luther Mott, *American Journalism: A History, 1690–1960* (New York: Macmillan, 1962).
3. Although Richard Hoe became the major supplier of printing equipment in the nation, he continued to produce saws and machines unrelated to publishing. Apparently he viewed himself as a general manufacturer, not a specialist in the printing and publishing field.
4. Harry W. Baehr, Jr., *The New York Tribune Since the Civil War* (New York: Dodd, Mead, 1936), p. 31.
5. James Melvin Lee, *History of American Journalism* (Boston: Houghton Mifflin, 1917), p. 329.
6. The *Herald* had a permanent Wall Street reporter in the late 1830s, but his material was always checked and rewritten by Bennett.
7. In 1898 a Bureau of Labor report indicated that 95 persons working 18.5 hours at 10 double-web machines were capable of producing as much as 4 persons at 10 hand presses could in 3,660 hours. United States, Bureau of Labor, *Hand and Machine Labor* (Washington, D.C.: U. S. Government Printing Office, 1898), pp. 68–69, 366–67.
8. Amos Cummings, a *Tribune* compositor, grumbled in 1869: "As a rule, thoroughly competent printers have better judgement and more newspaper tact than editors manufactured out of collegiate graduates. The majority of the printers of the *Tribune* office are

today better posted on general news matters than a majority of the *Tribune* editors. When will newspaper managers begin to use the raw material lying under their very noses? I have known owners of journals to run from one end of the country to the other in a vain search for a competent Managing Editor, when little fellows setting type in their own offices were fully able and competent to get out just such newspapers as were wanted in their various sections." Baehr, *New York Tribune*, p. 183.

9. There is no satisfactory biography of Ottmar Mergenthaler. But see Georges Iles, *Leading American Inventors* (Freeport, N.Y.: Books for Libraries Press, 1968 ed.), pp. 393–434 for a sketch of his life and career.
10. Elizabeth Faulkner Baker, *Printers and Technology* (New York: Columbia University Press, 1957), p. 69. This is an excellent study of labor-management relations in this period and the influence of the new technology.
11. New York *World*, May 11, 1883.
12. James W. Barrett, *Joseph Pulitzer and His World* (New York: Vanguard, 1941), p. 184.
13. George Juergens, *Joseph Pulitzer and the New York World* (Princeton, N.J.: Princeton University Press, 1966), pp. 19–26.
14. Gilson Gardner, *Lusty Scripps: The Life of E. W. Scripps* (New York: Vanguard, 1932) and Negley D. Cochran, *E. W. Scripps* (Garden City, N.Y.: Doubleday & Company, 1933) are interesting biographies of this highly idiosyncratic publisher.
15. Willard G. Bleyer, *Main Currents in the History of American Journalism* (Boston: Houghton Mifflin, 1927), p. 413. George Britt, *Forty Years—Forty Millions* (New York: Farrar and Rinehart, 1935) is a lively biography of Munsey.

Chapter 2

1. In the nineteenth century the word "profession" connoted occupation. Writing in the Jacksonian era, for example, Tocqueville said: "There are few rich men in America; hence almost all Americans have to take up some profession. Now, every profession requires an apprenticeship. Therefore the Americans can devote only the first years of life to general education; at fifteen they start on a career, so their education generally ends. . . ." In the 1920s, professions included those occupations that required a great deal of formal study and climaxed with certification by a professional organization of one's peers. It also came to imply a high calling, a variety of secular ministry. Thus teaching and

medicine were categorized as professions, while carpentry and maintenance work were not.

2. Albert A. Sutton, *Education for Journalism in the United States from Its Beginning* (Evanston, Ill.: Northwestern University Press, 1940), Chap. 2.
3. The best study of business-college relations is Merle Curti and Roderick Nash, *Philanthropy in the Shaping of American Higher Education* (New Brunswick, N.J.: Rutgers University Press, 1965).
4. What constitutes a college? There were many schools that called themselves colleges, but had more pretensions than performance. By some counts, there were as many as 563 of them in 1870. United States, *Historical Statistics of the United States, Colonial Period to 1957* (Washington, D.C.: U. S. Government Printing Office, 1958), p. 211.
5. For an interesting portrait of college life in this period—at Yale—see Andrew D. White (a future college president himself, at Cornell), *Autobiography* (New York: Century, 1905), Vol. I, p. 2.
6. For a study of Yale's "lost chances," see Edwin E. Slosson, *Great American Universities* (New York, Macmillan, 1910), pp. 34–43.
7. Laurence R. Veysey, *The Emergence of the American University* (Chicago: University of Chicago Press, 1965), p. 39.
8. Charles W. Eliot, *Educational Reform* (New York: Century, 1898), p. 1.
9. Criticisms of the elective system may be found in William Tucker, *My Generation* (Boston: Houghton Mifflin, 1919).
10. Veysey, *Emergence of the American University*, pp. 90–120, is an excellent discussion of Eliot's educational philosophy.
11. The similarity between the collegians of the late nineteenth century and campus reformers of the late 1960s should be evident, and is discussed in Chap. 12.
12. Amos Alonzo Stagg to his family, Jan. 10, 1891, in John S. Brubacher and Willis Rudy, *Higher Education in Transition* (New York: Harper & Row, 1968), p. 133.
13. Owen Johnson, *Stover at Yale* (Frederick A. Stokes, 1912), p. 246.
14. Henry Seidel Canby, *Alma Mater* (New York: Farrar and Rinehart, 1936), pp. 71–73.
15. John R. Tunis, *Was College Worth While?* (New York: Harcourt, Brace, 1936), pp. 58–59.
16. William Miller, "American Historians and the Business Elite," *Journal of Economic History*, Vol. IX, No. 3 (Nov. 1949), pp. 207ff.

17. An old Cornell joke was that after Ezra Cornell said he would open his school to all, critics noted that he would be flooded with students, to which the industrialist replied, "Wait till you see where I put the place."
18. Fritz Machlup, *The Production and Distribution of Knowledge in the United States* (Princeton, N.J.: Princeton University Press, 1962), pp. 77–78.
19. Tunis, *Was College Worth While?*, p. 21.
20. Canby, *Alma Mater*, pp. 60–61.
21. "The net result was that a German-style graduate school had to be built in America upon the foundation of the traditional English-style college. . . . Could the methods and purposes of those two aspects of learning—one aiming at general education and the other at the advancement of knowledge—be harmonized in the same framework of higher education?" Brubacher and Rudy, *Higher Education in Transition*, pp. 199–200.
22. Canby, *Alma Mater*, pp. 128–29.
23. Veysey, *Emergence of the Modern University*, p. 92.
24. Stephen Steinberg, *The Academic Melting Pot* (New York: McGraw-Hill, 1973), p. 23.
25. C. C. Brown, *The College Professor in America* (Philadelphia: Lippincott, 1938), p. 39.
26. Veysey, *Emergence of the Modern University*, p. 263.
27. As recently as 1939, male graduates of Harvard, Yale, and Princeton (which in any case were all-male in that period) over the age of forty reported an average income of $8,580, while that for all graduates in the age group was $4,020. Those who graduated from non-Big Ten midwestern colleges received $3,250. Elementary and secondary school teaching, a prime area for graduates of nonprestige schools, remained a low-paying job throughout the first half of the century, even though it carried a kind of shabby gentility. Seymour Harris, *The Market for College Graduates* (Cambridge, Mass.: Harvard University Press, 1949), pp. 4, 127.

Chapter 3

1. Slosson, *Great American Universities*, p. 210.
2. Lincoln Steffens, "Sending a State to College," *American Magazine*, Vol. 67 (Feb. 1909), p. 351.
3. Robert S. Maxwell, *LaFollette and the Rise of the Progressives in Wisconsin* (New York: Russell & Russell, 1956), pp. 128–72 passim.
4. Slosson, *Great American Universities*, p. 215.

5. Woodrow Wilson, "Princeton for the Nation's Service," *Science*, Vol. XVI (1902), pp. 721–30.
6. Ray Stannard Baker, *Woodrow Wilson: Life and Letters* (Garden City, N.Y.: Doubleday & Company, 1927), Vol. II, p. 213.
7. The most important of these involved a controversy regarding the location of the graduate school. Later on the struggle between Wilson and Dean West would appear monumental, but it was minor at the time. "I must confess," wrote Slosson, "that I have not been able to determine which side I am on, or even what the fuss is all about." Slosson, *Great American Universities*, p. 107.
8. Arthur S. Link, *Wilson: The Road to the White House* (Princeton, N.J.: Princeton University Press, 1947), pp. 98–99ff. Of course, there had been dark horses before in American politics, the most recent being William Jennings Bryan, and some had achieved their positions through newspapers—witness Hearst, who in 1906 hoped to become President someday. Wilson was the first academic figure to be considered seriously for high national office, and the only successful one in our history—although others after him would have ambitions in that direction.
9. This gulf would continue throughout the Wilson years, even though relations improved toward the end. In the 1920s it would be characterized as the difference between "sophisticates" and "provincials," and in the 1960s and early 1970s as between "effete eastern intellectuals" and "middle Americans." Under Wilson, the intellectuals were in the White House, the provincials in the press rooms; later on, in some administrations, the positions would be reversed.
10. George Creel, *Rebel at Large* (New York: G. P. Putnam's Sons, 1947), pp. 71–77.
11. Mark Sullivan, *Our Times*, Vol. V, *Over Here, 1914–1918* (New York: Charles Scribner's Sons, 1933), p. 425.
12. Creel, *Rebel at Large*, p. 158.
13. Robert Lansing, *War Memoirs of Robert Lansing* (Indianapolis, Ind.: Bobbs-Merrill, 1935), pp. 322–24.
14. This is not to say that Creel was necessarily the best selection for the position. Although most newspapers thought well of him, the New York *Times*, in an editorial of Apr. 16, 1917, could not find "any evidence of the ability, the experience, or the judicial temperament required to gain the understanding and co-operation of the press."
15. Of course, early Presidents utilized the party press to advantage. But although some of the editors held government posts, they

published their organs as private citizens. Wilson was the first President to maintain his own official propaganda apparatus within the White House.

16. The best studies of CPI organization and operations are James R. Mock and Cedric Larson, *Words That Won the War* (Princeton N.J.: Princeton University Press, 1939) and George Creel, *How We Advertised America* (New York: Harper & Brothers, 1920).
17. Ibid., p. 439.
18. Creel did not attempt to develop a prepublication policy, but instead tended to criticize stories after they appeared. After a while, however, his large-scale efforts had the effect of prepublication censorship.
19. Sullivan, *Our Times*, Part V, p. 440.
20. Mock and Larson, *Words That Won the War*, p. 202.
21. Charles Angoff, "The Higher Learning Goes to War," *American Mercury*, Vol. 11, No. 6 (June 1927), pp. 177–91; Harry Elmer Barnes, "The Drool Method in History," *American Mercury*, Vol. 1, No. 1 (Jan. 1924), pp. 31–38. *The American Mercury* became the leading anti-Wilsonian periodical for intellectuals in the 1920s.

Chapter 4

1. Guy Stanton Ford, *On and off the Campus* (Minneapolis: University of Minnesota Press, 1938), especially pp. 73–101.
2. Mock and Larson, *Words That Won the War*, pp. 136–37.
3. Creel, *Rebel at Large*, pp. 132–41.
4. Raymond Moley, *The Hays Office* (Indianapolis, Ind.: Bobbs-Merrill, 1945), p. 21; Gertrude Jobes, *Motion Picture Empire* (Hamden, Conn.: Archon, 1966), pp. 111–24; Mae D. Huettig, *Economic Control of the Motion Picture Industry* (Philadelphia: University of Pennsylvania Press, 1944), pp. 61–64; United States, *Historical Statistics of the United States, Colonial Times to 1957* (Washington, D.C.: U. S. Government Printing Office, 1960), p. 224.
5. A similar situation appeared when the first coin-operated soda water vending machines appeared. Banks of them were placed in arcades, and the curious came in to try them out, some purchasing and drinking several cups of soda just to see the machines in operation, not because they were thirsty. Earlier, visitors to Horn & Hardart Automats would do the same with the coin-operated food machines.

6. A. R. Fulton, *Motion Pictures* (Norman: University of Oklahoma Press, 1960), p. 18.
7. The vaudeville "wheels" may have provided the basis for the studio system of the 1930s. See Chap. 6.
8. Later on, other impresarios threatened the positions of the leaders. Among the newcomers were Martin Beck and Willie Hammerstein. Joe Laurie, Jr., *Vaudeville* (New York: Henry Holt, 1953), pp. 333–417.
9. Of course, not all were cut from the same pattern. Lewis Selznick was a small jewelry manufacturer, Joseph Schenck a retail druggist and his brother Nick a small showman, and Harry Cohn an office boy. Not all were Jewish—Cecil B. DeMille and Darryl Zanuck, both of whom arrived somewhat later, might still be placed among the pioneers, while Spyros Skouras was Greek. Still, the Jewish immigrant influence soon became dominant throughout the industry—even among non-Jews.
10. Although peep shows and nickelodeons were popular in all parts of the country, they did their best business in immigrant areas. The shows were cheap, offered glimpses into American life, and one did not have to have a knowledge of English to understand them. It may well have been the last two aspects of early films that attracted some of the pioneers to the field, although none of them indicate this was so. One can only wonder how the industry might have developed had Edison's ideas—a wedding of the film with the phonograph—been accepted.
11. Jobes, *Motion Picture Empire*, pp. 28–50, is a concise account of the industry wars of the period.
12. Terry Ramsaye, *A Million and One Nights* (New York: Simon & Schuster, 1926), pp. 465–72; Michael Conant, *Antitrust in the Motion Picture Industry* (Berkeley: University of California Press, 1960), pp. 18–19.
13. Joseph P. Kennedy, ed., *The Story of the Films* (A. W. Shaw, 1927), p. 61; Bosley Crowther, *The Lion's Share* (New York: E. P. Dutton, 1957), p. 131.
14. Daniel Frohman became a partner in Famous Players. He was an impresario like his brother, and went into the company because he was "temporarily embarrassed" by a lack of cash. Charles Frohman had mixed feelings about films at the time. "People who never came to the theatre at all because they had no sense for drama and comedy, now show a little from watching moving pictures. People who never thought at all now are inclined to think a little by the aid of yellow journalism." Unwittingly perhaps, he

perceived the linkage between men like Pulitzer and Zukor. Jobes, *Motion Picture Empire*, p. 89.

15. There were, of course, other problems, among them unionization of the labor force, which was talked about as early as 1910, but really began with an American Federation of Labor drive in 1916. By 1918 the Alliance of Theatrical Stage Employees and Motion Picture Machines Operators had been formed, and others followed. Actors' Equity was given jurisdiction over screen players in 1920, and the Authors' League of America protected the writers. But there were relatively few labor disputes in this period. Murray Ross, *Stars and Strikes* (New York: Columbia University Press, 1941), pp. 5–6ff.
16. Raymond Moley, *The Hays Office* (Indianapolis, Ind.: Bobbs-Merrill, 1945), p. 27.
17. Ibid., p. 34.
18. Will Hays, *See and Hear* (Motion Picture Producers' and Distributors' Association, 1929), pp. 2–54 passim; Jobes, *Motion Picture Empire*, p. 233.

Chapter 5

1. As late as 1893, Edison was able to write, in a letter to Edward Muybridge, "I have constructed a little instrument which I call the Kinetoscope, with a nickel and slot attachment. Some 25 have been made, but I am doubtful if there is any commercial feature in it, and fear they will not even earn their cost." Matthew Josephson, *Edison* (New York: McGraw-Hill, 1959), p. 392.
2. Robert V. Bruce, *Bell: Alexander Graham Bell and the Conquest of Solitude* (Little, Brown, 1973), p. 252.
3. Ramsaye, *A Million and One Nights*, pp. 69–70, 168, 419, 493–94.
4. The almost simultaneous arrival of the talkies and the depression had yet another result. The studios were able to fire their well-paid stars on the ground that they lacked voices, and then hire newcomers at far lower salaries. In addition, they were able to get rid of recalcitrant directors and producers in the same fashion. The artists of the silent era often came from the stage and vaudeville. As will be seen, those of the early sound period were developed by the studios, or came from radio.
5. David Sarnoff, in a 1934 statement to stockholders, conceded the point. "One of the main purposes of the investment was to provide at least one major motion-picture-producing and reproducing organization free to use RCA equipment in the motion-picture

field." Gleason L. Archer, *Big Business and Radio* (American Historical Company, 1939), p. 393.

6. "Marconi was eminently utilitarian," said British scientist Sir Ambrose Fleming. "His predominant interest was not in purely scientific knowledge per se, but in its practical application for useful purposes." W. Rupert Maclaurin, with the technical assistance of R. Joyce Harman, *Invention and Innovation in the Radio Industry* (New York: Macmillan, 1949), p. 30.
7. Helen M. Fessenden, *Fessenden: Builder of Tomorrows* (New York: Coward-McCann, 1940), p. 153.
8. Lee DeForest, *Father of Radio* (Wilcox and Follett 1950), pp. 225–35.
9. In 1944, Young recalled, "This interest was increased *later* [emphasis added] when I learned from engineers of its possibilities for entertainment." Maclaurin and Harman, *Invention and Innovation in the Radio Industry*, p. 104. David Sarnoff, then the commercial manager for RCA, had proposed another use for radio as early as 1915. "I have in mind a plan of development which would make radio a 'household utility' in the same sense as the piano or phonograph. The idea is to bring music into the house by wireless." David Sarnoff, *Looking Ahead: The Papers of David Sarnoff* (New York: McGraw-Hill, 1968), p. 31.
10. *The Radio Industry: The Story of Its Development* (A. W. Shaw, 1928), p. 194.
11. Sarnoff, *Looking Ahead*, pp. 33–34. The actual figures were close to the prediction: $11 million in 1922, $22.5 million in 1923, and $50 million in 1924, for a total of $83.5 million.
12. Eric Barnouw, *A Tower in Babel: A History of Broadcasting in the United States to 1933* (New York: Oxford University Press, 1966), p. 106; William P. Banning, *Commercial Broadcasting Pioneer: The WEAF Experiment, 1922–1926* (Cambridge, Mass.: Harvard University Press, 1946), p. 59.
13. Banning, *Commercial Broadcasting*, pp. 92, 118.
14. In 1924 Hoover said, "I can state emphatically that it would be most unfortunate for the people of this country, to whom broadcasting has become an important incident of life, if its control should come into the hands of any single corporation, individual, or combination. It would be in principle the same as though the entire press of the country were so controlled. . . . I believe, however, that everybody should be permitted to send out anything they like. The very moment that the government begins to determine what can be sent, it establishes a censorship through

the whole field of clashing ideas. . . ." Herbert Hoover, *The Memoirs of Herbert Hoover: The Cabinet and the Presidency, 1920–1933* (New York: Macmillan, 1952), pp. 139–43.

15. Sarnoff might have become an independent radio set producer, but by the time these companies had appeared, he was firmly entrenched in the RCA hierarchy.
16. As a result of an antitrust action in 1930, General Electric and Westinghouse were obliged to dispose of their RCA stock and terminate all crosslicensing agreements. With this action, RCA became a completely independent corporation, freed from its major parents—GE, AT&T, and Westinghouse.
17. Another network, the Mutual Broadcasting System, was formed in 1934, but it never became as powerful as NBC; even though it had 160 stations in 1940, most were small units in rural areas and minor cities.
18. Sarnoff, *Looking Ahead*, pp. 63–64.
19. Robert J. Landry, *This Fascinating Radio Business* (Indianapolis, Ind.: Bobbs-Merrill, 1946), pp. 202–4; Charles H. Wolfe, *Modern Radio Advertising* (New York: Funk & Wagnalls, 1949), p. 94.
20. Robert and Helen Lynd, *Middletown* (New York: Harcourt, Brace, 1949 ed.), pp. 270–71.
21. Ben Gross, *I Looked and I Listened* (New York: Random House, 1954), pp. 100–2.
22. Robert and Helen Lynd, *Middletown*, pp. 270–71.

Chapter 6

1. The same was true for singers. The early vocalists tended to sing as though at a concert or, in the case of band singers, as at a country-club dance. Not until the late 1920s did a new kind of singer—the "crooner"—appear, with a voice perhaps too low for an unamplified theater, but correct for the intimacy of radio. Russ Columbo and Bing Crosby were examples of this. On the other hand, some singers of the old school, such as Kate Smith, were also popular.
2. Edward W. Chester, *Radio, Television, and American Politics* (New York: Sheed & Ward, 1969), p. 16.
3. Theodore G. Joslin, *Hoover off the Record* (Garden City, N.Y.: Doubleday, Doran, 1935), p. 69.
4. Hadley Cantril and Gordon Allport, *The Psychology of Radio* (New York: Harper & Brothers, 1935), p. 40.

5. John Dos Passos, "The Radio Voice," *Common Sense* (Feb. 1934), pp. 17–18.
6. A Roosevelt critic remarked that during the fireside chats one had the feeling the President was talking and toasting marshmallows at the same time. A good contemporary analysis of the Roosevelt style may be found in Robert West, *The Rape of Radio* (Rodin, 1941), pp. 415–58.
7. "The important distinctions between the New Deal intellectuals and the rest of their countrymen began along rural and urban lines. One third of them were born in rural areas, while two thirds of the population was still, by the census definition, considered rural. In addition, 18 per cent of the New Deal elite was born on farms when 42 per cent of the national work force was still employed in agriculture. Conversely, two thirds of the New Dealers were born in urban areas when only one third of the population resided in them." Thomas A. Kreuger and William Glidden, "The New Deal Intellectual Elite: A Collective Portrait," *The Rich, the Well Born, and the Powerful*, ed. Frederic Cople Jaher (Urbana: University of Illinois Press, 1973), p. 346.
8. The company was known at the time as Famous Players-Lasky, of course. By the early 1930s, however, it had become Paramount. The best study of the antitrust activities in films is Conant, *Antitrust in the Motion Picture Industry*, especially pp. 84–220. Also see *Federal Trade Commission* v. *Famous Players-Lasky Corp.*, 57 F. 2d 152 (C.C.A. 2, 1932), 23, 27n, 202 and *United States* v. *Parmount Pictures,* 66 F. Supp. 323 (S.D.N.Y., 1946), 70 F. Supp. 53 (S.D.N.Y., 1947), 334 U.S. 131 (1948), viii, xviii, 35–105.
9. The members included Merlin Aylesworth of RCA, who was also president of RKO, and representatives from Twentieth Century-Fox, Paramount, Loew's, and Warner's. In addition, Universal and Republic were represented. According to one study, only two members were not connected with the trust in any fashion. United States, 76th Cong., 3d sess., Senate, Temporary National Economic Committee, Monograph No. 43, *The Motion Picture Industry—A Pattern of Control* (Washington, D.C.: U. S. Government Printing Office, 1941), p. 8.
10. Ellis W. Hawley, *The New Deal and the Problem of Monopoly* (Princeton, N.J.: Princeton University Press, 1966), pp. 365–67; Kenneth G. Crawford, *The Pressure Boys* (New York: Julian Messner, 1939), pp. 90–96.
11. In his admiring study of Hays, Raymond Moley—a major figure in the New Deal and an original member of the Brain Trust—

implies that the Neely-Pettengill Bill dealt with censorship, and avoids Hays' political activities and the matter of industry domination. As might be expected, his is a vigorous defense of the NRA approach to the industry. Moley, *The Hays Office,* pp. 202–10.

12. Leo C. Rosten, *Hollywood: The Movie Colony, the Movie Makers* (New York: Harcourt, Brace, 1941), p. 133.
13. United States, *Motion Picture Industry,* p. 9.
14. Rosten, *Hollywood,* p. 27.
15. The following section is not meant to be a deep analysis of film content from a critical point of view, but rather an illustration of the point that films were politically bland in this period, and so helped still whatever radical sentiments might have existed in the 1930s. There are many excellent collections of articles by critics and summaries of film stories and contents. Andrew Bergman, *We're in the Money* (New York: New York University Press, 1971), would be a good beginning. Also see James Agee, *Agee on Film* (Boston: Houghton, Mifflin, 1966 ed.) and Morgan Himelstein, *Drama Was a Weapon* (New Brunswick, N.J.: Rutgers University Press, 1963).
16. The film exegesis reached its peak with discussions of *King Kong,* which after World War II was described as a sensitive film with several layers of allegorical commentary. At the time of its release in 1933, however, it drew audiences interested in exciting drama, an exotic locale, and unusual special effects. For a selection of reviews of these and other films of the period, see *The New York* Times *Film Reviews* (New York: Quadrangle, 1971), Vols. 4–6.
17. One of the few films that the studios attempted—weakly—to suppress was King Vidor's *Our Daily Bread,* which was released in 1934 through United Artists. In it, a group of average Americans return to the soil and form what amounts to an agrarian collective farm—some saw it as an American soviet. But the film was not a call to revolution, but more an indication that the answer to the nation's ills might be a return to the rustic values of an older America.
18. In the early 1950s, when asked whether he believed there were Communists in Hollywood, Cooper had little to offer. He did say, however, that he didn't like Communists, "because they're not square shooters."
19. The nature of the movie palaces of this period—some of them ornate, semi-oriental edifices—added to the escapism of a trip to the movies in the 1930s. See Ben M. Hall, *The Best Remaining Seats* (New York: Clarkson N. Potter, Bramhall House, 1961).

20. Llewellyn White, *The American Radio* (Chicago: University of Chicago Press, 1947), p. 66.
21. The telephone talk shows, which first appeared in rural areas in the 1920s and then spread to lower-class urban ones in the early 1930s, were somewhat akin to Bell's concept of a wireless telephone network, resembling as they do what the inventor once talked of as a "national whispering gallery." The most popular of the early talk programs specialized in marital advice and discussions of personal problems by the host and his callers.
22. Robert S. Lynd and Helen M. Lynd, *Middletown in Transition* (New York: Harcourt, Brace, 1937), pp. 144, 263.
23. In this fashion, radio became what Hoover hoped it would be, "a magazine of the air." But the then Secretary of Commerce did not believe in advertising on radio, and the magazine format was made possible only through the use of advertising.
24. "When Arlene Francis, a 'March of Time' veteran, played a Bette Davis scene on *Forty-five Minutes in Hollywood,* it resulted in a phone call to Bette from her mother, congratulating her on her fine radio acting." Erik Barnouw, *The Golden Web* (New York: Oxford University Press, 1968), p. 104.
25. Frank Buxton and Bill Owen, *The Big Broadcast* (New York: Viking, 1972), is a program-by-program listing of radio shows in this period, complete with casts.
26. Under the NRA, minimum wages for large stations was twenty dollars a week. For an appreciation of performers' positions in the 1930s, see Mary Jane Higby, *Tune in Tomorrow* (New York: Cowles, 1968).
27. Quincy Howe, *The News and How to Understand It* (New York: Simon & Schuster, 1940), p. 161.
28. Barnouw, *A Tower in Babel,* p. 158.
29. Paul Lazarsfeld, *Radio and the Printed Page* (New York: Duell, Sloan and Pearce, 1940), p. 273.

Chapter 7

1. Edward L. Bernays, *Propaganda* (New York: Liveright, 1928), p. 145ff. Also see Edward L. Bernays, *Biography of an Idea: Memoirs of Public Relations Counsel, Edward L. Bernays* (New York: Simon & Schuster, 1965), pp. 426–36.
2. Karl A. Bickel, *New Empires: The Newspaper and the Radio* (Philadelphia: Lippincott, 1930), pp. 48–49.
3. Ibid., pp. 58, 81–85.
4. There were many radio fan magazines in the 1920s, but they

declined in the 1930s. Sarnoff's proposed magazine was on the order of a *TV Guide*, and at one time he prepared to put one out on his own. This plan never matured, however.

5. Most newsmen either were not interested in radio, or if they were, had poor speaking voices. On the other hand, announcers usually had no experience in journalism. Should newscasters be newspapermen-turned-radio personalities, or announcers who took an apprenticeship in news? The latter was chosen by most stations in the 1920s and early 1930s; with few exceptions, radio newsmen had little or no newspaper experience.
6. H. V. Kaltenborn, *Fifty Fabulous Years* (New York: G. P. Putnam's Sons, 1950), pp. 109–15.
7. Paul W. White, *News on the Air* (New York: Harcourt, Brace, 1947) contains the most complete record of these happenings, as well as being one of the best histories of the subject.
8. In 1932, Searchinger got Hitler to agree to a fifteen-minute broadcast to the United States for $1,500. CBS refused to pay that sum, and told the commentator to cover a musical event in Munich instead. Alexander Kendrick, *Prime Time: The Life of Edward R. Murrow* (Boston: Little, Brown, 1969), pp. 141–42.
9. The antitrust and related inquiries were concluded in 1941, at which time the government forced NBC to divest itself of one of its two networks as well as its talent bureau. NBC Blue was sold for $8 million to Edward J. Noble, who soon after transformed it into the American Broadcasting System. CBS was obliged to sell its talent bureau and refrain from several minor practices.
10. On Klauber's death, Edward R. Murrow saluted him. "I do not know whether he believed in the essential goodness or badness of man. But I do know that he believed passionately that the communication of information, unslanted, untarnished, and undistorted, was the only means by which mankind would progress." Kendrick, *Prime Time*, p. 375.
11. In addition, Swing refused to deliver commercials, and reserved the right to criticize his sponsors. Considered by his peers one of the most astute commentators of the time, he spent the war at MBS. Raymond (Gram) Swing, *Good Night!* (New York: Harcourt, Brace, 1964), pp. 196–222.
12. Kendrick, *Prime Time*, p. 266.
13. Elmer Davis, the veteran newsman who worked with Murrow at CBS, wrote that he was "painfully scandalized that such good reporting can be done by a man who never worked on a newspaper in his life." Fred Friendly, *Due to Circumstances Beyond Our Control* (New York: Knopf, 1967), p. xv.

14. Edward R. Murrow, *In Search of Light: The Broadcasts of Edward R. Murrow, 1938–1961* (New York: Knopf, 1967), pp. 4–5, 44–47.
15. Murrow's lack of comfort with impromptu shows became evident after the war, when he was the host of a television show, "Person to Person." On occasion he would appear ill at ease, at a loss for words, and unable to develop ideas fully. He was best when speaking to the audience, not discussing trivial matters with others.
16. Eric Sevareid, *Not So Wild a Dream* (New York: Knopf, 1946), p. 177.
17. In mid-1937, William Shirer wrote in his diary: "I have a job. I am to go to work for the Columbia Broadcasting System. That is, *if* . . . I have a job *if* my voice is all right. . . . Who ever heard of an adult with no pretenses to being a singer or any other kind of artist being dependent for a good, interesting job on his *voice?* And mine is terrible." William L. Shirer, *Berlin Diary: The Journal of a Foreign Correspondent, 1934–1941* (New York: Knopf, 1941), p. 78.
18. Sevareid, *Not So Wild a Dream*, p. 107.
19. At first, Murrow tried to use old-line newspaper reporters along with his new men. Thus, John Whittaker of the Chicago *Tribune* reported from Paris for CBS, while INS newmen Kenneth Downs and Pierre Huss represented the network in Berlin and Paris. Other newspaper reporters were used as stringers in other cities. As Murrow learned to orchestrate the news, men such as these were dropped in favor of others who were able to combine a news talent with a radio voice.
20. Even so, in 1944, 20.4 per cent of NBC's programming was news, against 16.5 per cent at CBS. The scope of the NBC effort may be gauged by considering that in 1939, NBC's news percentage was 3.8, and that at CBS, 10.9. White, *The American Radio*, p. 66.
21. Daniel Lerner, *Psychological Warfare Against Nazi Germany* (Cambridge, Mass.: MIT Press, 1971 ed.), Chaps. I and II.
22. For this overlapping authority during the war, see Eliot Janeway, *The Struggle for Survival* (New Haven, Conn.: Yale University Press, 1951).
23. One of these, not strictly in the information field, was the Office of Censorship, directed by Byron Price, executive news editor of the Associated Press. It relied primarily upon voluntary co-operation, but in early 1945 employed over fourteen thousand workers.

24. Corey Ford, *Donovan of OSS* (Boston: Little, Brown, 1970), pp. 126–28.
25. There is no history of the OWI, or even a satisfactory monograph on the subject. But see Wallace Carroll, *Persuade or Perish* (Boston: Houghton Mifflin, 1948), for an admittedly one-sided view of the subject. A former newspaperman, Carroll was decidedly opposed to the OSS and thought little of Sherwood.
26. A. A. Hoehling, *Home Front, U.S.A.* (New York: Crowell, 1966), p. 100.
27. Elmer Davis and Byron Price, *War Information and Censorship* (American Council on Public Affairs, n.d.), pp. 12–14.
28. Carroll, *Persuade or Perish*, pp. 235–37.
29. Carroll thought the conflict might be resolved through the establishment of two OWIs—"one for the clean business of information and the other for the dubious business of propaganda and psychological warfare"; he conceded this would have been difficult politically. Ibid., pp. 6–9, 236–38.
30. Considering that the industry was then fighting the Justice Department in a suit based on block booking, this last statement might have proved embarrassing for the producers. But Clark did not notice it. Moley, *The Hays Office*, pp. 120–27.
31. Of course, leading Hollywood male stars enlisted or were drafted into the service. Not to serve would be to indicate a lack of patriotism, and this would be deadly at the box office. Those who remained made certain to publicize their physical or age disabilities, as did the new stars who emerged during the war. Together with female stars, they engaged in bond drives, charities, and made overseas tours to indicate their support of the war.
32. Richard R. Lingeman, *Don't You Know There's a War On?* (New York: G. P. Putnam's Sons, 1970), p. 171.
33. Motion-picture artists were celebrities during World War I as well, and were used to help inculcate patriotism, both in films and at rallies. But the silent movies lacked much of the impact of the talkies of World War II, and of course there was no radio during World War I.

Chapter 8

1. In 1941, the public spent $607 million for radios, phonographs, records, and musical instruments. In 1945, the figure had dropped to $344 million. *Historical Statistics*, p. 224.
2. James Agee, *Agee on Film* (Universal Library, 1969), Vol. I, pp. 37–39.

3. Ibid., pp. 229–32.
4. *The Roaring Twenties*, released in 1939, was perhaps the best and most popular film dealing with the plight of returning World War I veterans, but it was really a crime picture, as its title indicates. *The Men* (1950) dealt with the paraplegic veterans, and although powerful, did not attempt to cover as wide a theme as did *The Best Years.*
5. The best study of Sherwood's career is Walter Meserve, *Robert E. Sherwood, Reluctant Moralist* (Indianapolis, Ind.: Pegasus, 1970).
6. John Howard Lawson, *Film: The Creative Process* (New York: Hill & Wang, 1964), p. 155. Lawson, a successful film writer during the war and founder of the Screen Writers' Guild, considered films like this soporifics. He was one of the first Hollywood writers to refuse to answer questions before the House Un-American Activities Committee, and for this he was blacklisted.
7. One of the new Republican members was Richard Nixon of California, just elected to his first term in the House of Representatives.
8. The best studies of the committee's Hollywood investigation are Walter Goodman, *The Committee* (New York: Farrar, Straus & Giroux, 1964), John Cogley, *Report on Blacklisting:* I: *Movies* (Fund for the Republic, 1956), and Robert K. Carr, *The House Committee on Un-American Activities, 1945–1950* (Ithaca, N.Y.: Cornell University Press, 1952).
9. Cogley, *Report on Blacklisting: Movies,* pp. 60–73.
10. "World War II came to a close in 1945, and it was not until about a year and a half later that the bulk of the social document films began to appear. Thus it was that the 1947 Hearings of the House Committee on Un-American Activities came in the year when social realism in Hollywood was just beginning to come into its own." Dorothy B. Jones, "Communism and the Movies," ibid., p. 218.
11. Ibid., p. 7.
12. For a study of press coverage of the hearings, see Carr, *The House Committee,* Chap. X.
13. The Hollywood Ten consisted of John Howard Lawson, Dalton Trumbo, Alvah Bessie, Ring Lardner, Jr., Albert Maltz, Samuel Ornitz, Lester Cole, Herman Biberman, Edward Dmytryk, and Adrian Scott.
14. Gordon Kahn, *Hollywood on Trial* (New York: Boni and Gaer, 1948), pp. 5–7. Although Kahn was strongly anticommittee and

pro-Hollywood Ten, this part of his narrative is in agreement with the facts as presented in less biased accounts.

15. Cogley, *Report on Blacklisting*, pp. 5–20 passim.
16. Herbert Biberman, *Salt of the Earth* (Boston: Beacon Press, 1965), p. 12.
17. This view is contrary to the *auteur* theory of films. For this view, see Andrew Sarris, *The American Cinema* (New York: Dutton, 1968).
18. Robert Rich, who won the Academy Award for best writing in 1956, was the pseudonym used by Dalton Trumbo.
19. In 1955, Murray Kempton wrote of a Union Square, New York, antifascist rally held four years before, at which Lawson appeared. A young man was addressing the audience. "One of his elders leaned over and said that John Howard Lawson was on the platform and should be introduced. The voice paused in its clangor. 'And now,' it rose again, 'I want to introduce a great antifascist, a great fighter for peace, a man you all know.' The young man stopped and turned to his mentor and, without bothering to put his hand over the microphone, asked for all to hear: 'What did you say his name was?' " Murray Kempton, *Part of Our Time* (New York: Simon & Schuster, 1955), p. 210.

Chapter 9

1. Hollywood did not produce a major film about the Korean War, perhaps due to the ambiguous nature of the conflict. Not until 1962, with *The Manchurian Candidate*, did a major director (John Frankenheimer) seek to utilize the new "yellow peril" theme in relation to the Chinese Communists.
2. This was not an entirely new phenomenon, since college and university faculties had had their time of glory in the Wilson administration. In 1919, Columbia's Nicholas Murray Butler, viewing the scene with satisfaction, noted that "The world at large is showing a new respect for men who have spent years in scholarly discipline and association. The President of the United States was for a quarter of a century a teacher of history and political science in three colleges; the president of the council in France once taught his native language and its literature to a group of American students at Stamford, Connecticut; the Prime Minister of Italy holds the chair of economics in the University of Naples; the first president of the Czechoslovak Republic is the most eminent teacher of philosophy among his people; one university professor has just resigned as American minister to China and an-

other is still serving as American minister to Greece; and so it goes through other European countries and in the South American republics. The fact of the matter is that the university teacher has some time since ceased to belong to a class apart, to an isolated group leading a life carefully protected and hedged about from contact with the world's affairs." Nicholas Murray Butler, *Scholarship and Service* (New York: Charles Scribner's Sons, 1921), p. 122. But the situation changed in the early 1920s, when the professors returned to the campuses.

3. Council of State Governments, *Higher Education in the Forty-eight States* (Council of State Governments, 1952), pp. 29–33, 170–72; Fritz Machlup, *The Production and Distribution of Knowledge in the United States* (Princeton, N.J.: Princeton University Press, 1962), pp. 77–92.
4. *Historical Statistics,* pp. 210–11.
5. Ibid., pp. 208–9. But see Machlup, *Knowledge in the United States,* p. 80, for slightly different figures.
6. Federal and state aid, the desire for vocational training, and educational experimentation resulted in a dramatic upsurge of interest in the two-year junior colleges, especially the public ones. There were 74,000 students in attendance in 1930, 122,000 in 1935, and 236,000 in 1940, when less than 20 per cent were in the private junior colleges, most of which were more finishing schools for wealthy women than anything else. *Higher Education in the Forty-eight States,* p. 33.
7. "Among the great heroes of football fame a year ago in our large colleges, I heard that Benny Oosterbaan, captain of the Michigan University football team, remarked that his name was easy as compared with many of those with whom he had football associations," noted an old-time faculty member, who went on to list the immigrant names on various squads. James A. Hawes, *Twenty Years Among the Twenty-year-olds* (New York: Dutton, 1929), p. 53.
8. At the University of Wisconsin, for example, the student population dropped from 11,376 in 1940–41 to 5,904 in 1943–44. Yet in the same period the school's budget rose from $9.5 million to $11.9 million, while state appropriations went from $3.6 million to $4.4 million. Keith W. Olson, *The GI Bill, the Veterans and the Colleges* (Lexington: The University Press of Kentucky, 1974), p. 88.
9. Davis R. B. Ross, *Preparing for Ulysses: Politics and Veterans During World War II* (New York: Columbia University Press,

1969), is the best study of the machinations that produced the legislation.

10. Dixon Wecter, *When Johnny Comes Marching Home* (Boston: Houghton Mifflin, 1944), p. 522. New York *Times* education editor Benjamin Fine thought those veterans who could not find employment might go to college. If conditions were very bad, he wrote, some million veterans might attend college under the GI Bill.
11. Olson, *The GI Bill*, p. 47.
12. The GI Bill was only one factor in this boom. One study indicates that of the 2,230,000 veterans who attended college under the legislation, only a half million might not have gone were it not for the benefits. Norman Frederiksen and William Schrader, *Adjustment to College* (Educational Testing Service, 1951), p. 326.
13. Olson, *The GI Bill*, p. 49.
14. While there was a Korean War GI Bill, it was not as generous as that for World War II returnees, and in any case there were fewer soldiers in the early 1950s than there had been seven years earlier, and the nation's social and economic structure was quite different.
15. The impact of the Korean War upon college and university enrollments was mixed. While World War II had resulted in fewer male students, the Korean War may have impelled young men to colleges, since by attending they might win deferments. In addition, the military science program's flourished, as candidates could hope to win commissions upon graduation. During World War II, officer training programs produced a large number of new second lieutenants. In the Korean War phase, the Reserve Officers' Training Corps in the institutions of higher learning achieved far greater popularity as the road to a commission.
16. It should be noted, too, that the Korean War GI Bill made flat payments to veterans, no matter whether they attended public or private schools. This encouraged them to seek the lowest-price education, and so was an additional incentive for them to attend the public colleges and universities.

Chapter 10

1. Seymour E. Harris, *The Market for College Graduates* (Cambridge, Mass.: Harvard University Press, 1949), pp. vi, 28, 33.
2. Harris had changed his mind by 1965, holding that "In the schools the supply of teachers is not adequate, and especially of the de-

sired quality." He hoped that a regular schedule of increased qualifications would be put into operation, but thought this not possible so long as the shortages continued. Harris also worried about the lack of qualified college professors. "It is expected that there should be a net rise of 100 per cent in the number of college teachers in fifteen years, an increase much beyond what is expected in competitive occupations." Yet the birthrate was declining rapidly in 1965, and within ten years the nation had its greatest oversupply of teachers in history. Seymour Harris, ed., *Challenge and Change in American Education* (Berkeley, Calif.: McCutchan Publishing Corp., 1965), p. 14.

3. The best study of this situation is David P. Gardner, *The California Oath Controversy* (Berkeley: University of California Press, 1967).
4. Clark Kerr, *The Uses of the University* (Cambridge, Mass.: Harvard University Press, 1963), pp. 87–88, 108–23.
5. Orrin E. Dunlap, Jr., *The Future of Television* (New York: Harper & Brothers, 1942), p. 157.
6. Sarnoff, *Looking Ahead*, p. 88; Lyons, *Sarnoff*, pp. 207–10.
7. Muriel Cantor, *The Hollywood TV Producer* (New York: Basic Books, 1971), pp. 71–116ff.
8. Live dramas were considered artistically pleasing in the early years, when miscues and other errors in performance could not be masked. The situation caused much anguish at the time, but later on was remembered fondly. This was the "golden age of television," and the title may have been merited, as young, fresh talent entered television. But the gold was in the writers, directors, and performers, not the technology.
9. Tape also gave a new life to the Hollywood studios. By the end of the 1960s, almost all weekly shows were produced there, often in the same locations as were the motion picture epics of the 1930s and 1940s. Thus, although Hollywood might no longer be the motion-picture capital of the nation, it remained the entertainment center. Without tape, New York might have retained many shows. Too, special made-for-television movies assisted the motion-picture industry in its new incarnation.
10. "In Washington, which lives on news as Milwaukee lives on beer, the nightly national news shows were staggered in fall 1970—Howard K. Smith at 6, David Brinkley at 6:30, Walter Cronkite at 7. At 6 in the Washington market, according to the November 1970 ratings sweep by the American Research Bureau, the most widely watched program in Washington was reruns of *I*

Love Lucy; at 6:30, reruns of *Petticoat Junction*; at 7, reruns of *Dick van Dyke*." Martin Mayer, *About Television* (New York: Harper & Row, 1972), p. 49.

Chapter 11

1. Joseph Barnes, *Willkie* (New York: Simon & Schuster, 1952), p. 165.
2. Oren Root wrote, thirty-four years later, "The *Fortune* article and the 'Information Please' appearance were part of the plan, together with a number of other appearances by Willkie on public platforms and in print." On the other hand, Root did not come out for Willkie until after the article had been printed. Other problems, some of which involved Willkie's personal life and purported support by Nazi groups, had to be stilled, and this was accomplished with skill by Davenport, Root, and others. Oren Root, *Persons and Persuasions* (New York: W. W. Norton, 1974), p. 27.
3. Later in his address, Brinkley moderated this view somewhat. "In about 15 years we have come from nothing to news programs that are a pretty good summary of the biggest of the news, fair and factual, reasonably imaginative, and all in color. But there is far more to be done and done better. . . ." Harry Skornia, *Television and the News* (Palo Alto, Calif.: Pacific Books, 1968), p. 5.
4. The newsreel, an art and informational form much neglected by historians and sociologists, is best covered and analyzed in Raymond Fielding, *The American Newsreel, 1911–1967* (Norman: University of Oklahoma Press, 1972).
5. Barnouw, *The Image Empire*, p. 49.
6. John Cogley, *Report on Blacklisting*: II, *Radio-Television* (Fund for the Republic, 1956), pp. 76–83 passim.
7. Gilbert Seldes, *The Public Arts* (New York: Simon & Schuster, 1956), pp. 216–22.
8. Barnouw, *The Image Empire*, pp. 52–53.
9. In 1954 Paul White, then executive editor at KFMB AM-TV in San Diego, recanted on his earlier view that objectivity was desirable. "An eleven-year-old quotation on the emasculation of commentator's opinions on radio or television has returned to haunt me," he wrote to *Newsweek* on April 8. "I have since changed my mind and have recanted publicly on several occasions. My nightly broadcast is proof that I no longer subscribe to that 1943 viewpoint." Edward Bliss, Jr., and John M. Patterson, *Writing*

News for Broadcast (New York: Columbia University Press, 1971), p. 181.

10. Robert Daley, "We Deal with Emotional Facts" (New York *Times Magazine*, Dec. 15, 1974), p. 54.

Chapter 12

1. The big-city morning dailies reported on happenings of the previous day, the stories written in the afternoons, and the press runs made at night, with two or even three editions possible. The afternoon and evening newspapers had to duplicate some of this, while at the same time printing short pieces on events that took place the same day. Several editions were possible, five or six in some unusual cases. Still, the reader of the morning newspaper did not want a rehash in the afternoon, and so the columns became a popular form for that part of the press.
2. As quoted in Timothy Crouse, *The Boys on the Bus* (New York: Random House, 1972), p. 30.
3. The most famous fictional reporter, of course, was Clark Kent, the disguise for Superman, on radio and television as well as in comics. Kent was "mild mannered," and his scoops came as a result of his Superman role. But his rival, Lois Lane, is presented as a tough, daring reporter, even though she often has to be rescued by Superman.
4. James M. Perry, *Us and Them* (New York: Clarkson N. Potter, 1973), pp. 3–8.
5. Major political parties have nominated men who lacked previous political experience—war heroes, for example. Dark-horse candidates have been nominated too—Alton Parker in 1908 and John Davis in 1924, both by Democrats. But in no case had the major parties selected men who had been created by the media. Even Greeley, who was the Democratic nominee in 1872, operated through the party bosses.
6. In 1952 Truman was challenged by Senator Estes Kefauver, who defeated him in the New Hampshire primary, and shortly thereafter the President withdrew from the race. Kefauver's reputation had been made as chairman of the select Senate committee investigating organized crime—hearings that were televised. Without television, it is doubtful that Kefauver could have risen so rapidly or gone so far.
7. Newton Minow, John Martin, and Lee Mitchell, *Presidential Television* (New York: Basic Books, 1973), pp. 34–38. The changing

roles of the press secretaries is covered in M. L. Stein, *When Presidents Meet the Press* (New York: Julian Messner, 1969).

8. See Arthur Schlesinger, Jr., *A Thousand Days* (Boston: Houghton Mifflin, 1965), for examples of how the Kennedys seduced intellectuals.
9. On one occasion, however, Kennedy barred the New York *Herald Tribune* from the White House.
10. CBS Reports, *Conversations with Walter Lippmann* (Boston: Little, Brown, 1965), p. 176.
11. Leo Bogart, *The Age of Television* (New York: Frederick Ungar, 1956), pp. 125–32. Sociologists also claimed that the children reared during World War II, when the fathers were in the service and the mothers at work, would become unbalanced socially. When this did not occur, the predictions were forgotten.

Chapter 13

1. "How could one be fair to Goldwater—by quoting what he said or by explaining what he thought? To quote him directly was manifestly unfair, but if he insisted on speaking thus in public, how could one resist quoting him? Later, when Goldwater would hang himself with some quick rejoinder, the reporters who had grown fond of him would laboriously quiz him again and again until they could find a few safe quotations that reflected what they thought he really thought." Theodore White, *The Making of the President, 1964* (New York: Atheneum, 1965), p. 112.
2. Michael Novak, *Choosing Our King* (New York: Macmillan, 1974), pp. 232–35.
3. *Crisis at Columbia: Report of the Fact-finding Commission Appointed to Investigate the Disturbances at Columbia University in April and May 1968* (New York: Vintage, 1968).
4. In early 1970, however, Cronkite conceded that in some areas television coverage of the convention had been weak. "We hadn't shown provocation in the streets of Chicago." Edith Efron, *The News Twisters* (Los Angeles: Nash Publishing Corp., 1971), p. 186.
5. Only one major television newsman, Howard K. Smith, believed Agnew's points were well taken. "Let us admit what we knew before Mr. Agnew said it: There is a problem," he observed on November 25. But Smith thought it a result of journalistic tradition, not left-wing bias. "The tradition deeply ingrained, of American journalism is negative. We are attracted mostly to what goes wrong in a nation where we must be doing something that is

right. The emigration of people trying to get out of this country are very few. The immigration figures of people trying to get in are high. They must know something we are not adequately reporting." Ibid., p. 182.

6. Edward P. Morgan, Max Ways, Clark Mollenhoff, Peter Lisagor, and Herbert G. Klein, *The Presidency and the Press Conference* (American Enterprise Institute, 1971), p. 34.
7. "Each political reporter, I suppose, just like taxi drivers and bartenders, has a special hang-up. Lindsay is mine. I have never been impressed by his administrative abilities or his intellect. He is, I believe, a true media candidate, more show than substance. To suggest all of this may be so is proper commentary, but there is an additional responsibility to deal with the essence of what a candidate is trying to say. I ducked that responsibility, and I'm sorry about it." Thus wrote James Perry of the *National Observer* after the election. Perry, *Us and Them*, p. 59.
8. Timothy Crouse, *The Boys on the Bus* (New York: Random House, 1973), p. 23.
9. In 1960, while Theodore White prepared to write *The Making of the President*, Allen Drury's book *Advise and Consent* was published, the first of a series of political novels that appeared somewhat farfetched at the time. Others followed, each one describing events more unusual than the first. On rereading, however, the books appear more "realistic" than what actually occurred in 1973–76. For example, had you been told in 1969 that five years later Gerald Ford would be President and Nelson Rockefeller Vice President, would you have been able to guess how they achieved their offices?

Selected Bibliography

MEDIA, GENERAL

Barnouw, Eric. A *Tower in Babel: A History of Broadcasting in the United States, I, -to 1933*. New York: Oxford University Press, 1966.

———. *The Golden Web: A History of Broadcasting in the United States, II, -to 1953*. New York: Oxford University Press, 1968.

———. *The Image Empire: A History of Broadcasting in the United States, III, -from 1953*. New York: Oxford University Press, 1970.

———. *Mass Communication*. New York: Rinehart, 1956.

Bernays, Edward. *Biography of an Idea: Memoirs of a Public Relations Counsel, Edward L. Bernays*. New York: Simon & Schuster, 1965.

———. *Propaganda*. New York: Liveright, 1929.

Boorstin, Daniel. *The Image*. New York, Harper & Row, 1961.

Boulding, Kenneth. *The Image*. Ann Arbor: University of Michigan Press, 1956.

Carroll, Carroll. *None of Your Business: Or My Life with J. Walter Thompson*. New York: Cowles, 1970.

Carroll, Wallace. *Persuade or Perish*. Boston: Houghton Mifflin, 1948.

Clarke, Athur. *Profiles of the Future*. New York: Harper & Row, 1960.

Coser, Lewis. *Men of Ideas*. New York: The Free Press, 1965.

DeFleur, Melvin. *Theories of Mass Communication*. New York: David McKay Co., 1966.

Duncan, Hugh. *Symbols in Society*. New York: Oxford University Press, 1968.

Ellul, Jacques. *The Technological Society*. New York: Alfred A. Knopf, 1964.

Farmer, Richard. *The Real World of 1984*. New York: David McKay Co., 1973.

Fenton, John. *In Your Opinion*. Boston: Little, Brown, 1960.
Finkelstein, Sidney. *Sense and Nonsense of McLuhan*. New York: International, 1968.
Flippen, Charles, ed. *Liberating the Media*. Washington, D.C.: Acropolis, 1974.
Giedion, Siegfried. *Mechanization Takes Command*. New York: Oxford University Press, 1948.
Kesey, Ken. *One Flew Over the Cuckoo's Nest*. New York: Viking Press, 1962.
———. *Sometimes a Great Notion*. New York: Viking Press, 1964.
Klapper, Joseph. *The Effects of Mass Communication*. New York: The Free Press, 1960.
Lyons, Russell. *The Tastemakers*. New York: Harper & Brothers, 1954.
Marcuse, Herbert. *One-dimensional Man*. Boston: Beacon Press, 1964.
Marx, Leo. *The Machine in the Garden*. New York: Oxford University Press, 1964.
Mayer, Martin. *Madison Avenue, U.S.A.* New York: Harper & Brothers, 1958.
McLuhan, Marshall. *Understanding Media*. New York: McGraw-Hill, 1964.
———. *The Gutenberg Galaxy*. Toronto: University of Toronto Press, 1962.
Mumford, Lewis. *The Myth of the Machine*. New York: Harcourt, Brace & World, 1966.
———. *Technics and Civilization*. New York: Harcourt, Brace & Company, 1934.
Packard, Vance. *A Nation of Strangers*. New York: David McKay Co., 1972.
Polanyi, Karl. *The Great Transformation*. Boston: Beacon Press, 1957.
Presbrey, Frank. *The History and Development of Advertising*. Garden City, N.Y.: Doubleday, Doran, 1929.
Rieff, Philip, ed. *On Intellectuals*. Garden City, N.Y.: Doubleday & Company, 1969.
Rivers, William. *The Opinionmakers*. Boston: Beacon Press, 1965.
Roper, Elmo. *You and Your Leaders*. New York: William Morrow & Co., 1957.
Rorty, James. *Our Master's Voice: Advertising*. New York: Day, 1934.
Seldin, Joseph. *The Golden Fleece*. New York: Macmillan, 1963.
Sennett, Richard and Cobbe, Jonathan. *The Hidden Injuries of Class*. New York: Alfred A. Knopf, 1972.
Toffler, Alvin. *Future Shock*. New York: Random House, 1970.

Tunstall, Jeremy, ed. *Media Sociology*. Urbana: University of Illinois Press, 1970.

Wallis, Robert. *Time: Fourth Dimension of the Mind*. New York: Harcourt, Brace & World, 1966.

Wells, Alan, ed. *Mass Media and Society*. Palo Alto, Calif.: National Press, 1972.

THE PRESS

Adler, Ruth, ed. *The Working Press*. New York: G. P. Putnam's Sons, 1966.

Alsop, Joseph and Alsop, Stewart. *The Reporter's Trade*. New York: Reynal, 1958.

Aronson, James. *The Press and the Cold War*. Indianapolis, Ind.: Bobbs-Merrill Co., 1970.

Barron, Jerome. *Freedom of the Press for Whom?* Bloomington: Indiana University Press, 1973.

Berger, Meyer. *The Story of the New York* Times, *1851–1951*. New York: Simon & Schuster, 1951.

Bickel, Karl. *New Empires: The Newspaper and the Radio*. Philadelphia: Lippincott, 1930.

Blumberg, Nathan. *One-party Press*. Lincoln: University of Nebraska Press, 1954.

Carlson, Oliver. *The Man Who Made News: James Gordon Bennett*. New York: Duell, Sloan & Pearce, 1942.

Cater, Douglass. *The Fourth Branch of Government*. Boston: Houghton Mifflin, 1959.

CBS Reports. *Conversations with Walter Lippmann*. Boston: Little, Brown, 1965.

Chase, Harold and Lerman, Allen, eds. *Kennedy and the Press*. New York: Thomas Y. Crowell Company, 1965.

Childs, Marquis and Reston, James, eds. *Walter Lippmann and His Times*. New York: Harcourt, Brace & Company, 1959.

Clapper, Raymond, ed. *Watching the World*. New York: McGraw-Hill, 1944.

Cook, Fred. *The Muckrakers*. Garden City, N.Y.: Doubleday & Company, 1972.

———. *What So Proudly We Hailed*. Englewood Cliffs, N.J.: Prentice-Hall, 1968.

Cooper, Kent. *Barriers Down*. New York: Farrar & Rinehart, 1942.

———. *Kent Cooper and the Associated Press*. New York: Random House, 1959.

Crouse, Timothy. *The Boys on the Bus*. New York: Random House, 1973.

Crozier, Emmet. *American Reporters on the Western Front, 1914–1918*. New York: Oxford University Press, 1959.

Desmond, Robert. *The Press and World Affairs*. New York: Appleton-Century, 1937.

Ernst, Morris. *The First Freedom*. New York: Macmillan, 1946.

Fisher, Charles. *The Columnists*. Washington, D.C.: Howell, Soskin, 1944.

Forrest, Wilbur. *Behind the Front Page*. New York: Appleton-Century, 1935.

Glessing, Robert. *The Underground Press in America*. Bloomington: Indiana University Press, 1970.

Hiebert, Ray, ed. *The Super Journalists*. Washington, D.C.: Acropolis, 1972.

Hohenberg, John. *The News Media*. New York: Holt, Rinehart & Winston, 1968.

Irwin, Will. *Propaganda and the News*. New York: McGraw-Hill, 1936.

Johnson, Michael. *The New Journalism*. Lawrence: The University Press of Kansas, 1971.

Joslin, Theodore. *Hoover off the Record*. Garden City, N.Y.: Doubleday, Doran, 1935.

Kempton, Murray. *Part of Our Time*. New York: Simon & Schuster, 1955.

Kobre, Sidney. *Modern American Journalism*. Tallahassee: Florida State University Bookstore, 1959.

Koop, Theodore. *Weapons of Silence*. Chicago: University of Chicago Press, 1946.

Lee, Richard, ed. *Politics and the Press*. Washington, D.C.: Acropolis, 1973.

Lindstrom, Carl. *The Fading American Newspaper*. Garden City, N.Y.: Doubleday & Company, 1960.

Lippmann, Walter. *Early Writings*. New York: Liveright, 1970.

Mankiewitz, Frank. *U.S.* v. *Richard Nixon: The Final Crisis*. New York: Quadrangle, 1975.

Mock, James. *Censorship, 1917*. Princeton, N.J.: Princeton University Press, 1941.

Mock, James and Larson, Cedric. *Words That Won the War*. Princeton, N.J.: Princeton University Press, 1939.

Mott, Frank. *American Journalism: A History, 1690–1960*. New York: Macmillan, 1962.

———, ed. *Journalism in Wartime.* Washington, D.C.: American Council on Public Affairs, 1943.
———. *The News in America.* Cambridge, Mass.: Harvard University Press, 1952.
Perry, James. *Us and Them.* New York: Clarkson N. Potter, 1973.
Pollard, James. *The Presidents and the Press.* New York: Macmillan, 1947 ed.
———. *The Presidents and the Press.* Washington, D.C.: Public Affairs Press, 1964 ed.
Powledge, Fred. *The Nixon Administration and the Press.* Washington, D.C.: American Civil Liberties Union, 1971.
Reston, James. *The Artillery of the Press.* New York: Harper & Row, 1967.
Ross, Lillian. *Reporting.* New York: Simon & Schuster, 1964.
Rowse, Arthur. *Slanted News.* Boston: Beacon Press, 1957.
Seldes, George. *Lords of the Press.* New York: Julian Messner, 1938.
———. *You Can't Print That.* Garden City, N.Y.: Doubleday, 1929.
Shirer, William. *Berlin Diary: The Journal of a Foreign Correspondent.* New York: Alfred A. Knopf, 1941.
Sinclair, Upton. *The Goose Step.* New York: Sinclair, 1922.
Smith, Merriman. *Thank You, Mr. President.* New York: Harper & Brothers, 1946.
Stein, M. L. *When Presidents Meet the Press.* New York: Julian Messner, 1969.
Stewart, Kenneth and Tebbel, John. *Makers of Modern Journalism.* Englewood Cliffs, N.J.: Prentice-Hall, 1952.
Swanberg, W. A. *Pulitzer.* New York: Scribner's Sons, 1967.
Talese, Gay. *The Kingdom and the Power.* New York: World, 1969.
Tebbel, John. *The Life and Good Times of William Randolph Hearst.* New York: E. P. Dutton & Co., 1952.
Villard, Oswald Garrison. *Fighting Years.* New York: Harcourt, Brace & Company, 1939.
Walker, Stanley. *City Editor.* New York: Stokes, 1934.
———. *Mrs. Astor's Horse.* New York: Stokes, 1935.
Wiggins, James. *Freedom or Secrecy.* New York: Oxford University Press, 1956.

MOTION PICTURES

Agee, James. *Agee on Film.* New York: Universal Library, 1969.
Andrews, Bert. *Washington Witch-hunt.* New York: Random House, 1948.

Balaban, Carrie. *Continuous Performance*. New York: G. P. Putnam's Sons, 1942.

Barret, Edward. *The Tenney Committee*. Ithaca, N.Y.: Cornell University Press, 1951.

Barth, Alan. *Government by Investigation*. New York: Viking Press, 1955.

———. *The Loyalty of Free Men*. New York: Viking Press, 1951.

Baxter, John. *Hollywood in the Thirties*. New York: Tantivy, 1968.

Belfrage, Cedric. *The American Inquisition*. Indianapolis, Ind.: Bobbs-Merrill Co., 1973.

Bergman, Andrew. *We're in the Money: Depression America and Its Films*. New York: New York University Press, 1971.

Bessie, Alvah. *Inquisition in Eden*. New York: Macmillan, 1965.

———. *The Un-Americans*. New York: Cameron, 1957.

Biberman, Herbert. *Salt of the Earth*. Boston: Beacon Press, 1965.

Bluem, A. William and Squire, Jason, eds. *The Movie Business*. New York: Hastings House, 1972.

Bowser, Eileen. *Biograph Bulletins, 1908–1912*. New York: Octagon, 1973.

Brown, John Mason. *The Ordeal of a Playwright: Robert E. Sherwood and the Challenge of War*. New York: Harper & Row, 1970.

———. *The Worlds of Robert E. Sherwood*. New York: Harper & Row, 1962.

Buckley, William F., Jr. *The Committee and Its Critics*. Chicago: Henry Regnery Co., 1962.

Cantor, Muriel. *The Hollywood TV Producer*. New York: Basic Books, 1971.

Carr, Robert. *The House Committee on Un-American Activities*. Ithaca, N.Y.: Cornell University Press, 1952.

Cerem, C. W. *Archeology of the Cinema*. New York: Harcourt, Brace & World, 1954.

Cogley, John. *Report on Blacklisting*: I, *Movies*. New York: Fund for the Republic, 1956.

Conant, Michael. *Antitrust in the Motion Picture Industry*. Berkeley: University of California Press, 1960.

Cowan, Lester, ed. *Recording Sound for Motion Pictures*. New York: McGraw-Hill, 1931.

Cowie, Peter. *Seventy Years of Cinema*. New York: A. S. Barnes, 1969.

Crowther, Bosley. *Hollywood Rajah*. New York: Holt, Rinehart & Winston, 1960.

———. *The Lion's Share*. New York: E. P. Dutton & Co., 1957.
Deming, Barbara. *Running Away from Myself*. New York: Grossman, 1969.
Dickinson, Thorold. *A Discoverer of Cinema*. New York: Oxford University Press, 1971.
Dickson, W. K. L. and Dickson, Antonia. *History of the Kinetograph, Kinetoscope, and Kinetophonograph*. New York: Arno Press, 1970 ed.
Dies, Martin. *Martin Dies' Story*. New York: Bookmailer, 1963.
———. *The Trojan Horse in America*. New York: Dodd, Mead, 1940.
Drinkwater, John. *The Life and Adventures of Carl Laemmle*. New York: G. P. Putnam's Sons, 1931.
Dyer, Frank. *Edison, His Life and Inventions*. New York: Harper & Brothers, 1929.
Emerson, John and Loos, Anita. *Breaking into the Movies*. McCann, 1921.
Fagan, Myron. *Red Treason in Hollywood*. New York: Cinema Educational Guild, 1949.
Faulk, John H. *Fear on Trial*. New York: Simon & Schuster, 1964.
Fielding, Raymond. *The American Newsreel, 1911–1967*. Norman: University of Oklahoma Press, 1972.
Forman, Henry. *Our Movie-made Children*. New York: Macmillan, 1933.
Franklin, Harold. *Sound Motion Pictures*. Garden City, N.Y.: Doubleday, Doran, 1929.
French, Philip. *The Movie Moguls*. Chicago: Henry Regnery Co., 1969.
Froug, William. *The Screenwriter Looks at the Screenwriter*. New York: Macmillan, 1972.
Fulton, A. R. *Motion Pictures*. Norman: University of Oklahoma Press, 1960.
Gelatt, Roland. *The Fabulous Phonograph*. New York: Appleton-Century-Crofts, 1965.
Gellermann, William. *Martin Dies*. New York: John Day, 1944.
Gelman, Barbara, ed. *Photoplay Treasury*. New York: Crown, 1972.
Goodman, Ezra. *The Fifty-year Decline and Fall of Hollywood*. New York: Simon & Schuster, 1961.
Green, Abel and Laurie, Joe, Jr. *Show Biz: From Vaude to Video*. New York: Holt, 1951.
Green, Fitzhugh. *The Film Finds Its Tongue*. New York: G. P. Putnam's Sons, 1929.

Griffith, Mrs. D. W. *When the Movies Were Young*. New York: Benjamin Blom, 1925.

Griffith, Robert and Theoharis, Athan, eds. *The Specter: Original Essays on the Cold War and the Origins of McCarthyism*. New York: New Viewpoints, 1974.

Handel, Leo. *Hollywood Looks at Its Audience*. Urbana: University of Illinois Press, 1950.

Hayden, Sterling. *Wanderer*. New York: Alfred A. Knopf, 1963.

Hays, Will. *The Memoirs of Will H. Hays*. Garden City, N.Y.: Doubleday & Company, 1955.

———. *See and Hear*. Hollywood: Motion Picture Producers' and Distributors' Association, 1929.

Hellman, Lillian. *An Unfinished Woman*. Boston: Little, Brown, 1969.

Hendricks, Gordon. *The Kinetoscope*. New York: Beginnings of American Film, 1966 ed.

———. *Origins of the American Film*. New York: Arno Press, 1972 ed.

Higham, Charles. *The Art of the American Film, 1900–1971*. Garden City, N.Y.: Doubleday & Company, 1973.

Huettig, Mae. *Economic Control of the Motion Picture Industry*. Philadelphia: University of Pennsylvania Press, 1944.

Inglis, Ruth. *Freedom of the Movies*. Chicago: University of Chicago Press, 1947.

Irwin, Will. *The House That Shadows Built*. Garden City, N.Y.: Doubleday, Doran, 1928.

Jacobs, Lewis. *The Rise of the American Film*. New York: Harcourt, Brace & Company, 1939.

Jarvie, I. C. *Movies and Society*. New York: Basic Books, 1970.

Jobes, Gertrude. *Motion Picture Empire*. New York: Archon, 1966.

Jones, Ken D. and McClure, Arthur. *Hollywood at War*. New York: A. S. Barnes, 1973.

Josephson, Matthew. *Edison*. New York: McGraw-Hill, 1959.

Kael, Pauline. *I Lost It at the Movies*. Boston: Little, Brown, 1965.

Kahn, Gordon. *Hollywood on Trial*. New York: Boni and Gaer, 1948.

Kallen, Horace. *Indecency and the Seven Arts*. New York: Liveright, 1930.

Kardish, Laurence. *Reel Plastic Magic*. Boston: Little, Brown, 1972.

Kennedy, Joseph, ed. *The Story of the Films*. New York: A. W. Shaw, 1927.

Klingender, F. D. and Legg, Stuart. *Money Behind the Screen*. New York: Lawrence and Wishart, 1937.

Lahue, Kalton. *Dreams for Sale*. New York: A. S. Barnes, 1971.
Latham, Earl. *The Communist Controversy in Washington*. Cambridge, Mass.: Harvard University Press, 1966.
Laurie, Joe, Jr. *Vaudeville*. New York: Holt, 1953.
Lawson, John Howard. *Film in the Battle of Ideas*. New York: Masses and Mainstream, 1953.
———. *Film: The Creative Process*. New York: Hill & Wang, 1964.
Lewis, Howard. *The Motion Picture Industry*. New York: Van Nostrand, 1933.
Macgowan, Kenneth. *Behind the Screen*. New York: Delta, 1967.
Madsen, Axel. *William Wyler*. New York: Thomas Y. Crowell Company, 1973.
McClure, Arthur, ed. *The Movies: An American Idiom*. Rutherford, N.J.: Fairleigh Dickinson University Press, 1971.
Meserve, Walter. *Robert E. Sherwood: Reluctant Moralist*. Indianapolis, Ind.: Pegasus, 1970.
Miller, Merle. *The Judges and the Judged*. Garden City, N.Y.: Doubleday & Company, 1952.
Moley, Raymond. *The Hays Office*. Indianapolis, Ind.: Bobbs-Merrill Co., 1945.
Momand, A. B. *The Hays Office and the NRA*. New York: Shawnee, 1935.
Nolan, William. *John Huston: King Rebel*. Hollywood: Sherbourne, 1956.
North, Joseph. *The Early Development of the Motion Picture, 1887–1909*. New York: Arno Press, 1973 ed.
Oberholtzer, Ellis. *The Morals of the Movies*. Philadelphia: Pennsylvania, 1922.
Peden, Charles. *Newsreel Man*. Garden City, N.Y.: Doubleday, Doran, 1932.
Powdermaker, Hortense. *Hollywood, The Dream Factory*. Boston: Little, Brown, 1950.
Pratt, George. *Spellbound in Darkness: A History of the Silent Film*. New York: New York Graphic Society, 1966.
Quigley, Martin and Gertner, Richard. *Films in America, 1929–1969*. New York: Golden, 1970.
Ramseye, Terry. *A Million and One Nights*. New York: Simon & Schuster, 1926.
Ross, Murray. *Stars and Strikes*. New York: Columbia University Press, 1941.
Rosten, Leo. *Hollywood: The Movie Colony, The Movie Makers*. New York: Harcourt, Brace & Company, 1941.

Rotha, Paul. *The Film Till Now*. New York: Funk & Wagnalls, 1948 ed.

Sands, Pierre. A *Historical Study of the Academy of Motion Picture Arts and Sciences, 1927–1947*. New York: Arno Press, 1973.

Sarris, Andrew. *The American Cinema*. New York: E. P. Dutton & Co., 1968.

Schickel, Richard. *The Disney Version*. New York: Simon & Schuster, 1968.

Schumach, Murray. *The Face on the Cutting-room Floor*. New York: William Morrow & Co., 1964.

Seabury, William. *The Public and the Motion Picture Industry*. New York: Macmillan, 1926.

Seldes, George. *Witch-hunt*. New York: Modern Age, 1940.

Sennett, Ted. *Warner Brothers Presents*. Castle Books, 1971.

Shayon, Robert L., ed. *The Eight Arts*. New York: Holt, Rinehart & Winston, 1962.

Sinclair, Upton. *Upton Sinclair Presents William Fox*. Los Angeles: Sinclair, 1933.

Stewart, George. *The Year of the Oath*. New York: DaCapo Press, 1971.

Talbot, Frederick. *Moving Pictures: How They Are Made and Work*. Philadelphia: J. B. Lippincott Co., 1923.

Taylor, Telford. *Grand Inquest*. New York: Simon & Schuster, 1953.

Thorp, Margaret. *America at the Movies*. New Haven: Yale University Press, 1939.

Trumbo, Dalton. *The Time of the Toad*. New York: Harper & Row, 1972.

United States, 76th Cong., 3d sess., Temporary National Economic Committee, Monograph No. 43. *The Motion Picture Industry—A Pattern of Control*. Washington, D.C.: United States Government Printing Office, 1941.

Van Zile, Edward. *That Marvel—The Movie*. New York: G. P. Putnam's Sons, 1923.

Vardac, A. Nicholas. *Stage to Screen*. Cambridge, Mass.: Harvard University Press, 1949.

Vaughn, Robert. *Only Victims*. New York: G. P. Putnam's Sons, 1972.

Wagenknecht, Edward. *The Movies in the Age of Innocence*. Norman: University of Oklahoma Press, 1962.

Wagner, Robert. *Film Folk*. New York: Century, 1918.

Walker, Alexander. *Stardom*. New York: Stein & Day, 1970.

White, David and Averson, Richard. *The Celluloid Weapon*. Boston: Beacon Press, 1972.

Whitney, Edward. *Antitrust Policies.* New York: Twentieth-century Fund, 1952.

Wilk, Max. *The Wit and Wisdom of Hollywood.* New York: Atheneum, 1971.

Zierold, Norman. *The Hollywood Tycoons.* New York: Hamilton, 1969.

HIGHER EDUCATION

Abeles, Elvin. *The Student and the University.* Indianapolis, Ind.: *Parent's* Magazine, 1969.

Adams, Henry. *The Education of Henry Adams.* Riverside, 1918.

Adams, John; Carpenter, C. R.; and Smith, Dorothy. *College Teaching by Television.* American Council on Education, 1958.

Altbach, Philip; Laufer, Robert; and McVey, Sheila, eds. *Academic Super Markets.* San Francisco: Jossey-Bass, 1971.

Angell, James. *The Higher Education.* Ann Arbor, Mich.: Board of Regents, 1879.

Angell, Robert. *The Campus.* New York: Appleton, 1928.

Avorn, Jerry et al., eds. *Up Against the Ivy Wall.* New York: Atheneum, 1968.

Bacciocco, Edward. *The New Left in America.* Stanford, Calif.: Hoover Institution Press, 1974.

Bailyn, Bernard. *Education in the Forming of American Society.* Chapel Hill: University of North Carolina Press, 1960.

Baker, Ray Stannard. *Woodrow Wilson: Life and Letters, Princeton, 1890–1910.* Garden City, N.Y.: Doubleday, Page, 1927.

———. *Woodrow Wilson: Life and Letters, War Leader, April 6, 1917–February 28, 1918.* Garden City, N.Y.: Doubleday, Doran, 1929.

Barton, Albert. *LaFollette's Winning of Wisconsin.* Homestead, 1922.

Barzun, Jacques. *The American University.* New York: Harper & Row, 1968.

———. *Teacher in America.* Boston: Little, Brown, 1945.

Bealle, John. *The History of Football at Harvard, 1874–1948.* Cambridge, Mass.: Columbia Publishing, 1948.

Bereday, George and Lauwerys, Joseph, eds. *The Education Explosion.* New York: Harcourt, Brace & World, 1965.

Berelson, Bernard. *Graduate Education in the United States.* New York: McGraw-Hill, 1960.

Bishop, Morris. *A History of Cornell.* Ithaca, N.Y.: Cornell University Press, 1962.

Bode, Carl. *The American Lyceum.* New York: Oxford University Press, 1956.

Bolte, Charles. *The New Veteran.* New York: Reynal & Hitchcock, 1945.

Boroff, David. *Campus U.S.A.* New York: Harper & Brothers, 1958.

Bowen, Robert. *The New Professors.* New York: Holt, Rinehart & Winston, 1960.

Bowman, Claude. *The College Professor in America.* Philadelphia: University of Pennsylvania Press, 1938.

Braden, William. *The Age of Aquarius.* New York: Quadrangle, 1970.

Bragdon, Henry. *Woodrow Wilson: The Academic Years.* Princeton, N.J.: Princeton University Press, 1970.

Brown, Francis. *Educational Opportunities for Veterans.* Washington, D.C.: Public Affairs Press, 1946.

Brubacher, John and Rudy, Willis. *Higher Education in America.* New York: Harper & Row, 1968.

Butler, Nicholas Murray. *Scholarship and Service.* New York: Charles Scribner's Sons, 1921.

Canby, Henry Seidel. *Alma Mater: The Gothic Age of the American College.* New York: Farrar & Rinehart, 1936.

———. *College Sons and College Fathers.* New York: Harper & Brothers, 1915.

Canfield, James. *The College Student and His Problems.* New York: Macmillan, 1902.

Christoffel, Tom; Finkelhor, David; and Gilbarg, Dan, eds. *Up Against the American Myth.* New York: Holt, Rinehart & Winston, 1970.

Collins, Varnum. *Princeton.* New York: Oxford University Press, 1914.

Commager, Henry Steele. *The Commonwealth of Learning.* New York: Harper & Row, 1968.

Cooper, Clayton. *Why Go to College?* New York: Century, 1912.

Coulton, Thomas. *A City College in Action.* New York: Harper & Brothers, 1955.

Council of State Governments. *Higher Education in the Forty-eight States.* Washington, D.C.: Council of State Governments, 1952.

Curti, Merle and Carstensen, Vernon. *The University of Wisconsin, 1848–1925.* Madison: University of Wisconsin Press, 1949.

Curti, Merle and Nash, Roderick. *Philanthropy in the Shaping of American Higher Education.* New Brunswick, N.J.: Rutgers University Press, 1965.

Dearborn, Ned. *The Oswego Movement in American Education.* New York: Columbia University Press, 1925.

DeVane, William. *The American University in the Twentieth Century.* Baton Rouge: Louisiana State University Press, 1957.

———. *Higher Education in Twentieth-century America.* New York: Harvard University Press, 1965.

Doan, Edward. *The LaFollettes and the Wisconsin Idea.* New York: Rinehart, 1947.

Dodd, William. *Woodrow Wilson and His Work.* Gloucester, Mass.: Peter Smith, 1932.

Eddy, Edward. *Colleges for Our Land and Time.* New York: Harper & Brothers, 1957.

Edwards, Richard; Artman, J. M.; and Fisher, Galen. *Undergraduates.* Garden City, N.Y.: Doubleday, Doran, 1928.

Eells, Walter. *The Junior College.* Boston: Houghton Mifflin, 1931.

Feuer, Lewis. *The Conflict of Generations.* New York: Basic Books, 1969.

Fine, Benjamin. *Democratic Education.* New York: Thomas Y. Crowell Company, 1945.

Fisher, Sydney. *American Education.* New York: R. G. Badger, 1917.

Foerster, Norman. *The American State University.* Chapel Hill: University of North Carolina Press, 1937.

Ford, Guy Stanton. *On and off the Campus.* Minneapolis: University of Minnesota Press, 1938.

Frederiksen, Norman and Schrader, William. *Adjustment to College.* Princeton, N.J.: Educational Testing Service, 1951.

Gard, Robert. *University Madison U.S.A.* Wisconsin House, 1970.

Gardner, David. *The California Oath Controversy.* Berkeley: University of California Press, 1967.

Gavit, John. *College.* New York: Harcourt, Brace & Company, 1925.

Gerberding, William and Smith, Duane, eds. *The Radical Left.* Boston: Houghton Mifflin, 1970.

Gerson, Mark. *The Whole World Is Watching.* New York: Viking Press, 1969.

Goldsen, Rose; Rosenberg, Morris; Williams, Robin; and Suchman, Edward. *What College Students Think.* New York: Van Nostrand, 1960.

Goodman, Paul. *The Community of Scholars.* New York: Random House, 1962.

———. *Growing Up Absurd.* New York: Vintage, 1960.

Gray, William. *Recent Trends in American College Education.* Chicago: University of Chicago Press, 1931.

Handlin, Oscar and Handlin, Mary. *The American College and American Culture*. New York: McGraw-Hill, 1970.

Harper, William Rainey. *The Trend in Higher Education*. Chicago: University of Chicago Press, 1905.

Harris, Seymour. *The Market for College Graduates*. Cambridge, Mass.: Harvard University Press, 1949.

———. *A Statistical Portrait of Higher Education*. New York: McGraw-Hill, 1972.

Harris, Seymour; Deitch, Kenneth; and Levensohn, Alan, eds. *Challenge and Change in American Education*. Berkeley, Calif.: McCutchan Publishing Corp., 1965.

Havemann, Ernest and West, Patricia. *They Went to College*. Harcourt, Brace, 1952.

Havighurst, Robert; Eaton, Walter; Baughman, John; and Burgess, Ernest. *The American Veteran Back Home*. New York: Longmans, Green, 1951.

Hawes, James. *Twenty Years Among the Twenty-year-olds*. New York: E. P. Dutton & Co., 1929.

Heath, Douglas. *Growing Up in College*. San Francisco: Jossey-Bass, 1968.

Hendel, Samuel, ed. *The Politics of Confrontation*. New York: Appleton-Century-Crofts, 1971.

Hill, Clyde. *A Decade of Progress in Teacher Training*. New York: Columbia University Press, 1927.

Hofstadter, Richard and Hardy, C. DeWitt. *The Development and Scope of Higher Education in the United States*. New York: Columbia University Press, 1952.

Hofstadter, Richard and Metzger, Walter. *The Development of Academic Freedom in the United States*. New York: Columbia University Press, 1955.

Hofstadter, Richard and Smith, Wilson, eds. *American Higher Education: A Documentary History*. Chicago: University of Chicago Press, 1961.

Hook, Sidney. *Heresy, Yes, Conspiracy, No*. New York: John Day, 1953.

Hook, Sidney; Kurtz, Paul; and Todorovich, Miro, eds. *The Idea of a Modern University*. Buffalo, N.Y.: Prometheus, 1974.

Hullfish, H. Gordon. *Educational Freedom in an Age of Anxiety*. New York: Harper & Brothers, 1953.

Hunt, Everett. *The Revolt of the College Intellectuals*. Chicago: Aldine, 1963.

Hunt, Frazier. *One American and His Attempt at Education*. New York: Simon & Schuster, 1938.

Hurd, Charles. *The Veterans' Program.* New York: McGraw-Hill, 1946.
Hutchins, Robert. *The Higher Learning in America.* New Haven, Conn.: Yale University Press, 1936.
Jencks, Christopher and Riesman, David. *The Academic Revolution.* Garden City, N.Y.: Doubleday & Company, 1968.
Joughlin, Louis, ed. *Academic Freedom and Tenure.* Madison: University of Wisconsin Press, 1967.
Kahn, Roger. *The Battle for Morningside Heights.* New York: William Morrow & Co., 1970.
Kelley, Robert. *The American Colleges and the Social Order.* New York: Macmillan, 1940.
Keniston, Kenneth. *The Uncommitted.* New York: Harcourt, Brace & World, 1965.
———. *Young Radicals.* New York: Harcourt Brace Jovanovich, 1968.
Kerr, Clark. *The Uses of the University.* Cambridge, Mass.: Harvard University Press, 1963.
Kiely, Margaret. *Comparisons of Students of Teachers Colleges and Students of Liberal Arts Colleges.* New York: Columbia University Press, 1931.
Koenig, Allen and Hill, Ruane, eds. *The Farther Vision: Educational Television Today.* Madison: University of Wisconsin Press, 1967.
Kolbe, Parke. *The Colleges in War Time and After.* New York: Appleton, 1919.
LaFollette, Bella Case and LaFollette, Fola. *Robert M. LaFollette.* New York: Macmillan, 1953.
LaFollette, Robert. *LaFollette's Autobiography.* Madison, Wis.: Robert M. LaFollette, 1911.
Lasch, Christopher. *The New Radicalism in America, 1889–1963.* New York: Vintage, 1967.
Lazarsfeld, Paul and Thielens, Wagner, Jr. *The Academic Mind.* New York: The Free Press, 1958.
Learned, William and Bagley, William. *The Professional Preparation of Teachers for American Public Schools.* New York: Carnegie Foundation, n.d.
Levenson, William and Stasheff, Edward. *Teaching Through Radio and Television.* New York: Holt, Rinehart & Winston, 1952.
Levitan, Sar and Cleary, Karen. *Old Wars Remain Unfinished.* Baltimore, Md.: The Johns Hopkins University Press, 1973.
Levitt, Morton, ed. *Youth and Social Change.* Detroit, Mich.: Wayne State University Press, 1972.
Liebling, A. J. *The Wayward Pressman.* Garden City, N.Y.: Doubleday & Company, 1947.

Lipset, Seymour and Wolin, Sheldon, eds. *The Berkeley Student Revolt*. Garden City, N.Y., Doubleday & Company, 1965.

MacIver, Robert. *Academic Freedom in Our Time*. New York: Columbia University Press, 1955.

Mallery, David. *Ferment on the Campus*. New York: Harper & Row, 1966.

Machlup, Fritz. *Education and Economic Growth*. Lincoln: University of Nebraska Press, 1970.

———. *The Production and Distribution of Knowledge in the United States*. Princeton, N.J.: Princeton University Press, 1962.

Mauldin, Bill. *Back Home*. New York: Sloane, 1947.

Maxwell, Robert, ed. *LaFollette*. Englewood Cliffs, N.J.: Prentice-Hall, 1969.

———. *LaFollette and the Rise of the Progressives in Wisconsin*. New York: Russell & Russell, 1956.

McCarthy, Charles. *The Wisconsin Idea*. New York: Macmillan, 1912.

McNeil, Mellicent. *A Comparative Study of Entrance to Teacher-training Institutions*. New York: Columbia University Press, 1930.

Metzger, Walter; Kadish, Sandford; DeBardeleben, Arthur; and Blaustein, Edward. *Dimensions of Academic Freedom*. Urbana, Ill.: University of Illinois Press, 1969.

Michener, James. *Kent State: What Happened and Why*. New York: Random House, 1971.

Miller, J. Harris and Allen, John. *Veterans Challenge the Colleges*. New York: King's Crown, 1947.

Millett, John. *The Academic Community*. New York: McGraw-Hill, 1962.

Minogue, Kenneth. *The Concept of a University*. Berkeley: University of California Press, 1973.

Monroe, Charles. *Profile of the Community College*. San Francisco: Jossey-Bass, 1972.

Moos, Malcolm and Rourke, Francis. *The Campus and the State*. Baltimore, Md.: The Johns Hopkins University Press, 1959.

Morison, Samuel. *The Centuries of Harvard, 1636–1936*. Cambridge, Mass.: Harvard University Press, 1936.

Olson, Keith. *The GI Bill, the Veterans, and the Colleges*. Lexington: The University Press of Kentucky, 1974.

Osgood, Charles. *Lights in Nassau Hall*. Princeton, N.J.: Princeton University Press, 1951.

Perkins, John. *Plain Talk from a Campus*. Newark: University of Delaware Press, 1959.

Pierce, Bessie. *Public Opinion and the Teaching of History in the United States*. New York: Alfred A. Knopf, 1926.

Richardson, Charles and Clark, Henry. *The College Book*. New York: Osgood, 1878.

Rogers, Carl and Wallen, John. *Counseling with Returned Servicemen*. New York: McGraw-Hill, 1946.

Root, E. Merrill. *Collectivism on the Campus*. Old Greenwich, Conn.: Devin-Adair Co., 1961.

Ross, Davis. *Preparing for Ulysses: Politics and Veterans During World War II*. New York: Columbia University Press, 1969.

Roszak, Theodore. *The Making of a Counterculture*. Garden City, N.Y.: Doubleday & Company, 1969.

Rudolph, Frederick. *The American College and University*. New York: Alfred A. Knopf, 1968.

Sale, Kirkpatrick. *SDS*. New York: Random House, 1973.

Schmidt, George. *The Old-time College President*. New York: Columbia University Press, 1930.

Simon, Kenneth and Grant, W. Vance. *Digest of Educational Statistics, 1968*. Washington, D.C.: United States Government Printing Office, 1968.

Slosson, Edwin. *Great American Universities*. New York: Macmillan, 1910.

Smith, G. Kerry, ed. *Twenty-five Years, 1945–1970*. San Francisco: Jossey-Bass, 1970.

Steinberg, Stephen. *The Academic Melting Pot*. New York: McGraw-Hill, 1974.

Stone, James and DeNevi, Donald, comps. *Portraits of the American University, 1890–1910*. San Francisco: Jossey-Bass, 1971.

Teodori, Massimo, ed. *The New Left*. Indianapolis, Ind.: Bobbs-Merrill Co., 1969.

Tewesbury, Donald. *The Founding of American Colleges and Universities Before the Civil War*. New York: Teacher's College, Columbia University, 1932.

Thorp, Willard, ed. *The Lives of Eighteen from Princeton*. Princeton, N.J.: Princeton University Press, 1946.

Thwing, Charles. *The American Colleges and Universities in the Great War*. New York: Macmillan, 1920.

———. *A History of Higher Education in America*. New York: Appleton, 1906.

Tunis, John. *Was College Worth While?* New York: Harcourt, Brace & Company, 1936.

Unger, Irwin. *The Movement: A History of the American New Left, 1959–1972*. New York: Dodd, Mead & Co., 1974.

Veysey, Laurence. *The Emergence of the American University.* Chicago: University of Chicago Press, 1965.

Waller, Willard. *The Veteran Comes Back.* New York: Dryden, 1944.

Walworth, Arthur. *Woodrow Wilson.* New York: Longman Green, 1958.

Wecter, Dixon. *When Johnny Comes Marching Home.* Boston: Houghton Mifflin, 1944.

Wertenbaker, Thomas J. *Princeton, 1746–1896.* Princeton, N.J.: Princeton University Press, 1946.

RADIO AND TELEVISION

Archer, Gleason. *Big Business and Radio.* New York: American Historical Society, 1938.

———. *History of Radio: To 1926.* New York: American Historical Society, 1938.

Arlen, Michael. *The Living-room War.* New York: Viking Press, 1969.

Arnold, Frank. *Broadcast Advertising: The Fourth Dimension.* New York: John Wiley & Sons, 1931.

Arons, Leon and May, Mark, eds. *Television and Human Behavior.* New York: Appleton-Century-Crofts, 1963.

Bagdikian, Ben. *The Information Machines.* New York: Harper & Row, 1971.

Baker, W. J. *A History of the Marconi Company.* New York: St. Martin's Press, 1971.

Banning, William. *Commercial Broadcasting Pioneer: The WEAF Experiment, 1922–1926.* Cambridge, Mass.: Harvard University Press, 1946.

Barrett, Marvin, ed. *Survey of Broadcast Journalism, 1969–1970.* New York: Grosset & Dunlap, 1970.

———. *Survey of Broadcast Journalism, 1970–1971.* New York: Grosset & Dunlap, 1971.

Belson, William. *The Impact of Television.* New York: Archon, 1967.

Bernstein, Julian. *Video Tape Recording.* New York: Rider, 1960.

Bliss, Edward. *In Search of Light: The Broadcasts of Edward R. Murrow, 1938–1961.* New York: Alfred A. Knopf, 1967.

Bliss, Edward and Patterson, John. *Writing News for Broadcast.* New York: Columbia University Press, 1971.

Bluem, A. William. *Documentary in American Television.* New York: Hastings House, 1965.

Bogart, Leo. *The Age of Television.* New York: Frederick Ungar Publishing Co., 1956.

Boyer, William. *Bureaucracy on Trial: Policy Making by Government Agencies.* Indianapolis, Ind.: Bobbs-Merrill Co., 1964.

Brokenshire, Norman. *This Is Norman Brokenshire.* New York: David McKay Co., 1954.

Bruce, Robert. *Bell: Alexander Graham Bell and the Conquest of Solitude.* Boston: Little, Brown, 1973.

Buxton, Frank and Owen, Bill. *The Big Broadcast.* New York: Viking Press, 1972.

———. *Radio's Golden Age.* New York: Easton Valley, 1966.

Cantril, Hadley and Allport, Gordon. *The Psychology of Radio.* New York: Harper & Brothers, 1935.

Carneal, Georgette. *A Conquerer of Space: An Authorized Biography of the Life and Work of Lee DeForest.* New York: Liveright, 1930.

Carson, Gerald. *The Roguish World of Doctor Brinkley.* New York: Holt, Rinehart & Winston, 1960.

Cary, William. *Politics and the Regulatory Agencies.* New York: McGraw-Hill, 1967.

Charnley, Mitchell. *News by Radio.* New York: Macmillan, 1948.

Chase, Francis. *Sound and Fury.* New York: Harper & Brothers, 1942.

Chester, Edward. *Radio, Television, and American Politics.* New York: Sheed & Ward, 1969.

Childs, Harwood and Whitton, John, eds. *Propaganda by Short Wave.* Princeton, N.J.: Princeton University Press, 1943.

Codding, George. *Broadcasting Without Barriers.* New York: UNESCO, 1959.

Cogley, John. *Report on Blacklisting:* II, *Radio-Television.* Washington, D.C.: Fund for the Republic, 1956.

Cole, Barry, ed. *Television.* New York: The Free Press, 1970.

Columbia University, Washington, D.C.: Bureau of Applied Social Research. *The People Look at Radio.* Chapel Hill: University of North Carolina Press, 1946.

Counterattack. *Red Channels.* New York: Counterattack, 1950.

Crosby, John. *Out of the Blue.* New York: Simon & Schuster, 1952.

———. *With Love and Loathing.* New York: McGraw-Hill, 1963.

Cushman, Robert. *The Independent Regulatory Commissions.* New York: Oxford University Press, 1941.

David, Elmer. *But We Were Born Free.* Indianapolis, Ind.: Bobbs-Merrill Co., 1954.

———. *Two Minutes to Midnight.* Indianapolis, Ind.: Bobbs-Merrill Co., 1955.

DeForest, Lee. *Father of Radio: The Autobiography of Lee DeForest.* New York: Wilcox & Follett, 1950.

Dunlap, Orrin. *The Future of Television.* New York: Harper & Brothers, 1942.

Efron, Edith. *How CBS Tried to Kill a Book.* Los Angeles: Nash Publishing Corp., 1972.

———. *The News Twisters.* Los Angeles: Nash Publishing Corp., 1971.

Elliot, William. *Television's Impact on American Culture.* East Lansing: Michigan State University Press, 1956.

Emery, Walter. *Broadcasting and Government.* East Lansing: Michigan State University Press, 1971.

Epstein, Edward Jay. *News from Nowhere.* New York: Random House, 1973.

Fang, I. E. *Television News.* New York: Hastings House, 1972 ed.

Felix, Edgar. *Television.* New York: McGraw-Hill, 1931.

Firth, Ivan and Erskine, Gladys. *Gateway to Radio.* New York: Macaulay, 1934.

Friendly, Fred. *Due to Circumstances Beyond Our Control.* New York: Alfred A. Knopf, 1967.

Gilbert, Robert. *Television and Presidential Politics.* New York: Christopher, 1972.

Goldsmith, Alfred N., et al. *Television,* Vols. I, II, and III. New York: RCA Review, 1944–46.

Green, Timothy. *The Universal Eye: The World of Television.* New York: Stein & Day, 1972.

Gross, Ben. *I Looked and I Listened.* New York: Random House, 1954.

Gunther, John. *Taken at the Flood: The Story of Albert D. Lasker.* New York: Harper & Brothers, 1960.

Harmon, Jim. *The Great Radio Heroes.* Garden City, N.Y.: Doubleday & Company, 1967.

Harris, Credo. *Microphone Memoirs.* Indianapolis, Ind.: Bobbs-Merrill Co., 1937.

Head, Sydney. *Broadcasting in America.* Boston: Houghton Mifflin, 1956.

Higby, Mary Jane. *Tune in Tomorrow.* New York: Cowles, 1966.

Hilliard, Robert, ed. *Understanding Television.* New York: Hastings House, 1972.

Howe, Quincy. *The News and How to Understand It.* New York: Simon & Schuster, 1940.

Hunt, Todd. *Reviewing for the Mass Media.* New York: Chilton, 1972.

Huntley, Chet. *The Generous Years.* New York: Random House, 1968.

Innis, Harold. *The Bias of Communication.* Toronto: University of Toronto Press, 1951.

Johnson, Nicholas. *How to Talk Back to Your Television Set.* Boston: Little, Brown, 1970.

Jolly, W. P. *Marconi.* New York: Stein & Day, 1972.

Jome, Hiram. *Economics of the Radio Industry.* Indianapolis, Ind.: A. W. Shaw, 1925.

Kaltenborn, H. V. *Fifty Fabulous Years.* New York: G. P. Putnam's Sons, 1950.

Kirschner, Allen and Kirschner, Linda, eds. *Radio and Television.* Indianapolis, Ind.: Odyssey, 1971.

Knight, Arthur. *The Liveliest Art.* New York: Macmillan, 1957.

Krasnow, Erwin and Longley, Lawrence. *The Politics of Broadcast Regulation.* New York: St. Martin's Press, 1973.

Kraus, Sidney, ed. *The Great Debates.* Bloomington: Indiana University Press, 1962.

Lackman, Ron. *Remember Radio?* New York: G. P. Putnam's Sons, 1970.

———. *Remember Television?* New York: G. P. Putnam's Sons, 1971.

Landry, Robert. *This Fascinating Radio Business.* Indianapolis, Ind.: Bobbs-Merrill Co., 1946.

Lang, Kurt and Lang, Gladys. *Politics and Television.* New York: Quadrangle, 1968.

Laurent, Lawrence, ed. *Equal Time: The Private Broadcaster and the Public Interest.* New York: Atheneum, 1964.

Lazarsfeld, Paul. *Radio and the Printed Page.* New York: Duell, Sloan & Pearce, 1940.

Lazarsfeld, Paul and Berelson, Bernard, eds. *The Effects of Mass Communication.* New York: The Free Press, 1960.

Lazarsfeld, Paul and Kendall, Patricia. *Radio Listening in America.* New York: Prentice-Hall, 1948.

Lazarsfeld, Paul and Stanton, Frank. *Radio Research, 1942–1943.* New York: Duell, Sloan & Pearce, 1944.

Lyons, Eugene. *David Sarnoff.* New York: Harper & Brothers, 1956.

Maclaurin, W. Rupert. *Invention and Innovation in the Radio Industry.* New York: Macmillan, 1949.

MacNeil, Robert. *The People Machine*. New York: Harper & Row, 1972.

Mayer, Martin. *About Television*. New York: Harper & Row, 1972.

McGaffin, William and Kroll, Erwin. *Anything but the Truth*. New York: G. P. Putnam's Sons, 1968.

Mehling, Harold. *The Great Time Killer*. New York: World, 1962.

Mickelson, Sig. *The Electric Mirror*. New York: Dodd, Mead, 1972.

Miessner, Benjamin. *On the Early History of Radio Guidance*. San Francisco: Pyramid, 1964.

Miller, Merle. *Only You, Dick Daring*. New York: Sloan, 1964.

Millerson, Gerald. *The Technique of Television Production*. New York: Communications Arts, 1961.

Minow, Newton; Martin, John; and Mitchell, Lee. *Presidential Television*. New York: Basic Books, 1973.

Noll, Roger; Peck, Merton; and McGowan, John. *Economic Aspects of Television Regulation*. Washington, D.C.: Brookings Institution, 1973.

Perry, Dick. *Not Just a Sound: The Story of WLW*. Englewood Cliffs, N.J.: Prentice-Hall, 1971.

The Radio Industry: The Story of Its Development. Indianapolis, Ind.: A. W. Shaw, 1928.

Read, Oliver and Welch, Walter. *From Tin Foil to Stereo: Evolution of the Phonograph*. Indianapolis, Ind.: Howard W. Sams & Co., 1959.

Roe, Yale. *The Television Dilemma*. New York: Hastings House, 1962.

Rosenberg, Bernard and Whit, David Manning, eds. *Mass Culture*. New York: The Free Press, 1964.

Sarnoff, David. *Looking Ahead*. New York: McGraw-Hill, 1968.

Schiller, Herbert. *Mass Communications and American Empire*. New York: Augustus M. Kelley, 1969.

Schmeckebier, Laurence. *The Federal Radio Commission: Its History, Activities and Organization*. Washington, D.C.: Brookings Institution, 1932.

Schneider, John. *The Golden Kazoo*. New York: Rinehart, 1956.

Schwartz, Bernard. *The Professor and the Commissions*. New York: Alfred A. Knopf, 1959.

Seldes, Gilbert. *The Public Arts*. New York: Simon & Schuster, 1956.

———. *The Great Audience*. New York: Viking Press, 1950.

Settel, Irving. *A Pictorial History of Radio*. New York: Citadel Press, 1960.

Sevareid, Eric. *Not So Wild a Dream*. New York: Alfred A. Knopf, 1946.

———. *This Is Eric Sevareid.* New York: McGraw-Hill, 1964.
Shayon, Robert. *The Crowd Catchers.* New York: Saturday Review Press, 1973.
Siepmann, Charles. *Radio, Television and Society.* New York: Oxford University Press, 1950.
Siller, Bob; White, Ted; and Turkel, Hal. *Television and Radio News.* New York: Macmillan, 1960.
Simonson, Solomon. *Crisis in Television.* New York: Living Books, 1966.
Skornia, Harry. *Television and Society.* New York: McGraw-Hill, 1965.
———. *Television and the News.* San Francisco: Pacific, 1968.
Skornia, Harry and Kitson, Jack, eds. *Problems and Controversies in Television and Radio.* San Francisco: Pacific, 1968.
Slate, Sam and Cook, Joe. *It Sounds Impossible.* New York: Macmillan, 1963.
Smith, William. *To Kill a Messenger: Television News and the Real World.* New York: Hastings House, 1970.
Steiner, Gary. *The People Look at Television.* New York: Alfred A. Knopf, 1963.
Summers, Harrison, ed. *A Thirty-year History of Programs Carried on National Radio Networks in the United States, 1926–1956.* Columbus: Ohio State University Press, 1958.
Swing, Raymond. *Good Night!* New York: Harcourt, Brace & Company, 1964.
Thomas, Lowell. *History as You Heard It.* Garden City, N.Y.: Doubleday & Company, 1957.
Thomson, Charles. *Television and Presidential Politics.* Washington, D.C.: Brookings Institution, 1956.
Trenaman, Joseph and McQuail, Denis. *Television and the Political Image.* New York: Metheun, 1961.
Tuchman, Gaye, ed. *The TV Establishment.* Englewood Cliffs, N.J.: Prentice-Hall, 1974.
Tyrell, Robert. *The Work of the Television Journalist.* New York: Communications Arts, 1972.
Waldrop, Frank and Borkin, Joseph. *Television: A Struggle for Power.* New York: William Morrow & Co., 1938.
Weinberg, Meyer. *TV in America.* New York: Ballantine, 1962.
Weiner, Peter. *Making the Media Revolution.* New York: Macmillan, 1973.
Wells, Alan. *Picture-tube Imperialism?* New York: Orbins, 1972.
West, Robert. *The Rape of Radio.* New York: Rodin, 1941.

White, Llewellyn. *The American Radio*. Chicago: University of Chicago Press, 1947.
White, Paul. *News on the Air*. New York: Harcourt, Brace & Company, 1947.
Williams, Albert. *Listening*. Freeport, N.Y.: Books for Libraries, 1968 ed.
Wolfe, Charles, ed. *Modern Radio Advertising*. New York: Funk & Wagnalls, 1949.
Wood, William. *Electronic Journalism*. New York: Columbia University Press, 1967.
Wylie, Max. *Clear Channels: Television and the American People*. New York: Funk & Wagnalls, 1955.
———. *Radio Writing*. New York: Farrar & Rinehart, 1939.
Yellin, David. *Special: Fred Freed and the Television Documentary*. New York: Macmillan, 1972.
Zworykin, V. K. and Morton, G. A. *Television*. New York: John Wiley & Sons, 1954 ed.

POLITICS AND THE MEDIA

Adler, Renata. *Toward a Radical Middle*. New York: Random House, 1969.
Alexander, Herbert. *Money in Politics*. Washington, D.C.: Public Affairs Press, 1972.
Alsop, Joseph and Kintner, Robert. *Men Around the President*. Garden City, N.Y.: Doubleday, Doran, 1939.
Barber, James. *The Presidential Character*. Englewood Cliffs, N.J.: Prentice-Hall, 1972.
Bazelon, David. *Power in America*. New York: New American Library, 1967.
Beck, Carl. *Contempt of Congress*. New York: Hauser, 1959.
Beichman, Arnold. *Nine Lies About America*. Freeport, N.Y.: Library Press, 1972.
Bernstein, Carl and Woodward, Bob. *All the President's Men*. New York: Simon & Schuster, 1974.
Berthoff, Rowland. *An Unsettled People*. New York: Harper & Row, 1971.
Boorstin, Daniel. *The Americans: The Democratic Experience*. New York: Random House, 1973.
Broder, David. *The Party's Over*. New York: Harper & Row, 1972.
Buchanam, Patrick. *The New Majority*. Philadelphia: Girard Bank, 1973.

Bunyan, James. *Intervention, Civil War, and Communism in Russia.* Baltimore, Md.: The Johns Hopkins University Press, 1936.

Burlingame, Roger. *The Sixth Column.* Philadelphia: J. B. Lippincott Co., 1962.

Burns, James MacGregor. *Roosevelt: The Soldier of Freedom.* New York: Harcourt Brace Jovanovich, 1970.

Casserley, J. V. *The Bent World.* New York: Oxford University Press, 1955.

Chafee, Zechariah. *Freedom of Speech.* New York: Harcourt, Brace & Company, 1920.

Chester, Lewis; Hodson, Godfrey; and Page, Bruce. *An American Melodrama: The Presidential Campaign of 1968.* New York: Viking Press, 1969.

Christian, George. *The President Steps Down.* New York: Macmillan, 1970.

Cornwall, Elmer. *Presidential Leadership of Public Opinion.* Bloomington: Indiana University Press, 1965.

Creel, George. *How We Advertised America.* New York: Harper & Brothers, 1920.

———. *Quatrains of Christ.* New York: Elder, 1908.

———. *Rebel at Large.* New York: G. P. Putnam's Sons, 1947.

———. *The War, the World and Wilson.* New York: G. P. Putnam's Sons, 1920.

———. *Wilson and the Issues.* New York: Century, 1916.

Cummings, Milton, ed. *The National Election of 1964.* Washington, D.C.: Brookings Institution, 1966.

Davis, Elmer and Price, Byron. *War Information and Censorship.* Washington, D.C.: American Council on Public Affairs, n.d.

DeVries, Walter and Tarrance, Lance. *The Ticket Splitters: A New Force in American Politics.* Grand Rapids, Mich.: Eerdmans, 1972.

Didion, Joan. *Slouching Toward Bethlehem.* New York: Farrar, Straus & Giroux, 1968.

Domhoff, G. William. *Who Rules America?* Englewood Cliffs, N.J.: Prentice-Hall, 1967.

Drury, Allen. A *Senate Journal, 1943–1945.* New York: McGraw-Hill, 1963.

Drury, Allen and Maroon, Fred. *Courage and Hesitation.* Garden City, N.Y.: Doubleday & Company, 1971.

Duchene, François, ed. *The Endless Crisis: America in the Seventies.* New York: Simon & Schuster, 1970.

Dutton, Frederick. *Changing Sources of Power.* New York McGraw-Hill, 1971.

Dyer, Murray. *The Weapon on the Wall: Rethinking Psychological Warfare*. Baltimore, Md.: The Johns Hopkins University Press, 1959.

Eisenhower, Milton. *The President Is Calling*. Garden City, N.Y.: Doubleday & Company, 1974.

Evans, Rowland and Novak, Robert. *Lyndon B. Johnson: The Exercise of Power*. New York: New American Library, 1966.

Faber, Harold, ed., for the New York *Times*. *The Road to the White House*. New York: McGraw-Hill, 1965.

Ford, Corey. *Donovan of OSS*. Boston: Little, Brown, 1970.

Frost, David. *The Presidential Debate, 1968*. New York: Stein & Day, 1968.

Goodman, Jack, ed. *While You Were Gone*. New York: Simon & Schuster, 1946.

Goodman, Walter. *All Honorable Men*. Boston: Little, Brown, 1963.

Grattan, Harley. *Why We Fought*. New York: Vanguard, 1929.

Greene, Bob. *Running*. Chicago: Henry Regnery Co., 1973.

Goldman, Eric. *The Tragedy of Lyndon Johnson*. New York: Alfred A. Knopf, 1969.

Halberstam, David. *The Best and the Brightest*. New York: Random House, 1972.

Hassett, William. *Off the Record With FDR, 1942–1945*. New Brunswick, N.J.: Rutgers University Press, 1958.

Hinshaw, David. *The Home Front*. New York: G. P. Putnam's Sons, 1943.

Hoehling, A. A. *Home Front, U.S.A.* New York: Thomas Y. Crowell Company, 1966.

Hoffman, Abbie. *Revolution for the Hell of It!* New York: Dial Press, 1968.

Hofstadter, Richard. *Anti-Intellectualism in American Life*. New York: Alfred A. Knopf, 1963.

———. *The Paranoid Style in American Politics*. New York: Random House, 1965.

Hoult, Thomas. *The March to the Right*. Cambridge, Mass.: Schenkman Publishing Co., 1972.

Jaher, Frederick Cople, ed. *The Rich, the Well Born, and the Powerful*. Urbana: University of Illinois Press, 1973.

Janeway, Eliot. *The Struggle for Survival*. New Haven, Conn.: Yale University Press, 1951.

Johnson, Donald. *The Republican Party and Wendell Willkie*. Urbana: University of Illinois Press, 1960.

Johnson, Lyndon. *The Vantage Point*. New York: Holt, Rinehart & Winston, 1971.

Lansing, Robert. *War Memoirs of Robert Lansing*. Indianapolis, Ind.: Bobbs-Merrill Co., 1935.

Lasswell, Harold. *Propaganda Techniques in the World War*. New York: Alfred A. Knopf, 1927.

Lawrence, Bill. *Six Presidents, Too Many Wars*. New York: Saturday Review Press, 1972.

Lerner, Daniel. *Psychological Warfare Against Nazi Germany*. Cambridge, Mass.: MIT Press, 1971 ed.

Lingeman, Richard. *Don't You Know There's a War On?* New York: G. P. Putnam's Sons, 1970.

Link, Arthur. *Wilson: The Road to the White House*. Princeton, N.J.: Princeton University Press, 1947.

———. *Wilson: Campaigns for Progressivism and Peace, 1916–1917*. Princeton, N.J.: Princeton University Press, 1965.

Lipset, Seymour and Schlaflander, Gerald. *Passion and Politics*. Boston: Little, Brown, 1971.

Lora, Ronald. *America in the '60s*. New York: Wiley & Sons, 1974.

McCarthy, Eugene. *The Year of the People*. Garden City, N.Y.: Doubleday & Company, 1969.

McCoy, Donald. *Calvin Coolidge: The Quiet President*. New York: Macmillan, 1967.

MacDonald, Dwight. *Against the American Grain*. New York: Random House, 1962.

McGinniss, Joe. *The Selling of the President, 1968*. New York: Trident Press, 1969.

Mailer, Norman. *The Armies of the Night*. New York: New American Library, 1968.

———. *Miami and the Siege of Chicago*. New York: World, 1968.

Millis, Walter. *Road to War*. Boston: Houghton Mifflin, 1935.

Mills, C. Wright. *The Power Elite*. New York: Oxford University Press, 1965.

———. *White Collar: The American Middle Class*. New York: Oxford University Press, 1951.

Monson, R. Joseph and Cannon, Mark. *The Makers of Public Policy*. New York: McGraw-Hill, 1965.

Morris, Lloyd. *Not So Long Ago*. New York: Random House, 1949.

Napolitan, Joseph. *The Election Game*. Garden City, N.Y.: Doubleday & Company, 1972.

Neustadt, Richard. *Presidential Power: The Politics of Leadership*. New York: John Wiley & Sons, 1960.

Nixon, Richard. *Six Crises*. Garden City, N.Y.: Doubleday & Company, 1962.

Novak, Michael. *Choosing Our King*. New York: Macmillan, 1974.
Novak, Robert. *The Agony of the GOP, 1964*. New York: Macmillan, 1965.
Oberdorfer, Don. *Tet!* Garden City, N.Y.: Doubleday & Company, 1971.
Ogburn, William, ed. *American Society in Wartime*. Chicago: University of Chicago Press, 1943.
Osborne, John. *The First Two Years of the Nixon Watch*. New York: Liveright, 1971.
———. *The Third Year of the Nixon Watch*. New York: Liveright, 1972.
———. *The Fourth Year of the Nixon Watch*. New York: Liveright, 1973.
———. *The Fifth Year of the Nixon Watch*. Liveright, 1974.
Paxton, Frederic. *America at War, 1917–1918*. Boston: Houghton Mifflin, 1939.
Perrett, Geoffrey. *Days of Sadness, Years of Triumph*. New York: Coward, McCann & Geoghegan, 1973.
Perry, James. *The New Politics*. New York: Clarkson N. Potter, 1968.
Peterson, H. C. *Propaganda for War*. Norman: University of Oklahoma Press, 1939.
Peterson, H. C. and Fite, Gilbert. *Opponents of War, 1917–1918*. Seattle: University of Washington Press, 1957.
Rather, Dan and Gates, Gary Paul. *The Palace Guard*. New York: Harper & Row, 1974.
Reedy, George. *The Presidency in Flux*. New York: Columbia University Press, 1973.
———. *The Twilight of the Presidency*. New York: World, 1970.
Reich, Charles. *The Greening of America*. New York: Random House, 1970.
Reisman, David. *Abundance for What?* Garden City, N.Y.: Doubleday & Company, 1964.
Root, Oren. *Persons and Persuasions*. New York: W. W. Norton & Company, 1974.
Rosenbloom, David. *The Election Men*. New York: Quadrangle, 1973.
Salinger, Pierre. *With Kennedy*. Garden City, N.Y.: Doubleday & Company, 1966.
Sanford, Charles. *The Quest for Paradise*. Urbana: University of Illinois Press, 1961.
Scammon, Richard, ed. *America at the Polls*. Pittsburgh, Pa.: University of Pittsburgh Press, 1965.

Scammon, Richard and Wattenberg, Ben. *The Real Majority*. New York: Coward-McCann, 1970.

Schlesinger, Arthur M., Jr. *The Crisis of Confidence*. Boston: Houghton Mifflin, 1969.

———. *A Thousand Days*. Boston: Houghton Mifflin, 1965.

———. *The Imperial Presidency*. Boston: Houghton Mifflin, 1973.

Sevareid, Eric, ed. *Candidates, 1960*. New York: Basic Books, 1959.

Shadegg, Stephen. *How to Win an Election*. New York: Taplinger, 1964.

———. *What Happened to Goldwater?* New York: Holt, Rinehart & Winston, 1965.

———. *Winning's a Lot More Fun*. New York: Macmillan, 1969.

Sherwood, Robert. *Roosevelt and Hopkins*. New York: Harper & Brothers, 1948.

Shuman, R. Baird. *Robert E. Sherwood*. New York: Twayne, 1964.

Sidey, Hugh. *A Very Personal Presidency*. New York: Atheneum, 1968.

Sisson, Edgar. *100 Red Days*. New Haven, Conn.: Yale University Press, 1931.

Smith, R. Harris. *OSS: The Secret History of America's First Central Intelligence Agency*. Berkeley: University of California Press, 1972.

Stouffer, Samuel. *Communism, Conformity and Civil Liberties*. New York: John Wiley & Sons, 1966.

Strakhovsky, Leonid. *Origins of American Intervention in North Russia*. Princeton, N.J.: Princeton University Press, 1937.

Thompson, Hunter. *Fear and Loathing on the Campaign Trail, '72*. San Francisco: Straight Arrow, 1973.

Thomson, Charles. *Overseas Information Service of the United States Government*. Washington, D.C.: Brookings Institution, 1948.

Valentine, Alan. *1913: America Between Two Worlds*. New York: Macmillan, 1962.

Wattenberg, Ben and Scammon, Richard. *This U.S.A.* Garden City, N.Y.: Doubleday & Company, 1965.

White, Theodore. *The Making of the President, 1960*. New York: Atheneum, 1961.

———. *The Making of the President, 1964*. New York: Atheneum, 1965.

———. *The Making of the President, 1968*. New York: Atheneum, 1969.

———. *The Making of the President, 1972*. New York: Atheneum, 1973.

Wicker, Tom. *JFK and LBJ: The Influence of Personality Upon Politics*. Baltimore, Md.: Penguin, 1968.

Wilson, Edith Bolling. *My Memoir*. Indianapolis, Ind.: Bobbs-Merrill Co., 1938.

Wise, David. *The Politics of Lying*. New York: Vintage, 1973.

Wise, David and Ross, Thomas. *The Invisible Government*. New York: Random House, 1964.

Witcover, Jules. *85 Days: The Last Campaign of Robert F. Kennedy*. New York: Ace, 1969.

———. *The Resurrection of Richard Nixon*. New York: G. P. Putnam's Sons, 1970.

———. *White Knight: The Rise of Spiro Agnew*. New York: Random House, 1972.

Wolfe, Tom. *The Electric Kool-Aid Acid Test*. New York: Farrar, Straus & Giroux, 1968.

———. *Radical Chic and Mau-Mauing the Flak Catchers*. New York: Farrar, Straus & Giroux, 1970.

Wycoff, Gene. *The Image Candidates*. New York: Macmillan, 1968.

Zevin, B. D., ed. *Nothing to Fear: The Elected Addresses of Franklin D. Roosevelt, 1932–1945*. Boston: Houghton Mifflin, 1946.

Zinn, Howard. *Postwar America, 1945–1971*. Indianapolis, Ind.: Bobbs-Merrill Co., 1973.

Index

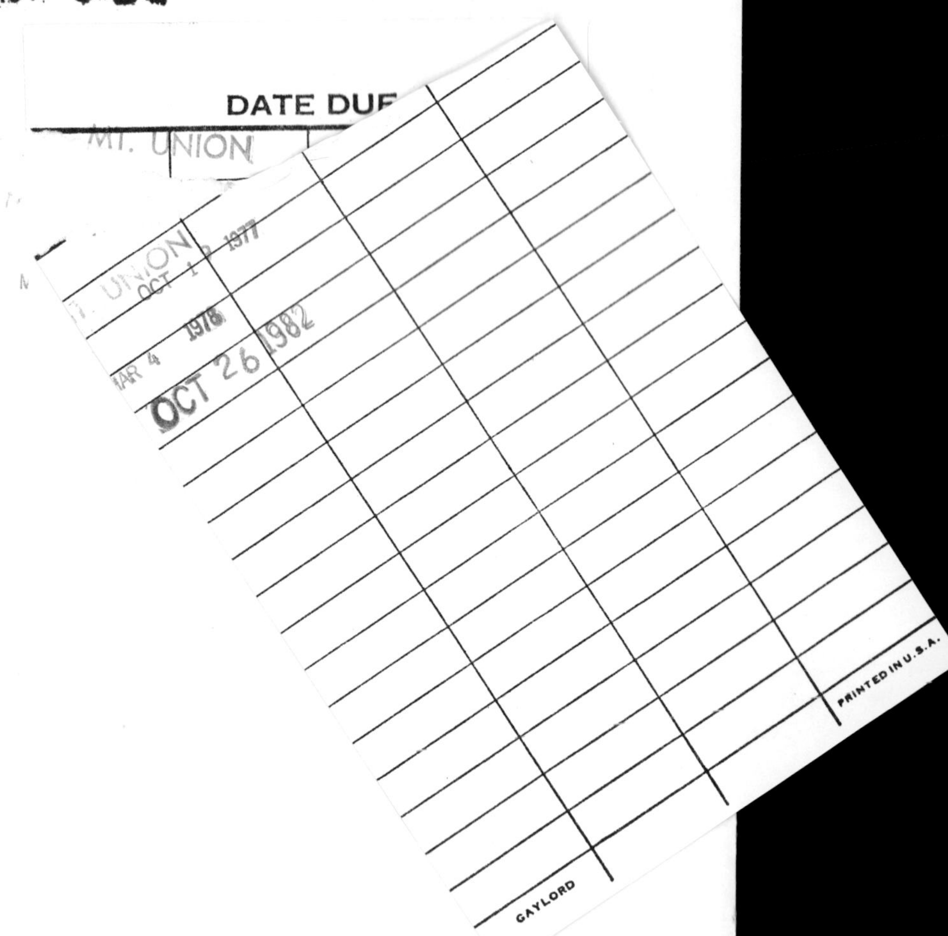